Merry Christmas, Gene

1994

D0466995

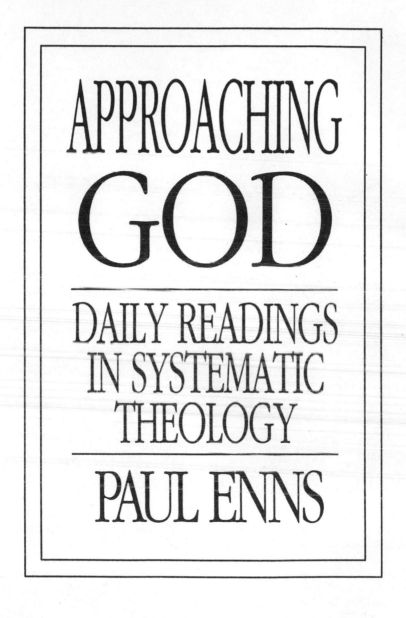

APPROACHING
GOD

DAILY READINGS IN SYSTEMATIC THEOLOGY

PAUL ENNS

MOODY PRESS
CHICAGO

In memory of my mother,
who went home to be with the Lord
during the writing of this book

CONTENTS

PREFACE

One spring when I was working in an architect's office I asked Larry if the office would be closed on Good Friday.

"What is Good Friday?" he queried.

"That's the day we remember when Christ died on the cross for our sins," I replied.

"I don't understand what you mean," was his final response.

Larry was raised in an evangelical home and had made a public profession of faith, but he was unaware of the meaning of Good Friday and the substitutionary atonement of Christ. Larry is not alone; for various reasons, many Christians do not know the elements of the Christian faith. That is why this book was written.

What is this book? *Approaching God* is a daily devotional book with a distinctive format. It is written to give you a basic understanding of the doctrines of the Christian faith. What is God like? Are there errors in the Bible? Was Jesus both God and man? What is demon possession? What is the nature of angels? What will happen during the Tribulation? Such questions will be answered in this book.

The readings will take you systematically through biblical doctrine, beginning with God, then moving on to the Bible, Christ, the Holy Spirit, man, sin, salvation, the church, angels, Satan, demons, and prophecy. Since the readings follow logically and consecutively, *Approaching God* will be most beneficial if you read it systematically, beginning with the January 1 reading. *Approaching God* covers the entire scope of Bible doctrine, but it is broken up into concise daily readings, with illustrations and applications, and is written in nontechnical, understandable language. It is intended for the average reader, who does not have a background in biblical studies.

Why was this book written? *Approaching God* was written to meet a need. A prominent preacher once said that Mormons win more converts to their cult from his evangelical denomination than from any other. Perhaps that statement exposes the need for this book. Since most Christians do not hear a series of sermons on Bible doctrine and since most Christians do not read theological books, *Approaching God* was written to fill that void. Of course, this book does not replace normal daily Bible reading; rather, it is designed to give understanding to your Bible study.

For whom was this book written? Perhaps you are a parent who wants to firmly ground your children in the doctrines of the Bible. This book is written for you. Or perhaps you have wanted to know about the doctrines of the Christian faith but you haven't known where to begin. This book is written for you as well. It was written for those who are afraid to attempt reading a doctrinal book but have an interest in learning what Christians believe. And it is written in bite-sized chunks so that you can readily understand it.

You are also encouraged to look up the Scripture references that are mentioned in the daily readings—that will strengthen your understanding of the doctrine.

Why is this book important? Because right living is based on right doctrine. "All Scripture is inspired by God and profitable for teaching, for reproof, for correction, for training in righteousness; that the man of God may be adequate, equipped for every good work" (2 Timothy 3:16-17). It is through a knowledge of the truth that we are enabled to live the truth. And ultimately godliness must be the result. Scripture exhorts us to teach "doctrine conforming to godliness" (1 Timothy 6:3). That is my purpose and prayer in this book.

Part 1
The Lord God

GOD EXISTS:
THE PROOF FROM CAUSE-EFFECT

For every house is built by someone,
but the builder of all things is God. (Hebrews 3:4)

I have always been partial to Bulova watches because my father was a jeweler and always wore a Bulova wristwatch. A wristwatch is a precision instrument—it is small, intricately made, amazing in its ability to keep accurate time. If I were to open my wristwatch it would probably state, "Made in Switzerland." Although I have never been to Switzerland or a watch factory I know that somewhere there is a watch factory that manufactures wristwatches. How do I know? Because my wristwatch bears witness of the fact. Every effect demands a cause. Something does not come from nothing. A wristwatch demands that there is a watchmaker; a book demands that there is a publisher; a house demands that there is a carpenter—and a creation demands a Creator. Since the world exists there must be a cause for its existence; it did not come into being by accident.

However, some who deny God's existence suggest that the universe is eternal in spite of the indication of the second law of thermodynamics that the universe is running down. The law states that although the amount of energy remains the same, there is less available for work. Similarly, the law of entropy indicates that there is a decrease of order and organization in the world. Symptoms throughout the world reveal there is a "devolution" from order to chaos. A hot cup of coffee does not become hotter; it gradually turns cold. Man begins to die as soon as he is born; there is a constant deterioration of the human body—black hair turns gray, teeth decay, organs become weak.

All those things imply that the universe is not eternal and self-sustaining; rather, it has been created by an all-wise God. All of nature speaks a testimony of an all-wise Creator. The beautiful hibiscus, the majestic mountains, the magnificent hummingbird—all remind us of an all-wise Creator who desires fellowship with us. How wonderful that this great Creator has also deigned to share His eternal life with you and me (1 Corinthians 1:9)! Enjoy this day in fellowship with the majestic Creator God!

LESSON: *The existence of the world demonstrates the existence of God who created it, the majestic God with whom we may enjoy fellowship.*

GOD EXISTS:
THE PROOF FROM MAN

They show the work of the Law written in their hearts,
their conscience bearing witness, and their thoughts
alternately accusing or else defending them. (Romans 2:15)

Some years ago the Canadian National Railway opened what it termed a "Conscience Fund." Over a period of time a number of individuals had written letters confessing that they had taken train rides without paying for them. After living with their dishonesty for many years, they wanted the guilt erased from their conscience.

What is it inside a person—believer or unbeliever—that plagues him when he has sinned? Animals do not have this inner witness. I have watched my two Siamese cats. Whenever the younger cat, Sam, sees her mother walking toward the bowl to eat, she walks toward the bowl, "nudges" her mother out of the way, and stands in front of the bowl herself. She is not interested in eating; she is simply jealous. I have never seen Sam repent or express regret for her action, but God has placed a conscience inside every human being, and no one can escape the moral obligation that the conscience dictates.

God created man in His own image (Genesis 1:26), suggesting that man is created as a moral being with a relationship to Almighty God. But that relationship demands accountability. Man has a sense of obligation or "oughtness." That sense of obligation is placed there by God in man's conscience (Romans 2:15). All humans, educated or uneducated, civilized or uncivilized, have a conscience that dictates moral accountability to a righteous God. Violation of God's law as written on the conscience causes condemnation within the heart. That knowledge apart from the gospel cannot save a person but is preparatory, leading him to see his need of the salvation that Jesus Christ has provided.

Man has a conscience so that he may respond to God. Mankind is lost because of the Fall of the human race, but the conscience provokes men and women to recognize their need and respond in faith to the call of the gospel. Have you heard the still small voice of your conscience? Have you responded to the promptings of the Holy Spirit through it?

LESSON: *Man's conscience reminds him of his accountability to a righteous God and enables him to respond to God.*

GOD EXISTS:
THE PROOF FROM DESIGN

The heavens are telling of the glory of God; and the
firmament is declaring the work of His hands. (Psalm 19:1)

E verywhere in the universe there is evidence of a Master Designer. The sun at 93,000,000 miles from the earth is precisely the right distance to permit life on earth. Were it closer, the earth's surface would be too hot to sustain life; were it farther away, the earth would be too cold for habitation. The moon, at 240,000 miles, is also just the right distance from the earth. Were it closer, the gravitational pull would be stronger, producing tidal waves of enormous proportions.

One may also look at life on earth. Have you ever considered the wonder of the human body? The eardrums are recessed sufficiently to prohibit children from poking their fingers into their ears and damaging them. Have you ever considered that if your nostrils were turned upward you could drown in a rainstorm? The human body is magnificent in its design—clearly the production of a Master Creator. Everywhere in the universe is evidence of harmony and intelligence.

The magnificence of creation bears witness to God's existence. The harmony in our world could no more come about by accident—or evolution—than a monkey left alone in a room with a typewriter could produce a Shakespearean play.

God has not left Himself without a witness; there is tangible proof that He exists. The harmony in the universe is inexplicable apart from God. Why is there not chaos in the universe? How do we explain the order, symmetry, and harmony in creation apart from God? Order and harmony do not happen by accident—they are the resultant work of a loving, all-wise, and merciful God.

God's general revelation is designed to lead people to a knowledge of Him and ultimately to faith (Romans 10:17-18). Have you responded to the God who has revealed Himself? Perhaps you want to approach God on a rational basis. The intricate design and harmony in the universe, the world, and nature demonstrate His existence. He has spoken! Will you speak to Him? "Whoever will call upon the name of the Lord will be saved" (Romans 10:13).

LESSON: *The order and harmony in the universe testify that there is an all-wise God who has created all things.*

GOD EXISTS:
THE PROOF FROM INTUITION

In Him we live and move and exist. (Acts 17:28)

David Livingstone traveled extensively in Africa and later announced that he knew of no people on earth, no matter how primitive, who did not have a concept of God. Everywhere he went even the most primitive people had a basic awareness that God exists.

The knowledge of God's existence is, of course, unique to man. Animals do not have that understanding. My Siamese cat does not know that God exists. It is an intuitive knowledge that God has placed within the heart of every person. No one is without that awareness. Because man is made in the image of God, he bears the brand of God. Man knows that God exists. It is intuitive.

In Acts 17:28, Paul reminds the Athenians of their common knowledge of God's existence. Epimenides, a Cretan who was not a Christian, expressed awareness of God's existence when he stated, "For in Him we live and move and exist." Another poet, Aratus, stated, "For we also are His offspring."

Paul used that common knowledge as a basis for bringing the people of Athens the gospel of Christ. The Athenians knew that God exists, but they didn't know Him in truth. They acknowledged their unawareness when they erected an altar "To an Unknown God." Paul had a common foundation with the Athenians. They both agreed that God exists. Then Paul explained the truth concerning God—that He revealed Himself in Jesus Christ.

God has engraved the knowledge of Himself on the heart of each person, that he or she might come to know Him in truth. Most people in America and around the world do acknowledge a belief in God, but mere recognition of His existence is inadequate for fellowship with Him and assurance of eternal life. That comes through personal faith in Jesus Christ.

LESSON: *All people have the inner witness that God exists.*

January 5

GOD IS
INDEPENDENT

And God said to Moses, "I AM WHO I AM";
and He said, "Thus you shall say to the sons of Israel,
"I AM has sent me to you." (Exodus 3:14)

An unborn child is entirely dependent upon its mother for nourishment and life. It can do nothing to sustain itself; it is dependent on someone else. Animals are dependent on nature for survival and life. They are dependent on other animals, rainfall, and vegetation. Trees, plants, and vegetation are dependent on the proper amount of sunshine and rainfall for survival. During a drought or flood the vegetation may dry up or drown. Everything that has life is dependent upon someone or something else for survival. Except God.

God alone is independent. He is not dependent upon anyone or anything else for survival because God has life in Himself. The basis for His existence is within Himself. That is particularly evident in His name. When God commissioned Moses to lead the Israelites out of Egypt into Canaan, Moses asked, "What is [Your] name?" (Exodus 3:13). God explained to Moses, "I AM WHO I AM" (v. 14). In the following verse God identifies Himself as Lord. Many people understand the name *Lord* to be related to the Hebrew verb "to be"; hence, to say, "I AM WHO I AM" would be similar to saying, "My name is Lord." But what does it mean?

When God referred to Himself as I AM WHO I AM, He was saying that He is the continually existing One. God is not bound by time; He had no beginning, and He has no end. He is the One who continually exists. For Him everything is in the present. God's very name emphasizes His self-existence, that He is independent of anything and anyone. He has life in Himself.

The wonder of this truth is that whereas God has life in Himself, so does Jesus Christ since Christ is God (John 5:26). Further, God has extended His grace to us that we might live in Him, for "in Him we live and move and exist" (Acts 17:28). Whether we recognize it or not, every breath we take is a result of His daily gift of grace. Surely every vestige of pride should vanish as we consider our complete dependence upon Him.

LESSON: *God is independent of all things; He is self-existent, having life in Himself.*

January 6

GOD IS
UNCHANGING

I, the Lord, do not change. (Malachi 3:6a)

Change. The world is filled with it. Perhaps it is the only thing we can count on. The other day I turned to the classical music station only to discover it had switched its format to contemporary music. When my weed-eater broke and I tried to buy another just like it, I found that they had discontinued it. I bought an "improved" model with an automatic line feed, but I couldn't use it. But that isn't all. They changed the ingredients in my deodorant. And now they use staples to attach the labels in my tea bags.

On a more serious level, churches change, colleges and seminaries change, and unfortunately, not always for the better. But God does not change! While the world around us changes, He remains the same.

Think of where we would be if God were also subject to change. It would mean His promises are not reliable. He could decide that He no longer loves the world and reverse His promise of John 3:16. He could change His mind about our security (see John 10:28). He could stop being patient and longsuffering; instead He could mete out judgment immediately. Surely the immutability—the unchanging nature of God—is important!

Change is always for better or for worse; therefore, it is impossible for God to change. He cannot improve or deteriorate in His deity. God "does not change like shifting shadows" (James 1:17, NIV*). He continues to be a God of grace; He is the author of "every good thing bestowed and every perfect gift . . . from above" (James 1:17a). And because God does not change, His "faithfulness continues throughout all generations" (Psalm 119:90a). What a blessed and important truth! Each morning you can rely on the patience, grace, and love of God. No matter how you feel, God does not change. His faithfulness endures forever!

LESSON: *God is unchanging in His being, His purposes, and His promises.*

New International Version.

GOD IS
ONE

Hear, O Israel! The Lord is our God,
the Lord is one! (Deuteronomy 6:4)

A young Hindu man growing up in India was told by his Hindu priest that he could choose which God he wanted to serve and ignore the others. But that created a dilemma for him. Which one should he choose? What if he ignored the stronger God and chose a weaker one? The decision caused him to search for the true God, and he was converted to Christ.

The beautiful words of Deuteronomy 6:4 form part of the *Shema* (meaning, "to hear"), the great confession of Jewish faith that faithful Jews recited every morning and evening. At the heart of Hebrew (and Christian) faith is the belief in the absolute uniqueness of God. He alone is God. He is the only God, and He is one. From the beginning—in contrast to the surrounding cultures—Jews and Christians have tenaciously held to monotheism—the belief that there is only one God.

This verse stresses the uniqueness of God. There is none like Him. The Hebrews make a similar statement after their deliverance from Egypt: "Who is like Thee among the gods, O Lord?" (Exodus 15:11). The "Egyptian gods" were inept in their ability to stop the Exodus. God is absolutely unique; He has no equal.

How does one approach this unique God? It is well to know that the Lord is the only unique God, but how does one come to know Him? God has provided a mediator. "For there is one God, and one mediator also between God and men, the man Christ Jesus" (1 Timothy 2:5). God is accessible through Jesus Christ, who is the bridge, the ladder, the way to God. Christ gave Himself as a ransom that we might have access to the one and only God (1 Timothy 2:6).

John's concluding words in his first epistle warn, "Little children, guard yourselves from idols" (1 John 5:21). Allowing anything in our lives to take the place that God alone should have is idolatry. Because He is unique, He should receive our wholehearted devotion.

LESSON: *God alone is God. He has no peer, and there is no other like Him.*

GOD IS
TRUTH

God is not a man that He should lie. (Numbers 23:19)

A Mennonite farmer in Minnesota walked into an insurance office and inquired about a policy. After the agent explained the benefits of the insurance policy the farmer told him that he believed him, was satisfied, and would take the policy. Later, a group of Mennonite farmers also approached the same insurance agent and told him they would like to take out the same insurance policy as their friend. "Let me explain it to you," said the insurance agent. "That won't be necessary," they said. "Our friend has explained it to us, and his word is good enough."

How wonderful when a simple word can be trusted. Unfortunately that is becoming less and less common. Agreements from appliance rentals to house purchases are covered by large swaths of documents. Why? Because people's word cannot be trusted.

Not so with God. God's every word can be trusted. When God gives a promise, it is true and reliable because it is impossible for Him to lie. That is an encouragement to us because we can count on His Word (Hebrews 6:18). Man may fail to keep his word, but God "is not a man that He should lie" (Numbers 23:19).

To say that God is truth is to say "that He is consistent with Himself, that He is all that He should be, that He has revealed Himself as He really is, and that He and His revelation are completely reliable" (Ryrie, *Basic Theology*, p. 44). He alone is the true God (John 17:3). Though every man could be a lying unbeliever, still God is true (Romans 3:4); He will never go back on His Word (2 Timothy 2:13).

Of what significance is that? It is a cause for rejoicing, because our hope of eternal life is based on the promise of a God who cannot lie (Titus 1:2). Jesus Christ has enabled us to know Him who is true, and we are in Him (1 John 5:20). Moreover, God is faithful and true to those who belong to Him (1 Thessalonians 5:24). You can confidently rest in the promises God has made to you.

LESSON: *God is truth. His person, knowledge, words, and revelation are in complete accord with reality.*

GOD IS
LOVE

*In this is love, not that we loved God, but that He loved us
and sent His Son to be the propitiation for our sins. (1 John 4:10)*

A seminary student in Chicago drove a transit route on which a group of thugs boarded the bus, refused to pay their fares, and intimidated the passengers. The seminarian called a policeman aboard, who made the thugs pay their fares. When the policeman and the rest of the passengers had disembarked, the thugs beat up the seminary student, leaving him unconscious. The seminarian pursued them, finally found them, and brought them to trial. When the judge sentenced the thugs to prison, the student stood up, told them about the love of Christ, and said he wanted to serve their sentence. His demonstration of God's love resulted in the conversion of at least one of the thugs.

That remarkable story beautifully illustrates the love of God. God's love is not a Hollywood-type emotion; it is a rational love that loves mankind though mankind is entirely unlovely. Love is basic to God's nature since "God is love" (1 John 4:8). *Agape,* a Greek word for love, does not emphasize a love based on emotion but rather a reasoned love that loves the object regardless of the worth of the object or whether the love is returned. That love is a primary attribute of God.

Love demands communication. Love does not reveal itself in isolation, does not live in a vacuum; hence, God demonstrated His love in sending "His only begotten Son that whoever believes in Him may have eternal life" (John 3:16). God also loves the Son (Matthew 3:17), Israel (Deuteronomy 7:8), and believers (John 14:33). Further, God's love is not simply sentimental but based in His truth and holiness. God has expressed His love because He seeks to redeem man from his sinful estate.

God has especially exhibited His love for believers, loving them while they were sinners (Romans 5:8) and lavishing His love on them to name them His children (1 John 3:1). But love is unfulfilled if it does not receive response. Have you responded to God's love?

LESSON: *God is love and portrays that love by communicating to man through sending His Son, Jesus Christ.*

GOD IS
HOLY

*Consecrate yourselves therefore,
and be holy; for I am holy. (Leviticus 11:44)*

Holiness is a confusing word to many people. Some envision a church choir singing, "Holy, holy, holy." Others understand it to be a perfectly pious person who even parts his hair exactly the right way. Actually the word *holy* simply means "set apart." We demonstrate this principle in every area of life. We set apart clean laundry from dirty laundry; we select the good fruit from the spoiled fruit in a grocery store; we hoe our vegetable gardens to separate the vegetables from the weeds; we even separate convicted criminals from the rest of society.

Holiness has several senses. First, it means that God is set apart from His creatures and exalted above them in majesty. It emphasizes God's "transcendence," which means that God is exalted above His creation and is without peer. Isaiah 57:15 states, "For thus says the high and exalted One Who lives forever, whose name is Holy, 'I dwell on a high and holy place.'" It is also emphasized in Exodus 15:11, "Who is like Thee among the gods, O Lord? Who is like Thee, majestic in holiness, awesome in praises, working wonders?"

Holiness also has an ethical sense, meaning that God is entirely separated or set apart from moral evil and sin. God is pure; He has no relationship with sin. Habakkuk 1:13 declares, "Thine eyes are too pure to approve evil, and Thou canst not look on wickedness with favor."

Many consider holiness the greatest, most basic attribute of God. Every attribute, characteristic, and action reflects His holiness. It is seen in His love, mercy, truth, and justice. Moreover, because God is holy He called Israel to be a holy people, giving them many laws that simply emphasized that they were special, set apart for the Lord. Similarly, Christians are special, set-apart people.

God has called us to be holy (1 Peter 1:15-16). What does that mean to you? How does it affect your behavior? your speech? your thoughts? your television viewing? your recreation? your business habits? your marital conduct? Do you have the same hatred for sin that God has?

LESSON: *God is infinitely exalted above His creation and is entirely pure, separated from evil.*

January 11

GOD IS
WISDOM

O Lord, how many are Thy works! In wisdom
Thou hast made them all. (Psalm 104:24)

Although both God and man can be said to be wise, any comparison between divine and human wisdom will only reveal contrasts. Socrates, one of the world's wisest men, acknowledged that his wisdom could be summed up in the fact that he knew that he knew nothing! God, on the other hand, not only knows all things but in wisdom has planned all things.

The wisdom of God is the application of God's unlimited knowledge. God's wisdom is displayed everywhere in the world and in the universe. Reflecting on the world, the psalmist sees the imprint of an all-wise God. In mysterious wisdom, God has set the world in space "so that it will not totter" (Psalm 104:5). In wisdom He created the water runoff from the mountains, forming valley springs and providing water for the wild donkeys (vv. 10-11). In wisdom God causes the grass to grow, providing food for animals; He also causes the plants to grow, providing food for man (v. 14). Both on earth and in the universe God has appointed everything in its place: high mountains for wild goats, cliffs for rock badgers, and the moon to mark off the seasons, and the sun for its rising and setting (vv. 18-19). God is wise!

Do you realize God has called you and me to share His wisdom? The epitome of God's wisdom is Christ (Ephesians 3:10). When we trust Christ, God places us in union with Him who becomes to us "wisdom from God" (1 Corinthians 1:30), a wisdom not found in this world system (1 Corinthians 1:21). All the philosophies and speculations of this world cannot compare with the wisdom you enjoy in Christ. In Christ "are hidden all the treasures of wisdom and knowledge" (Colossians 2:3).

H. B. Smith has stated that God's wisdom means He "produces the best results with the best possible means." Do you understand the implication? It means that in His wisdom God has planned the very best goal for us and the best path for us to travel toward that goal. He has planned that path not for our gain but for His glory. The deep riches of God's wisdom have directed our path for one purpose: that we live for the glory of God (Romans 11:33-36).

LESSON: *God in His wisdom has planned our path so that through Christ our lives may reflect His glory and wisdom.*

GOD IS
JEALOUS

You shall not worship any other god, for the Lord,
whose name is Jealous, is a jealous God. (Exodus 34:14)

I was standing in line in a government building when I overheard the conversation of two men behind me, which, to my grief, was liberally sprinkled with profanities misusing the name of Christ. I finally turned around and said, "Pardon me, but that is a very precious name that you are misusing." My heart was pained over their abuse of God's name. God wants us to be jealous for His name because He is a jealous God.

God jealous? It sounds contradictory, doesn't it? We think jealousy is negative because it reflects envy. But there is also a positive jealousy. The Hebrew word can also be translated "zealous," meaning a strong emotion expressing desire or possession of an object. Thus David had a zeal for God's house (Psalm 69:9) as did Christ (John 2:17).

How is God jealous? He is jealous for His name. In the Ten Commandments He instructed Israel to refrain from idolatry because the Lord alone is to be worshiped (Exodus 20:4-5). The Israelites provoked the Lord, arousing His anger and jealousy when they fashioned idols and worshiped them (Psalm 78:58). They ignored the Lord's warnings, so He disciplined them by sending them into captivity in Babylon (Ezekiel 16:42). God is jealous for the singular honor that He is to receive since He alone is God.

God is also jealous for His people. He wants their complete devotion. For that reason God warned Israel to tear down the idolatrous altars in the land (Exodus 34:10-16). We can arouse God's jealousy by giving Him half-hearted attention (1 Corinthians 10:22).

Not only is God jealous for us; we should be jealous for God! Elijah the lonely prophet was consumed with righteous jealousy for the Lord as he stood up to wicked King Ahab (1 Kings 19:14); when Phinehas saw his people disobey God he acted out of a zeal for righteousness (Numbers 25:6-13). When we see the Lord's name defamed and misused in profanity our hearts should grieve; when His moral standards are violated we should be pained and filled with passion for righteousness. We are called as a redeemed, purified people to be "zealous for good deeds" (Titus 2:14).

LESSON: *God is jealous for His holy name and for holiness in His people; similarly, we should be jealous for God's name to be honored.*

GOD POSSESSES
ETERNITY

From everlasting to everlasting, Thou art God. (Psalm 90:2)

Eternity is surely one of the most difficult concepts for finite man to consider. Since we have a beginning and an ending, since all of our history has a beginning and an ending, we cannot conceive of anything as never beginning or ending. I couldn't understand that as a child, and I still don't understand it! We try to illustrate it in a variety of ways. Picture a bird visiting an island once every thousand years and carrying one grain of sand away from the island. When the bird will have removed all the sand from the island, eternity will have only begun.

Eternity looks backward and forward. God never had a beginning. We cannot, of course, answer the question, "Where did God come from?" He is eternal. He alone has always existed. Moses recognized that prior to the creation of the world God existed (Psalm 90:2). Moreover, God has ruled as King forever (Psalm 102:12).

All of that means that God is not bound by a succession of events; He is timeless, above time. He is not affected by time—He does not age, grow tired, advance, or deteriorate. He remains the same.

Although God is not bound by time that does not mean time is not real to Him. Whereas God sees everything in an eternal present, He still sees a succession of events in history.

God is called the "everlasting God" (Genesis 21:33). His name, Lord, more correctly understood as Yahweh, comes from the Hebrew verb "to be"; hence, His name emphasizes that He is the continually existing One (Exodus 3:14). He has life in Himself and is not dependent on anyone or anything else for life. He has existence within Himself and is therefore eternal.

The eternity of God is a reminder to us that our lives on earth are temporal. Our lives are like a vapor that quickly vanishes (James 4:14); we are but dust (Psalm 90:3). Our temporary existence on earth and God's eternal existence ought to instruct us to spend our sojourn here wisely.

LESSON: *God is eternal, having no beginning and no ending; He is not bound by time nor succession of events.*

GOD IS
ALL-KNOWING

O Lord, Thou hast searched me and known me. (Psalm 139:1)

A young boy discovered that his neighbors, who had a delicious apple tree, were leaving their farm for the day. Watching their car depart, the boy hurried toward the neighbor's apple tree. He shinnied up the tree and began to stuff his jacket full of apples, certain that no one was watching him. However, another neighbor had recently purchased a pair of binoculars and was enjoying his new purchase by scanning the horizon. The binoculars focused on the boy stealing the apples! Although the boy was unaware, a neighbor watched the entire proceedings.

God is not spying on people, trying to catch them in a fault, but He is omniscient, meaning that He knows all things. David found that truth comforting, not frightening (Psalm 139:1-6). He recognized that God knew his life from the time he got up in the morning to the time he lay down at night. God knew his thoughts, and even before he spoke a word, God knew what it would be.

God knows things as they actually are. He knows the number of stars, and He gives names to each of them (Psalm 147:4). He also knows all possibilities that could happen. Jesus knew that had He performed miracles in Tyre and Sidon they would have repented (Matthew 11:21). God also knows future events. God revealed the successive empires that would rule for centuries into the future (Daniel 2:36-45). Jesus explained the course of events that will occur at the end of the age (Matthew 24-25).

God's knowledge is intuitive; it is not acquired. Any knowledge you and I have is acquired through study and learning. Not so with God. His knowledge is innate and complete.

What is the significance of this? For the believer it is a great comfort. Nothing happens to you that escapes the notice of your Father. He who sees the sparrow fall from the tree also sees your grief. For the unbeliever this is a solemn realization. You cannot hide from God, for He sees your heart. He knows everything about you—*everything*. Don't run any longer. Come to Christ in faith.

LESSON: *God knows all things that have already happened, that potentially could happen, and that will happen in the future.*

GOD IS
PRESENT EVERYWHERE

Where can I go from Thy Spirit? Or where
can I flee from Thy presence? (Psalm 139:7)

We live in an age of disappearing people. Children disappear. Mothers disappear. Fathers disappear. Of course, they disappear for different reasons. Tragically, many children disappear because they are kidnapped. Some parents, however, disappear because they willfully leave. Some mothers get tired of the drudgery of housework; fathers become weary of their responsibilities in the home, or they break the law and decide to run away. One prominent bank manager disappeared, and then his bank discovered considerable money was missing. A pastor abandoned his wife and family and ran away with the church secretary.

Those are sad stories, incidents wherein homes are broken and churches hurt. However, "disappearing people" cannot disappear from God. They may escape responsibility by hiding from other people, but they cannot hide from God. The Scriptures teach that God is omnipresent—He is everywhere. David recognized he could not run or hide from God. He said that if he could flee to heaven God is there, or if he descended to Sheol, the netherworld, God is there also. Could he swiftly take wings and escape to the beyond or hide in the depths of the sea, God would be there. No one can escape from God (Psalm 139:7-12)!

God is present everywhere in the totality of His person: "'Do I not fill the heaven and the earth?' declares the Lord" (Jeremiah 23:24). However, that is not pantheism, which says God is in everything. Nor does it mean that part of God is in one place and part in another. His entire being is in every place. Yet He is specially in some places: His glory uniquely dwelt in the Holy of Holies; He is uniquely present with believers; He is not in hell as He is in heaven; He is not with animals as He is with man.

God's omnipresence is a great comfort to believers; Christ taught it to encourage the disciples (Matthew 28:20). Amid our service for Him, amid our trials, He is with us! God's omnipresence is also a warning to unbelievers and to Jekyll-and-Hyde Christians: they cannot escape God's presence. He sees everything and is present everywhere. He is the divine detective!

LESSON: *God is present everywhere in the totality of His being.*

GOD IS
ALL-POWERFUL

Nothing is too difficult for Thee. (Jeremiah 32:17)

S keptics sometimes challenge Christians with questions: "Is there anything God can't do?"
"No, He can do everything."
"Can He create a rock so big that He can't move it?" Of course, that is a trick question. There *are* things that God cannot do. He cannot act contrary to His nature. But the fact is that most people have too small a concept of God, not recognizing that He is all-powerful. J. B. Phillips wrote a book titled *Your God Is Too Small,* in which he exposed people's caricatures of God. Many people have a God of their own making—but it is not the biblical God.

God can do anything He pleases that is in harmony with His nature. God "works all things after the counsel of His will" (Ephesians 1:11); "He does whatever He pleases" (Psalm 115:3). Nothing can hinder God's plan and purpose. Whatever He decides to do will come to pass.

Almighty is a word that describes God's power. As God Almighty (*El Shaddai*) He could make ninety-nine-year-old Abram a father (Genesis 17:1); He caused cunning Jacob to be the father of nations and kings (35:11), and one day He will judge the world in the Great Tribulation (Revelation 4:8).

God's power also goes beyond what He actually does. "Is anything too difficult for the Lord?" asked the angel (Genesis 18:14). No. He can enable a ninety-year-old mother to conceive and bear a child, and He can do even more. John the Baptist said that God could turn stones into faithful Israelites—but He didn't (Matthew 3:9). Jesus said He could appeal to the Father to send seventy-two thousand angels to rescue Him—but He didn't (26:53).

There are things God cannot do. He can't associate with sin (Habakkuk 1:13), He can't go back on His word (2 Timothy 2:13), He can't lie (Hebrews 6:18).

The greatest expression of God's power was the bodily resurrection of Jesus (2 Corinthians 13:4). And the power of God that raised Jesus from the dead is operative in believers (Ephesians 1:19)! Think of it! Are you living by faith in the all-powerful God? Or do you carry the weight of the world as if God were not powerful? Remember, "Nothing is too difficult for God!"

LESSON: *God is all-powerful and able to do whatever He wills and whatever is consistent with His nature.*

GOD IS MERCIFUL

God [is] rich in mercy. (Ephesians 2:4)

Following the San Francisco earthquake of 1989, Mark Smith won a $15,000 Mazda Miata sports car in a radio contest and promptly turned the sports car over to the Red Cross to help earthquake victims. The disc jockey and radio station management were thunderstruck, so they decided to give Smith another $15,000 Miata sports car. Said Smith, "I still don't know what I'm going to do. I may yet give this one up, too." Smith's donation sparked a rash of other donations. Human expressions of mercy are wonderful, but the greatest expressions of mercy come from God Himself.

Mercy is an attribute of God that expresses His love to mankind; it is God's pity for man, regardless whether man deserves it or not. Mercy is free—God is not obligated to show His mercy any more than Mark Smith was obligated to donate his sports car. If it is obligatory, then it becomes a debt. But God's mercy rises out of His pity for sinful humanity's estate. Hence, God is "rich in mercy" (Ephesians 2:4), a mercy that moves to action because of His love.

God's mercy generally expresses itself in two ways. First, God extended His mercy to us when we were dead in sin and rebels toward Him. He gave us life by joining us to Christ (Ephesians 2:4-5). God saved us according to His mercy and gave us life (Titus 3:5). Second, God moves to meet people's temporal needs. When Naomi sent her daughters-in-law away she prayed, "May the Lord deal kindly with you" (Ruth 1:8), expressing the hope they would each acquire a husband to care for them. God also promised that if He gave believers the greater gift (Christ) He would surely also give them the lesser—temporal needs (Romans 8:28).

Peter praises God because of His mercy that gives us a living hope and a future inheritance in heaven (1 Peter 1:3). God's gift of Christ is the ultimate expression of His mercy (Romans 8:32). But it would be a great tragedy if God's mercy received no response. How have you responded to God's great act of pity on man's misery? Do you reflect God's nature by showing mercy? Jesus said, "Be merciful, just as your Father is merciful" (Luke 6:36).

LESSON: *God is merciful, showing compassion and pity on sinners by making both physical and spiritual provisions for them.*

GOD IS
A PERSON

I am the Lord, and there is no other;
besides Me there is no God. (Isaiah 45:5)

D uring the 1950s there was an epidemic of polio. Many people—
teenagers and young married people included—succumbed to
the dreaded disease. Some who survived it were confined to an
iron lung, having completely lost the use of their bodies. Although they had
no functional bodies, they proved that a body is not necessary to personality. One young married woman who was immobilized through polio was a
great encouragement and blessing to her visitors because of her radiant
faith in Christ.

God does not have a body, yet He is a person. What, then, constitutes
personhood? A person is someone who has a will. Animals do not have a
will; they function according to instinct and conditioning. The vegetable
world does not have a will. Human beings have a will because they are
made in the image of God. God reveals His personality in the display of His
will; He makes choices. For example, He chose Jacob rather than Esau to
be the one through whom He would display His blessings (Romans 9:11).

A person is also someone with intellect. God displayed His intellect in
His observation of the Israelites' suffering; He listened to their cries, and He
responded to their suffering (Exodus 3:7).

A person has emotion. God reveals that He is a person in His display
of emotion: when God saw the wickedness of man on earth He was grieved
in His heart and sorry that He had made him (Genesis 6:6).

A person is also self-conscious, that is, he is aware of his existence;
he is able to relate his feelings and thoughts to himself. An example of this
is Isaiah 45:5: "I am the Lord, and there is no other; besides Me there is no
God."

Is it significant that God is a person? Indeed. Otherwise it would be
impossible for us to have fellowship with Him. Paul Tillich taught that God
is an impersonal force, "the ultimate ground of all being." It is impossible to
have fellowship with a god like that! Thankfully, God, though He does not
have a body, is indeed a person.

LESSON: *God is a person, having self-consciousness, intellect, emo-*
tion, and a will in order that we might have fellowship with Him.

GOD IS
SPIRIT

*God is spirit; and those who worship Him
must worship in spirit and truth. (John 4:24)*

Who has not seen a picture of the magnificent painting in the Sistine Chapel ceiling in the Vatican? In Michelangelo's painting of the creation of man he painted God as an old man with long white hair extending His finger to create Adam. As a work of art, Michelangelo's work is monumental. As a depiction of biblical truth, it is wrong.

Actually that concept of God is probably not unusual. Many homes have pictures of Jesus with long hair and blue eyes—even though we have no knowledge of what He looked like. Non-Christian cultures have physical depictions of God, whether a wooden totem pole, a statue of Buddha, or a representation of a dragon.

It is the nature of man to think in tangible terms, to visualize in physical forms. For that reason it becomes difficult to think of God without some physical visualization. But Jesus taught, "God is spirit." That means God is not material or visible. He cannot be reduced to a physical form nor confined to spacial limitations. He is spirit, and therefore His presence pervades everything.

It is because God is spirit that He cannot be confined to a house or one location (Acts 7:48). He is not *a* spirit, for then He would be localized. If He were physical, He would be confined to space and thus would not be God. He would not have all the qualities of God. Being spirit, He stands in contrast to finite, human beings.

Moreover, since God is spirit it is wrong to produce a physical image of Him (Exodus 20:4). In any case, it would be a wrong representation. Any physical depiction of God limits Him. He is greater than any physical representation and larger than any space can accord Him!

But because God is spirit, all of us, no matter where we are—China or Chicago—can approach Him, knowing He is present. And because He is spirit He can dwell with all believers everywhere.

LESSON: *God is spirit; He does not have a physical form and cannot be confined to a physical image or place.*

GOD IS JUST

[God] will render to every man
according to his deeds. (Romans 2:6)

A young man was caught smoking marijuana and brought to trial. He had never been charged with a criminal act before. Although he was not selling the drug, he was caught with it in his possession. The judge sentenced the young man to forty years in prison. Was that justice? Undoubtedly not. People will debate the justice of sentencing Jim Bakker to forty-five years in prison for a "while collar crime," because the average convicted murderer is sentenced to less time. One man who murdered another man was sentenced to twelve months in the workhouse. Is a human life only worth twelve months in prison?

Unfortunately there is little genuine justice in the world. But God is just and righteous in all His acts (Psalm 99:4). God is entirely correct and consistent in everything He does. There is never any unfairness. There are no wrong decisions. He never rewards or punishes someone too much or too little.

There are two aspects of God's justice. First, God rewards those who love Him for countless generations (Deuteronomy 7:9). Those who persist in doing good, seeking God's honor in daily life, will be rewarded accordingly (Romans 2:7). At the end of his life Paul looked to the "righteous Judge" to reward him for having fought the good fight (2 Timothy 4:8). Second, God punishes those who violate His law and His justice (Romans 2:9); in fact, lawbreakers are aware that God is righteous in judging them (1:32). God will severely judge the world at the end of the age (Revelation 16:5-7).

What an encouragement to faithfulness! Are you discouraged in your attempt to be faithful? Do you think it worthless to live a righteous life in a sinful world? Not at all! Persist in living according to God's Word. Be faithful to the Lord. A day is coming when all wrongs will be made right, the faithful rewarded, and the lawbreakers punished.

LESSON: *God is entirely just in all His dealings with people, fairly rewarding the faithful and punishing the evildoers.*

GOD IS THE
CREATOR OF ALL THINGS

And God saw all that He had made,
and behold, it was very good. (Genesis 1:31)

Scientists suggest the earth was born 15 billion years ago in a great explosion—"the big bang." The big bang produced protons and neutrons that, after one year, formed atoms. In 300,000 years the atoms coalesced to eventually form stars, and in 2 to 3 billion years galaxies were formed. But what produced the big bang? Where did the protons and neutrons come from?

There is a better answer to the origin of the universe than the big bang theory: "In the beginning God created the heavens and the earth" (Genesis 1:1). God, who alone is eternal, brought the temporal universe into existence. That is the only possibility since all else had a beginning, and something cannot come from nothing. The earth did not create itself!

God created the universe, the world, and man directly—not through any form of evolution. On the first day, God created light. The source of light was not the sun (created on the fourth day) but light from a fixed source outside the earth, instituting the light-darkness cycle called "day" (Davis, *Paradise*, p. 49). The light caused a separation from the darkness (Genesis 1:3-5).

On the second day, God created an expanse (the atmosphere), separating the waters on the earth from the waters above the earth (vv. 6-8). The waters above, which were unleashed during the Flood, formed a canopy, creating a greenhouse effect, enabling man to live longer.

On the third day God separated the land from the seas and created the individual species of plants "after their kind" (vv. 9-13). The fourth day God created the sun, moon, and stars, necessary since plants require sunlight to grow (vv. 14-19). The fifth day God created the individual species of fish and birds, each "after its kind" (vv. 20-23). On the sixth day God created the individual species of animals to fill the earth, and He created Adam and Eve, the first pair from whom all humanity has descended (vv. 24-31). He created man and woman in His image that we might have fellowship with Him. And although the fellowship was broken through the Fall, the path to fellowship is open again through the Lord Jesus.

LESSON: *God created the universe, the earth, all vegetation, animals, and Adam and Eve directly, apart from any form of evolution.*

GOD IS
A TRINITY

Hear, O Israel! The Lord is our God,
the Lord is one! (Deuteronomy 6:4)

1 + 1 + 1 = 1. New math? No—the doctrine of the Trinity. The Father is God, the Son is God, and the Holy Spirit is God. Although all three are called God, there is only one God, not three. The Trinity can be illustrated in several ways. An egg has a shell, a white, and a yoke. Each is distinct; the shell is not the white, the white is not the yoke, and the yoke is not the shell. There is only one egg, but at the same time the yoke may be referred to as one egg, and likewise the white or the shell may each be called an egg. The Trinity can also be illustrated by a cake. A cake can be ingredients, layers, and slices. The Father may be compared to the ingredients, the Son to the layers by which the cake has come down to us, and the Holy Spirit to the slices by which He is passed around (Bolce, *Foundations*, p. 112).

At the heart of Hebrew-Christian faith is the truth that there is only one God. Morning and evening faithful Hebrews rightly recited, "Hear, O Israel! The Lord is our God, the Lord is one!" (Deuteronomy 6:4). It is true that there are three persons in Scripture called God. The Father is called God (1 Corinthians 8:6). In contrast to the surrounding cultures, Hebrews and Christians recognized but one God, the Father. The Son is called God (John 1:1). The Son, who is called "the Word," has existed from all eternity in fellowship with the Father. The Holy Spirit is also called God (Acts 5:3). Peter reminded Ananias that to lie to the Holy Spirit is to lie to God.

One of the wonders of the Trinity is that God has sent all three to indwell the believer. The Holy Spirit is the Comforter who indwells believers forever (John 14:16), but Jesus promised that the Father and the Son would also indwell believers: "If anyone loves Me, he will keep My word; and My Father will love him, and We will come to him, and make Our abode with him!" (John 14:23). What an amazing provision God has made for His people! The Spirit, the Father, and the Son all make their home with the believer. Draw comfort from those comforting words spoken by the Lord Jesus.

LESSON: *There are three distinct persons who exist as God, yet there is only one God.*

January 23

THREE IN
AUTHORITY

*The grace of the Lord Jesus Christ, and the love of God,
and the fellowship of the Holy Spirit, be with you all.
(2 Corinthians 13:14)*

In the fourth century a man named Arius taught that Christ was not equal with the Father, nor was Christ eternal. He taught that Christ was of a different substance than the Father and was in fact a created being. A great controversy erupted in the church, particularly between Arius and Athanasius. Athanasius taught that Christ was of the same substance of the Father and therefore equal with the Father and eternal. The church eventually recognized that Athanasius taught the orthodox, biblical view.

The mention of the Father, the Son, and the Holy Spirit together is important in recognizing their equality as persons and in authority. For example, Jesus instructed the apostles to "make disciples of all the nations, baptizing them in the name of the Father and the Son and the Holy Spirit" (Matthew 28:19). Since some cults deny the personality of the Holy Spirit, that statement would then indicate that we baptize disciples in the name of two persons and one thing! Some cults also deny the deity of the Son. But if that were true, then Jesus would be commanding His followers to baptize their converts in the name of one who is superior and two who are inferior. That, too, is unlikely.

Even stronger is the benediction: "The grace of the Lord Jesus Christ, and the love of God, and the fellowship of the Holy Spirit, be with you all (2 Corinthians 13:14). Grace, love, and communion come from the three persons of the Trinity. Surely those words demand the equality of the Father, Son, and Holy Spirit.

Other statements indicate that the Son and Holy Spirit are equal in authority to the Father. For example, the Son is to be worshiped just as the Father (John 5:23)—and Christ willingly received worship (Matthew 14:33). Blasphemy against the Holy Spirit can never be forgiven, indicating the Spirit's authority and importance (Matthew 12:31).

The Trinity multiplies God's blessing to us: grace from Christ, love from the Father, and fellowship with the Holy Spirit.

LESSON: *Three persons exist within the Godhead, who are equal in authority, power, and honor.*

NAMES OF GOD:
YAHWEH

I appeared to Abraham, Isaac, and Jacob,
as God Almighty, but by My name, Lord,
I did not make Myself known to them. (Exodus 6:3)

What's in a name? A name is important because it identifies a person. Most of us have common names. But some stand out as prominent names on the social register. Rothschild. Rockefeller. DuPont. Ford. They are well-known names, some having centuries of historical prominence. The Rothschilds were financial barons of the great Austrian empire during the eighteenth and nineteenth centuries, having developed a large banking empire. They were so powerful that they negotiated loans for Denmark, aided England during the war with Spain, and enabled the British government to pay subsidies to European princes.

Another name, however, is above every name. God has revealed facets of Himself through His names. When Moses was commissioned to lead the Israelites out of Egypt Moses asked God for His identification. God revealed Himself as "I AM WHO I AM . . . the Lord. . . . This is My name forever" (Exodus 3:14-15). The name *Lord* is more properly pronounced "Yahweh" and occurs 6,828 times in the Old Testament. It comes from the Hebrew verb meaning "to be"; hence, God is the eternally existing One. His name reveals His timeless, eternal existence.

It was by the name *Lord* that God revealed Himself as the covenant God of Israel. When the Lord appeared to Moses He told him that He had not revealed Himself as Yahweh to the patriarchs Abraham, Isaac, and Jacob (6:3). However, as Israel's covenant God, He would establish His covenant with them, deliver them from Egyptian bondage, and redeem them by bringing catastrophic judgments upon Egypt (vv. 4-6). He promised to enter into a covenant relationship with them in which they would be His special people and He would be their God, bringing them into the Promised Land (vv. 7-8).

Jesus uttered many unique "I AM" statements in which He identified Himself with Yahweh (John 6:35; 8:12; 10:9, 11; 11:25; 14:6; 15:1). Jesus claimed deity in those statements, but He was also reminding us of our special relationship with Him. He is our shepherd, our resurrection, our life!

LESSON: *By His name* Yahweh, *God has revealed Himself as a covenant-keeping God who rescues and redeems His people.*

NAMES OF GOD:
ELOHIM

*In the beginning God created
the heavens and the earth. (Genesis 1:1)*

We prize power. Anyone who has seen and heard the gigantic rockets roar, then lift the space shuttle from its fiery launch pad at Kennedy Space Center, is awestruck by the power. Solid rockets propel the assembled shuttle, normally weighing 4.5 million pounds at liftoff, into orbit around the world. Together with the engines on the orbiter the rockets produce more than 7 million pounds of thrust. That is awesome power! Yet it is insignificant when compared to God, who has revealed Himself as awesome.

In the Old Testament God is known by the name *Elohim,* which is translated "God." The name occurs more than two thousand times and emphasizes that God is above all others that are called God. He stands unique. The name God probably comes from a root word meaning "to be strong." Thus He is the Strong One. That is seen at the outset of Scripture: "In the beginning God created the heavens and the earth" (Genesis 1:1).

When Jacob was about to flee for his life because he deceived his brother, Esau, Isaac blessed Jacob with the promise "May God Almighty bless you and make you fruitful and multiply you, that you may become a company of peoples" (28:3). It was the strong God who would secure Jacob's future despite his dismal condition. Later, God reminded Jacob, "I am God Almighty" (35:11). God promised Jacob descendants, a great nation, and possession of the land that He had promised to his forefathers. Jacob could have hope in the future because his God was strong.

Our strong God gives encouragement to His people. The same God who resolved seemingly insurmountable obstacles for His people in the past can resolve our difficulties in the present. Are you carrying your own burdens today, or are you allowing God to carry them for you?

LESSON: *By His name* Elohim, *God has revealed Himself as a strong God, able to help His people amid troubles.*

NAMES OF GOD:
ADONAI

The Lord your God is the God of gods and the Lord of lords, the great, the mighty, and the awesome God. (Deuteronomy 10:17)

A man stole a car from a used car lot in Lynchburg, Virginia, but was arrested when he arrived in Florida. "The Lord put me in this car and showed me the way to Florida," the man told police. "The Lord above saw a way for me to get to Florida." The man was jailed anyway. Clearly he did not know the Lord or acknowledge Him as Master. He was using the Lord's name in vain, treating God as a genie to help him get to Florida.

The Lord is known by His name *Adonai*, which occurs 449 times in the Old Testament. *Adonai* comes from a root word meaning "lord" or "master" and is used to describe a master-servant relationship. For example, Eliezer described Abraham as his master (*adonai*) and saw himself as Abraham's servant (Genesis 24:9). When Joseph rose to prominence in Egypt he exercised authority as a "lord," or master, over the people of Egypt (45:8).

The psalmist viewed God as Lord of the universe and addressed Him with a title of respect in a master-servant relationship (Psalm 8:1). By His name *Lord* He is viewed as the God who has no equal; He is without peer, Lord of all (Deuteronomy 10:17).

The Israelites understood this concept since in their entire religion they assumed a "king-vassal" (master-servant) relationship. They were given detailed instructions on how to assemble the Tabernacle, transport it, and approach God in the Tabernacle. Only the high priest could approach the Lord once a year in the Holy of Holies; only the worshiper who brought a sacrifice could approach the inner court. Every ritual was designed to remind Israel that the Lord was their Master and they were His servants. When the Israelites carried the Ark across the Jordan into the Promised Land, "the Lord of all the earth" was crossing over the Jordan with them (Joshua 3:11). The Master was going before them into Canaan.

God's name *Adonai* is a reminder that He is our Lord. He is not our genie that we should rub His lamp when we want something from Him. The name *Adonai* reminds us that we are His servants; He is the Master, and we are to stand in awe of His majesty. He is worthy of our worship and respect.

LESSON: *By His name* Adonai, *the Lord has revealed Himself as Master of all people.*

NAMES OF GOD:
EL SHADDAI

I am God Almighty. (Genesis 17:1a)

Most people enjoy the mountains. Who has visited central Colorado and not been awestruck by the "fourteeners"—Mounts Harvard, Yale, and Princeton? Or stood in amazement at the grandeur of Mount Edith Cavel in Jasper National Park in Alberta? On a day when the desert valley was free of smog I could stand in my front yard in southern California and view the spectacular, snow-capped Mount Gorgonio, piercing the sky at well over eleven thousand feet. It made me think of God.

That is significant since God's name *Shaddai* probably means mountain. The compound name, *El Shaddai,* likely means "God of the mountain," the dwelling place of God. Thus, mountains remind us of God's greatness and power.

What is the significance of the name *El Shaddai?* As *El Shaddai* God revealed Himself to the patriarchs as a powerful God who could perform what He promised. As *El Shaddai* He is the God of the impossible. When Abram was ninety-nine years old and childless, God reminded him that He was *El Shaddai*—the Strong One who would fulfill His covenant (Genesis 17:1). And that meant that Abram would have an infinite number of descendants—a hopeless prospect for Abram alone, but possible through a powerful God. Because He is *El Shaddai,* God could say, "I will establish My covenant . . . I will multiply you. . . . I will make you the father of a multitude of nations. . . . I will make you exceedingly fruitful" (Genesis 17:2-6). God is able to perform what He has promised!

Is your God that big? Is your God the God of the impossible? Do you know *El Shaddai?* Or are you living a mediocre existence, groveling in self-pity, doubting God's ability? Come to *El Shaddai!* Heed His words: "Walk before Me, and be blameless" (Genesis 17:1), and see Him fulfill His "I will" on your behalf. What does He expect of you? Obedience and trust. As you live before *El Shaddai* in obedience and belief, you will see His strong arm come to help you. The God of the mountains is your strength!

LESSON: *As El Shaddai God reveals Himself as a powerful God, able to perform what He promises to those who walk in obedience.*

NAMES OF GOD:
EL OLAM

Before the mountains were born, or Thou didst
give birth to the earth and the world, even
from everlasting to everlasting, Thou art God. (Psalm 90:2)

Have you ever been in a country general store? The smells and sights take one back forty or fifty years. The old Coca Cola signs, the ornate postcards, the manual cash register, the candy in jars, and the old-fashioned radio are all reminiscent of yesteryear. And they remind us how much the world has changed.

But God does not change; He is untouched by time. And because He is everlasting, He represents continuity. When Abraham came to Beersheba, he planted a tamarisk tree, a durable wood similar to the cypress tree, to remind him of the eternal, enduring God (Genesis 21:33). Abraham had gained new insight into the nature of God. God is *El Olam*—the everlasting God. Through his experiences Abraham came to believe in the stability of God and His unchanging nature. As the tamarisk is an enduring tree, so God continues forever; He is enduring, providing continuity and hope.

Predicting when the Israelites would be held captive in distant Babylon, Isaiah promised hope by reminding them of the everlasting God: "Do you not know? Have you not heard? The everlasting God, the Lord, the creator of the ends of the earth does not become weary or tired" (Isaiah 40:28). Because He is eternal He is unchanging, never wearying. And because He is unchanging, He remains faithful to His promises. He helps His people. His eternality is a reminder that His people may dwell in fellowship with the eternal God (Psalm 90:1-2), enjoying His lovingkindness forever (100:5; 103:17).

So what is the import? "He gives strength to the weary, and to him who lacks might He increases power. . . . Yet those who wait for the Lord will gain new strength; they will mount up with wings like eagles, they will run and not get tired, they will walk and not become weary" (Isaiah 40:29, 31). Because God is eternal, He is stable, faithful, and consistent. That means He is able to help us. We can find refuge in the eternal God and allow Him to surround us with His everlasting arms of grace (Deuteronomy 33:27).

LESSON: *As* El Olam *God reveals Himself as the everlasting God, One who is stable and continues forever and therefore can help His people.*

NAMES OF GOD:
EL ELYON

Blessed be Abram of God Most High, Possessor of heaven and earth; and blessed be God Most High, who has delivered your enemies into your hand. (Genesis 14:19-20)

The great golden eagle is considered a symbol of power and courage because of the high altitudes to which it soars. The eagle's supremacy is further enhanced when it builds its nest in high, remote rocks and cliffs. Its young are ably protected under the wings of this powerful bird. Even so, God is a Most High God, majestic and sovereign in the heavens but simultaneously sheltering His own.

When Abram returned from rescuing Lot from the destruction of Sodom and Gomorrah, he was met by Melchizedek, king of Salem, who blessed the God of Abram as *El Elyon*—God Most High. *Elyon*, meaning "Most High," conveys the idea is that God is exalted. It stresses His supremacy and overwhelming majesty. He is omnipotent—the Most High speaks but a word, and hailstones and coals of fire put enemies to flight (Psalm 18:13). For that reason the Most High is protection for His people (9:2). As the young eagles seek refuge under the mighty pinions of their mother, so the child of God finds protection in the shelter of the Most High (91:1). Even the king, supreme though he is on earth, finds his own security and steadfastness in the faithfulness of the Most High God (21:7). Indeed, *El Elyon* is the supreme, exalted God (78:35). But the wicked are ignorant of Him, thinking they can escape when they arrogantly mock Him. *El Elyon* is also supreme in knowledge. Even the pagan Balaam told of His supreme knowledge (Numbers 24:16).

In a time of trouble there is tranquillity in the presence of the Most High (Psalm 46:4). Though the earth changes, the nations are in an uproar, and the world crashes around him, he is at peace who dwells in the presence of the Most High (vv. 1-6). What does that mean to you? It means that your circumstances need not dictate your comfort level. You can enjoy tranquillity despite the turmoil in your world. You may find refuge under the wings of the Most High God, high above the storm.

LESSON: *As El Elyon God is exalted, majestic, and supreme, ruling heaven and earth and protecting those who seek refuge in Him.*

January 30

NAMES OF GOD:
THE LORD WILL PROVIDE

And Abraham called the name of that place
The Lord Will Provide, as it is said to this day,
"In the mount of the Lord it will be provided." (Genesis 22:14)

We had driven about five miles along the Blue Ridge Parkway in North Carolina when we stopped to take a picture at a scenic turnout. From the car we heard, "Sssss." I turned around and saw green fluid running from the radiator. But it wasn't long until we were treated to Southern hospitality as two gentlemen supplied us with two gallons of water and directions to get the water pump replaced. Days later as we were homeward bound on the interstate, I felt a thumping and pulled to the shoulder. A flat tire. To my dismay I discovered my lug nut wrench had been stolen. My wife and I spent the afternoon walking down the interstate to get help.

Although those were not major dilemmas, when we are in difficult circumstances, we need help. And the Lord provides—He is *Yahweh-Jireh.* In a much more serious lesson than our escapades on the highway, God revealed Himself to Abraham. When the aged patriarch and his son ascended Mount Moriah, Isaac asked, "Where is the lamb for the burnt offering?" (Genesis 22:7). "God will provide for Himself the lamb for the burnt offering, my son," Abraham responded. But Abraham's faith was severely tested. When they reached the altar, Abraham placed the wood around it and reluctantly bound his teenaged son in the place where the lamb should have been. Knife uplifted, he was about to plunge it into his son when the angel of the Lord called to him. God had made an alternate provision. A lamb, caught in a thicket, became the burnt offering. God had provided a substitute.

The name *Jireh* actually means "to see"; hence, "Yahweh will see to the problem." But Abraham "was also reflecting on the fact that it is God's abiding character that prompts Him to see to our problems and that at His appointed time He would undoubtedly provide for the great problem of sin. God would provide a Savior" (Boice, *Genesis,* 2:224). Jesus became the final Lamb of God, given by His Father as a sacrifice. He made the greatest provision by being the "Lamb of God which takes away the sin of the world" (John 1:29). Have you availed yourself of God's greatest provision?

LESSON: *God has revealed Himself as* Yahweh-Jireh—*the Lord Will Provide—by providing a Savior for our sins.*

NAMES OF GOD:
LORD OF HOSTS

How lovely are Thy dwelling places,
O Lord of hosts! (Psalm 84:1)

June 6, 1944, is a date that will long be remembered in the annals of war. On that day, General Dwight D. Eisenhower, supreme Allied commander, launched an armada from the coast of England against the Axis powers on the European continent that would eventuate in the destruction of the Third Reich. The fleet of ships was so enormous that when the first ships had arrived at the coast of France, the other end of the fleet was still in England. That great naval assault magnified the Allied powers. Similarly, the attendants surrounding the Lord magnify Him.

The name "Lord of Hosts" is taken from two words: *Yahweh,* God's covenant name with Israel (Exodus 3:14-15), and *Sabaoth,* a root word meaning "to wage war" and thereby implying the armies of heaven. The name, then, means the Lord of the armies of heaven. It is an exalted title, announcing Yahweh's kingship over all the nations and His headship over all the armies.

But how is it used? "Lord of Hosts" is frequently used in connection with a great national crisis or need. Because God is the "Lord of the armies," He can help. Perhaps this was best illustrated when Joshua met the "captain of the host of the Lord" (Joshua 5:14), prior to entering the Promised Land. The "Lord of Hosts" would bring victory to the Israelites when they engaged in warfare. He is the Lord of the armies of Israel.

But He is more. He is also the universal ruler, commander of the armies of earth and heaven and has authority over all people. When David met Goliath, he declared, "I come to you in the name of the Lord of hosts, the God of the armies of Israel" (1 Samuel 17:45). The "Lord of Hosts," who also demanded Philistine submission, gave David victory. A day is coming when the "Lord of Hosts" will establish Messiah as King on Mount Zion (Psalm 24), and He will receive the worship of the nations (Zechariah 14:16). On festive days as they entered the Temple in a triumphal procession, Israel sang, "Lift up your heads, O gates, and lift them up, O ancient doors, that the King of glory may come in! Who is the King of glory? The Lord of hosts, He is the King of glory" (Psalm 24:9-10).

LESSON: *The "Lord of Hosts" is an exalted title meaning the God of the armies, not only of Israel, but of heaven and earth. He is the ruler of the universe.*

NAMES OF GOD:
THE LORD IS MY BANNER

And Moses built an Altar, and named it
The Lord Is My Banner. (Exodus 17:15)

M any wars have been fought in the name of God. The tragic Crusades of the Middle Ages, where children died en route to fight in the Holy Land, invoked the Lord's name in battle. Some of Hitler's soldiers inscribed the slogan "God With Us" on their belt buckles. It is doubtful that the Lord sanctioned those and other wars attributed to Him. But there are occasions where He has fought on behalf of His people.

On their way to the Promised Land, the Israelites encountered the Amalekites in battle at Rephidim, near Mount Sinai. While Joshua and the Israelites fought the Amalekites, Moses, Aaron, and Hur invoked God's help with uplifted hands on the mountain overlooking the battlefield. While their hands were upheld, the Israelites prevailed. God gave them the victory. As a memorial, Moses built an altar and named it *Yahweh-Nissi*, "The Lord Is My Banner" (Exodus 17:15). It was a reminder that God was the One who had given them the victory. It was a name of God, extolling His power in fighting on behalf of His people. "The Lord Is My Banner" was the One who would fight their battles and defeat their enemies in bringing them into the Promised Land.

The "banner" (*nissi*) was a rallying point or standard around which people gathered to receive important information. It was usually a high pole, sometimes with an attached ensign, raised high as a focus of hope. When Moses, Aaron, and Hur raised their hands toward heaven, it was a reminder that they were not following an earthly standard. Their standard-bearer was God. The flag they followed was the God of heaven!

A future day is coming when Christ "will stand as a banner for the peoples; the nations will rally to him, and his place of rest will be glorious" (Isaiah 11:10, NIV). Not only Israel, but the repentant nations of the world will submit to Christ, the Commander-in-chief who will triumph over sin, Satan, and all subversive forces. As the flag-bearer of all believers, He will triumph over evil and inaugurate God's kingdom on earth (Revelation 19:11-16). We look up to Christ, our victorious Standard-bearer.

LESSON: *"The Lord Is My Banner" reveals God as the One who leads His people to battle, bringing them the victory.*

NAMES OF GOD:
THE LORD THAT SANCTIFIES

You shall consecrate yourselves therefore and be holy
. . . I am the Lord who sanctifies you. (Leviticus 20:7-8)

I f you were to ask a man on the street, "What does it mean to be holy?" he would probably answer something like this: "A holy man is someone from India who wears white robes and a turban and sits cross-legged meditating all day." That, of course, is not what it means to be holy.

The Lord revealed Himself to Israel as a God who is holy, and as a holy God He demands holiness from His people. But what does it mean to be holy? Holy means "to set apart." His people are to be set apart from the world and set apart to God. When God called the Israelites as His people and established them as a nation, He commanded Moses, "Go to the people and consecrate them today and tomorrow, and let them wash their garments" (Exodus 19:10). Washing clothes was a symbol of consecration and holiness. God established a dwelling place in their midst, but to remind them of His holiness, the Lord was "set apart" from the people in the Holy of Holies (26:33). God also appointed a special priesthood to serve Him; even their garments were holy—they were set apart in service for Him (28:2-5).

What does all that teach us? That God is a holy God. He is entirely set apart from His creatures and His creation, and He demands that His people be set apart for fellowship with Him and separate from the world. Christians are called to be holy (1 Peter 1:16). What does that mean? It means that we are to guard our minds from impure thoughts (v. 13); we should abandon our former lifestyle though we once followed fleshly desires (v. 14). It means that we are to love one another (v. 22) and declare God's excellencies in an unholy world (2:9).

Child of God, are you living a holy life? It is not an option. In a day when distinctions between Christians and non-Christians have become increasingly blurred, there is a greater need than ever for Christians to take seriously our Lord's injunction: "You shall be holy, for I am holy."

LESSON: *The Lord who sanctifies is holy, set apart from evil. He calls His people to be set apart from the world and to Himself.*

NAMES OF GOD:
THEOS

Now to the King eternal, immortal, invisible, the only God,
be honor and glory forever and ever. Amen. (1 Timothy 1:17)

Christianity and Judaism have stood virtually alone in believing there is only one God. Throughout history people have been polytheistic believing in many gods. The ancient Egyptians, for example, worshiped about eighty gods. Not only did they worship men such as Amun and Osiris but also the Nile River and animals, including the lion, wolf, dog, cat, vulture crocodile, cobra, frog, locust, and insects! (Shades of this are seen in the Mother Earth movement.) Against such beliefs Christianity stands unique.

God (*Theos*) is one God, and He is absolutely unique. There is none like Him (Mark 12:29, 32). He is the only God, having no equal, therefore He alone deserves honor and glory (1 Timothy 1:17; Jude 25). He is the only sovereign God by whom everyone and all things exist (Ephesians 4:6).

The belief that there is only one God is critical to Christianity and is strongly emphasized in the Bible. Although non-Christian people worship idols, those idols are not gods they are meaningless since "there is no God but one" (1 Corinthians 8:4). As there is only one God there is also only one mediator—only one who can introduce us to God Jesus Christ (1 Timothy 2:5). *Theos* is the only true God; He is the only one whom people need to know to have eternal life, and Jesus Christ is the way to the knowledge of Him (John 17:3). He is the one God of all people, whether Jews or Gentiles (Romans 3:29).

God is not only Creator of heaven and earth, but He has authority and sovereignty over His created realm (Acts 17:24). He is infinite in His being, One who cannot be localized or confined to a building as though He were an image of wood. Although He Himself is independent, everything and everyone depends on Him because He is the sustainer of life (v. 25). Because of His sovereign authority, power, and eternality, He alone is worthy of worship and adoration (Revelation 11:15-17). He alone deserves the love of our entire being (Mark 12:30). How can we know Him? Through Jesus Christ because Christ Himself is also called God (John 20:28).

LESSON: *As* Theos, *God is the only true, unique God, without peer, sovereign, and the only One worthy of our worship.*

NAMES OF GOD:
KURIOS

Every tongue should confess that Jesus Christ is Lord,
to the glory of God the Father. (Philippians 2:11)

Throughout the centuries, from Roman emperors to modern gu-
rus, mortal men have proclaimed their own deity and lordship.
As the guru of the Divine Light Mission, Maharaj Ji receives the
worship of his devotees as one who is the incarnation of God. I wondered
about this when I read that the guru was ill and had to be hospitalized. God
in a hospital bed? Mortals may proclaim their lordship, but they get sick and
die like other mortals. God alone is Lord.

Another name for God is *Kurios,* translated "Lord." It is the equivalent
of the Old Testament name *Yahweh. Kurios* can be used in a nontechnical
sense, as a master over his slave (Matthew 18:25) or an employer over his
employee (Luke 16:3) or even as a husband over the wife (1 Peter 3:6). The
name *Kurios* means one having power or authority, one who is a ruler and
has control. The Lord is Master of heaven and earth (Matthew 11:25).

As Lord, God is the almighty, eternal God (Revelation 1:8). The Lord is
holy—set apart from His finite creatures—and as Lord and Master receives
worship (4:8; 11:17). Because He is holy and righteous, He must judge the
unrighteous, and His judgments are just (16:7). Ultimately, because He is
Master, the Lord will one day reign on the earth (19:6; 21:22).

An important revelation of Scripture is the fact that Jesus is Lord,
meaning that He is God. Acknowledging that is critical to becoming a Christian (Romans 10:9). Having seen the nail prints in His hands and the
wounds in His side, Thomas made this confession: "My Lord and my God!"
(John 20:28). Since Jesus rose from the grave, He proved that He is God,
summoning everyone to worship Him and confess that He is God (Philippians 2:10-11). Psalm 102:25, which is ascribed to the Lord God in the Old
Testament, is applied to Jesus in the New Testament, reminding us that
since He is God, Jesus is Creator, eternal, and unchangeable (Hebrews
1:10-11). What a phenomenal privilege we have—the One who is Master of
heaven and earth also sympathizes with our weaknesses and listens to our
cry.

LESSON: *The Lord, who is also Jesus, is Master of heaven and earth,*
holy and exalted in heaven, and receives the worship of His creatures.

NAMES OF GOD:
FATHER

*Every good thing bestowed and every perfect gift is from above,
coming down from the Father of lights. (James 1:17)*

Although my father died when I was only nine years old, I remember him well. From his laughter as he slipped his opponent an extra marble in Chinese checkers, to his lavish Christmas presents, to his sense of justice that demanded obedience in his children (he selected willows that whipped well!), to the sense of security he provided by his bearing and presence.

There is a correlation between our earthly father and our heavenly Father as the name itself indicates. The first commandment on the first table of the law was "You shall have no other gods before Me" (Exodus 20:3), whereas the first commandment on the second table of the law was "Honor your father and your mother" (v. 12). If a child has an unloving, ungracious father the child will have a wrong image of God. What an awesome responsibility it is to bear the name *father!*

God's title as Father is used hundreds of times in the Bible. He was Israel's Father, even though they disobeyed Him and forgot His fatherly kindnesses (Deuteronomy 32:6). As an earthly father has compassion on his children so the heavenly Father demonstrates His lovingkindness by removing His children's sins as far away as east is from the west (Psalm 103:12-13).

But to whom is God Father? Some have used the statement "the Fatherhood of God and the brotherhood of man" to suggest that spiritually all people are brothers, and all have God as Father. That, of course, is not true. The only way one can have a father is to be born into the family; even so, no one has God as Father except he is spiritually born into His family through the new birth (John 1:12; 3:3). Only then can we enjoy the benefits of a family relationship.

In that family relationship our heavenly Father strengthens us through His Spirit and His grace (Ephesians 3:14, 16). But as an earthly father disciplines his children so God corrects us—it is a sign we are in the family (Hebrews 12:8-10)! Yet we must be mindful that our heavenly Father only bestows good gifts on His children (James 1:17), particularly through His provision of a heavenly home (John 14:2) and a way to that home (John 14:6). Are you in the family? Do you know the heavenly Father?

LESSON: *God reveals Himself as Father to those who have been reborn, guiding, disciplining, and providing an eternal home for them with Him.*

THE IMMENSITY
OF GOD

Will God indeed dwell on the earth? Behold, heaven
and the highest heaven cannot contain Thee. (1 Kings 8:27)

I n a Christian college the students determined to display their affection for a professor, so they "papered" his room one evening. When he approached his office the next day, the students peeked around corners to watch his reaction. As he attempted to open the door he was confronted with an obstacle. The room was entirely filled with wadded newspaper. There wasn't a vacant spot in the office—one part was as filled with newspaper as another.

The immensity of God is slightly different from the omnipresence of God. Immensity teaches that whereas God is present in every place with His entire being, He is not limited to space; He is above it. Immensity thus emphasizes God's transcendence—that He is entirely above and beyond finite being—whereas omnipresence stresses that God fills all space with His entire being (my illustration breaks down here!).

Solomon built a magnificent Temple, lavishly embossed with gold and silver. But it was not adequate to contain God, for He cannot be confined to any building. God is above and beyond earthly buildings, yea, beyond heaven itself (1 Kings 8:27). Our bodies are bound to space and limited by it, but not God. He cannot be limited to space nor localized by it.

In combining thoughts both of immensity and omnipresence, the Lord exclaimed to Jeremiah, "Am I a God who is near . . . and not a God far off? Can a man hide himself in hiding places, so I do not see him? Do I not fill the heaven and the earth?" (Jeremiah 23:23-24). The God who is near emphasizes His omnipresence, that He fills all places and condescends to fellowship with man. On the other hand, God is transcendent—He is a God far off—He is "wholly other." As the infinite God, He is above mankind and above the limitations of space. How amazing that He who fills all space and is beyond all space deigns to dwell with man! This very God, whom heaven cannot contain, dwells with believers! Jesus said, "If anyone loves Me . . . My Father will love him, and we will come to him, and make Our abode with him" (John 14:23).

LESSON: *The immensity of God teaches that whereas God fills every space, He cannot be limited by space—He is beyond it.*

THE SOVEREIGNTY
OF GOD

We have obtained an inheritance, having been
predestined according to His purpose who works
all things after the counsel of His will. (Ephesians 1:11)

A friend of mine accidently backed his car into a gasoline bowser, resulting in an accident. He later confided to me, "I don't know why God allowed me to back into that gas bowser. I know He is sovereign. I don't understand why this had to happen." Every one of us could cite similar questions relating to God's sovereignty.

The historic Westminster Confession defines God's sovereignty: "The decree [sovereignty or plan] of God is His eternal purpose, according to the counsel of His own will, whereby, for His own glory, He hath foreordained whatsoever comes to pass." That takes your breath away! It's a good and accurate statement, based entirely on Scripture. Yet many people have trouble with this idea. What are the options? There are only two: (1) God is sovereign and has absolute control over the universe, or (2) God is not sovereign, and the universe carries on in defiance of His holy will, and He does not have the power to control it. We need to understand there is no middle ground. We cannot compose a "half and half" doctrine. Either God is in control or He is not—and if He is not, then man is in control. Some people look at the tragedies of life and conclude God is not in control. One well-known rabbi saw the lengthy suffering of his dying son and concluded God could not be in control.

All things—everything that happens, the good and the bad—are included in God's sovereign will. But that does not mean God is responsible for sin. He is not. God directly causes some things to come to pass ("the directive will of God"), for example, choosing Paul as an apostle (Romans 1:1) and calling us to salvation (Ephesians 1:4). On the other hand, He may permit events to come to pass ("the permissive will of God"), but He is not responsible for sinful action. For example, when the Israelites demanded a king it was within the sovereign will of God (Genesis 17:6), yet the Israelites were responsible for their sinful action, not God (1 Samuel 8:19-22).

It is a genuinely comforting thought to realize everything that happens to me is because of the plan of a wise, sovereign God. That knowledge brings peace.

LESSON: *In His sovereign will, God has planned and ordained everything that comes to pass, yet He is not the author of evil.*

WHAT IS THE SOVEREIGN PLAN OF GOD?

He does according to His will in the host of heaven and among the inhabitants of earth. (Daniel 4:35)

God's sovereign plan is a single plan that includes everything that happens. If God is all-powerful, He must also have an all-wise plan that encompasses all things. Things cannot just happen at random. As Master Architect, God has laid out the blueprints for everything that transpires. He has the master plan, and He drew it according to His own will. He didn't consult with anyone else.

God's plan was not made in consultation with man, nor did He wait to see what man would do. God does not "react," waiting for man to make his decisions; rather, God "acts" apart from man. Moreover, God made His plan in eternity past. For example, He appointed us to salvation in eternity past (Ephesians 1:4; 2 Timothy 1:9).

God's master plan is a wise plan because God is wise. Since God knows all things, including all the variables and possibilities, He guides all events for His glory and for our good. To be sure, we cannot fathom it— even if you think you can, you haven't! Paul couldn't fathom it. But when He considered the sovereignty of God he concluded with an emotional doxology (Romans 11:33-36).

God's master plan is according to His sovereign discretionary will. He does as He pleases (Daniel 4:35). (Especially remember, at this point, that He is an all-wise, loving Father). No one has counseled or informed God, nor has He consulted with anyone. If man assisted in God's sovereign plan it would introduce failure and error into it since man is sinful. Therefore, God must establish the master plan by Himself.

Why do some people resist this important and wonderful teaching of Scripture? Because of pride. Man wants to be the captain of his own ship. Some also think it robs them of their freedom. But God does not treat us like robots; He holds us responsible for our decisions. In a turbulent world it is comforting to know an all-wise God is controlling all things.

LESSON: *God has a single, all-wise, master plan that He established in eternity past and that is for His glory and our good.*

February 9

How Can We Understand the Sovereign Plan of God?

*This [Jesus], delivered up by the predetermined plan
and foreknowledge of God, you nailed to a cross
by the hands of godless men and put Him to death. (Acts 2:23)*

Some things are difficult to understand. There are teachings in
Scripture that teach opposite truths, yet both are equally true.
That is called an antinomy ("against the law"), something that is
contrary to finite, human reason. We mortals cannot grasp such things with
our finite minds. For example, Jesus is both God and man; how can we
understand that? There is only one God, yet the Father, the Son, and the
Holy Spirit are all God. We cannot comprehend that. Those are antinomies.

The sovereign plan of God is also an antinomy, namely, although God
has planned all things in eternity past, man is responsible for his sinful
actions. For example, Peter said that Christ died on the cross because God
had sovereignly planned it from eternity past, yet in the same breath Peter
indicted the Jewish leaders and Roman soldiers for killing Him. We cannot
grasp that—but both statements are true.

When the prophet Habakkuk saw the sinfulness of his people he cried
to God to do something. God reminded Habakkuk that He was doing something: "I am raising up the Chaldeans" (1:6). In His sovereign plan God was
taking His disobedient people into the divine woodshed, using the Chaldeans as His stick to punish His people. Yet, after the Chaldeans had inflicted
punishment on Judah, God would hold the Chaldeans responsible for what
they had done (v. 11).

Although God has planned everything that comes to pass, people are
responsible for their actions. God has chosen believers from eternity past
for salvation, but no one is saved apart from evangelism. Someone must
present the gospel to the unbeliever, and the unbeliever must respond by an
act of the will and believe the gospel to be saved (Acts 16:31).

We cannot understand all these things—and it isn't necessary that we
do. Although we can rest secure that every part of God's sovereign plan will
be completely carried out (Psalm 33:11), we are also responsible to respond to the gospel and live in obedience to the Scriptures.

LESSON: *God's sovereign plan is an antinomy—though God has foreordained everything that happens, man is responsible for his actions.*

GOD'S SOVEREIGN PLAN
IN THE PHYSICAL REALM

*Man's days are determined; you have decreed the number of
his months and have set limits he cannot exceed. (Job 14:5, NIV)*

Have you ever read the obituary page in the newspaper? You
scan the ages of the deceased, and you read 76 . . . 85 . . .
79 . . . 51 . . . 18. Why do some live to be 85 and some die at
18? My grandmother lived to be 96, but my father died at 48—and achieved
the oldest age in a family of ten. We don't understand, but God has a reason. The answer is wrapped up in the sovereign plan of God.

In His sovereign plan God created the heavens and the earth (Psalm
33:6). And what a magnificent creation it is! From "purple mountain majes-
ties" to "fruited plain" God has created a breathtakingly beautiful world. It
was part of His sovereign plan.

When God established the nations on earth, He also established their
boundaries. It is God who determines where the people of the earth will
live. Surely the sovereign plan of God can be seen behind the changing face
of Eastern Europe. Who could have foreseen the demise of Communism?
Who could have expected freedom for millions of previously enslaved people? God acted. God has established the boundaries of people, "having determined their appointed times, and the boundaries of their habitation"
(Acts 17:26).

On a personal level, God has determined the length of our lives (Job
14:5; 21:21), even the manner of our departure from this life (John 21:19).
That knowledge provides peace and comfort when we fail to understand
why a young life is snuffed out like a beautiful flower that hasn't had a
chance to open, or why some lives linger for years amid great suffering. Our
lives are in God's hands.

God's sovereign plan has also determined that some will be alive at
the time of the trumpet call. Some will not die but will hear the trumpet and
be changed in a moment (1 Corinthians 15:51-52)! Surely it is a consolation
to know that God has sovereignly planned our lives according to what is
best for us. God's sovereign plan is tailor-made specifically for each of us
because He knows what is best.

LESSON: *God's sovereign plan includes everything in the physical
realm—creation of the world, habitation of countries, and length of our
lives.*

GOD'S SOVEREIGN PLAN
REGARDING SIN

There were gathered together against Thy holy Servant Jesus,
whom Thou didst anoint, both Herod and Pontius Pilate,
along with the Gentiles and the peoples of Israel, to do whatever
Thy hand and thy purpose predestined to occur. (Acts 4:27-28)

Although God's sovereign plan includes all things, God is never the author of sin, nor does He entice people to sin. People sin when they are carried away by the desires of their sinful nature and sin comes to fruition (James 1:17). We are responsible for our sins. Yet sin does not frustrate God's plan.

How does God deal with sin in His sovereign plan? He may permit people to manifest sin. When a society is bent on sinning, God may give that society over to its sin (Romans 1:24-32). Perhaps that explains the sinful brazenness that is evident today—adultery, immorality, and homosexuality—those are indulged in as normal lifestyles. It may be that God has given people over to their corruption, but even immorality does not frustrate God's sovereign plan.

In fact, God may use sinful acts to accomplish His purpose. When Herod sought the death of Jesus, when Pilate ordered His execution, when the Jews called for His crucifixion, when the Romans executed Jesus—all that happened because God's purpose had predestined that Jesus' crucifixion should occur (Acts 4:27-28). Whereas God was not responsible for their sinful acts, His sovereign plan determined that His purpose would be fulfilled.

But God also puts boundaries on evil. Hitler was not permitted to completely obliterate the Jewish people. Nikita Khrushchev could not bury America. Sin has boundaries. When Satan sought to test Job, God imposed limitations on Satan. He could do nothing that God would not permit (Job 1:6-12). God overrules evil. Perhaps nowhere is our comfort so genuine as when we recognize that in this sinful world, controlled by "the god of this world," we are safe because our sovereign God has imposed limitations on evil. Nothing—absolutely nothing—happens that is not allowed by our loving, wise, and sovereign God.

LESSON: *God's sovereign plan permits sin, but God is never the author of it, and He determines the boundaries of evil.*

GOD'S SOVEREIGN PLAN
IN THE POLITICAL REALM

It is He who changes the times and the epochs;
He removes kings and establishes kings. (Daniel 2:21)

I f you look at a forty-year-old atlas of the world, you will notice many changes. In South America, nations such as British, Dutch, and French Guiana have all changed. In Africa, new nations have emerged. Gone are British Rhodesia, the Belgian Congo, French Equatorial Africa, and others. Ceylon is now Sri Lanka. New nations have emerged. How has it all happened?

God revealed His sovereign plan of history to Daniel in a vision. Although Daniel was living in the Babylonian era (612-539 B.C.), God revealed to him the successive world empires that He would establish according to His sovereign plan. God announced that Medo-Persia (539-331 B.C.) would succeed Babylon and in turn would be destroyed by Greece (331-68 B.C.) under Alexander, the mighty young general. Greece would continue until Rome conquered it in 68 B.C. Daniel blessed the God of heaven, recognizing that it is not through battle or the ballot box that governments change; it is God who removes and establishes rulers (Daniel 2:21). Even the mighty Nebuchadnezzar recognized that God is the one who "does according to His will in the host of heaven and among the inhabitants of earth" (4:35).

Of course, that is true not only of Babylon and Rome; it is true of America, the Soviet Union, and the other nations of the world today because "there is no authority except from God, and those which exist are established by God" (Romans 13:1). God has established the governments that exist. It is He who determines whether a Republican or Democrat wins the presidency. Moreover, it is God who will bring the empires of the world to their dissolution. Although the nations rebel against the Lord and His Messiah (Psalm 2:1-3), He will subdue them and establish Messiah as reigning monarch of the world (vv. 4-9). As we read of the opening of eastern Europe and of changes in the Soviet Union, we are mindful that God controls history. In His sovereign plan He is carrying the course of history forward to the ultimate establishment of Messiah as ruler. What a blessed day! One day all the nations of this world will submit to Messiah because of God's sovereign plan.

LESSON: *God's sovereign plan controls the course of history, establishing the rise and fall of nations.*

Part 2

The Bible

February 13

GOD'S REVELATION
IN THE UNIVERSE

---

*The heavens are telling of the glory of God; and
the firmament is declaring the work of His hands. (Psalm 19:1)*

When Voyager 2 was some 2.8 billion miles from earth, after traveling to the outer fringes of our solar system, it sent back pictures of Neptune before it headed into interstellar space. Voyager 2 had previously relayed pictures of Jupiter, Saturn, and Uranus to earth. Information sent from Neptune revealed the planet's day to be only sixteen hours in length, that Neptune has five rings circumventing it, and that it contains clouds of frozen methane gas. As Voyager 2 speeds beyond our universe, it will continue for another twenty-five years before ending communication with earth. But it carries a recording titled "Sounds of Earth" (should it encounter beings in outer space), a greeting from former President Carter concluding with the words, "This record represents our hope and our determination and our goodwill in a vast and lonely universe."

We cannot fathom the immensity of the universe. Neither could the psalmist, who declared, "The heavens are telling of the glory of God" (Psalm 19:1). Psalm 19 teaches God's general revelation in nature. General revelation is truth about Himself that God has made known to everyone. No one is without the revelation of God in nature. Everyone can look into the sky and consider with amazement the vastness of the universe.

The psalmist indicates that general revelation continues: "Day to day pours forth speech, and night to night reveals knowledge" (v. 2). It is not encoded in a book; it is without words: "There is no speech, nor are there words" (v. 3). It is a worldwide revelation; everyone has received it: "Their line has gone out through all the earth, and their utterances to the end of the world" (v. 4).

Since the universe is immense beyond human comprehension, how immense, how powerful, how great the God who has created it must be! How small is man in comparison with the greatness of God. What should be man's opinion of himself? What should be man's opinion of God? What should be your response to this great God?

LESSON: *God has revealed Himself in the universe to all mankind so that man may discover the greatness of God and the humility of humanity.*

GOD'S REVELATION
IN NATURE

*Since the creation of the world His invisible
attributes, His eternal power and divine nature,
have been clearly seen. (Romans 1:20)*

God has revealed many truths about Himself in nature. If we take the time to study nature, we will observe those truths. When Hurricane Hugo roared through Charleston, South Carolina, the fury of its 135-mile-per-hour winds devastated the southern city where the Civil War began, causing $3 billion in damage. Sixty-five percent of the coastal buildings from Charleston to the North Carolina border were destroyed, airplanes were flipped over, sailboats heaped in piles like dead fish washed ashore, buildings flipped about and ripped apart like toys.

Hurricane Hugo is an illustration of the general revelation of God in nature. God has revealed truths about Himself for all humanity to see. No one is without this witness. Romans 1:20 testifies, "Since the creation of the world His invisible attributes, His eternal power and divine nature, have been clearly seen." God's invisible attributes are observed in creation, which affirms His omnipotence, or power. Who can stare at the starry heavens and not recognize the power of God? Who can behold the beauty of nature and not recognize His majesty?

His eternal power is understood in hurricanes or earthquakes. With all his modern technology, man can do nothing to avert the devastation of a hurricane. We may listen to news reports and be warned of the impending destruction, but its coming is certain. We cannot avoid it.

God's divine nature is understood in His patience in withholding judgment, affirming that God is indeed a God of mercy and grace. Although man is deserving, God does not judge immediately. He patiently waits for man to repent, providing an opportunity for rescue from divine judgment (Romans 2:4).

General revelation renders man guilty before God; man is without excuse since he has received the testimony of nature that God is a God of power, judgment, and grace (1:20). Since He is a God of grace, He offers opportunity for man to change his mind and through faith receive forgiveness and peace. God's grace is surely an exhortation to respond.

LESSON: *Although God has revealed Himself in nature as a God of judgment, He is also a God of grace, permitting people to turn to Him in faith.*

GOD'S REVELATION
IN ANIMAL KINGDOM

Thou dost make him to rule over the works of Thy hands;
Thou hast put all things under his feet. (Psalm 8:6)

One evening when we were living in Dallas my family and I observed an unusual phenomenon. I was in the backyard and noticed a cicada (a large brown locust) climbing up our clothesline pole. I had read about how cicadas live in the ground for seventeen years and then undergo a metamorphosis. I called for my wife to rouse our two young sons from bed, and together the four of us observed this spectacle for nearly two hours. The cicada climbed up the clothesline pole and while resting in a vertical position his back began to split open. Slowly emerged a lime green insect, looking much like a grasshopper, from the shell of the cicada. The "new" cicada left the shell of the "old" cicada, climbed further along the clothesline pole and spread his wings to dry. When they were dry he flew into a nearby tree and began to sing in unison with thousands of other cicadas. The entire shell of the old cicada remained attached to the clothesline pole.

What an illustration in nature, teaching the truth of the resurrection! As the psalmist observes the earth he is overwhelmed by the divine evidence all around him. He is amazed that God should concern Himself with humanity, that God should care for him and crown him as the apex of His creation. Although man has fallen, God has destined him for glory. Through the resurrection, man is destined to rule in a renewed earth. The last Adam, Christ, will restore to this world all that the first Adam forfeited. During His earthly ministry Christ revealed that He was the last Adam, who had come to subject all nature to His authority. He came to rescue, redeem, and resurrect fallen humanity and restore a fallen earth.

Redeemed people will rule with Christ, having undergone their own metamorphosis, having received new, glorified, resurrection bodies. Rejoice, Christian, even nature bears witness of the new day when we with glorified bodies will live in a renewed earth!

LESSON: *Nature reveals that believers will received new, glorified, resurrection bodies and reign with Christ in a renewed world.*

GOD'S REVELATION
IN CONTROL OF HISTORY

The Lord will scatter you among all peoples, from one end
of the earth to the other end of the earth. (Deuteronomy 28:64)

Following a favorable vote by the United Nations General Assembly, the modern state of Israel was born on May 14, 1948, as David Ben-Gurion became the new nation's first prime minister. The tiny nation of some 600,000 Jews, living at the navel of the world, represented a modern miracle. In 586 B.C., when Nebuchadnezzar invaded Israel, carrying the Jewish people captive into Babylon, Israel ceased to exist as a nation—but not as a people. For some 2,500 years the Jewish people continued to exist but without a homeland. Never before in the annals of human civilization had a people continued as a distinct group after removal from their homeland for so a long period. Israel's rebirth in 1948 demonstrated God's providential control of history and His preservation of the Jewish people.

Daniel discovered that God "removes kings and establishes kings" (2:21). In His sovereign control of history, God is the One who deposes one government and inaugurates another. Nations only exist by divine design. God has ordained the nations that govern the people of the world. It was true in ancient Israel, and it is true of modern America.

God outlined Israel's future to the patriarch Moses (Deuteronomy 28:15-68). Should the nation disobey God, Israel would be defeated by her enemies (v. 25), exiled, sent into captivity (vv. 36, 41), besieged by a foreign nation (v. 52), and scattered over the earth (v. 64). Those events were precisely fulfilled when the Assyrians carried the ten northern tribes captive in 722 B.C. and the Babylonians took the southern kingdom captive in 586 B.C. Israel was also scattered by the Romans in A.D. 70. But God has also foreordained that Israel will be reestablished as a nation when He will bring them back to the land (30:1 10). Although that prophecy was not fulfilled in 1948, the creation of the state is a harbinger of an approaching day when Israel will turn to the Messiah.

God's control of history gives great comfort. Christians should not worry about world events. God controls the destiny of America, Russia, China, and all other nations. He will lead history to its God-ordained destiny.

LESSON: *God's providentially controls history, determining the rise and demise of nations.*

GOD'S REVELATION
IN PROVIDING FOR MANKIND

He causes His sun to rise on the evil and the good, and
sends rain on the righteous and the unrighteous. (Matthew 5:45)

S outhern California is a spectacular place of beauty. Motoring up
the mountain at Glen Avon, near San Bernardino, you can see the
luscious orange groves in the hotter climate at the bottom of the
mountain. As you climb the mountain you arrive at a higher, cooler level,
where you can stop at the roadside stands and enjoy a variety of delicious
apples fresh from the orchards. As you continue up the winding road you
come to cherry orchards. And you can enjoy any of this fruit, freshly picked
from the trees.

In chatting with the man at the apple orchard I discovered he was a
brother in Christ. Among the fruit growers of California there are also unbelievers, perhaps even atheists. Yet the beautiful orange groves and apple
orchards all receive the same sunshine and rainfall that provide for the ma-
turation of the oranges and apples. That is God's general revelation, revealing His providential goodness—He does not distinguish between believers
and unbelievers when He sends sunshine and rainfall (Matthew 5:45). His
providential goodness extends to all mankind—this is also called "common
grace." Although believers are the objects of His special love, all humanity
partakes of the benefits of God's goodness.

In a time of drought or flood people become woefully aware that they
are dependent upon Someone greater than themselves. They can do nothing to avert natural disaster. Mankind is dependent upon God for sunshine
and rainfall. That ought to remind us of God's greatness and goodness. Every breath we take, every hour we live, every day we enjoy the benefits of our
environment we need to remind ourselves that it is a beneficent God who
gives us these blessings. Are you aware of God's daily blessings to you, or
do you take His blessings for granted? Are you thankful for His daily providential goodness?

LESSON: *All humanity enjoys the benefits of a beneficent God—*
whether they recognize it or not.

GOD'S REVELATION
THROUGH CONSCIENCE

They show the work of the Law written in their hearts,
their conscience bearing witness, and their thoughts
alternately accusing or else defending them. (Romans 2:15)

The Internal Revenue Service received some cash in the mail with an attached anonymous note reading, "I have not been able to sleep at night because I cheated the government on my income tax return. I am enclosing some money. If I still can't sleep, I'll send the rest!"

Why did that man send money to the IRS? They didn't know his name, and he likely would never have been found out. But God has placed an inner moral monitor within man that reminds each person of his or her moral conduct. Although the conscience is not entirely reliable and may be affected by the environment, nonetheless it reminds people when they have defaulted in moral matters.

Romans 2:15-16 indicates that Gentiles who do not have the law of God may in fact do the dictates of the law because of the prompting of the conscience within. Paul teaches that the conscience alternately accuses or defends the individual's action, accusing the individual when he errs and defending him when he does right. In Paul's view the conscience is to the Gentile what the law is to the Jew. It gives moral direction. Indeed, it convicts upon failure to pay taxes (Romans 13:5)!

The conscience, of course, needs to be guided by the Scriptures and the Holy Spirit (Romans 9:1); only then can the inner guidance be reliable. Peter exhorts us to "keep a good conscience" (1 Peter 3:16) as does Paul (1 Timothy 1:5, 19), that we may have a good testimony toward unbelievers. It is possible to develop a "seared conscience" (1 Timothy 4:2). May we be sensitive to the inner monitor that gives us moral directives. God forbid that we should grow hardened and callous to the internal monitor within.

LESSON: *God has placed a conscience within every person as a witness to His concern for righteousness and holiness.*

February 19

GOD'S REVELATION
IN PRESERVATION

*And He is before all things, and in Him
all things hold together. (Colossians 1:17)*

One of the unique, valuable conveniences of the twentieth century is super glue. We use super glue with almost everything: broken vases, children's toys, broken book spines, fingernails, shoes, and endless other items. One super glue manufacturer advertises its glue as so strong it is able to lift a car. We even use super glue in the manufacture of chipboard, where glue holds bits of wood together, producing a useful building material.

What is the value of glue? It adheres several items together. It unites and holds them together where otherwise they would fall apart.

Colossians 1:17 declares that in Christ "all things hold together." Since the preceding verse is speaking about the universe, it means that Jesus Christ is the cohesive force of the universe. He is the One who holds the universe together. The universe is infinitely vast, yet it is orderly, as in our solar system, with planets revolving around the sun and moons revolving around the planets. Who holds the universe in its orderly pattern? Why doesn't it explode into all directions? Because Jesus Christ holds it together. He is the super glue. He is both Creator and Sustainer of the universe. He is the One who creates that unity and solidarity, making it a cosmos, or an orderly design, instead of a chaos (Lightfoot, *Colossians*, p. 156).

Hebrews 1:3 develops this thought further by emphasizing that Christ carries all things to their predetermined conclusion. Not only does He sustain and hold the universe together, He is carrying it along its appointed course. You and I can function in peace because Jesus Christ is at work in sustaining the universe.

LESSON: *Jesus Christ holds the universe together by His power and carries it to its predetermined destiny.*

GOD'S REVELATION
IN JESUS CHRIST

---

*No man has seen God at any time; the only begotten God, who
is in the bosom of the Father, He has explained Him. (John 1:18)*

Nearly two thousand years ago there lived a man who was reared
in poverty. He had little formal education, nor did he come
from an influential family. He never traveled more than 150
miles from his home. He never became wealthy, never even owned a home.
He never wrote a book. His people and even his brothers rejected him, and
in his mid-thirties he was executed on criminal charges. Yet two thousand
years later one day each week is set aside in honor of Him. Coinage, monetary bills, legal documents, and business transactions are all dated from His
birth.

No one has influenced history like Jesus Christ. God has revealed
Himself to the human race in Him. He has revealed Himself to mankind in a
variety of ways called general revelation, but His revelation in Christ is
called special revelation. It is a unique revealing of God's person and nature. Jesus Christ gives us a true picture of what God is like. John 1:18
affirms that Jesus "has explained" the Father to us. He has given us a "full
account" of the Father. What was previously a mystery has now been revealed. A French translator suggests that it means that Jesus "has led the
way into the bosom of the Father."

Near the end of His life Jesus said, "He who has seen Me has seen the
Father" (John 14:9). He taught people what God was like (3:11); moreover,
His words were life-giving (6:63). Jesus' works also revealed the Father
(5:36).

Jesus is the only unblemished man ever to penetrate this planet. He
alone spoke pure words, did righteous deeds, held pure motives. In all
things He has given us a perfect revelation of God. Love of that magnitude
demands response. "See how great a love the Father has bestowed upon
us" (1 John 3:1). Such revelation, such love, invites a response of love.

LESSON: *God has revealed Himself in Jesus Christ, the apex of His
revelation.*

GOD'S REVELATION
IN THE BIBLE

*All Scripture is inspired by God and profitable
for teaching, for reproof, for correction,
for training in righteousness. (2 Timothy 3:16)*

B illy Graham recounts the crisis in his life concerning the Bible: "Early in my life I had some doubts about the Word, but one night in 1949 I knelt before a stump in the woods near Forest Home, California. I opened my Bible and I said, 'O God, there are many things in this Book I do not understand, but I accept it by faith as Your infallible Word from Genesis to Revelation.' I settled that, and from that moment on I have never had a single doubt that this is God's Word. So when I quote the Bible, when I preach it, I know that I am preaching the truth of God" (*Decision*, 10/89, p. 2).

Indeed, the Bible is God's special revelation to mankind. Whereas nature may tell us that God exists and that He is all-powerful, the Bible gives us comprehensive understanding of God, man, and the world. The Bible explains why we live in a world filled with crime, suffering, and tragedy. It reveals how God chose one man through whom would come a special people—the Jews—through whom God would bring the Messiah and bless the human race.

The Bible explains God's Father-heart in dealing with His people—blessing them when they obeyed Him and disciplining them when they were wayward. It reveals God's hatred for sin and the extent He would go to resolve the problem of sin. The Bible tells the greatest love story ever told in God's sending His only Son, who would live the perfect life upon earth, perfectly revealing the Father and teaching man how to live. It tells that the Son would die for the sins of mankind and reveals the glorious future for those who respond to God's grace. It tells of the bodily resurrection of Christ and the glorious future hope that God has given. The Bible tells of a utopia—the millennial kingdom—that Jesus Christ will inaugurate at His second coming.

Indeed, the Bible is good news and a special revelation of God to the human race! Read it to know God, the world, yourself, and your future!

LESSON: *The Bible is God's special revelation to mankind telling us of His special Son.*

THE BIBLE:
SUPERNATURALLY WRITTEN BY MEN

*No prophecy was ever made by an act of human will,
but men moved by the Holy Spirit spoke from God. (2 Peter 1:21)*

Early Saturday morning you pick up the newspaper from your driveway and saunter back into the house. You notice that Penney's is having a sale on lamps that would enhance your living room decor. You quickly drive to Penney's. Since the sale is on the second floor of the store you rush toward the escalator and in your haste to get to the sale you walk up the moving stairway. How did you get to the second floor? You walked—but you were also carried by the escalator.

Second Peter 1:21 teaches that the Scriptures were written by man, but it also teaches that the writers were supernaturally carried along by the Holy Spirit. Peter emphasizes that Scripture does not have a human origin. The last phrase in verse 21 provides the explanation: "men moved by the Holy Spirit spoke from God." The word *moved* is in the passive form, suggesting that although men actively wrote the Scriptures, there is a sense in which they were passive; the Holy Spirit was carrying them along. Just as the escalator carries the shopper to the second floor of the department store, so the Holy Spirit carried the writers of Scripture along so that the very words they used were the words God intended.

The same word *moved* is used of a ship's being carried along by the wind (Acts 27:15, 17). Although a captain pilots the ship, it is the wind that moves the ship along. So it was with the writing of Scripture. The Holy Spirit carried the writers along, ensuring the complete accuracy of the material they recorded.

Why is it important to know that the Bible is supernaturally authored? Peter wrote his second letter urging us to diligently pursue spiritual qualities, that we may be effective and productive for the Lord (1:5-8). But Peter exhorts us because what he spoke was true; these are truths based on a supernatural Bible. Are you diligently pursuing spiritual qualities because you know the Bible is inspired and must be obeyed?

LESSON: *The Holy Spirit supernaturally guided the writers of Scripture, ensuring the complete accuracy of all that was written.*

THE BIBLE:
BREATHED BY GOD

All Scripture is inspired by God and profitable
for teaching, for reproof, for correction,
for training in righteousness. (2 Timothy 3:16)

As a young boy growing up in Winnipeg, Canada, I endured many cold winter days. An actual temperature of 35 degrees below zero was not uncommon. On those frigid days we would sometimes exhale onto the windowpane. The moisture from our breath would freeze on the window, creating a layer of frost.

Second Timothy 3:16 states that Scripture is the "exhalation" of God. Just as one may breathe out, creating frost on a windowpane, so God has "breathed out," creating the Scriptures. The phrase translated "is inspired by God" is but one word in Greek, *theopneustos*, meaning God-breathed. Hence, one may read the verse, "All Scripture is God-breathed." God didn't breathe divine power into human writings; rather, the Scriptures are the result of God's breathing out. The Bible is the product of the exhalation of God.

The word "God-breathed" is not active, as though the Scriptures are purely a human product, but passive, meaning that the Scriptures have their origin with God, not man. That is also consistent with many Old Testament passages that state, "God spoke all these words" (cf. Exodus 20:1; Deuteronomy 5:22), or, "the Lord speaks" (Isaiah 1:2), or, "thus says the Lord" (Isaiah 44:2), or, "the word of the Lord came to me saying" (Jeremiah 1:4). The emphasis in those passages is that God spoke, and the result was a perfect word. That is the idea of the Scriptures as stated in 2 Timothy 3:16. God spoke forth, and the Scriptures were the result.

The purpose for the God-breathed Bible is found in verse 17: "So that the man of God may be thoroughly equipped for every good work" (NIV). God has "completely outfitted" us that we may produce "every good work" as we actively put the Word of God to work in our lives. Depend on His Word at work in you to produce beautiful, Christlike works!

LESSON: *The Scriptures are the product of the creative, out-breathing of God and are therefore perfect and able to equip us for every good work.*

INSPIRATION OF
THE WHOLE BIBLE

*Until heaven and earth pass away, not the smallest
letter or stroke shall pass away from the Law,
until all is accomplished. (Matthew 5:18)*

D id Jesus believe the entire Bible to be inspired? In reading the four gospels, it is fascinating to study Jesus' use of the Old Testament Scriptures. From that observation we can learn an important lesson—surely, our view of Scripture ought to be as high as Jesus' view. How, then, did Jesus view the Bible?

When Jesus met the two disciples on the road to Emmaus and they failed to understand why Christ had to die, Jesus traced the Old Testament Scriptures from the Pentateuch to the prophets, explaining how the prophecies had to be fulfilled (Luke 24:26-27). He showed them the accuracy of the entire Old Testament.

When confronted by religious opponents, Jesus quoted from Isaiah 61:1-2a and exclaimed, "Today this Scripture has been fulfilled in your hearing" (Luke 4:21). Jesus had complete confidence that what had been written in Isaiah was now fulfilled. Moreover, He terminates His quotation in the middle of verse 2—had He continued the quotation, "and the day of vengeance of our God," He could not have concluded with the statement "Today this Scripture has been fulfilled in your hearing." It shows Jesus believed in the precise and total inspiration of the Old Testament.

And at the critical hour of His earthly mission, while hanging on a criminal's cross, Jesus turned to the Psalms crying out, "My God, My God, why hast Thou forsaken Me?" (Matthew 27:46). He recognized He was fulfilling His mission as foretold by David in Psalm 22. When death was near He turned to the childlike prayer of Psalm 31:5, "Into Thy hands I commit My spirit" (Luke 23:46). Could Jesus have done that without complete confidence in the entire Scriptures?

If the entire Old Testament were not inspired, Jesus could not have argued with His opponents as He did. Does that give you confidence in the Scriptures? Because Jesus had absolute confidence in the trustworthiness and accuracy of the entire Scriptures, we may also trust the complete Bible completely.

LESSON: *Jesus quoted many of the Old Testament books, revealing His complete confidence in the trustworthiness of the entire Bible.*

INSPIRATION OF
THE OLD AND NEW TESTAMENTS

For the Scripture says, "You shall not
muzzle the ox while he is threshing," and
"The laborer is worthy of his wages." (1 Timothy 5:18)

Some people draw a sharp dichotomy between the Old and New Testaments. Years ago, G. Bromley Oxnam called the God of the Old Testament "a dirty bully" (Harris, *Inspiration & Canonicity*, p. 40). Some people, failing to understand their significance, find fault with God's laws in the Old Testament; others cannot comprehend God's ordering the Israelites to exterminate the Canaanites and for that reason reject the Old Testament. On the other hand, conservative followers of Judaism accept the Old Testament but not the New Testament as inspired.

In fact, the Old and New Testaments are equally inspired. The same God inspired them; they are both inerrant and God's authoritative Word. In 1 Timothy Paul argues that those who give themselves to teaching and preaching the Word of God should receive remuneration (1 Timothy 5:17). Leaders are to be honored by giving them appropriate pay. Paul defends his thesis by a quotation from the Scriptures. Which Scripture is Paul quoting? Although he prefaces his statement with "the Scripture says," he is not quoting only one Scripture passage. Actually, Paul combined an Old Testament and New Testament passage. "You shall not muzzle the ox" is taken from Deuteronomy 25:4, but "the laborer is worthy of his wages" comes from Luke 10:7. This is an important statement since Paul regards both of these statements as equal in authority, defending the right of the preacher to receive remuneration for his ministry. From that passage we see that the New Testament is as inspired as the Old Testament, and the Old is as inspired as the New.

Perhaps one fault Christians have in Bible reading is the neglect of the Old Testament. If we read the Old Testament more, we would be spiritually richer—and we would know the New Testament better because it builds on the Old. Read the law, and note the holiness of God; read the psalms, and be comforted and encouraged; read the prophets, and see how God will bring history to its predicted conclusion.

LESSON: *The Old and New Testaments are equally inspired.*

INSPIRATION OF
THE PARTS OF THE BIBLE

It is written, "Man shall not live on bread alone, but on every word that proceeds out of the mouth of God." (Matthew 4:4)

One theologian has written, "We can trust the Bible when it tells us about salvation, but we may expect that errors have crept into other parts." The question is, How can we separate the parts that tell us about salvation from the parts that supposedly have errors? We cannot. Discussions about salvation are intertwined with historical information. We must conclude that not only is the Bible inspired in its entirety, but the individual parts are inspired as well.

As we look at how Jesus viewed the Scriptures, we can learn an important lesson about the inspiration of the parts of Scripture. During His temptation by Satan, Jesus turned to Deuteronomy, the Old Testament book of obedience. In answering the onslaught of temptation, Jesus continually stated, "It is written . . . it is written . . . it is written" (Matthew 4:4, 7, 10). He demonstrated His complete confidence in the trustworthiness and accuracy of the parts of Scripture.

When Jesus debated the unbelieving Jews because they denied His deity, He exhorted them to search the Scriptures because "it is these that bear witness of Me" (John 5:39). Jesus would have been thinking of all the various parts of Scripture. As the Jews would read the various parts of the Old Testament, they would discover that the Scriptures refer to Jesus.

When the scribes and Pharisees approached Jesus demanding a sign, He replied by quoting Jonah 1:17, illustrating His impending death and resurrection by Jonah's sojourn in the fish (Matthew 12:40). The legitimacy of Jesus' argument depended on the accuracy of the book of Jonah. Jesus believed the book of Jonah to be true.

If any those passages were in error Jesus could not have made His point. The fact is that Jesus quoted from a great variety of passages, revealing His belief in the inspiration of all the various parts of Scripture. You and I may read from Genesis, Psalms, Malachi, or Hebrews, or any other Scripture, and rest in complete assurance that all the parts of Scripture are inspired. Read with confidence, and be nourished in God's Word!

LESSON: *The Bible is inspired in all its various parts.*

INSPIRATION OF
THE NEW TESTAMENT

---

*The Helper, the Holy Spirit, . . . He will teach you all things, and
bring to your remembrance all that I said to you. (John 14:26)*

Going to speak at a Bible conference, a seminary professor drove
his car from Dallas to Houston. When the conference was over
he took a plane home—but when he couldn't find his car at
home he reported it stolen! That brings to mind the saying that a certain
sign of old age is forgetfulness.

Have you ever wondered how in their old age the disciples remembered the details of the life of Christ to write the gospels? How could they
possibly remember the detailed conversations? Think of the Sermon on the
Mount (Matthew 5-7) or the Upper Room discourse (John 14-16). How
could Matthew and John have remembered the details of Jesus' teaching
when Matthew wrote at least twenty years after the event and John may have
written sixty years after it?

Jesus promised the disciples help in remembering His teaching. He
promised them a supernatural Helper—the Holy Spirit. He would teach
them all things and "bring to your remembrance all that I said to you." In
that statement Jesus promised the accurate recording of His conversations
and thereby the inspiration of the New Testament. They could not possibly
have remembered all the details of Christ's words, but He promised that the
Holy Spirit would cause them to remember the things He had said. Jesus
promised, "When the Helper comes, whom I will send to you from the Father, that is the Spirit of truth, who proceeds from the Father, He will bear
witness of Me" (John 15:26). Jesus also promised that the Holy Spirit would
guide them into all the truth (16:13), so that as they wrote the New Testament it would be accurate.

We may read the New Testament with complete confidence that the
Holy Spirit has guided and reminded the writers to accurately remember
and record the truth.

LESSON: *Christ guaranteed the inspiration of the New Testament,
promising that the Holy Spirit would remind the disciples of all that He
taught.*

INSPIRATION OF
PAUL'S NEW TESTAMENT WRITINGS

As also in all [Paul's] letters, speaking in them of these things, in which are some things hard to understand, which the untaught and unstable distort, as they do also the rest of the Scriptures, to their own destruction. (2 Peter 3:16)

In his book *Man As Male and Female,* Paul K. Jewett charges that the apostle Paul is wrong in his explanation of the role relationship of men and women in Paul's appeal to the order of creation in Genesis 1-2 (pp. 134 45). Letha Scanzoni and Nancy Hardesty, writing in *All We're Meant to Be,* say that Paul reflected the culture of his day, but it is not normative for our day.

Those charges are very serious. They go far beyond the singular issue of the biblical teaching on men and women, which is a separate issue. The charge that Paul was in error in his writing cuts at the jugular vein of inspiration. All the sixty-six books of the Bible were written by mortal men just like Paul. If Paul was in error so were the other writers.

In his second epistle, Peter wrote to encourage suffering believers to look for Christ's return and to be blameless in their Christian conduct. Peter reminded them that Paul also spoke of the Lord's patience in rendering judgment and that Paul wrote things "in which are some things hard to understand" (3:16). Because of the difficulty in understanding some of Paul's teaching, the ignorant and unstable would twist Paul's teachings "as they do also the rest of the Scriptures" (v. 16). Note Peter's words "as they do also the rest of the Scriptures." With that remark Peter equated Paul's writings with the rest of Scripture. That means Paul's writings are on par with Jesus' words in the Sermon on the Mount, with the Lord's words to Moses at Sinai, and with all other Scripture.

It is unfortunate that some Bibles are printed in "red letter editions" because they give the faulty impression of two degrees, or levels, of inspiration. But if the Holy Spirit guided all the writers of Scripture, then all sixty-six books of Scripture, including Paul's writings, are as inspired by God as any other part. We need to heed the words penned by the apostle Paul and superintended by the Holy Spirit as the true, inspired words of Scripture that they are.

LESSON: *Paul's New Testament letters are inspired and equal in inspiration and authority to the other books of the Bible.*

February 29

THE BIBLE:
INSPIRED IN ITS WORDS

*The Lord said to My Lord, "Sit at My right hand,
until I put Thine enemies beneath Thy feet." (Matthew 22:44)*

Words are important. A couple decided to marry, and all proceeded well until the preacher asked the young man, "Do you take this woman to be your lawfully wedded wife?" There was a pause. After a moment of silence the young man responded, "No, preacher, I don't believe I will." And he walked out of the church, never to be heard from again! Words are important!

When the Pharisees confronted Christ about His messianic claims, Jesus asked them a question: "What do you think about the Christ, whose son is He?" Their response was simply, "The son of David" (Matthew 22:42). The Pharisees only thought of the Messiah as a man, a human deliverer who would free them from Roman oppression. In His response Jesus demonstrated from the Old Testament that their view of Messiah was faulty. He was more than a man—He was God.

Jesus turned their attention to Psalm 110:1 where David says, "The Lord says to My Lord, sit at My right hand." An interesting statement. If the Pharisees were correct that Messiah was only a man, why did David—Israel's greatest king—call his descendant, "My Lord"? That was not reasonable if David's descendant was only a man, but as the quotation indicates, David recognized that Messiah would be greater than he was. The point of Jesus' argument with the Pharisees hinges on His use of "My Lord" in His quotation from Psalm 110:1. Jesus based His entire argument on the fact that Psalm 110:1 was inspired in its very words; He argued that the Scriptures stated the precise words "My Lord." If the Scriptures were inspired only in their ideas or concepts Jesus could not have argued according to the precise wording of the Psalm 110:1.

As you read the Scriptures, pay attention to the words. Read them carefully. The precise words of Scripture can give us great encouragement. Consider: "Casting *all* your anxiety upon *Him*, because He cares for you" (1 Peter 5:7); "The *Lord* is *my* shepherd" (Psalm 23:1). The exact words are important.

LESSON: *Biblical inspiration extends to the precise words of Scripture as given in the original writings.*

THE BIBLE:
INSPIRED IN ITS LETTERS

*Until heaven and earth pass away, not the smallest
letter or stroke shall pass away from the Law,
until all is accomplished. (Matthew 5:18)*

When we lived on the Atlantic coast in Florida my wife and I enjoyed walking the beach, searching for sharks' teeth. As the waves splashed up on the sandy beach, they washed up many sea shells and sharks' teeth—and occasionally hammerhead sharks! Early one Saturday morning we came to the beach. The sun was just coming up and had cast its golden beams across the Atlantic. The ocean was still and looked like a mirror with the sun's reflection on its calm waters. It was a spectacular sight that might have inspired an artist to paint a picture or a poet to write a poem.

We use the same word, *inspired*, to describe the work of God in supernaturally producing the Scriptures. Are the words to be understood in the same way? Some people understand the inspiration of the Scriptures in only the same way as an artist is inspired to paint a picture. That, however, would be human inspiration, and the Bible would be no different than the writings of William Shakespeare or George Bernard Shaw. However, when applied to the Bible, the term *inspired* emphasizes divine inspiration.

Biblical inspiration extends to the very letters of Scripture, as given in the original writings. In Matthew 5:18 Jesus says, "Not the smallest letter or stroke shall pass away from the Law, until all is accomplished." The smallest letter was the *yodh*, equivalent to an apostrophe. The stroke was the minor difference between two letters. In English it is a tiny stroke that distinguishes an *O* from a *Q*.

Is that important? Most assuredly! Jesus promised us that every part of the Word of God, down to the very letters, will be fulfilled. It means God's Word is reliable. You can believe it and trust it implicitly.

LESSON: *Biblical inspiration is more than a natural, human inspiration; it extends to the very letters of Scripture in the original writings.*

VERBAL PLENARY
INSPIRATION

Then the Lord said to Moses,
"Write down these words. . . . " (Exodus 34:27)

What then is the correct view of inspiration? There are three important words necessary to a proper definition of inspiration: *verbal, plenary,* and *autographs. Verbal* means that we believe that inspiration extends to the very words of Scripture, not merely the ideas or concepts. Words were important to Moses: "Moses wrote down all the words of the Lord" (Exodus 24:4). Words were also important to God, for He instructed Moses, "Write down these words" (34:27). The Lord told the prophet Jeremiah, "Behold, I have put My words in your mouth" (Jeremiah 1:9; cf. Isaiah 51:16; Ezekiel 2:7-8). Jesus also proclaimed the importance of the words of Scripture: "Heaven and earth will pass away, but My words shall not pass away" (Matthew 24:35). The apostle John too recognized he was writing the "true words of God" (Revelation 19:9; 21:5; 22:6).

The second important word in our definition is *plenary,* meaning "full." It means that more than just part of the Bible is inspired in its words—not just the law at Sinai or the Sermon on the Mount. The Bible is "fully" inspired. All sixty-six books—every verse, every chapter, every book.

The third word is *autographs,* meaning the original writings. An orthodox statement of faith says that we believe the Bible is fully inspired in its words in the original writings—the manuscripts written by Moses, Malachi, Matthew, and the others. A translation is only as good as it is faithful to the original languages. That is why the Jehovah's Witnesses' *New World Translation* cannot be considered the Word of God. Fortunately, we have many good translations that accurately reflect the original writings.

Obedience is linked to the words of Scripture. Moses reminded the people, "All that the Lord has spoken we will do, and we will be obedient!" (Exodus 24:7). What would they obey? The words God had given. And it is obedience to the words God has given that is incumbent on us.

LESSON: *The Bible is fully inspired in its words in all sixty-six books in the original writings.*

ILLUMINATION
OF THE BIBLE

Who among men knows the thoughts of a man except the spirit
of the man which is in him? Even so the thoughts of God
no one knows except the Spirit of God. (1 Corinthians 2:11)

I wondered why the sign specified that a child had to be at least six years old as my family and I prepared to walk through one of the world's longest underground caves in the Black Hills of South Dakota. As we began our trek I realized the reason. The cave was not only horizontal—part of it was vertical! As I descended the ladder in one of the vertical shafts, I held my young son with one hand around his waist, and with the other hand I held the lantern. I desperately needed a third hand to hold the ladder! Although it was a fascinating underground journey, it was also a relief to arrive at the mouth of the cave once more. But as we walked the several miles, it would have been impossible had we not had a lantern to guide us.

Similarly, we need God's internal lantern, the Holy Spirit, to illuminate our understanding that we might comprehend the truth of His Word. Man's mind has been darkened through sin (Romans 1:21), preventing him from properly understanding God's Word. Man cannot understand God's truth apart from God's divine enablement (Ephesians 4:18).

God's truth has remained a mystery, even to religious leaders—apart from His supernatural intervention (1 Corinthians 2:8). How then is it possible to understand God's Word? Providing understanding of God's Word is the work of the Holy Spirit called illumination, which is provided for every believer (v. 10).

Man understands the things that pertain to man. God understands the things that pertain to God; hence, God must reveal the things about Himself to man (1 Corinthians 2:11). For that reason God has sent His Holy Spirit to indwell all believers, that each believer may understand His truth (v. 12). In the Upper Room Jesus reminded the disciples that He would send them another Helper, the Holy Spirit, who would teach them all things (John 14:26). He would guide them into spiritual truth, illuminating their path amid the world's darkness, that they might see the light of God's truth (16:13). How gracious of God to lift our minds out of this world and illuminate our spiritual path!

LESSON: *Christ sent the Holy Spirit to indwell all believers that He might illuminate their minds concerning God's truth.*

APPLYING
THE BIBLE (I)

*All Scripture is inspired by God and profitable
for teaching, for reproof, for correction, for training
in righteousness; that the man of God may be adequate,
equipped for every good work. (2 Timothy 3:16-17)*

Friedrich Nietzsche, the atheistic philosopher, admonished Christians by saying, "You Christians will have to look a lot more like your Christ if I am to believe in him." Nietzsche's remark points out the great need for Christians to practice what they preach. It is undoubtedly true that we speak a better faith than we live. Contrary to what some Christians think, the Bible was not given merely to teach us some facts. The Bible was given to teach us how to live! When we read it we must learn to apply it to our daily living.

We begin by asking, "What did this passage mean to the original readers?" That will help us interpret its meaning. For example, in Corinth meat was sacrificed to idols and later sold at a reduced price at the market. Some Christians refused to eat that meat, whereas other Christians thought they had the liberty to eat the half-priced food (1 Corinthians 8). That is the interpretation, and there is only one interpretation for any passage.

Next we ask, "What does this passage mean to me today?" That is application, and there are many applications—to different people in different cultures in different ages. I may apply this passage by concluding, "I will avoid _____ (it will vary in different cultures) to keep from offending a brother" (1 Corinthians 8:13).

Probe the passage with questions. Is there something for me to believe? Does it teach me something about God, Christ, the Holy Spirit, sin, or salvation? Is there a promise to believe? The Psalms are full of encouraging promises to apply. Is there a warning to heed? The Proverbs give many warnings. Is there a command to obey? Some commands were given to Israel and are not possible for us to fulfill (i.e., traveling to Jerusalem three times a year, Deuteronomy 16:16). Keep a notebook, and write down your application each day. It will help you remember what you read and the important meaning it has for you.

LESSON: *As I read the Bible I must learn to apply it to my everyday living in order to grow as a Christian.*

March 5

APPLYING
THE BIBLE (II)

Greet one another with a holy kiss. (Romans 16:16)

When I took my wife to a seafood restaurant on our anniversary, the waiter ushered us to a table by the window overlooking the St. John's River where it flows into the Atlantic Ocean. When we ordered our favorite seafood dinner—scallops—we didn't consider that this was not permissible for us, even though Leviticus 11:10 forbids it.

Some Old Testament passages teach restrictive truths for the nation Israel that are difficult for us to apply. For example, Leviticus 11 specifies the dietary laws for ancient Israel, but what application do they have for us now? The prohibition concerning pork, seafood, and other foods was probably to remind Israel that they were different from other nations, and the restriction was removed in Acts 10. I may apply Leviticus 11 by concluding that I should not abuse my body by eating improper foods.

Other passages describe ancient customs and practices that must be applied with care. Paul exhorts, "Greet one another with a holy kiss" (Romans 16:16), yet most Christians recognize that as cultural. A handshake may be a comparable greeting. New Testament women covered their heads with a veil (1 Corinthians 11:5), a difficult parallel to observe today. But we must be careful not to assign controversial passages to culture, relieving us of our responsibility to obey them. Ask, What principle can I learn from this passage?

Some passages describe universal situations that are easier to apply. John 3:16 is a timeless truth and easy to apply. "Whoever" includes everyone in every age. Psalm 5:11-12 is always true: the one who takes refuge in the Lord will be glad. Proverbs 28:13 also expresses the timeless truth concerning confessing and forsaking sin. It is always true that we should not worry but in every circumstance commit our burdens to the Lord (1 Peter 5:7).

The Bible provides principles more often than specifics; it doesn't specifically tell which forms of entertainment are acceptable or which habits are wrong. But it provides principles that can be applied to many situations: "Whatever you do, do all to the glory of God" (1 Corinthians 10:31).

LESSON: *We need to exercise care in applying the Bible: some passages are restricted whereas other passages contain timeless truths.*

THE BIBLE:
ITS ETERNAL ENDURANCE

The grass withers, the flower fades,
but the word of our God stands forever. (Isaiah 40:8)

Despite opposition and persecution, the Bible remains a bestseller. As of 1804, the British Bible Society had distributed 409 million Bibles; as of 1932 the German Bible Society had apportioned 1 billion, 330 million Bibles. In 1966 alone the American Bible Society distributed 87 million copies. In the same year the Bible had appeared in 240 languages and dialects, and one or more books had been translated into 739 additional languages. Yet all that has been amid persecution and vilification.

In A.D. 303 Emperor Diocletian issued an edict ordering churches to be razed and their Scriptures to be burned. Voltaire (1694-1778), the French rationalist and opponent of Christianity, exclaimed that in one hundred years Christianity would pass from existence. But fifty years after Voltaire's death, the Geneva Bible Society used Voltaire's house and printing press to print and distribute Bibles! (Doesn't God have a sense of humor?)

A modern attempt to discredit to trustworthiness of the Bible is called higher criticism. It is an ingenious and subtle attack of Satan. In its attack on historical reliability, higher criticism has attempted to undermine trust in the Bible by suggesting that Moses didn't write the Pentateuch, Isaiah didn't write Isaiah, Paul didn't write the pastoral epistles, and the historical narratives are not historical. Yet the Bible continues to survive such attacks. It continues to be read, trusted, and obeyed. We may freely place our entire confidence in its reliability, trust it implicitly, and reap the rewards of faith. "The grass withers, the flower fades, but the word of our God stands forever" (Isaiah 40:8).

LESSON: *Though the Bible is attacked by its opponents, it has survived and will continue to survive.*

CONTINUITY
OF THE BIBLE

The judgments of the Lord [Scriptures] are true;
they are righteous altogether. (Psalm 19:9b)

The Book of Mormon, first published in 1825, is the cornerstone of Mormon belief. According to Lamoni Call, by 1898 it had undergone 2,038 corrections, and Arthur Budvarson indicated that by 1959 more than 3,000 changes in grammar and doctrine had been made (Hoekema, *Mormonism*, 91-92). That raises serious questions. If God is the author, should one expect 3,000 errors to need correcting?

The Bible is a truly unique book. There is no other book like it. Consider, for example, that the Bible was written over a span of fifteen hundred years on three continents by more than forty different authors! Image forty people with different backgrounds writing on philosophy, the interpretation of history, and ethics. Consider some of the writers. Moses, who wrote the first five books of the Old Testament, was educated in Egyptian schools; Solomon was reared in the luxury of the royal courts of Israel. By contrast, Amos was a poor sheepherder from the hills south of Bethlehem, and Peter was a simple fisherman, obviously uneducated (Acts 4:13). Luke, on the other hand, was a Gentile medical doctor and Paul a zealous Jew who trained under the renowned Gamaliel. Could all these men (and many more) realistically write on the same subject and agree?

Add to that the fact that they wrote over a period of fifteen hundred years. Things change in that period of time! Consider what it would be like to have a king, a carpenter, a fisherman, a bookkeeper, and an engineer from the days of St. Augustine, Charlemagne, William of Orange, Christopher Columbus, Napoleon, and George Bush writing on the same subject. And the writers of Scripture wrote from three different continents—Europe, Asia, and Africa. Yet the Bible is entirely accurate and in perfect harmony, agreeing on every subject it discusses. There is only one conclusion. God is the Author, superintending all the writers to bring about continuity and perfect agreement.

LESSON: *The Bible was written over a period of fifteen hundred years by more than forty authors on three continents, yet it is in perfect harmony.*

March 8

WHAT IS
INERRANCY?

Thy Word is truth. (John 17:17b)

If I told you, "The sunrise on the Atlantic ocean is a spectacular sight," you would agree with my statement. Though we both recognize the sun does not actually "rise," we would understand the statement as "language of appearances." I could say, "To travel to Jerusalem is to go back in time two thousand years. You will see merchants hawking their wares as in the days of Christ, women transporting their goods in large baskets carried on their heads, and old men riding their laden donkeys to market." Someone else could counter, "Jerusalem is a fully modern city. It boasts modern architecture and modern technology—taxi drivers even drive Mercedes Benz cars." Both statements would be correct.

"The inerrancy of the Bible means simply that the Bible tells the truth. Truth can and does include approximations, free quotations, language of appearances, and different accounts of the same event as long as those do not contradict" (Ryrie, *What You Should Know About Inerrancy*, p. 30). We must be careful not to impose our Western culture, language rules, and precision in language on scriptural statements. For example, when Jesus was resting at the well John remarks, "It was about the sixth hour," which means it was around noon. But what time was it exactly? Twelve o'clock? Probably not. It may have been 11:41 A.M. or 12:13 P.M. To the Semitic mind it was "about the sixth hour." And that is a true statement.

The writer of Hebrews says, "One has testified somewhere, saying . . . " (2:6) as he provides a free quotation from Psalm 8:4-6. Although he has not given a precise rendering of Psalm 8:4-6, what he said is true. Both Psalm 8:4-6 and Hebrews 2:6-8 are entirely true in their statements.

Similarly, the gospel writers may provide different details about the resurrection of Christ, yet each writer provides an accurate and true account of the way it was. All gospel accounts are entirely correct and true. Sometimes we may not have all the information we need to resolve seeming differences, but we can still rest with complete assurance that the Scriptures are entirely true in all that they say.

LESSON: *Inerrancy allows for approximations, free quotations, language of appearances, and different accounts of the same event.*

THE BIBLE'S CLAIM
TO INERRANCY

If any one thinks he is a prophet or spiritual,
let him recognize that the things which I write
to you are the Lord's commandment. (1 Corinthians 14:37)

Muhammad Ali, former world heavyweight boxing champion, made many boastful claims during his boxing career. "I am the greatest," he would boast. And for a number of years he was. He backed up his boasts with his boxing ability. When a claim is made, it is important that it be backed up.

The Bible claims to be inerrant. Some 3,808 times the Bible declares, "God said" or, "Thus says the Lord." When Moses received the law from God on Mount Sinai, the account is preceded by the words "God spoke all these words, saying . . . " (Exodus 20:1). In examining Psalm 69 we note David's cry of distress, but when we read Peter's remark "The Holy Spirit foretold by the mouth of David," in reference to Psalm 69, we are reminded that the ultimate author is not just David. It is God the Holy Spirit.

The prophet Jeremiah had a difficult life and ministry. People plotted against his life, his own family hated him, he was imprisoned a number of times—he even sank in the mud when he was thrown into the cistern Why would he endure all that opposition? For his own philosophy? Not likely. It was because he knew he was conveying the Word of God, and he accepted the suffering for it. "The word of the Lord came to [Jeremiah]" (Jeremiah 1:11).

Similarly, Isaiah had a difficult message, calling his own people by the metaphorical names of "Sodom" and "Gomorrah" because of their wickedness (Isaiah 1:10). Why would he suffer such ignominy? Because he knew he was standing for the Word of God. Paul, too, recognized that he was writing the Word of God when he stated, "Let him recognize that the things which I write to you are the Lord's commandment" (1 Corinthians 14:37). Over and over the Bible claims to be inerrant because God is its Author. The human authors knew God was speaking through them and that they were recording His eternal Word. It is not for us to "adjust" the Word to suit us because it is not a human word; it is God's very Word.

LESSON: *The Bible claims that God is its Author 3,808 times, speaking through human messengers.*

INERRANCY
IS IMPORTANT

The Scripture cannot be broken. (John 10:35)

A prominent theologian has commented on Jesus' remark that the mustard seed is "smaller than all other seeds" (Matthew 13:32). He says, "Botanists know of seeds even smaller than the mustard seed. . . . Jesus in his omniscience, knew perfectly well that there were smaller seeds, but he used this facet of the culture of the people to whom he was speaking. . . . Had Jesus spoken of the seed which was indeed the smallest, he would have been scientifically more accurate." That remark represents two problems. If the thesis is correct, then there are errors in the Bible. Further, it also suggests Jesus was a deceiver. But the mustard seed is the smallest *cultivated* seed.

That illustration reveals the importance of inerrancy. The character of God is at stake. If the Bible is in error, then it impugns the character of God. It makes Him to be a liar.

If the Bible is not inerrant, then we should want to know what those errors are. What if there are errors in doctrinal statements? If Jesus wasn't accurate in His statement about the mustard seed, how can I know He was accurate in saying, "He who believes in the Son has eternal life" (John 3:36)?

Not only is the Bible entirely accurate and without error in everything it says—scientifically and historically as well as doctrinally—but Jesus was accurate in every statement He spoke. He did not deceive His hearers. In telling the disciples about the heavenly home He was going to prepare, He assured them of the truthfulness of His words, saying, "If it were not so, I would have told you" (John 14:2). Those words can be applied to all other areas. If it were not so, Jesus would have told us. The doctrine of inerrancy is important, and we can believe it. And because of that we can believe all the precious doctrinal truths of Scripture.

LESSON: *Inerrancy is important because the Bible claims to be inerrant; if it were not inerrant we could not be assured of our beliefs.*

March 11

INERRANCY
ALLOWS FOR VARIETY

And as they were going out from Jericho, a great
multitude followed Him. And behold, two blind men
sitting by the road ... (Matthew 20:29-30a)

If you and some friends take a trip to southern California, and all of you send postcards home, some of the cards may read as follows. "We enjoyed the big waves at the ocean, but the water was cool." "Southern California is very hot—it gets up to 120 degrees." "Big Bear is a wonderful place for snow skiing." Are these statements contradictory? Not at all. They are all true. They all describe southern California from different viewpoints.

Inerrancy allows for variety in explaining the same event. For example, Matthew says that when Jesus left Jericho, two blind men approached Him, begging Him to heal them (20:29-34). Mark describes the same event, mentioning that as Jesus approached Jericho a blind beggar named Bartimaeus met Him (10:46-52). Describing the same event, Luke states that Jesus was approaching Jericho when a certain blind man met Him (Luke 18:35-43).

Critics may suggest these accounts are contradictory, yet they can be harmonized very simply. In Jesus' day there were two Jerichos, an old Jericho and a new Jericho. Matthew considered the event from the perspective of old Jericho; hence, his statement is correct in saying Jesus was leaving Jericho. Mark and Luke viewed the event from the standpoint of new Jericho. Their statements are also correct. There were two blind men, one named Bartimaeus, who was well known. Mark and Luke focused on the well-known blind man, whereas Matthew emphasized that two men were healed. Both statements are correct. Two blind men were healed, one of whom was known to everyone.

An important principle can be established here. Although we cannot resolve every difficulty (we don't have all the necessary information), we can, through this example, see that it is possible to solve supposed contradictions in Scripture. The Bible does not contradict itself. The different writers of Scripture may tell the same story from a different perspective, but all accounts are true. How wonderful that you and I can have complete confidence in the absolute trustworthiness of God's Word!

LESSON: *The writers of Scripture may describe the same event in different ways, but they are all true; the Bible does not contradict itself.*

PROPHECY AND INERRANCY

They pierced my hands and my feet. . . .
They divide my garments among them,
and for my clothing they cast lots. (Psalm 22:16, 18)

A newspaper carried the story of an evaluation of all the prophecies made by mediums, horoscope writers, and other self-styled prophets in the year 1986. They made predictions concerning the economy, the presidency, and other topics—both general and specific. Of the six hundred predictions that had been made, only thirty were actually fulfilled! In the early 1980s one economist predicted that the Dow Jones stock market would plummet below 500 within the near future. Since that time, the stock market has climbed above 2000. Predictions originating with man are replete with error.

The Bible contains many predictions, but unlike purely human predictions, every prediction of the Bible is true. There are some 332 prophecies concerning Jesus Christ, given hundreds of years before His birth, that have been fulfilled. The following is a sampling:

Subject	Prediction	Fulfillment
Virgin Birth	Isaiah 7:14	Matthew 1:23
Birthplace	Micah 5:2	Matthew 2:1, 5, 6
Life in Egypt	Hosea 11:1	Matthew 2:15
Triumphal Entry	Zechariah 9:9	Matthew 21:5
Rejection	Daniel 9:26	Luke 19:42
Crucifixion	Psalm 22:16	John 20:25
Resurrection	Psalm 16:8-11	Acts 2:27-31

The fact that the Bible's predictions concerning Christ's first advent have all been precisely fulfilled demonstrates the Bible's total accuracy. Someone has calculated that the chance of fulfilled prophecy as found in the Bible is as remote as one chance in 884 plus ninety zeroes! The Bible's fulfilled prophecies bear witness to its divine authorship. Since the Bible is accurate in its promises concerning Christ, it is also accurate in its promises to us. We may firmly believe every promise and encouragement! Is your heart anxious? Rely upon the timeless truths of God's promises in the Bible!

LESSON: *The prophecies of the Bible are literally fulfilled, demonstrating that the Bible is accurate, trustworthy, and reliable.*

ARCHAEOLOGY AND INERRANCY

They became aware of it and fled to the cities of Lycaonia,
Lystra and Derbe, and the surrounding region. (Acts 14:6)

S ir William Ramsey's conversion is an unusual and fascinating story. Ramsey did not believe that the book of Acts was a first-century document and began an archaeological investigation to
demonstrate his disbelief. Ramsey at first considered the statement in Acts
14:6, "cities of Lycaonia, Lystra and Derbe," to be an erroneous geographical statement. Four centuries earlier Iconium had belonged to Phrygia, but
the border shifted and Ramsey thought Luke was unaware of it. But Ramsey
discovered that Luke's statement identifying Lystra and Derbe as cities of
Lycaonia and implying that Iconium was a city of Phrygia (Acts 13:51) was
precise and accurate. For a brief period in the middle of the first century,
Iconium was again a Phrygian city. Hence, Luke grouped Lystra and Derbe
as cities of Lycaonia but not Iconium. That precise accuracy in Luke's statement caused Sir William Ramsey to change his mind about the integrity of
the Holy Scriptures.

Another example of archaeological witness to the Bible's accuracy
concerns the Hittite civilization. The Bible mentions that ancient civilization, but prior to the twentieth century there was no evidence outside the
Bible that the Hittites ever existed. Critics of the Bible ridiculed the scriptural statements, arguing that the Bible was in error because the Hittites had
never existed. In 1906-7, Hugo Winckler, a German archaeologist, discovered thousands of clay tablets in Boghazkeui (modern Turkey), identifying it
as the ancient Hittite capital. Moreover, he discovered that the Hittites had
been a great civilization, ruling from approximately 1900-1200 B.C. and extending from Asia Minor to the Tigris-Euphrates area. The Bible was true in
its statements about the Hittite civilization.

The archaeologist's spade is the believer's friend. Archaeological evidence, if interpreted correctly, will always confirm the truthfulness of the
Bible. The Word of God is a solid rock, a sure foundation.

LESSON: *Archaeological findings, correctly interpreted, will always*
confirm the truthfulness of the Bible.

HISTORY AND
INERRANCY

But as for you, Bethlehem ... from you One will
go forth for Me to be ruler in Israel. (Micah 5:2)

In a Columbus Day poll it was found that one-fourth of American college seniors did not know that Christopher Columbus landed in the Western Hemisphere prior to 1500. In the same test, nearly 60 percent of the students did not know that the Korean War began during the Truman administration. Forty-two percent did not know during which half of the nineteenth century the Civil War began.

History is important. It affects beliefs. History is also important in Scripture. Some may say the historicity of Adam and Eve in Genesis 1-2 is not important. Is that true? In Romans 5:12-21 Paul draws an analogy between Adam and Jesus. What the first Adam lost, bringing sin, condemnation, and death—the last Adam, Jesus Christ, won, bringing righteousness, justification, and life. In Paul's argument it is important that both Adam and Jesus are historical people. The analogy breaks down if Jesus is historical, but Adam is not.

Similarly, the geography of Micah 5:2 is important. Micah announced that in Bethlehem, a tiny, insignificant town in Judah, the Messiah would be born. He would be "ruler in Israel. His goings forth are from long ago, from the days of eternity." That is an important statement announcing the eternality of Jesus Christ, a vital doctrine to Christians. But the doctrine of Christ's eternality is tied to a statement about geography—His birth would be in Bethlehem. If we cannot believe for certain that Christ was born in Bethlehem, can we be certain about His eternality?

We can rest in complete assurance that the Bible is true and trustworthy in all its statements. Aren't you glad that you don't need to wonder about the accuracy of each statement of Scripture?

LESSON: *The Bible is true and without error in all its statements, including geography, history, and science.*

ARE THERE HISTORICAL ERRORS IN THE BIBLE?

Moses finished writing the words
of this law in a book. (Deuteronomy 31:24)

Years ago *Time* magazine ran an issue with a feature article on Nelson Glueck, a Hebrew archaeologist. Although a brilliant scholar, Professor Glueck took a simplistic view of the Bible. He read the Old Testament, believing that it recorded accurate historical events and engaged his archaeological digs on that basis. And he was successful.

Critics have argued that the life of Abraham and his family are unhistorical and untrustworthy. But in excavating Ur, Abraham's ancient home, archaeologists found it to be a large, flourishing city with an advanced civilization around 2000 B.C., just as the Bible depicts. A tablet has also been found, recording a farmer named Abarama, who rented an ox.

Some have argued that writing was unknown prior to the time of David (ca. 1000 B.C.), and therefore Moses could not have written the first five books of the Bible. In 1929, Schaeffer made an enormous discovery at Ras Shamra, ancient Ugarit, of writing in a language closely related to Hebrew. Also found in the early 1900s was the Gezer calendar (dating about 925 B.C.), a schoolboy's exercise, revealing that writing was so common throughout Israel at that time that even children were taught to write.

Others argue that the Bible contains errors in chronology, citing the reigns of Hebrew kings. The solution is that some kings reigned in a coregency (where father and son reigned together and their monarchies overlapped). On occasion even three kings reigned together. For example, Amaziah reigned 796-767, Uzziah 790-736, Jotham 751-736, and Ahaz 743-728. From 743-736 there were three kings ruling.

We do not need to attempt to separate doctrine from historical statements. The Bible is trustworthy and true in all its statements—doctrinal and historical.

LESSON: *The Bible is accurate in its historical accounts.*

WHY IS THE APOCRYPHA NOT PART OF THE BIBLE?

You shall not add to the word which I am commanding you, nor take away from it, that you may keep the commandments of the Lord your God which I command you. (Deuteronomy 4:2)

What is the Apocrypha? The word *Apocrypha* means "hidden" and refers to fourteen (or fifteen) historical and fictional books written in Israel between 300 B.C. and A.D. 100. Because of their esoteric content the word *Apocrypha* came to mean false or heretical to early Christian leaders.

Why do some people believe the Apocrypha? When Luther and other Reformers challenged doctrinal views taken from the Apocrypha at the Council of Trent, the counter-reformation movement pronounced eleven of the books as canonical, meaning they have the stature of inspired Scripture.

Why do we reject the Apocrypha as part of the Bible? The books of the Apocrypha are never quoted in the New Testament. That is unusual since Matthew alone quotes twenty-five of the thirty-nine Old Testament books. Only Esther, Song of Solomon, and Ecclesiastes are not quoted in the New Testament.

Second, although He quoted from many Old Testament books, Christ never indicated that He recognized the apocryphal books as part of the Bible. The same is true of the Jews of Jesus' day.

Third, the apocryphal books don't claim to be inspired. They are simply historical books or books of fiction. That is also recognizable in reading them—they don't read like Scripture. The reader notices a contrast between books of Scripture and the Apocrypha.

Fourth, they contain historical, geographical, and chronological errors. For example, the book of Judith says Nebuchadnezzar reigned over the Assyrians (false: it was the Babylonians) and that Nineveh was captured by Nebuchadnezzar (false: it was his father, Nabopolassar).

Also, the apocryphal books contradict Scripture. Second Maccabees advocates prayer for the dead, justifies suicide, suggests that almsgiving atones for sin, and teaches the preexistence of souls and that the end justifies the means.

Finally their teaching is rejected in Malachi 4:4-6, which anticipates no writing between the Old and New Testaments.

We may read the sixty-six books of our Bible with complete confidence that we have the entire Bible—not more, not less.

LESSON: *The apocryphal books are not part of the Bible because they contain error, contradict Scripture, and Christ never acknowledged them.*

WHICH BOOKS BELONG
IN THE OLD TESTAMENT? (I)

*All things which are written about Me in the Law of Moses
and the Prophets and the Psalms must be fulfilled. (Luke 24:44)*

A s our boys were growing up we measured their growth by marking their height, with the date, on the wall. Then we measured the height with a yardstick. The yardstick was the standard by which their height was measured.

When we speak of the canonicity of Scripture we are referring to a spiritual yardstick—the standard of measuring which books belong in Scripture. Other books were written when the Scriptures were written. Why are those thirty-nine books included in the Old Testament and not others? All the books are measured against the spiritual standards to determine which books belong in the Old Testament.

Tests were applied to the writings to determine which were inspired. If they met the tests, the books were deemed canonical. What are those standards for the Old Testament?

1. *Did the book indicate God was the author?* For example, many passages in the Old Testament begin, "God spoke all these words," or, "the Lord spoke to _____ " (Exodus 20:1; Joshua 1:1; Isaiah 2:1).

2. *Was the book related to Moses?* Genesis through Deuteronomy were considered "the law" and were identified as having been written by Moses and were therefore judged to be Scripture (Joshua 1:7-8). God's Word was equated with Moses' writings in these five books (Deuteronomy 31:24; 1 Kings 2:3).

3. *Was the human author a spokesman (such as a prophet) for God?* For example, Samuel's writings were recognized as inspired (1 Samuel 10:25). The prophets received revelation directly from God, which they recorded and which was considered inspired (Jeremiah 1:2; Ezekiel 1:3; Hosea 1:1).

At a time when some self-styled prophets suggest that they are receiving divine revelation, we may rest assured that there is no new revelation being given today—no new books are being added to the Bible. We have all that we need for our spiritual maturity in the thirty-nine Old Testament books (and the New Testament writings). So we need to read them!

LESSON: *The law, the prophets, and the writings, covering all thirty-nine Old Testament books, were recognized as inspired.*

WHICH BOOKS BELONG
IN THE OLD TESTAMENT? (II)

*All things which are written about Me in the Law of Moses
and the Prophets and the Psalms must be fulfilled. (Luke 24:44)*

Which books belong in the Bible? Which books are truly inspired? Roman Catholicism acknowledges the sixty-six books of the Old and New Testaments but also accepts the Apocrypha as inspired and belonging to the sacred Scriptures. Seventh Day Adventists recognize the writings of Ellen White as inspired. Christian Science acknowledges Mary Baker Eddy's *Science and Health with Key to the Scriptures,* whereas Mormons use the Book of Mormon (and other writings) in addition to the Scriptures. What books—to the exclusion of all others—are truly inspired?

Through the centuries, believers adopted a spiritual yardstick called a "canon" (meaning "measuring rod") to determine which books are inspired. Several tests were applied to the Old Testament writings.

1. *Was the book historically accurate?* Historical errors can be found in the Apocrypha, the Book of Mormon, and others.

2. *How was the book received by the Jews?* The thirty-nine books of the Old Testament were eventually gathered into three groups: the law, the prophets, and the writings. The Jews recognized those three groups (our thirty-nine books) as Scripture. Josephus, Philo, and Christ Himself recognized those books as inspired (Luke 24:44).

3. *How was the book received by the church?* The New Testament quotes all the Old Testament books except Esther, Ecclesiastes, and Song of Solomon. The church also recognized the threefold category of Old Testament writings.

Jesus acknowledged the thirty-nine books of the Old Testament as inspired (Luke 24:44). Because Jesus believed the Scriptures to be inspired surely you and I can put our trust in the Scriptures! Read them in confidence; trust them for your spiritual profit.

LESSON: *Jesus and the church affirmed that the thirty-nine books of the Old Testament are inspired.*

WHICH BOOKS BELONG IN THE NEW TESTAMENT?

*When you received from us the word of God's message,
you accepted it not as the word of men, but for what
it really is, the word of God. (1 Thessalonians 2:13)*

In the year A.D. 138 (or 139) a man of considerable wealth named Marcion came from Pontus to Rome, joined the church, and bestowed some of his wealth on the church. But he had a falling out with the church and was removed from fellowship. Marcion formed a separate church and began expounding his unique teachings. He taught that the Old Testament God was evil and that the New Testament writers had obscured the true gospel by combining it with Judaism. He said the New Testament God was a God of love who had revealed Himself in Jesus. Furthermore, Jesus did not have a genuine body but only appeared to have one. Marcion taught that only Paul properly understood the gospel; hence, Marcion accepted ten of Paul's letters and an edited version of Luke's gospel as inspired. He rejected the rest of the New Testament.

Marcion's action forced the church to consider a crucial question: Which books belong in the New Testament? Which New Testament books— to the exclusion of all others—are inspired?

Certain tests were applied to determine which books were a part of the New Testament.

1. *Was the author an apostle or did he have some connection with an apostle?* Mark, for instance, wrote under Peter's authority, and Luke wrote under Paul's authority.

2. *Did the church at large accept the book?* By this test false books were rejected if the church at large did not accept the book. The Spirit's witness to all believers in different communities was important.

3. *Did the book reflect doctrine that was consistent with the historic faith?* False writings were rejected as a result of this test.

4. *Did the book reflect the quality of inspiration?* Was there the Holy Spirit's inner witness that it was inspired? It was important that the book reflect the high moral and spiritual values of a work inspired by the Holy Spirit.

5. *Was the book used in early Christian worship?*

By those tests the twenty-seven books of the New Testament—no more, no less—were determined to be inspired. We are the beneficiaries of serious prayer, study, and consideration by devout Christians in the early centuries. Only those twenty-seven books are authoritative. Let us not be enslaved to false writings by false teachers.

LESSON: *God guided the early Christians to conclude that the twenty-seven books of the New Testament are inspired.*

INTERPRETING THE BIBLE
IN CONTEXT

Open my eyes, that I may behold
wonderful things from Thy law. (Psalm 119:18)

A woman entered the Democratic primary for governor of the state of Texas. She was convinced that the Bible had told her she would win the nomination. When she received the official list of names from the primary she saw her name printed last. Then she read in her Bible, "Many that are first will be last, and the last first" (Matthew 19:30). On the basis of that verse she thought God was telling her she would win. But she lost.

Someone has well said, "A text without a context is a pretext." What principles should we then follow? In applying a verse, read the surrounding context, several paragraphs before and after the passage. It will shed new light on the subject.

For example, adherents to the "health and wealth gospel" quote Deuteronomy 7:13, suggesting that we can claim wealth on the basis of that verse. But note the context. It is for the covenanted people Israel (v. 9) when they entered the Promised Land (v. 1). We are not Israel!

Next, look at the more remote context by studying the surrounding chapters. How do they shed light on the subject? Notice Deuteronomy 5:1: "Moses summoned all Israel, and said to them, 'Hear, O Israel, the statutes and the ordinances which I am speaking today in your hearing, that you may learn them and observe them carefully.'" Moses is addressing ancient Israel, not twentieth century money-minded people! These chapters are part of the law of Moses. If they applied to us, we would then also need to reimpose the Sabbath (5:12) and bind Scriptures on our hands and foreheads (6:8).

Finally, look at the context of the entire book. To whom was it written? Why was it written? The opening words of Deuteronomy indicate "these are the words which Moses spoke to all Israel across the Jordan in the wilderness" (1:1). Those words tell us that Deuteronomy was a reiteration of the law to the new generation of Israelites that was about to enter the land of Israel. New Testament believers are "not under law but under grace" (Romans 6:14).

It is important that we handle the Word of God carefully because it is just that—the Word of God. Read and apply the words of Scripture, but study the surrounding context to make certain you are interpreting it correctly.

LESSON: *We should consider the immediate, more remote, and overall context of the book when interpreting a passage.*

INTERPRETING THE BIBLE GRAMMATICALLY

Which things we also speak, not in words taught by human wisdom, but in those taught by the Spirit, combining spiritual thoughts with spiritual words. (1 Corinthians 2:13)

A man was taken to court on a marijuana possession charge. He pled his case arguing that the Bible encourages using marijuana. He quoted Genesis 1:29, "I have given you every herb bearing seed, which is upon the face of all the earth . . . to you it shall be for meat" (KJV*). He lost the case. He was misinterpreting the words of Scripture.

When studying Scripture, grammar is important in interpretation. Since we believe in verbal inspiration (that the words of Scripture are inspired) it is incumbent upon us to consider the words of Scripture. But what should we look for? Look at the verbs, the action words. For example, after Paul and Silas were beaten and tortured in the stocks, they "were praying and singing hymns of praise to God and the prisoners were listening" (Acts 16:25) Is that unusual? Most assuredly! The prisoners expected to hear curses, but they heard praises! Verb tenses are important. The wonder of John 3:16 is that believers *have* eternal life. The present tense reinforces that it is a present position. Look at the nouns and pronouns.

Peter caught the incongruity of Jesus' washing his feet: "Lord, do *You* wash *my* feet?" (John 13:6). The pronouns shout forth the distinction between Jesus and Peter. Prepositional phrases are also significant. The phrase "in just the same way" in Acts 1:11 reminds us that we look for the physical, visible return of Jesus Christ from glory. In Philippians 4:19 Paul says God will supply all our needs "according to His riches in Christ Jesus." Will God throw us a few peanuts? No. He will supply our needs "according to" His lavish riches in Christ! Prepositions are significant. Matthew says the Son of Man came "to give His life a ransom *for* many" (Matthew 20:28). "For" means Christ died in our place, as our substitute. That minuscule word takes on major importance.

To enrich your Bible reading, read carefully. Get a good study Bible. Pay attention to the precise words of Scripture. Learn, grow, and rejoice at your riches in Christ!

LESSON: *Interpret the Bible grammatically, paying attention to nouns, pronouns, verbs, conjunctions, and prepositions.*

* King James Version.

March 22

INTERPRETING THE BIBLE LITERALLY

Now all this took place that what was spoken by the Lord through the prophet might be fulfilled, saying, "Behold, the virgin shall be with child, and shall bear a Son." (Matthew 1:23)

While attending a Monday night Bible class, a major league baseball player became a Christian. Reading in the King James Version that a believer should go into his closet to pray (Matthew 6:6), every morning he took his flashlight and his Bible into his closet, shut the door, and read his Bible. He explained that he was very uncomfortable, but he learned a lot about the Bible! He was right in interpreting the Bible literally, but he needed a new translation of Matthew 6:6.

Why is literal interpretation important? It is necessary to understand the plain or normal meaning of the Bible. We should not look for allegorical or "hidden" meanings or attempt to give unnatural meanings to ordinary words. We can readily understand the Bible when we interpret it literally. The account of creation, the Exodus from Egypt, the life, death, and resurrection of Jesus—all are understood in their literal or normal meaning.

Reading the Bible literally also guards us from the imaginative ruminations of the cults. For example, the Christian Science cult sees the Bible as one vast allegory; hence, the devil is not a person, only "a lie, error." Heaven becomes "harmony," hell becomes "lust, remorse, hatred," and Jesus becomes "the highest human corporeal concept of the divine idea." When literal interpretation is abandoned, all objectivity—all normal understanding is lost. Imagination takes over.

Old Testament prophecies have been fulfilled literally, giving us a precedence for literal interpretation. It was literally prophesied and literally fulfilled that Jesus would be born of a virgin (Isaiah 7:14; Matthew 1:22), that He would be born in Bethlehem (Micah 5:2; Matthew 2:6), that soldiers would gamble for His garments (Psalm 22:18; John 19:24).

We need not look for mystical, hidden meanings behind the plain words of Scripture. Though we recognize figures of speech, we interpret the Bible in its ordinary meaning. That is a comfort. God did not intend that only seminary trained people could grasp the Scriptures. He wants all of us, from all walks of life, to read, understand, believe, and enjoy His Word.

LESSON: *The Bible is to be interpreted literally, understanding the words in their normal meaning.*

INTERPRETING THE BIBLE HISTORICALLY

*But when the fulness of time came, God sent forth His Son,
born of a woman, born under the Law. (Galatians 4:4)*

T he historical background of the Bible is important because the
Bible must be understood in its context. What is that context? In
Genesis 12 God calls Abraham, the father of the Jewish people,
who, because of a famine, goes down to Egypt. As the book of Exodus
opens, the family of seventy-five has grown to more than two million people. God delivered them from oppression, bringing them to Sinai, where He
gave them a constitution (which covers Exodus-Deuteronomy).

The Israelites entered the land under Joshua, fell into apostasy
(Judges), and begged for a king (1 Samuel). God gave them Saul, David,
and Solomon, each ruling the twelve tribes for forty years (1050-931 B.C.).
Then the nation split into the northern kingdom of Israel (ten tribes) and the
southern kingdom of Judah (two tribes). The Old Testament prophets ministered to the nation during this time, calling the people back to obedience
under the Mosaic Covenant. Samuel, Kings, Chronicles, and the major and
minor prophets provide the historical background for these events.

Because the northern kingdom never had a godly king, Israel was destroyed in 722 B.C. and taken captive by Assyria. But Judah had reforming
kings, who called people back to obedience under the law; for that reason
Judah continued until 586 B.C. when Jerusalem was destroyed by Nebuchadnezzar and the people were carried captive to Babylon. After seventy years
of captivity, God fulfilled Daniel's prophecy and brought the Jews back into
the land (Ezra, Nehemiah, Haggai, Zechariah, Malachi), enabling them to
rebuild Jerusalem and also, under Zerubbabel, the Temple.

After the four hundred "silent years," God again revealed Himself to
the nation by sending Jesus of Nazareth, the promised Messiah. The four
gospels record His glorious life, death, resurrection, and ascension into
heaven. Acts relates the story of the church that Jesus came to build. The
epistles describe the significance of Jesus' coming—He came to rescue us
from sin, that we might be justified by faith and not by works of the law
(Galatians 2:16). And Revelation captures the climax—Jesus is coming
again to establish His glorious kingdom. As you read the Bible, using a
Bible handbook, ask yourself, "What is the historical background in which
this passage is written?"

LESSON: *All the books of the Bible were written in a historical context
that must be considered in interpretation.*

STUDY THE BIBLE
GEOGRAPHICALLY

And He had to pass through Samaria. (John 4:4)

Wwhen the revolution occurred in former Belgian Congo following independence, Christian missionaries, particularly those who were Americans, were in grave danger. A Canadian missionary whose wife was American, attempted to emigrate by placing his Canadian passport over his wife's American passport. The official, assuming both were Canadians, asked another official, "Where is Canada?" "Oh, it's somewhere in South America," replied the other. The missionaries' lives were saved because of a lack of geographical knowledge.

In studying the Bible a knowledge of geography is important. For example, why did Joshua invade the Promised Land at Jericho? There were three main valleys leading into the land of Israel, so Joshua invaded where he could directly attack the inhabitants.

Why was Jerusalem built on Mts. Moriah and Zion? Those hills are at the highest point of the central Judean hills running through the length of the land. By building Jerusalem on the highest point in the Judean hills, the Lord indicated the premier importance of that city.

Why did Jesus walk through Samaria when the other Jews wouldn't? John says, "[Jesus] had to pass through Samaria" (John 4:4). Traditionally, Jews walking from Jerusalem to Galilee walked east, crossing the Jordan, then northward in Perea, and once they were past Samaria crossed the Jordan again. All that added many miles to the trip. Jesus rejected tradition by walking through Samaria, the most direct route to Galilee. By doing so, He was breaking down barriers between Jews and Samaritans.

What was significant about the Macedonian man's calling Paul to Philippi (Acts 16:9)? It meant the gospel would spread westward, toward Europe, instead of eastward. We in the West are the beneficiaries of the westward movement of the gospel.

There is considerable geographical information that will help us understand the Bible. Obtain a Bible atlas to help you in your study. As you study the geographical background, your eyes will be opened to more exciting biblical truth.

LESSON: *A knowledge of the geography of the Holy Land is important in aiding our understanding of the Bible.*

STUDY THE BIBLE
CULTURALLY

*Now one of the Pharisees invited Jesus to have
dinner with him, so he went to the Pharisee's
house and reclined at the table. (Luke 7:36, NIV)*

The best way to obtain insight into the culture of the Bible is to take a trip to Israel. As you enter the old city of Jerusalem you will see examples of life as it was in Jesus' day—women on their way to market carrying large baskets of bakery goods or clothes; rugged-looking men riding donkeys with big bundles tied behind them; people in the narrow streets hawking their products. In the countryside you will see Bedouin living in tents much like Abraham (except for the TV antenna) and shepherds on the Judean hills. It all reveals the culture of the Bible—a culture much different from our own.

In ancient Israel ordinary people lived in tents or small, one-room cottages with dirt floors. Beds were mats unrolled on the floor. Roofs were flat and used for drying grain or for prayer and refuge.

Food was simple. Meat was reserved for special occasions, but fish was a staple. Unleavened bread similar to crepes was used to scoop up the food with the hand (Matthew 26:23). Utensils were not normally used. "Why use a fork when God has given man so many fingers?" they said. People drank milk from goats and camels, and when it curdled it became lunch (Isaiah 7:15)! Olives were eaten as food and when crushed served as butter, but the oil also provided fuel and medicine. At mealtime family members sat cross-legged on cushions, whereas at banquets they reclined on couches (Luke 7:36).

Hospitality was very important (Genesis 18:1-8). Both men and women wore tunics and robes, but women's robes were more ornate. A cloak, which also served as a peasant's bedding (Exodus 22:26-27), was worn in cold weather. Women wore veils in public, still true of many Arab women today. Homes were patriarchal, and when the father died, the oldest son became ruler of the family, yet women were treated with respect. Parents arranged marriages (Genesis 24:58), and love came after the marriage (Titus 2:4). A groom's failure to provide a proper wedding feast could result in a lawsuit (John 2:3).

The culture of the Bible is both fascinating and important. A book such as Ralph Gower's *New Manners & Customs of Bible Times* (Moody) has beautiful pictures and is very helpful. Study the culture for added insight into the Bible.

LESSON: *Understanding the culture of the Bible is important in interpreting the Word of God.*

RECOGNIZE
FIGURES OF SPEECH

*The mountains and the hills will break forth
into shouts of joy before you, and all the trees
of the field will clap their hands. (Isaiah 55:12b)*

That'll rot your socks!" boomed the professor. "You'll get nailed to the wall! You'll get shot out of the saddle!" On graduation day the Asian student thanked the Lord for letting him graduate, even when he didn't understand the strange speech of the professor. The student had encountered figures of speech that were difficult to understand.

Since the Bible also uses figures of speech, it is important to recognize and accurately interpret them. We must understand the figure of speech as well as its application. What are some figures of speech?

1. A simile compares two things, using *like* or *as*. "'Is not My word like fire?' declares the Lord, 'and like a hammer which shatters a rock?'" (Jeremiah 23:29). The Word of God is like a hammer that shatters the rock of human resistance.

2. A metaphor suggests a likeness simply by stating it: "The Lord is My Shepherd" (Psalm 23:1). The Lord protects, nourishes, and quiets His people just as a shepherd cares for His sheep.

3. Personification attributes human characteristics to inanimate things. For example, "The wilderness and the desert will be glad, and the Arabah [desert] will rejoice . . . with rejoicing and shout of joy" (Isaiah 35:1-2a). No one has ever heard the desert shout, but when Christ inaugurates His kingdom on earth, even nature is pictured as being happy.

4. Irony is satire or sarcasm, stating the opposite of what is meant. When Job answered Zophar, "With you wisdom will die" (12:2b), he was being sarcastic because his three friends had "all" the answers.

5. Anthropomorphism attributes human characteristics to God. "They heard . . . the Lord God walking in the garden" (Genesis 3:8). God the Father does not have legs, but His presence in the Garden is pictured by His walking.

As you read the Bible, ask yourself, "Does this make sense in its normal (literal) meaning, or is that nonsense?" If it makes no sense in its normal meaning (God has wings, Jesus is a door, the hills clap their hands, and so on), then it is likely a figure of speech. Then ask, "What does the figure mean, and what lesson is it intended to teach?"

LESSON: *A figure of speech is an illustration teaching something other than its literal meaning.*

WHY DIFFERENT BIBLE VERSIONS?

*From childhood you have known the sacred writings
which ... give you ... wisdom that leads to salvation
through faith ... in Christ Jesus. (2 Timothy 3:15)*

Which is the best Bible version? That question could raise a heated discussion! Some will argue that the *New American Standard* is the best study Bible; others will say the *New International Version* is the best. Still others will suggest that children understand the *Living Bible* best, whereas some will say the King James is the only Bible.

Why are there different versions? Versions in themselves are necessary because most of us don't read Hebrew and Greek, the languages the Bible was inspired in. A translation is only as good as it accurately reflects the original Hebrew and Greek. Translations are also necessary because languages continue to change. For example, in 2 Thessalonians 2:7, speaking of the restrainer, the King James reads, "Only he who now letteth will let." "Letteth" today means allow, but when the King James was written it meant the opposite; it meant to hinder. And in 1 Peter 3:1, Peter says unsaved husbands "may without the word be won by the conversation of the wives." That sounds contradictory, but "conversation" formerly meant conduct, not talking. Hence, the need for new translations.

The discovery of new Greek manuscripts has also made new translations necessary since it assures us that our text will most accurately represent the original manuscripts, which we do not have. Although there were only six Greek manuscripts available when the King James was translated, modern translations are based on the study of more than five thousand Greek manuscripts, assuring their accuracy.

Some translations indicate biases against the deity of Christ or the virgin birth. A good translation is faithful to the vernacular. It must be properly understood in the modern language. And a good translation should not take liberties to obscure biblical doctrines.

Which is the best translation? Someone has answered by saying, "My mother's." "Which one was that?" "The one she constantly read." Indeed, that is the best translation—the one that is read. We may have the best translation, but it is of little value if it is not read.

LESSON: *Translations are necessary because languages change and because new Greek and Hebrew manuscripts are discovered.*

Part 3
Christ

March 28

PREEXISTENCE OF CHRIST

Before Abraham was born, I AM. (John 8:58)

Jesus Christ made some amazing statements. He once infuriated His opponents by telling them, "I existed before Abraham was born" (Williams). Since Abraham lived two thousand years before Christ, Jesus' words were unusual indeed. They knew Him to be a man in His thirties, a carpenter born in Bethlehem and living in Nazareth. How could He have existed before Abraham? A preposterous idea!

But numerous biblical passages actually teach the preexistence of Christ. A particularly pointed passage is Micah 5:2. This verse identifies Bethlehem as the birthplace of Jesus. One born in Bethlehem will one day be a Ruler in Israel. However, Micah teaches something else. Concerning the same Ruler, Micah also declares, "His goings forth are from long ago, from the days of eternity." The prophet indicates that although this Ruler is born in Bethlehem, that is not His beginning. In fact, He does not have a beginning; He has existed from eternity past.

John also teaches the preexistence of Christ—that He existed prior to His birth in Bethlehem. John declared that Christ created all things, that nothing has come into existence without Christ's creating it (John 1:3). If Christ is the Creator, then He must have existed prior to His earthly sojourn. John further remarks that no one has ascended into heaven except Christ, who has come down from heaven (John 3:13); moreover, Christ can explain about heaven since He has been there (v. 31). In His prayer to the Father, Jesus Himself stated that He had the glory of God before the world existed (17:5).

What a great Savior we have! He not only became partaker of our nature so that He might understand us and come to our aid, He also existed prior to His earthly life. He is the eternal God and has come to earth to reveal the Father to us that we might know the true and living God.

LESSON: *Jesus existed before His earthly life, as evidenced by His work in creation, His fellowship with the Father, and His having come down from heaven.*

ETERNALITY OF CHRIST

In the beginning was the Word, and the Word
was with God, and the Word was God. (John 1:1)

Although Jesus' human existence began when He was born in Bethlehem, He nonetheless has existed as God from timeless eternity. John enunciates this profound truth in his opening statement: "In the beginning was the Word." John's remark is reminiscent of Genesis 1:1, taking the reader back to the beginning of history and the "root of the universe." Although the universe had a beginning, the Word did not. The Word (identified as Jesus Christ in John 1:14) already existed at the dawn of the universe.

John also explains what Christ was doing in eternity past: "The Word was with God." That means that in eternity past Christ was in face-to-face fellowship with the Father. Kenneth Wuest translates it, "And the Word was in fellowship with God the Father." That phrase further reinforces Christ's eternal existence. Not only was He in existence from all eternity, but He was the second Person of the Trinity, in fellowship with the Father. Jesus continually shared the divine glory with the Father before the world's beginning (John 17:5).

John was quick to remind readers that Christ created all things: "All things came into being through Him; and apart from Him nothing came into being that has come into being" (1:3). Speaking to fallen humanity, John saw the need to remind us twice that Christ created "all things" and that "nothing" has come into being apart from Him. The conclusion is clear. If Christ created all things and nothing exists apart from His creation, then Christ Himself must be uncreated. Christ is eternal.

Of what significance is Christ's eternality to us? John reminds us that "in Him was life" (v. 4). Because Christ is eternal, He must have life in Himself. His life is inherent to His eternal nature; it is not derived from someone else. And because He is life, He can give us life. He gives us qualitative life in the present and quantitative life—endless, joyous fellowship with Him forever. Is the eternality of Christ important? Yes!

LESSON: *Jesus Christ is eternal, having existed in fellowship with the Father from all eternity.*

JESUS CHRIST
IS CREATOR

*All things came into being through Him; and apart from Him
nothing came into being that has come into being. (John 1:3)*

Scientists have been studying a supernova, a massive star dying in
a violent explosion that has outshone hundreds of millions of
stars put together. A supernova is a large star that runs out of fuel
and collapses under its own weight, blowing off outer layers of gas. A neu-
tron star, or a black hole, is all that remains. Early in March 1987, the supernova was as bright as 100 million suns and matched the brilliance of a
billion stars. Dubbed 1987A, the supernova is the brightest star and most
important happening in astronomy since 1604. This amazing event occurred
at the edge of the Milky Way (*Time*, March 9, 1987, pp. 70-71).

The magnitude of the universe is staggering to the limitations of a finite mind. In recognizing the vastness, the believer also considers that Jesus Christ is the Creator of this immensity. John said, "All things came into
being through Him and apart from Him nothing came into being that has
come into being" (John 1:3). Jesus Christ created everything that exists
—from the enormous supernovas in the universe, to the sweet smelling
roses, to the colorful cardinals, to the majestic mountains, to the turquoise
lakes—Jesus Christ is the Creator of it all! That fact stresses His deity and
His eternality. He performs the works of God.

Paul affirms the same truth in Colossians 1:16. Christ has created the
visible and the invisible; there is nothing anywhere that Christ has not created. He has also created angels and everything in the invisible sphere.

Jesus Christ is worthy of our worship, not only as our Redeemer but
also as the eternal Creator God. Paul concludes that because Christ has
created all things, all creation ought to be subject to Him, "so that He Himself might come to have first place in everything" (Colossians 1:18). Because Jesus Christ is the supreme Creator, He ought to have supremacy in
everything. Consider your life: your thoughts, time, activities, abilities, fi-
nances—does Jesus Christ have first place in all things?

LESSON: *Jesus Christ created all things, affirming that He is God
since He performs the creative works of God.*

CHRIST UPHOLDS ALL THINGS

*And He is before all things, and in Him
all things hold together. (Colossians 1:17)*

Occasionally we read in the newspaper that a newborn infant has been found abandoned in a trash can or on the doorstep of a government agency. The mother of an abandoned baby has failed in her responsibility as mother.

How different is Christ! Not only is He Creator, but He also sustains all things. The one who brought the world and universe into being is the one who holds it together and carries it forward to its predetermined destiny. Think of it! Paul's statement that in Christ "all things hold together" concludes a train of thought that begins, "[In Christ] we have redemption, the forgiveness of sins" (Colossians 1:14). Christ not only redeemed us through His blood but delivered us from the domain of darkness and will bring us and all things to their appointed conclusion. Although world events may not make sense to us, everything—individually and nationally—is guided along a path by Christ our Savior.

The writer of Hebrews also states that Christ "upholds all things by the word of His power" (1:3). Christ is carrying all things along to their predetermined destiny. Years ago I enjoyed traveling the Supercontinental passenger train in Canada. As I relaxed in the coach, the train carried me along to a determined destination. So also Christ carries all things forward on their appointed course. But it is not something He will do in the future; He is doing it now.

How does He do it? By the "word of His power." Just as Christ spoke the word and all things were created, so He simply speaks the word and all creation is sustained and carried along. That is not an abstract truth. It means He is carrying you and me along on our appointed course! Does that encourage you? It should because it is parallel to Romans 8:28. The things that happen to us are appointed and designed by our loving Savior and are therefore for our good. Nothing can hinder God's divine design for us. The evil one will have no victory over us because Christ's Word is stronger, and it is by His Word we are sustained.

LESSON: *Just as Christ has created all things, so He also sustains and carries all things along (including us) according to His loving plan.*

CHRIST IS
THE FIRSTBORN

[Christ is] the firstborn of all creation. (Colossians 1:15b)

While Queen Elizabeth II rules over the British Empire, Prince Charles waits in the wings. Upon her death or abdication, Charles will assume the throne as King of England because of his preeminent position—he is the firstborn. As the firstborn he has a position of priority: he is heir to the throne with all the sovereign authority accompanying the position of king of England.

In what sense is Christ the "firstborn"? Firstborn does not mean that Christ has a beginning—as God He has always existed. Firstborn is a title meaning superiority, dignity, and status. It means Christ is prior to all creation. Because Christ is the firstborn, "in Him all things were created, both in the heavens and on earth, visible and invisible, whether throne or dominions or rulers or authorities—all things have been created through Him and for Him" (Colossians 1:16). If Christ created *all* things, then He is uncreated and therefore eternal. And if all things were created *for* Him, then He is the sovereign Lord.

Firstborn also means that Christ is sovereign over all creation. As firstborn, the Messiah is "highest of the kings of the earth" (Psalm 89:27); He will rule over all the nations of the earth. Because of His priority, Christ will have dominion over the whole earth (Hebrews 1:2). Ancient Jews understood this. Rabbi Bechai gave God the title of "Firstborn of the World," describing God's preeminence over creation. That is Christ's position. Because Christ is the "firstborn from the dead" (Colossians 1:18), He is "to have first place in everything."

As God Christ is eternal, and as firstborn He is to have first place. As firstborn Christ receives worship—a privilege of deity alone (Hebrews 1:6). If we could enter the presence of Queen Elizabeth, we would make some submissive gesture. How much more so when we enter Christ's presence! He is preeminent—not only theoretically but experientially for us. He is to be preeminent in our lives.

LESSON: *As the firstborn Christ has superior rank and dignity; as the eternal God-Man He is to have first place in everything.*

CHRIST
NEVER CHANGES

Jesus Christ is the same yesterday and today,
yes and forever. (Hebrews 13:8)

M y cousin passed away a few months ago. I can hardly believe it—she wasn't very old and was always so full of life. When I think of her, I can see her friendly face—always smiling, laughing, talking. But now she is with the Lord. When a loved one departs it is a reminder of change. We would like to think we have drunk from the fountain of eternal youth, but we get older, our friends pass on, and eventually we do too. Death is a solemn reminder of the continuing cycle of change.

But Jesus Christ never changes! He remains forever the same in His person. What does that mean? It means that He forever retains His humanity, and thus He understands us. He sympathizes with our weaknesses because He has partaken of our humanity (Hebrews 2:15). Because He is also God He is able not only to understand us but to lift the burden from our back (Philippians 4:13). It means He is unchanging in His grace toward us.

Unlike the religions of this world, Christ does not meet us on the basis of our works. He meets us on the basis of His grace—and it is endless: "For of His fullness we have all received, and grace upon grace" (John 1:16). Do you need God's grace? Because Jesus Christ is unchanging He will give you grace, and you will never exhaust it. Use it up, and He will give you more. And because Christ is unchanging, His love for us is constant. We cannot grasp the width, length, height, and depth of Christ's love (Ephesians 3:18). It is unchanging.

Of what significance is it that Jesus Christ does not change? It is because He does not change that He is able to help us. The One who never changes (Hebrews 13:8) is also the One who never deserts us (v. 5). For that reason we can say, "The Lord is my helper, I will not be afraid. What shall man do to me?" (v. 6). Jesus Christ remains the same to help us.

What is your burden today? Christ is unchanging toward you in His love, His mercy, and His grace. Will you leave your burdens with the unchanging Christ today?

LESSON: *Because Jesus Christ is forever unchanging, He is always able to help His people.*

SOVEREIGN
AUTHORITY OF CHRIST

*Jesus came up and spoke to them, saying, "All authority
has been given to Me in heaven and on earth. (Matthew 28:18)*

There are many things in life we cannot explain. The death of a
loved one, an extended illness, loss of a job, persecution and
withheld promotions at work, loneliness, emotional struggles—
the list is endless. Why do such things happen? Is anyone in control?

One thing is certain—you and I will never explain the puzzles and
perplexities of life. We do not know why things happen. But we do know
one thing: Jesus Christ is sovereign, and He is in control. He said, "All authority has been given to Me in heaven and on earth." Think of it! There is
no realm where Jesus does not have "all authority." But what does that
mean?

"Authority" *(exousia)* means two things. It means Jesus has the right,
or prerogative, to do something. As the incarnate Son of God He has authority over every realm in heaven and on earth. Of course, that alone does not
mean anything. Even the president of the United States is limited in power if
his bills are not approved by Congress and the Senate. The real question is,
Does Christ have the power to carry out His given authority? That is the
second point. Not only does Christ have heaven's authority, but He has the
inherent power to carry it out. When a hurricane roars toward land, I could
say, "Peace be still." But it wouldn't mean anything; the hurricane would
invade land despite my pleading. But Christ could say, "My son, your sins
are forgiven" (Mark 2:5), and they would be. Or He could say to the sea,
"Hush, be still" (4:39), and the sea would be still. To the blind beggars
Jesus could say, "Be it done to you" (Matthew 9:29), and they would receive
sight. Jesus sustains all things simply by the authority of His word (Hebrews
1:3). He speaks, and it is done.

Actually Matthew 28:18 says that Christ is carrying all things forward to
their predetermined destiny. What does that do for you? Does that relieve
your fret factor? Does it comfort your heart? Jesus is sovereign—He has absolute control over every situation—including your life. Believe it and rest.

LESSON: *Jesus is sovereign, having authority over every realm in
heaven and upon earth.*

THE ONLY BEGOTTEN SON OF GOD

*For God so loved the world, that He gave His
only begotten Son, that whoever believes in Him
should not perish, but have eternal life. (John 3:16)*

Jesus is no longer the only begotten Son of God. . . . God sees you
the same way He sees Jesus. He wants to treat you like He treats
Jesus—so let Him! . . . You are not a spiritual schizophrenic—
half-God and half-Satan—you are all-God. . . . Jesus was in right-standing
with the Father during His earthwalk and the results He obtained were outstanding. As a child of God and joint-heir with Jesus, you should expect to
receive the same results."

Those are the words of a television evangelist. Do you believe them?
They make Jesus no more than we are—or they lift all believers to a status
of deity, similar to the Mormon doctrine of a plurality of gods. That is wrong.
Jesus is unique. Although we are "children of God," we are not sons of God
in the same way that Jesus is. He reminded Mary of the difference when He
said, "I ascend to My Father and your Father" (John 20:17). He did not say
"our Father" because His relationship with the Father is not like ours. He is
the eternal Son of God.

John could say, "We beheld His glory, glory as of the only begotten
from the Father" (John 1:14). Glory describes the Shekinah, the brilliant
light coming from the presence of God Himself. It was Christ. He radiated
the glory of God. No human can do that.

The glory was reflected from the "only begotten" of the Father. What
does "only begotten" mean? The word *begotten* does not come from the
word *to beget*, as if to come into existence. It means "unique," "the only
one of a kind." That is our Savior. He is one of a kind. God has no other
sons like Jesus. We are not like Him. As the only begotten He is the only
one who can reveal the Father (John 1:18). Mortals cannot see God, but
Jesus reveals the Father to us. That was His mission.

As the absolutely unique and only Son of God, Jesus has revealed the
Father (John 1:14, 18) and the Father's love (1 John 4:9); He has provided
eternal life (John 3:16), and He judges those who refuse to believe in Him
(John 3:18). Rejoice in the Son. He is the only begotten Son of God, and
there is no other like Him.

LESSON: *As the only begotten Son, Jesus is unique, the only one of a
kind that can reveal the Father and provide eternal life.*

April 5

CHRIST IS THE
ANGEL OF THE LORD

The angel of the Lord said to him, "Why do you ask
my name, seeing it is wonderful?" (Judges 13:18)

In the Old Testament there are numerous appearances by a man identified as the "angel of the Lord" and sometimes simply as the "Lord." These are known as "theophanies," or "Christophanies," that is, the appearance of God in human form. Theophanies are identified with Christ; Christians believe that they were physical appearances of Christ on earth before His birth in Bethlehem.

On one occasion three men unexpectedly visited Abraham, and the old patriarch immediately recognized the uniqueness of the visitors. Abraham slaughtered a choice calf, suggesting that it was a special occasion (Genesis 18:7). One of the visitors became a spokesman for the three, and later he is identified as "Lord" (v. 13). We understand the theophany to be Christ since the Father and the Spirit do not reveal themselves in physical form (Exodus 33:20; John 1:18).

When Israel was experiencing oppression by the Midianites, the angel of the Lord visited Gideon (Judges 6:11). He instructed Gideon to deliver the Israelites from their sufferings, promising, "I will be with you" (v. 16). Like Abraham, Gideon recognized his unusual visitor and prepared a special meal for Him. The text clarifies this further by identifying the visitor as "Lord" (v. 14). Gideon had been visited and commissioned by the pre-incarnate Christ.

It is interesting to note that in many of the appearances of Christ in the Old Testament He comes with encouragement. He brought a message of hope to Abraham and Sarah—that they would have a son; He exhorted Gideon to a victory battle, promising "I will be with you"; to a couple without children He promised a splendid child (Judges 13:3). The message is significant: the appearances of Christ as the angel of the Lord are to comfort, exhort, encourage, and guide His people. Although the angel of the Lord no longer appears after Jesus' birth, Christ's ministry is still the same. He comforts and encourages us. Although we experience trials in the world, we can also live in Christ and experience His peace and comfort.

LESSON: *Christ appears in the Old Testament as the angel of the Lord and is thereby recognized as God.*

JESUS CLAIMED
TO BE GOD

That all may honor the Son, even as
they honor the Father. (John 5:23)

C S. Lewis, once a professor at Cambridge University and a former agnostic, wrote: "I am trying here to prevent anyone saying the really foolish thing that people often say about [Christ]: 'I'm ready to accept Jesus as a great moral teacher, but I don't accept His claim to be God.' That is the one thing we must not say. A man who was merely a man and said the sort of things Jesus said would not be a great moral teacher. He would either be a lunatic—on a level with the man who says he is a poached egg—or else he would be the Devil of Hell. You must make your choice. Either this man was, and is, the Son of God; or else a madman or something worse" (*Mere Christianity*, pp. 40-41).

The claims of Christ are enormous. A mere human teacher could not make those claims. Jesus claimed to be the Son of God—which the Jews understood to mean equality with God. They attempted to stone Him for that supposedly blasphemous claim (John 5:18). Jesus claimed to have the power to give life in the very same way as the Father—a boastful claim, unless Jesus is really God (v. 21). Moral man cannot give life; it is God's prerogative (Deuteronomy 32:39). Jesus had the power to lay down His own life and to take it up again (John 10:18).

Jesus claimed to have authority to judge humanity (John 5:22); moreover, through Christ's authority as Judge, all people are to give honor—worship—to Christ in the same way that they honor and worship the Father (v. 23). Again, that would be the blatant blasphemy if Jesus were not God. God is jealous for His honor and shares it with no one.

Jesus also claimed that He was one with the Father (10:30); He was claiming to be of the same essential essence as the Father. He is God.

Jesus' claims of deity are a comfort and encouragement to us. As God He gives life. Who has not stood by the grave of a loved one and wept? Because Jesus is God He will wipe away all tears. Because He is God He can say, "I am the resurrection and the life" (11:25). Put your confidence in Him who is God and who has the power to give life.

LESSON: *Jesus claimed equality with God, and He claimed the prerogatives of God as One who gives life, judges, and receives worship.*

JESUS IS GOD:
HE KNOWS ALL THINGS

*He did not need any one to bear witness concerning man
for He Himself knew what was in man. (John 2:25)*

We admire people who have unusual intelligence. We are awed by Marilyn Vos Savant who is listed in the Guinness Book of World Records as having the highest IQ ever. Her weekly column demonstrates her unusual knowledge and ability to answer complicated questions. We respect Albert Einstein, recognized as the world's greatest scientist, whose research led to the quantum theory, which made inventions such as automation systems and television possible. His research on the theory of relativity was verified in the power released in atomic explosions and astronomical predictions.

But as brilliant as those people have been, they are nonetheless limited in their knowledge. Only one Man has comprehensive knowledge of all things—Jesus Christ. His complete knowledge verifies that He is more than a man; He is God.

There are many instances in the life of Jesus that reveal that He knows all things. When He spoke to Peter He knew that the vacillating, unpredictable apostle would one day be spiritually strong and stable (John 1:42). In speaking with Nathanael Jesus knew that Nathanael was an honest, unpretentious person (v. 47). When many believed in Him Jesus refused to believe in any of them, recognizing the superficiality of their belief (2:24). Jesus also foreknew the manner and place of His death, as well as His resurrection three days later (Matthew 16:21; 17:22-23).

The classic example of Jesus' omniscience is His encounter with the Samaritan woman. When she simply told Him, "I have no husband," He responded by reminding her that she had had five husbands and was now living with a man who was not her husband. He knew all about her—observable in her astonishment (John 4:17-19).

Of what significance is Jesus' omniscience? Just as He knew the Samaritan woman, so He knows us completely—our thoughts, hopes, aspirations, fears, and sins. He knows the weakness of my frame, my frailty, my fears. He knows my failures. It is a comfort to know that my Savior cares.

LESSON: *Jesus knows all things—He is omniscient—demonstrating that He is God.*

JESUS IS GOD:
HE IS EVERYWHERE PRESENT

I am with you always, even to the
end of the age. (Matthew 28:20)

David Livingstone once addressed a group of students at Glasgow University. The scars from his hardships in Africa lined his body. Severe sickness on dozens of occasions had drained him of health and strength. His left arm hung limp at his side, having been crushed by a lion. After describing his sufferings, he exclaimed, "Would you like me to tell you what supported me through all the years of exile among people whose language I couldn't understand and whose attitude to me was uncertain and often hostile? It was this, 'Lo, I am with you always, even unto the end of the world.' On these words I staked everything and they never failed."

Livingstone espoused the doctrine of the omnipresence of Christ—the teaching that Jesus is everywhere present. That is true only of God. Man cannot be present everywhere. You and I are localized; we cannot be in two places at the same time. If we are at the grocery store we are not at home. If we are driving in the car we are not in the office. But Christ is present everywhere because He is God. With this teaching Christ gave hope to the disciples. As He thrust them into the world, He reminded them that He was always present with them (Matthew 28:20).

But how could Jesus be everywhere present if He had a human body? Since Jesus is the God-Man, some things are true only of His deity, whereas other things are true only of His humanity. In His humanity Jesus is not omnipresent—He is localized at the right hand of the Father in heaven. But in His deity He is omnipresent. For that reason Paul could encourage the Colossian believers with the comforting words "Christ in you, the hope of glory" (1:27).

It is only because Jesus is God and therefore everywhere present that we can believe that Jesus indwells each of us. It is the omnipresent Christ indwelling us that enables us to go on to maturity, loving one another (Ephesians 3:17).

Amid the cares and concerns of life, remember there is One who, because He is God, has promised, "I will never desert you, nor will I ever forsake you" (Hebrews 13:5). He is with you always.

LESSON: *Jesus is everywhere present—He is omnipresent—demonstrating that He is God.*

JESUS IS GOD:
HE CAN DO ALL THINGS

In order that you may know that the Son of Man
has authority on earth to forgive sins. (Matthew 9:6)

Words are cheap. Religious leaders may make grandiose statements but cannot validate them. One has said, "Man is incapable of sin, sickness and death." But reality has disproved his claims because he died. Another says, "I absolve thee from thy sins." But that is impossible because sinful man cannot forgive another sinful man. Another, proclaiming that Jesus failed in His mission and saying he would succeed where Jesus failed, remarked: "I have talked with many, many Masters, including Jesus. . . . They have subjected themselves to me in terms of wisdom." But that false leader has failed. They have all failed because they are finite and false.

Jesus alone can validate the strong claims He has made. By His words and by His works Jesus has demonstrated that He is God of very God. "All authority has been given to Me in heaven and on earth," Jesus announced, and He demonstrated that He had heaven's authority (Matthew 28:18).

When He healed the paralytic, Jesus boldly announced, "Your sins are forgiven" and then reminded the doubters that He had authority to forgive sins (9:2-6). Not only did Jesus have the prerogative to forgive sins, He had the power to do it. That is entirely unique since only God can forgive sins (Isaiah 43:25).

Awakened by the frightened disciples during the furious storm on the Sea of Galilee, Jesus first admonished the unbelieving men and then hushed the waves—with a word (Matthew 8:26). Who has the power to speak to a storm on the sea and silence it? Only God. The psalmist says, "[The Lord] caused the storm to be still" (Psalm 107:29). On another occasion, as Jesus departed from Jericho, two blind men approached Him, and He healed them (Matthew 9:29). Jesus healed the blind more frequently than He performed any other miracle, yet there is no record of anyone else ever healing the blind. Only God can do that (Psalm 146:8).

It is awesome to consider the works of our Savior. Surely He has demonstrated that He is more than man—He is also God! What is there in your life that Jesus, because He is God, can resolve for you?

LESSON: *Jesus can do all things—He is omnipotent—demonstrating that He is God.*

JESUS IS
THE MESSIAH

*As for you, Bethlehem Ephrathah, too little
to be among the clans of Judah, from you One
will go forth for Me to be ruler in Israel. (Micah 5:2)*

Rudolf Hess died on August 17, 1987, at the age of ninety-three. Hess was the deputy führer, serving Adolf Hitler as the number three man in Nazi Germany during World War II. Hess regarded Hitler as a messiah who would lead the Germans to greatness. "There is one man, who is always above criticism. That is the führer. This is because everyone knows and feels he is always right and always will be right." All that Germany needed to achieve glory, he claimed, was "faith without criticism, surrender to the führer, not to ask why, but the silent carrying out of his orders."

Numerous men have appeared on the pages of history who have claimed to be messiahs; however, there is but one Messiah. Jesus Christ alone has the correct credentials. Many Old Testament prophecies, announced centuries before Christ's birth, reveal He is the true Messiah. He would be of the line of Shem (Genesis 9:26-27), a descendant of Abraham, bringing blessing to many (12:1-3), a king, a descendant of the tribe of Judah, bringing all people in subjection to His authority (49:10). As king He will establish an eternal dynasty and kingdom; His rule will never be replaced by another's (2 Samuel 7:16). He will rule the entire world in righteousness and justice, bringing peace to the world (Isaiah 9:6-7). His rule will be fair, judging sin and exalting righteousness (11:4).

Yet it was prophesied that He would be born in a lowly, insignificant town, too little for the official town lists (Micah 5:2), but He would also have a unique birth, being born to a virgin (Isaiah 7:14). He would die a substitutionary death (Isaiah 53) but be raised from the dead (Psalm 16:10).

Many false voices divert the allegiance of people from the true Messiah to false messiahs. But Messiah was not prophesied to be born in Korea, nor would He establish His headquarters in Boston. Jesus of Nazareth alone has the credentials of the true Messiah. He is the true Shepherd, worthy of our trust. Our faith is not misguided when we wholly rely on Him.

LESSON: *Jesus Christ alone has the proper credentials of the true Messiah.*

JESUS IS
CALLED GOD

Of the Son He says, "Thy throne, O God,
is forever and ever, and the righteous scepter
is the scepter of His kingdom." (Hebrews 1:8)

M y doorbell rang on a Saturday morning, presenting me with a clean-cut teenager, briefcase in hand. I became suspicious, and my suspicion proved correct—he was a member of the Watchtower Society, peddling the doctrine that Jesus is not God. We had a lengthy discussion at my front door centered on the Person of Christ.

Is Jesus God? An important testimony to Christ's deity is found in the words of the writer of Hebrews as he contrasts Jesus to the angels. Whereas the angels are servants, the Son has a more significant status. In Hebrews 1:8 the writer prefaces his Old Testament quotations with the statement "But of the Son He says . . . " Everything that follows refers to the Son. He quotes Psalm 45:6, stating, "Thy throne, O God, is forever and ever." The Son is called the eternal God. In verse 9 he states, "Therefore God, Thy God, hath anointed Thee." The first reference to "God" refers to the Son whereas the second refers to the Father. God the Father has anointed God the Son as King, as Messiah. In verse 10 the writer comments, "Thou, Lord, in the beginning didst lay the foundation of the earth." Here Jesus is called Lord (*Yahweh*), Creator of the universe who alone is eternal (v. 11). The statements "O God," "therefore God," and, "Thou Lord" refer to the Son mentioned in verse 8. Three times the Son is explicitly addressed as God in Hebrews 1:8-10. That Jesus is God could not be clearer.

In the Upper Room, following the resurrection, Thomas recognized Jesus as the risen Lord and exclaimed, "My Lord and my God!" (John 20:28). Having been convinced that Jesus had risen from the dead, Thomas was also convinced that Jesus was Lord and God. If Jesus were not God He should have rebuked Thomas—but He didn't; He accepted the accolade. The Jehovah's Witnesses suggest that Thomas was simply swearing!

Thomas wasn't swearing. God gave him spiritual insight to see that Jesus was indeed all He claimed to be. Jesus is God. To those who do not believe He says, "Be not unbelieving, but believing" (John 20:27*b*).

LESSON: *Jesus is called God.*

JESUS IS
CALLED YAHWEH

If you confess with your mouth Jesus as Lord,
and believe in your heart that God raised Him
from the dead, you shall be saved. (Romans 10:9)

While at St. Helena, Napoleon was struck that millions were ready to die for the crucified Nazarene who founded a spiritual empire by love, whereas no one would die for Alexander or Caesar or himself, who founded a temporal empire by force. In that Napoleon saw a convincing argument for the deity of Christ, declaring, "I know, and I tell you, men, Christ was not a man. Everything about Christ astonished me. There is no comparison between him and any other being. He stands single and alone" (Schaff, 1:110). The doctrine that Jesus is God is the bedrock of Christianity.

While chatting with my Saturday morning visitor, we discussed Romans 10:9-13. Verse 9 reads, "That if you confess with your mouth Jesus as Lord . . ." Paul was referring to a Christian confession that believers would make; as such, the statement belongs in quotation marks: "Jesus is Lord." What is the meaning of Lord? Does it only mean that He is our Master? No, it means much more. "Lord" is the New Testament equivalent of the Old Testament *Yahweh*, or Jehovah. No one can make that confession or understand its truth without being born by the Spirit, because "no one can say, 'Jesus is Lord,' except by the Holy Spirit" (1 Corinthians 12:3).

When Jesus came to Jerusalem for the Passover Feast, John notes that He performed many signs, yet the people refused to believe in Him, like the people in Isaiah's day. But John notes, "These things Isaiah said, because he saw His glory and spoke of Him" (John 12:41). Whose glory? Christ's! That is the context. John saw Christ's glory, but the reference is to Isaiah 6, where Isaiah saw "the Lord sitting on a throne, lofty and exalted" (v. 1). Isaiah saw the glory of the exalted Jesus, enthroned as Yahweh in heaven.

That Jesus is none other than Yahweh of the Old Testament is a truth that God wants all people to know. It is His desire that "every tongue confess that Jesus Christ is Lord" (Philippians 2:11). Have you acknowledged Jesus as Lord God and submitted to His authority?

LESSON: *Jesus is Yahweh, the Lord God.*

April 13

CHRIST IS
JUDGE

*Not even the Father judges any one, but He
has given all judgment to the Son. (John 5:22)*

Who has the right to judge? Most will agree that judgment is a prerogative of God. That is His privilege. Jesus demonstrated His unity with the Father by claiming the prerogatives of judgment when He said, "Not even the Father judges any one, but He has given all judgment to the son . . . and He [Father] gave Him [Son] authority to execute judgment because He is the Son of Man" (John 5:22, 27). The Father and the Son share the responsibilities of judgment because both are God. If Jesus were not God, the Father would not share the office of judge with Him.

David reminds us that "the Lord abides forever; He has established His throne for judgment, and He will judge the world in righteousness" (Psalm 9:7-8a). God is the judge. Jesus also claims He has the authority to judge. What is He saying? He is claiming deity.

When Matthew pictures Christ returning in triumph, he says, "Then He will sit on His glorious throne and all the nations will be gathered before Him; and He will separate them from one another" (Matthew 25:31-32). At His return Christ will assume the office of judge.

Another passage depicts God in the same role: "He [the Lord] is coming; for He is coming to judge the earth" (Psalm 96:13a). Who is coming? The Lord. But Jesus applies it to Himself as Judge of the nations at His return. Moreover, at the unleashing of the disastrous judgments of the Tribulation, Christ alone has the right to open the book releasing the horrifying judgments upon the earth (Revelation 5:2-14). The seals, trumpets, and bowls, hailing the plagues and fire from heaven come from Christ, the Judge of the world.

Though humans may reject Him and His authority, heaven's citizens recognize Christ's authority as Judge and worship Him as the One who is worthy to judge (Revelation 5:9-10). Of course, Christ need not be your Judge. He can be your Savior and Deliverer instead. His purpose in coming was to save the world. The one who believes in Him will never come into judgment, but the one who refuses to believe already stands under judgment (John 3:18). Avail yourself of His grace, and avert His judgment.

LESSON: *Since He is God, Jesus has the authority to execute judgment on the world.*

April 14

CHRIST RECEIVES WORSHIP

That all may honor the Son, even as they honor
the Father. He who does not honor the Son
does not honor the Father who sent Him. (John 5:23)

In Sarasota, Florida, the minister of a church invited women to take part in "Cakes for the Queen of Heaven," a day celebrating goddesses. The minister led the women in singing "guided fantasy, self-growth experiences and personal exploration of ancient and current goddess-centered spiritual rituals." The women planned to bake and eat cakes in honor of goddesses.

Who is to receive worship? Fundamental to the Judeo-Christian faith is the conviction that only God receives worship. No one else—not a goddess in the heavens, not Mary, not "the saints"—no one except God. The first two of the Ten Commandments state it clearly: "You shall have no other gods before Me. . . . You shall not worship them or serve them; for I, the Lord your God, am a jealous God" (Exodus 20:3, 5). Each day, morning and evening, faithful Israelites recited the "Shema": "Hear, O Israel! The Lord is our God, the Lord is one! And you shall love the Lord your God with all your heart and with all your soul and with all your might" (Deuteronomy 6:4-5).

In that light Jesus' statement to the Jews becomes highly significant, He told them that all should honor the Son just as they honor the Father (John 5:23). If an ordinary mortal made that statement it would be blasphemous. But Christians are to honor Him just as they honor the Father. That can only mean that Jesus is equal with the Father—and that was what He claimed. The Jews recognized His claim of equality and tried to stone Him to death for it (John 5:18). When Jesus rode into Jerusalem at the Triumphal Entry, the pilgrims cried out, "Hosanna to the Son of David" (Matthew 21:9). But when the religious leaders rebuked Jesus for it, He reminded them of Psalm 8:2, "Out of the mouth of infants and nursing babes Thou has prepared praise for Thyself" (v. 16). Jesus accepted their worship; He applied the worship accorded the Father to Himself (Psalm 8:1-2). Jesus is more than our Savior and Friend; He is our God, who desires our worship.

LESSON: *Since Jesus is God, He is to receive our worship in the same way that we worship the Father.*

JESUS IS GOD:
HE REFLECTS THE FATHER

*He is the radiance of His glory and the exact
representation of His nature, and upholds
all things by the word of His power. (Hebrews 1:3)*

I f you look at a quarter you will notice that one side has a picture of George Washington and the other has a picture of an eagle. The quarter reflects the die from which it was struck. Although most of us have never seen it, somewhere there is a die having the bust of George Washington and an eagle. We know precisely what it looks like because we have seen the image that bears its precise resemblance.

Just as the quarter reveals the exact nature of the die, so Jesus reveals the precise nature of the Father. Jesus is the "radiance of His glory" (Hebrews 1:3). As the rays of the sun emit the brightness of the sun so Christ radiates the nature of the Father. The Shekinah glory of God shines forth from Christ. Jesus does not merely reflect God's glory; He is the source of it. Christ's life constantly bore the image of God. The centurion saw it and remarked, "Truly this man was the Son of God!" (Mark 15:39). The disciples saw God's glory shine forth from Christ on the mountain and fell on their faces; they feared they were dying, for they knew they were in God's presence (Matthew 17:2, 6).

Jesus is also the "exact representation of [God's] nature" (Hebrews 1:3). He is the "precise character" of God. Just as an engraving tool engraves a mark, so Jesus has made the mark of God on this world. He has completely revealed the Father to us. He told the disciples, "He who has seen Me has seen the Father" (John 14:9).

But Jesus is even more than that. He "upholds all things by the word of His power" (Hebrews 1:3). That actually means that Jesus is carrying all things forward to their predetermined course or destiny. He is more than Charles Atlas holding up the world. He is carrying all events on their predetermined course.

What is God like? Look at Jesus! We see the likeness of the Father reflected in Jesus. Jesus' mission was to manifest the Father and to show us the way to Him.

LESSON: *In His words and works Jesus radiated the Father, proving that He is God.*

JESUS IS
THE SON OF GOD

That all may honor the Son, even
as they honor the Father. (John 5:23)

W hat does "Son of God" mean? The phrase has confused many people. In the fourth century a historic debate on the subject between Athanasius and Arius lasted for decades. Arius, a handsome man and eloquent preacher from Alexandria, Egypt, taught that "the Son has a beginning but that God is without beginning." He also taught that since Christ was the Son, He was subordinate to the Father. Opposing Arius was Athanasius, who argued that the Son was of the very same substance as the Father. Moreover, Athanasius defended the deity and eternality of Christ, arguing that the Father as a father was no older than the Son as a son. If there was a time when the Son did not exist, then the Father was not a father.

When Jesus spoke of God as His Father, thereby identifying Himself as the Son of God, the Jews tried to stone Him to death. The reason they gave was that He "was calling God His own Father, making Himself equal with God" (John 5:18). They understood that when Jesus claimed to be the Son of God He was claiming equality with God. As the Son, Jesus claimed He could do "whatever the Father does" (v. 19). That would be possible only if Jesus is God. Otherwise it would be an arrogant, blasphemous utterance.

The Son also has the power to give life just as the Father does (v. 21). Giving life is a prerogative of God (Deuteronomy 32:39). If the Son was not God He could not give life. In addition, the Son has the authority to judge (John 5:22, 27)—which is also the privilege of deity (Genesis 18:25). Perhaps the crowning criterion revealing that the Son of God is equivalent to God is the statement that the Son receives worship "even as they honor the Father" (John 5:23). God is a jealous God and will not share His glory with anyone. If the Son is not God then it would be blasphemous to suggest that the Son receives worship. The truth is evident: the Son of God is equivalent to God.

What a blessed truth that the Son came to have fellowship with us: "He who has the Son has life" (1 John 5:13). We are privileged to enter into fellowship with the Son and have Him make His abode with us (John 14:23).

LESSON: *Jesus, as the Son of God, has all the prerogatives of God and is acknowledged as God.*

April 17

CHRIST
THE CORNERSTONE

*For no man can lay a foundation other than the one which
is laid, which is Jesus Christ. (1 Corinthians 3:11)*

The summer had been unusually hot with very little rain when my wife and I returned from vacation. As we walked through the house after several weeks' absence, my eyes fastened on a half-inch crack that ran from floor to ceiling in our dining room wall. After investigating the problem I discovered that we had purchased a house with an improper foundation. Because of the dry weather, the faulty foundation had allowed the house to settle, causing the wall to crack.

A foundation is important. In the construction of our spiritual building—the church—Jesus Christ is the cornerstone, the building block that ties the building together. Although the apostles and prophets are the foundation of the church, Jesus Christ Himself is the cornerstone, the anchor (Ephesians 2:20).

These New Testament references in 1 Corinthians and Ephesians undoubtedly build on Isaiah 28:16, where the Lord promised, "Behold, I am laying in Zion a stone, a tested stone, a costly cornerstone for a foundation, firmly placed. He who believes in it will not be disturbed." Amid Israel's apostasy God promised a future day when God would lay an expensive cornerstone who would bring spiritual stability to the nation.

It is a prophecy of Christ. He is a "tested stone"—He has been tested through His temptations and found to be the pure, impeccable Son of God (Matthew 4:1-11). This is also a "costly cornerstone." Money could not purchase it; its price was "precious blood" (1 Peter 1:18-19), and for that reason it is a precious cornerstone. And to the one who believes there is no disappointment (1 Peter 2:6). Moreover, this cornerstone is "firmly placed"—it is a reliable foundation. When the day of judgment comes, illustrated by the rain, flood, and wind, this house will stand (Matthew 7:24-27).

What we believe makes a difference. Jesus Christ demonstrated His credentials through His temptations, teachings, and miracles. He is the true Messiah and cornerstone of our faith. If we put our faith in Christ, our spiritual house will never crack or collapse.

LESSON: *Jesus Christ in the purity of His person, in His death, and in His resurrection is the secure cornerstone of our faith.*

CHRIST AUTHENTICATED
BY HIS WORDS

The multitudes were amazed at His teaching;
for He was teaching them as one having authority,
and not as their scribes. (Matthew 7:29)

Words are important. Winston Churchill, the great British prime minister during World War II, was known for his great words. Complimenting the renowned R.A.F. fighter pilots he remarked, "Never in the field of human conflict was so much owed by so many to so few." Perhaps his most momentous speech was on June 4, 1940, when he addressed the House of Commons to rally the British to victory, "We shall go on to the end, . . . we shall fight in the seas and oceans, . . . we shall fight on the beaches, we shall fight on the landing grounds, we shall fight in the fields and in the streets, we shall fight in the hills; we shall never surrender."

The words of Jesus Christ were recognized as entirely unique. His words carried authority. Jewish rabbis had to depend on some other teacher to authenticate their words; they had a derived authority and appealed to other human teachers. Jesus, however, had authority in Himself. Repeatedly He taught, "You have heard . . . but I say to you" (Matthew 5:21, 22, 27, 28). He corrected the false teaching of others and appealed to no other human teacher. When Jesus concluded the Sermon on the Mount the people were amazed at His teaching; they recognized His authority (7:28-29). Jesus traversed the land, teaching and preaching, thereby revealing His messiahship (4:23). In His own town the people recognized His unusually attractive speech and were puzzled since they only knew Him as a carpenter (Luke 4:22). They were astonished at the wisdom reflected in His teaching (Mark 6:2).

The Old Testament foretold Messiah's profound teaching (Isaiah 2:3; 11:2). When Jesus came, His teaching and preaching ministry revealed that He was the Messiah, for no one had ever reflected such wisdom as He exhibited. Jesus revealed that the words He spoke were in union with the Father (John 12:49). He had come to reveal the Father, and when He spoke, He reflected the Father's words (John 17:8).

Since Jesus' words revealed the Father and His own authority as Messiah, we should heed His words. He has given us words of eternal life (John 6:63, 68) and comfort (16:33). Do not pin your hopes on the futile words of man; find your refuge, hope, and peace in the authoritative, comforting words of Christ.

LESSON: *The words of Jesus Christ verified His authority and authenticated Him as Messiah.*

April 19

CHRIST AUTHENTICATED
BY HIS WORKS

*The works which the Father has given Me to
accomplish, the very works that I do, bear witness
of Me, that the Father has sent Me. (John 5:36)*

During His earthly ministry Jesus performed mighty works demonstrating that He was no ordinary man but the long-awaited Messiah. Isaiah promised that when Messiah came the blind would see, the deaf hear, the lame walk, and the dumb shout for joy (Isaiah 35:5-6). Jesus performed precisely those miracles that His people would know Messiah was in their midst. When two blind men met Jesus near Jericho, He healed them of blindness (Matthew 9:30). There are no examples of anyone except Jesus healing the blind in all the Scriptures, and there are more recorded miracles of Jesus' healing the blind than any other miracle. Further, healing the blind is a work of God (Psalm 146:8). Messiah has authority over blindness.

The rabbis considered healing a leper as difficult as raising the dead; no leper had been healed since the days of Elisha—eight hundred years before—yet Jesus healed a leper (Matthew 8:3). Jesus reminded John that healing a leper was a messianic sign (11:5). Messiah has authority over leprosy and sickness.

When Jesus crossed the Sea of Galilee a great storm was unleashed on the tiny sea, threatening the lives of the disciples. Jesus merely spoke to the sea, "Hush, be still" (Mark 4:39), and the wind stopped, and the sea became calm. The Master had spoken. Who has that kind of authority? Only God. Jesus' miracle demonstrated that He is Messiah, God come in the flesh, for only God has authority over nature (Psalm 107:29). Messiah has authority over nature.

When Jesus and the disciples arrived on the east side of the sea Jesus expelled the demons from two men into a herd of swine (Matthew 8:32). God is the one who has authority over Satan (Revelation 20:1-3). Confronted by a paralyzed man, Jesus not only healed him but also forgave his sins, showing Messiah has authority to forgive sins—which also is a work of God (Matthew 9:1-8; Isaiah 43:25). Jesus' climactic miracle was raising the dead—destroying man's greatest obstacle (Matthew 9:25). Messiah has authority over death.

Are you aware that the particular problems that beset you are precisely the areas over which Jesus has authority? Sin, sickness, Satan, suffering—Jesus has authority over them all. You can find comfort and rest in your great Savior, who can still the storm in your life.

LESSON: *The works of Jesus Christ verified His authority in every realm and authenticated Him as the Messiah.*

JESUS HAS A HUMAN BODY, SOUL, AND SPIRIT

*Jesus kept increasing in wisdom and stature,
and in favor with God and men. (Luke 2:52)*

Although Jesus is God, He is also man, with a genuine human body. He is not a phantom who came to indwell a human body for a time. He is a man. In speaking to Him at the well, the Samaritan woman recognized Him as a Jewish man. No doubt His appearance and accent distinguished Him as being a Jew. And as a man He experienced the limitations of a human body. Following a day of teaching He was tired and needed to sleep. When He was scourged and crucified he felt the horror of pain.

As a man Jesus also has a human soul and spirit, experiencing the normal feelings and emotions of a human being. Coming to the grave of His friend Lazarus, Jesus experienced considerable emotional turmoil within Himself as He saw the ravages of sin in the human race bring grief and death. He also grieved at His friend's death (John 11:33, 35).

When Jesus saw dishonesty He became angry. He overthrew the tables of the money changers who were fleecing the worshipers, and He chased them out of the Temple precincts with a whip (2:12-16). Jesus expressed indignation, denouncing the hypocrisy of the religious leaders (Matthew 23). He felt compassion for the common people, who were harassed by the religious leaders (9:36). When the crowds were tired and without food Jesus had compassion on them (15:32).

As a man Jesus felt human emotions, feeling pain, sorrow and grief. But He didn't have to. He could have remained in heaven, enjoying eternal fellowship with the Father and the Spirit. But He left heaven's glories, took on humanity, that He might redeem distressed mankind. Can we ever fully appreciate what it cost Him? Can we ever realize the depths to which He stooped when He left the splendor of heaven and came to earth to be scorned by His own people? He did it for but one reason. Because of His infinite love, He willingly assumed suffering and sorrow that He might rescue fallen humanity from the ravages of sin.

LESSON: *Jesus took on genuine humanity—body, soul, and spirit—that as a man He might represent and redeem fallen humanity.*

JESUS HAS
HUMAN CHARACTERISTICS

*We do not have a high priest who cannot sympathize
with our weaknesses, but one who has been tempted
in all things as we are, yet without sin. (Hebrews 4:15)*

Jerry Singleton was a prisoner of war in Viet Nam for seven years. While imprisoned he heard a man complain of hunger though Jerry still had food; then the day came when he too was hungry. He saw a man taken away and locked up in solitary confinement though he was still with the other men; then the day came when Jerry was locked up in solitary confinement. He heard a man screaming as he was beaten by a guard; then the day came when Jerry was beaten by the guards. It was then that Jerry experienced the sufficiency of Christ. "I discovered that Christ is all I need," he said.

How can Christ be all we need? Because He was bone of our bone and flesh of our flesh. Although Jesus was God of very God, He was also a man—genuine humanity with feelings, emotions, and limitations. Jesus suffered the same limitations that we battle day after day. After He had fasted in the wilderness He became hungry and was tempted by the devil (Matthew 4:2). After walking long distances and climbing the steep hills in Samaria, He became tired and had to rest (John 4:6). Traveling in the desert regions He became thirsty and longed to slake His thirst with a drink of water (v. 7). Jesus experienced grief and great emotion when His friend Lazarus died (11:33, 35). When He saw distressed people He felt compassion for them (Matthew 9:36). Jesus experienced all our limitations, not only that He might understand us but that He might help us.

Does it mean anything to you that the Son of God became tired and had to rest? that He experienced the same temptations that you experience? that He understands you? People may fail you and misunderstand you, but not Christ. He has been there—He understands your struggles, agony, and weariness. "Because he himself suffered when he was tempted, he is able to help those who are being tempted" (Hebrews 2:18, NIV).

LESSON: *As a man Christ has the characteristics of a human being, suffering the limitations of humanity that He might comfort us.*

April 22

Jesus Is
a Prophet

*No man has seen God at any time; the only begotten God, who
is in the bosom of the Father, He has explained Him. (John 1:18)*

In 1965 Jeanne Dixon predicted the existence of a special child in
the Middle East who would revolutionize the world by bringing an
all-embracing faith to mankind. She prophesied that he would "be
doing his stuff by 1980." "He's in Egypt now," she announced in March,
1980. "We're going to see him by the mid-1980s. We're really going to be
seeing him." The mid-1980s are gone, and the so-called leader from the
Middle East has not materialized. Jeanne Dixon's prophecy has been proved
wrong—as have most of her prophecies.

There is only One who consistently prophesied the truth. His name is
Jesus Christ. Moses, who himself established the prophetic office, announced the coming of a prophet greater than he—Jesus Christ (Deuteronomy 18:15-18; Acts 3:22). Whereas the people did not always heed Moses, the
ancient prophet predicted that they would listen to Christ, the greater
Prophet.

What is a prophet? Why is a prophet important—or necessary? A
prophet is one who represents God to man. He receives truth directly from
God and reveals that truth to man. Jesus Christ has done precisely that.
Although no one has ever seen God, Jesus has come from the bosom of the
Father to explain the Father to us (John 1:18). "To explain" is frequently
used for "publishing or explaining of divine secrets." As the Prophet, Jesus
came to earth from heaven to explain God's divine secrets to us.

What is God like? We would never know God had not Jesus revealed
Him to us. Jesus revealed the Father in two ways: through His teaching and
through His miracles. His prophecies always came true, and the miracles
further authenticated Him as a prophet who came from God.

John was overwhelmed by Christ's prophetic revelation. He could say,
"We beheld His glory, glory as of the only begotten from the Father" (John
1:14). As they looked at Christ, the disciples saw the Father. They saw His
majesty, they grasped grace, and they heard His truth. Jesus remains the
only prophet that has given us a complete and true understanding of God.
As the Father Himself announced, "Hear Him!"

LESSON: *Jesus fulfills the office of Prophet, fully representing and revealing God to mankind.*

JESUS IS
A PRIEST

He is able to save forever those who draw near
to God through Him, since He always lives
to make intercession for them. (Hebrews 7:25)

In the fourteenth and fifteenth centuries a dark blot of immorality fell upon the ecclesiastical priesthood. Because of the doctrine of celibacy, many priests sought sexual expression by keeping concubines or consorting with female members of the congregation. Other priests indulged in luxurious living. In the papacy, church offices were bought and sold (which ultimately sparked the Reformation), and relatives were accorded prominent positions—all by priests who purported to mediate between man and God.

There is but one capable mediator and Priest between God and men: Jesus Christ. In Israel, a priest had to be of the tribe of Levi, and since Christ was of the tribe of Judah, He did not qualify for the levitical priesthood. However, Christ has been appointed an eternal High Priest according to the order of Melchizedek (Hebrews 7:17). He is entirely qualified to represent man to God since He has completed His work as Priest. Whereas Old Testament priests never finished their work—indicated by their constant standing in the Temple—Christ, through His death and resurrection, finished His work and sat down (1:3).

Jesus is also qualified because the Father appointed Him as Priest; He was not appointed by men (5:1-10). Christ serves as a better priest, seen in the abolition of the levitical priesthood (7:18-19). And He is able to serve us continually as our High Priest since He is not subject to death. Levitical priests—or any human priests—were ineffective since they were subject to death. Because Christ lives forever He serves as our secure High Priest forever (vv. 23-24). Our salvation is secure! We cannot lose our salvation nor our position of acceptance before the Father because Christ faithfully and continually serves as our mediator and High Priest (v. 25).

What comforting assurance! Our security, our acceptance before the Father, is not dependent on weak, finite, failing men. We are accepted in the Beloved. We are secure and confident before the heavenly bar of justice because of our faithful, ever-living Priest, who successfully represents us on the basis of His pure and indestructible life.

LESSON: *Jesus fulfills the office of Priest, in adequately and faithfully representing man to God.*

JESUS IS
A KING

He will reign over the house of Jacob forever;
and His kingdom will have no end. (Luke 1:33)

One of the outstanding monarchs of British royalty was Queen Victoria, who ruled from 1837-1901. Queen Victoria was exemplary in her home life, in her personal integrity, and in her involvement in the affairs of state. Her marriage was unusual for the monarchy inasmuch as it was marked by love, devotion, and happiness. She was greatly admired for her personal honesty and respected for her support and unity with British government leaders with whom she disagreed. Although Queen Victoria left a great legacy as a capable and wise monarch, there is but one Monarch who is destined to rule with absolute pure and just leadership. For that the world awaits the rule of Jesus Christ.

The New Testament opens with the genealogy of Jesus, linking Him to David (Matthew 1:1). Why does it begin with a genealogy listing? Matthew reminds us that Jesus is a descendant of David, of the kingly tribe of Judah. God gave a great promise to David. Although he was Israel's greatest king, God promised him a descendant greater than he. That future descendant will build a stronger kingdom than David (although David expanded Israel's kingdom tenfold over King Saul). He will establish a permanent dynasty and will rule over many people. And He will have a throne of authority that will last forever (2 Samuel 7:16). No ordinary king could expect that. It was a prophecy predicting Jesus' future millennial reign (Revelation 20:4).

In appearing to Mary, the angel told her that the ancient prophecy given to David would be fulfilled in Jesus (Luke 1:33). However, Jesus' reign demands a response by His people. When He came to earth and offered the kingdom to the nation they rejected Him (Matthew 12:24). A king cannot reign when he is rejected; hence, the kingdom is held in abeyance until the King's people receive Him as their King (Zechariah 12:10-14). Although we see injustices and inequities in this world, we rejoice at the anticipation of Christ's future righteous rule (Isaiah 11:4-5).

LESSON: *Jesus fulfills the office of King, having the correct credentials, and is destined to reign over the entire world in the millennial kingdom.*

April 25

JESUS IS
BOTH GOD AND MAN

The Word was God ... the Word became flesh. (John 1:1, 14)

L ife has numerous, inexplicable mysteries. So does the Bible, where we discover seemingly opposing truths. We call this an antinomy, something contrary to law or human reason. For example, Einstein concluded that time was relative only to the motion of our solar system. Hypothetically, one could take a trip to the star Alpha Centauri in one month traveling at the velocity of the speed of light. However, the people on earth would have aged ten years since time would flow at two different rates! (Boa, *God, I Don't Understand,* p. 88).

An example of an antinomy is that Jesus is both God and man. That is impossible to comprehend; how can Jesus be infinite God, all-knowing and all-powerful, and yet be finite man with all the limitations of humanity? We cannot grasp that, yet we believe it because the Bible teaches that Jesus is both natures in one person.

Many passages reflect both Jesus' deity and humanity. John declared, "The Word [Jesus] was God," but then affirmed, "The Word became flesh and dwelt among us" (John 1:1, 14). The One who eternally had fellowship with the Father and shared the Godhead became flesh—He took on humanity. Paul places Jesus' deity and humanity side by side as well. He speaks of the "Son, who was born of the seed of David according to the flesh" (Romans 1:3). The fact that He was born, was a descendant of David, and partook of human flesh—all those phrases emphasize His humanity. Paul also remarks that Jesus "was declared with power to be the Son of God by the resurrection from the dead according to the Spirit of holiness" (v. 4). The emphasis that He was "declared" rather than born, that He was the Son of God, that He was raised "according to the Spirit of holiness"—all those phrases stress His deity. Jesus also "existed in the form of God," an expression bespeaking His deity (Philippians 2:6), yet He was "found in appearance as a man" (v. 8).

The Bible teaches that Jesus was both God and man—incomprehensible to us but true nevertheless. It was necessary that Jesus be man to represent man at the cross, and He had to be God for His death to have infinite value. That remains a mystery but a blessed truth necessary for our redemption.

LESSON: *Jesus is both God and man, two distinct natures existing in one Person, without any intermingling.*

PROPHECIES OF
CHRIST'S LINEAGE

*The scepter shall not depart from Judah, nor the ruler's
staff from between his feet, until Shiloh comes, and to him
shall be the obedience of the peoples. (Genesis 49:10)*

The prophetic failures of psychic Jeanne Dixon are well known. She predicted that World War III would begin in 1954; the Vietnam War would end in 1966; union leader Walter Reuther would run for president in 1966; and that in 1970 Fidel Castro would be overthrown in Cuba and be forced to leave the island (McDowell & Stewart, *Handbook*, p. 183).

Humans fail, but the Bible has made amazing prophecies about Christ that have been minutely fulfilled— though prophesied centuries before they occurred. Immediately following Adam's eating the forbidden fruit, God proclaimed the "good news" for the first time, promising a Deliverer from sin who would be born of a virgin (Genesis 3:15).

Who would He be? He would be born of the lineage of Shem (9:26) and descend from the patriarch Abraham (12:2). God chose aged Abraham from ancient Ur to be the father of a new people through whom would come the Messiah. But not all Abraham's descendants would be heirs of the messianic line—only those of the lineage of Isaac (17:19) and of Isaac's son Jacob (28:13). Messiah would come from Jacob's line, destroying the enemies and establishing dominion on the earth (Numbers 24:17-19). Specifically, Jesus would be from the family of Judah, the kingly line. He was destined to rule as a monarch to whom the people would give their obedience (Genesis 49:8-10). Judah's line would continue until the Messiah comes to rule and inaugurate a worldwide reign of peace. Christ would descend from David (2 Samuel 7:12-16), having an enduring dynasty and a people and territory over which He will rule.

Those are amazing prophecies, foretelling of Christ's genealogy hundreds of years prior to their occurrence—and they have been precisely fulfilled. Yet we await the fulfillment of the final prophecy—His rule. Surely, living in a tired world that longs for the transformation that Messiah will bring, we too anxiously await the final fulfillment of Christ's future return and reign.

LESSON: *The prophecies that Christ's descent would be through Shem, Abraham, Isaac, Jacob, and Judah have been accurately fulfilled.*

PROPHECIES OF 🏃
CHRIST'S BIRTH

As for you, Bethlehem Ephrathah, too little
to be among the clans of Judah, from you One
will go forth for Me to be ruler in Israel. (Micah 5:2)

If you peruse the Rand McNally Road Atlas you will find thousands of small towns in the United States. Some of our presidents and great leaders have been born in these small towns, but who could have anticipated it? In the year A.D. 1250, for example, who would have guessed that Dwight D. Eisenhower would be born in Denison, Texas?

Yet the Bible provides astoundingly precise prophecies of Christ's birth. Writing seven hundred years before Christ's birth, Micah predicted that Jesus would be born in Bethlehem of Judea (5:2). Bethlehem was so small and considered so insignificant that it was not included in the official list of towns in the book of Joshua. Christ's prophesied birth in Bethlehem was well known, however, for when the magi came to Bethlehem and inquired of the chief priests, scribes, and people, the answer was readily available—in Bethlehem, in the land of Judah.

What would be the manner of His birth? Also writing seven hundred years before the event, Isaiah predicted that Christ would be born of a virgin: "Behold, a virgin will be with child and bear a son, and she will call His name Immanuel" (Isaiah 7:14). What a remarkable prophecy! Isaiah specifically used a Hebrew word, *almah*, that meant an unmarried woman, namely a virgin. There is no occurrence in the Old Testament where that word does not mean an unmarried woman—and by inference, a virgin. Had Isaiah not intended to mean a virgin he would have used the Hebrew word *bethulah*, the usual word for a married woman. Moreover, when Matthew quoted Isaiah 7:14 to explain its fulfillment in the birth of Christ, he used the normal Greek word for virgin (*parthenos*). Isaiah clearly predicted that Jesus would be born of a virgin.

Isaiah also prophesied that the child who would be born would be "a son given to us" (Isaiah 9:6). That infant would also be the eternal Son of God, given by the Father for the redemption and rule of mankind. What a generous gift the Father has given us!

LESSON: *The Old Testament prophesied Christ's birth in Bethlehem and His unique birth by a virgin.*

April 28

PROPHECIES OF
THE LIFE OF CHRIST

The eyes of the blind will be opened, and the ears
of the deaf will be unstopped. (Isaiah 35:5)

John the Baptist was a rugged man, living in the desert of Judea on a diet of locusts and wild honey. He had a unique mission. We could call him "the Great Introducer" because it was his honored privilege to introduce Jesus Christ, the Son of God, to the nation Israel. Seven hundred years before John was born, Isaiah prophesied he would come as a voice in the wilderness, calling the nation to prepare for Messiah's advent. Malachi predicted that John would be Messiah's "messenger," preparing the people for Messiah (Isaiah 40:3).

Isaiah also explained that Messiah would "bring good news to the afflicted" (61:1). The Holy Spirit would empower the Messiah, who would heal the sick, bring liberty to the oppressed, and solve the suffering of sin. Isaiah announced that Messiah would not be contentious and quarrelsome like the Pharisees; He would be gentle. He would not snuff out the smoldering wick—He would not crush the people who were already depressed and devastated by the legalistic Pharisees (42:2-4).

But how would the people identify the Messiah? How would they know when He had come? Isaiah promised that Messiah's presence would be known by the signs He performed: He would give sight to the blind, open the ears of the deaf, give legs to the lame, enable the dumb to shout for joy (35:5-6). When John the Baptist was confused and in prison, Jesus sent messengers to him, reminding him that the miracles revealed Jesus was the Messiah (Matthew 11:2-6).

Moses foretold that Jesus would be the greater prophet, who through His teaching would reveal the Father (Deuteronomy 18:15-18). And with those credentials confirming His messiahship He would present Himself to the nation, riding into Jerusalem on an unbroken colt—revealing that even nature is submissive to the Messiah (Zechariah 9:9). Sadly, His people spurned His offer to rule over them—He was rejected (Psalm 118:22). For that reason His promised blessings to the nation were held in abeyance.

What a glorious picture of a great Savior the Old Testament paints for us!

LESSON: *Christ's coming was foretold by the forerunner, and His messiahship was proved by His teaching and His miracles.*

PROPHECIES OF
THE DEATH OF CHRIST

He was pierced through for our transgressions,
He was crushed for our iniquities; . . .
and by His scourging we are healed. (Isaiah 53:5)

Seven centuries before Christ's birth, Isaiah promised that Messiah would become our sin bearer. Isaiah was so certain of the prophecy's fulfillment, that he wrote in the past tense: "Our griefs He bore, our sorrows He carried. . . . He was pierced through for our transgressions, He was crushed for our iniquities" (Isaiah 53:4-5). That was ultimately why Messiah came. He did not come to be simply an example or martyr. He came as our substitute. He took on Himself what we could never bear and paid what we couldn't pay. Isaiah said, "The Lord has caused the iniquity of us all to fall on Him" (v. 6). He paid the full price for sin. Hence, Jesus could shout on the cross, "*Tetelestai!*"—"It is finished!" (John 19:30). He fully paid the price for sin.

An astounding psalm prophesying details of Christ's death was penned by David a thousand years before Christ was crucified. Psalm 22:1 gives Christ's exact words from the cross: "My God, my God, why hast Thou forsaken me?" The Psalm also describes the taunts of the mockers gathered around the cross (v. 7). They sneer at Him: "He trusts in the Lord; let the Lord rescue him, let him deliver him, since he delights in him" (v. 8). With mouths wide open in taunting, they appear as roaring lions against Christ (v. 13). David describes Christ's dreadful suffering—the agony of crucifixion: "They pierced my hands and my feet" (v. 16), the body's painful distortion on the cross: "All my bones are out of joint" (v. 14), the loss of strength and courage: "I am poured out like water . . . my heart is like wax" (v. 14). He describes dehydration: "My strength is dried up like a potsherd, and my tongue cleaves to my jaws" (v. 15), and His emaciated frame is visible: "I can count all my bones" (v. 17). Meanwhile the soldiers gambled, unconcerned, for His clothing (v. 18).

What an awesome portrayal of the suffering and death of our Savior. Why did he die? It was not for a "cause"; it was for people—for sinners. It was for you and me. Do you grasp it? Can you fathom the enormity of His love, that He should willingly die a horrible death that you might live forever?

LESSON: *The Old Testament predicts Christ would die a horrible death with great suffering, but it would be substitutionary, on behalf of all people.*

April 30

PROPHECIES OF
THE RESURRECTION OF CHRIST

*Because you will not abandon me to the grave, nor will
you let your Holy One see decay. (Psalm 16:10, NIV).*

The originator of a new religion came to the great French diplo-
mat-statesman Charles Maurice de Talleyrand-Perigord and complained that he could not make any converts. "What would you
suggest I do?" he asked. "I should recommend," said Talleyrand, "that you
get yourself crucified and then die, but be sure to rise again the third day"
(Green, *Illustrations,* p. 305).

David gave a great confession of faith, believing that life would not
end in the grave but that he would be resurrected, yet David's statement
passes beyond his own experience (Psalm 16:10). It was also a prophecy of
Christ's resurrection. In explaining Christ's resurrection, Peter quoted Psalm
16 and reminded his readers that the statement did not find fulfillment in
David because David died and was buried—and did undergo decay (Acts
2:29). David rather spoke of one of his descendants, Christ, whom God the
Father raised up, preventing Jesus from undergoing decay (v. 31).

Moreover, Peter explained that he and the apostles were witnesses of
the resurrection of Christ. They saw the visible fulfillment of Psalm 16:10.
The fact that Christ sent the Holy Spirit revealed that Christ had not only
risen from the dead but ascended into heaven from whence He sent the
Spirit (v. 33). Paul spoke of the same truth in his sermon at Antioch (13:33-
36). Paul also quoted Psalm 2:7, "Thou art My Son; today I have begotten
Thee," explaining that the resurrection verified the Sonship of Christ. Jesus
is the Son of God from all eternity, and His resurrection vindicated His Son
ship. Paul gives the same thought in Romans 1:4.

The resurrection of Christ is also implied in other Old Testament passages. Psalm 22:22 is quoted in Hebrews 2:12, describing victory over sin.
The resurrection is a logical inference because Christ's name is praised following His triumph. That can only mean the resurrection. Similarly, at the
conclusion of Isaiah 53, which describes Christ's suffering, there is also the
implication of the resurrection (Isaiah 53:10). The resurrection of Christ was
a genuine hope in the Old Testament. Indeed, it is the only genuine hope
we have. Nothing else really matters.

LESSON: *The Old Testament prophesied that Christ would not undergo decay in the grave but would be raised from the dead.*

JESUS WAS
BORN OF A VIRGIN

Behold, the virgin shall be with Child, and shall
bear a Son, and they shall call His name Immanuel,
which translated means, God with us. (Matthew 1:23)

History has recorded some very unusual births. In 1961 a fifty-four-year-old woman in Rangoon, Burma, gave birth to a three-pound calcified baby following a twenty-five year gestation period. On July 25, 1978, the world's first "test-tube baby" was born to Lesley Brown in Lancashire, England. The child had been conceived outside the mother. In the eighteenth century, a peasant woman living east of Moscow, gave birth to sixty-nine children (sixteen twins, seven triplets, and four quadruplets). Sixty-seven survived infancy (1990 *Guinness BOWR*, pp. 14ff.).

But the birth of Jesus Christ was entirely unique and stands above all others. Seven hundred years before His birth, a Judean prophet announced that His birth would be a sign to Israel that God was with them—He would be born of a virgin (Isaiah 7:14). In detailing the extraordinary event, Matthew explains that Jesus' conception was during Mary's engagement to Joseph and before she lived with him as his wife. Matthew explains that the Holy Spirit, not Joseph, was responsible for it (1:18). Luke also states, "The Holy Spirit will come upon you, and the power of the Most High will overshadow you; and for that reason the holy offspring shall be called the Son of God" (1:35). Mary expressed surprise at the angel's announcement, "How can this be, since I am a virgin?" (v. 34).

Joseph knew he was not Jesus' father and wanted to divorce Mary because of her pregnancy, not knowing it was by the Holy Spirit. But an angel comforted him by explaining that the Child that had been conceived in Mary was through the Holy Spirit. Moreover, the angel explained Jesus' mission, announcing, "He will save His people from their sins." But He could do that only if He was "Immanuel—God with us" (Matthew 1:19-23).

Is the virgin birth important? Definitely. Had Jesus been born through natural procreation, He would have inherited the same sin nature that motivates each human being to sin. Instead He was the impeccable Son of God, entirely pure, altogether without sin. Only thus could He be the sinless, spotless Lamb of God, a pure sacrifice for sin. Yes, Jesus was born of a virgin.

LESSON: *Jesus Christ's birth was the result of His mother, Mary, conceiving by the Holy Spirit, ensuring the sinless humanity of Christ.*

JESUS
DID NOT SIN

*We do not have a high priest who cannot sympathize
with our weaknesses, but one who has been tempted
in all things as we are, yet without sin. (Hebrews 4:15)*

I magine that a deranged man takes a BB gun into a rowboat, pad-
dles alongside the USS Saratoga, and fires his BB gun at the ship.
The news report could read that the USS Saratoga had been attacked. Would the attack have been real? Yes. Was there any possibility of
the ship being sunk by the attack? No.

In some measure that could explain the nature of Jesus' temptation by
the devil (Matthew 4:1-11). In considering whether Jesus could have sinned
it is important to remember the purpose of His temptation: it was not to
determine whether He could sin, but rather to show that He could not. Suppose a magnificent bridge is built over a large chasm. Before the bridge is
put into use two locomotives slowly cross the bridge and meet in the center.
What is the purpose? Is it to see whether the bridge will collapse? No. It is to
show that the bridge will not collapse. Similarly, Jesus' temptation shows us
what kind of a Savior we have—He is One who could not sin.

The temptation was initiated by the Holy Spirit, not the devil (Matthew
4:1). If Jesus could have sinned, then God the Holy Spirit would have been
soliciting Him to sin, but God promised He would never do that (James
1:13). Further, if Jesus was only a man, He could have sinned, but He is the
God-man.

Jesus is unchangeable (Hebrews 13:8). If He could have sinned while
on earth then He could sin now while He is in heaven. That would destroy
our confidence in Him. Jesus also declared that He has all power and authority (Matthew 28:18), which would preclude Him from sinning. Sin is
based on deception, but Jesus is all-knowing (John 2:25) and cannot be
deceived.

Sin takes place when the inner sin nature responds to the outward
temptation, but Christ had no sin nature to respond to temptation. Finally,
Christ had the authority to dismiss Satan with a word (Matthew 4:10-11). If
Christ could have sinned it would have been strange not to dismiss Satan
immediately. The temptation is designed to show us what a great Savior we
have. He did not sin, and He could not sin. We have security in our Savior!

LESSON: *Jesus was tempted in all things as we are to show us that
as God-Man He could not sin.*

REJECTION
OF CHRIST

*The Pharisees said, "This man casts out demons only
by Beelzebul the ruler of the demons." (Matthew 12:24)*

When the Shah of Iran attempted to modernize his country and
still hold to some of the traditions, he failed to appease either
side of the controversy. Although he was the rightful ruler of
Iran, he was rejected by his people, driven from power, and forced into
exile, where he died. He could no longer rule Iran because the people refused him as their monarch.

Some of the most tragic words found in the Bible are those in Matthew
12:24, where the nation of Israel rejects Christ as their rightful ruler. It was
the Pharisees' evaluation of Christ after they had seen His works and heard
His words. "He came to His own, and those who were His own did not
receive Him" (John 1:11).

When Jesus came to the Israelites, He came with impeccable credentials. He could claim the throne of David because He was a descendant of
David (Matthew 1:1), but He was not polluted with the "Jeconiah curse" of
David's line (Jeremiah 22:30) because He was born of a virgin (Matthew
1:22-23). And whereas John the Baptist introduced Him to the nation from
earth (3:1-12), the Father introduced His Son from heaven, "This is My beloved Son, in whom I am well pleased" (v. 17). When Jesus was tempted by
the devil He proved He was the impeccable, sinless Son of God (4:1-11).

As Jesus began His public ministry He continually revealed His messiahship in two realms: His words and His works. In preaching to the people
and healing the sick (4:23) He was announcing the imminency of the kingdom. The King was coming! And the people knew it because they were
surrounded by the witness of His words. When He preached the Sermon on
the Mount (5-7) the people were astonished, "for He was teaching them as
one having authority, and not as their scribes" (7:29). And He followed His
teaching with miracles—healing the lepers and the blind, stilling the storm
on the sea, casting out demons, raising the dead (8-9).

They were all signs of the Messiah. He was in their midst. But what did
they say? That He did it all through the power of Satan. Tragedy of tragedies!
The promised kingdom would now be held in abeyance. What greater sin is
there than to reject the grace of God and to scorn His Son?

LESSON: *Jesus authenticated His messiahship through His teaching
and through His miracles but was rejected by the nation Israel.*

THE HUMILIATION
OF CHRIST

*[Christ] emptied Himself, taking the form of a bondservant,
and being made in the likeness of men. (Philippians 2:7)*

James the Fifth of Scotland on certain occasions removed his royal
robes, disguised himself as a peasant, and freely mingled among
his people incognito. He would talk with them about their problems, aspirations, and concerns, trying to enter into a proper understanding
of their way of life. Upon his return, James became a better ruler because he
had united himself with his people. Jesus Christ did even more than that;
He actually became a man, living among to men that He might understand.
us and represent us to the Father.

Although He took on humanity, Jesus was God of very God. On the
Mount of Transfiguration, Jesus removed the veil, and the splendor of the
Shekinah glory of God shone forth from His being (Matthew 17:2). When the
soldiers came to arrest Him in the garden, He merely spoke the word, and
they fell over as dead (John 18:6). He had authority in His word.

Although He was God and remained God, Jesus "emptied Himself"
(Philippians 2:7). That is an unusual statement and the cause of considerable discussion. What does it mean? It cannot mean He emptied Himself of
His deity since He displayed His deity consistently; He showed that He was
all-powerful by His miracles, and He showed He was all-knowing by His
infinite knowledge of people. Nor does it mean He chose not to use His
divine attributes, because He did reveal them on many occasions. The emptying of Jesus was not a subtraction but an addition. In His humiliation
Jesus took on an additional nature, a human nature. Thereafter He was and
remains the God-Man. The humiliation or emptying of Christ is explained in
the following phrases: "Taking the form of a bondservant, and being made
in the likeness of men. And being found in appearance as a man, He hum-
bled Himself" (vv. 7-8). It is a solemn reminder of Christ's infinite love for
you and me, that He would leave heaven's splendor to take on the humiliation of humanity—being rejected, ridiculed, scorned in order to bring us
safely home to heaven. Are you trusting in Him alone? There is no one else
—no church, no system—that can bring you safely home to heaven (Acts
4:12).

LESSON: *Christ did not divest Himself of His deity; rather, in His humiliation He took on the limitations of humanity while retaining His deity.*

JESUS ROSE
FROM THE DEAD

*He was raised on the third day according
to the Scriptures. (1 Corinthians 15:4)*

Not far from the Damascus Gate in the old city of Jerusalem is a serene garden. Within this garden is a rock-hewn tomb in the side of a hill only yards from Gordon's Calvary—"the place of the skull." It is of particular interest to Christians because many believe that Christ's body was laid in that tomb. The rectangular opening is about four feet high, the channel still revealing where the circular stone "door" was rolled to seal the entrance. Many factors suggest it may have been the actual tomb where Christ was buried: it was used by a wealthy Jew during Herodian times, it was hewn in rock, it was in a garden near the place of crucifixion.

If that was the actual place where Jesus was buried, then it was also the place where He rose from the dead. On that first Easter morning Peter and John raced to the tomb. John won the foot race and glanced into the tomb. Peter brushed past John and looked at the evidence. He saw more than John. Peter "beheld the linen wrappings" and theorized that something had happened. Peter saw the head wrapping "rolled up in a place by itself" (John 20:7). Then John entered the tomb, "saw, and believed" (v. 8).

What did John see? What did Peter theorize? Peter and John saw the linen wrappings that had been around the body. The head wrapping still retained its circular shape. The seventy-five pounds of spices that had been placed between the wrappings had caused the linen wrappings to cave in slightly, but they still retained the shape of a body. Yet the body was gone! That was what impacted the disciples—they saw the wrappings in the shape of a body, but the body was gone. There was no way someone could have unwrapped the body and rewrapped the linen wrappings in that shape. There was only one conclusion: Jesus had risen from the dead.

What a glorious truth! Because of the resurrection we have hope for the future. Because Christ lives, we shall live also. He is the firstfruits of the resurrection. More resurrections shall follow. Every believer in Jesus Christ has a genuine, living hope in a bodily resurrection (1 Corinthians 15:22).

LESSON: *Jesus Christ rose bodily from the grave.*

IMPORTANCE OF
THE RESURRECTION

And if Christ has not been raised, your faith is worthless;
you are still in your sins. (1 Corinthians 15:17)   •

One theologian said, "It wouldn't hurt my faith one bit if they found the bones of Jesus." Is the resurrection of Christ really important?

The resurrection of Christ is very important. For one thing, the resurrection is part of the gospel message (1 Corinthians 15:4). If He did not rise from the dead, the gospel is not true. The good news of the gospel is not only that Christ died for our sins but that He rose again on the third day. The resurrection validates the Christian faith. If it is not true, we are still in our sins (1 Corinthians 15:17).

The resurrection also validates the claims of Christ. Since "the sting of death is sin" (v. 56) and Christ claimed to be sinless (John 8:46), false claims of resurrection would imply that He was not at all what He claimed to be.

The resurrection is the guarantee that the Father has accepted the Son's work as sufficient and effective payment for sin. If Christ did not rise, then the Father did not accept the Son's work. It would mean that the Father didn't hear the Son. Yet Hebrews 5:7 says that the Father heard His prayer when Jesus prayed to Him who was "able to save Him from ["out of"] death."

The resurrection is essential in the sequence of events in God's program. Christ promised His disciples, "It is to your advantage that I go away; for if I do not go away, the Helper shall not come to you; but if I go, I will send Him to you" (John 16:7). The resurrection was necessary for the ascension, and the ascension was necessary for Christ to send the Holy Spirit. Had Christ not risen from the dead there could have been no Pentecost, no ministry of the Holy Spirit, and therefore no church.

Yes, the resurrection of Christ is important. There is no gospel without it, no forgiveness of sins, and no victory. The sting of death is gone. We can face death with faith; since Christ was raised, we too shall be raised.

LESSON: *The resurrection of Christ is a necessary part of the gospel to guarantee our forgiveness and to validate Christ's claims.*

JESUS ASCENDED INTO HEAVEN

*He was lifted up while they were looking on, and
a cloud received Him out of their sight. (Acts 1:9)*

The Mount of Olives east of Jerusalem is an important biblical site, especially as it relates to the Lord Jesus. From that hill the glory of God departed prior to Nebuchadnezzar's destruction and sacking of Jerusalem. On Olives' eastern slope lay Bethany, a town where Jesus often retired to visit His friends. From the mountain Jesus descended into the city of Jerusalem, offering Himself as the nation's Messiah as He passed through the golden gate. On the slopes Jesus frequently spent the night sleeping outdoors. And on that mountain Jesus took His last steps on earth. From the Mount of Olives He ascended into heaven.

Luke pictures Jesus ascending into heaven, being lifted up into the clouds just as a sail is hoisted up on a ship. As the disciples gazed intently into the sky, He was borne into heaven by the clouds, the heavenly draperies, to take His authoritative seat at the right hand of God.

What is the meaning of the ascension of Christ? It ended the limitations He imposed on Himself by taking on humanity. The ascension ended His period of humiliation. The glory of God, always resident in Jesus because He was always God, was nonetheless veiled during His earthly humiliation. With the ascension Jesus was glorified and exalted in heaven. He now possesses a name above all others, a name at which every knee will bow (Philippians 2:9). Jesus' ascension made the descent of the Holy Spirit possible (John 16:7).

Jesus' ascension also reminds us that the first resurrected man has entered heaven. The first member of the human race, with a resurrected, glorified body, is now in heaven. Hebrews encourages us on this basis. Because Jesus has entered heaven we should remain steadfast in our faith (4:14). Moreover, we can approach God's throne with confident prayer because we have a representative in heaven who is one of us. Because He has shared our weaknesses (but without sinning), He empathizes with us. We can approach God boldly and receive grace to help us in our need (vv. 15-16).

LESSON: *Jesus has bodily ascended into heaven to take His place of authority at the right hand of the Father.*

JESUS' PRESENT WORK:
HEAD OF THE BODY

He is also head of the body, the church. (Colossians 1:18a)

A ll of us carry a computer with us twenty-four hours a day—our brain. That little organ weighing only three pounds and about the size of a grapefruit is much more complex than the most sophisticated computer. Our brain governs every move we make—voluntary or involuntary—and every emotion we feel. The brain sends messages via the network of nerves, directing actions, emotions, and bodily functions. As a result of those messages from the brain we can think, talk, eat, breathe, sleep, walk, and perform all essential functions necessary for life and survival. A most amazing organ, the brain is our "control center."

As head of His spiritual Body, Christ gives direction to the church, just as the head of the human body gives direction to the physical body. Christ's spiritual Body is being formed as He baptizes each born-again believer into the Body of Christ at the moment of conversion (1 Corinthians 12:13). As its Head, Christ is also the Savior of the Body—its protector, provider, and defender (Ephesians 5:23).

Today Christ nourishes His Body, the church (Ephesians 5:29-30). Faithful parents nurture their children to maturity; similarly Christ is nourishing the church, building it up to maturity.

Part of Christ's present work also involves cleansing the church by washing her with the Word (v. 26). Christ brings the church to maturity through the instrumentality of the Word. That emphasizes the necessity of the believer's absorption with the Word.

Following His ascension into heaven, Christ gave gifts to believers (4:7-13). Just as the Roman armies conquered her enemies and gave the spoils of war to Roman citizens, so Christ has conquered Satan, sin, and death and now gives spiritual gifts to believers, also to produce maturity.

Jesus Christ's work did not end on the cross. He continues to work on our behalf, giving us spiritual gifts, nurturing us through the Word—all to promote our spiritual maturity before we are promoted to heaven.

LESSON: *Christ is presently at work, directing, nurturing, and cleansing the church, which is His Body.*

CHRIST'S PRESENT WORK:
OUR HIGH PRIEST

*Hence also He is able to save forever those who
draw near to God through Him, since He always
lives to make intercession for them. (Hebrews 7:25)*

When a person breaks the law and is caught, he must hire someone to capably represent him. His future hinges on the capability of his attorney. If his lawyer fails he may pay a stiff fine or be sentenced to prison. A good attorney can make the difference between being found guilty or being acquitted.

An important present ministry of Christ is as our defense attorney. At the present, Jesus is at the right hand of the Father, interceding for us (Hebrews 7:25). It is a wonderful truth that Jesus saves us completely and for all time. Both thoughts are bound up in that verse. Christ saves us "fully and completely" so that we may rest secure in our salvation. His is not a partial salvation. He also saves us "for all time." Our salvation never terminates; it is forever. What a matchless Savior He is!

How is He able to save us completely? Our security rests in Christ's undying and unending continuity as our High Priest. In ancient Israel the people were represented by the Aaronic priests. But those priests died, and the people never knew if the next priest would be an acceptable representative. Christ never dies! He never stops representing us. He has risen from the dead never to die again. He "abides forever" (v. 24); He "lives forever" (v. 25) to intercede for us. As Christ prayed for His own while on earth (Luke 22:32; John 17), He now continually prays for His own in heaven.

Can our present sin cause eternal loss? No. John says, "If anyone sins, we have an Advocate with the Father, Jesus Christ the righteous" (1 John 2:1). As our Advocate, Jesus is our defense attorney, pleading our case for us. On the basis of His own merits, Jesus is able to appear on our behalf in the presence of the Father.

Our security depends on Christ's capability as our intercessor. Has Christ ever lost a case? Can anyone defeat our divine Defense Attorney? If we could lose our salvation it would mean that Christ could be ineffective and fail as our representative. Perish the thought! He is our faithful and enduring High Priest.

LESSON: *Jesus is presently in heaven interceding on our behalf as our defense attorney, assuring the security of our salvation.*

CHRIST AS
KINSMAN-REDEEMER

Now Naomi had a kinsman of her husband,
a man of great wealth, of the family of
Elimelech, whose name was Boaz. (Ruth 2:1)

Everyone likes to have important relatives. A friend of ours is able to trace her lineage to Benjamin Harrison, twenty-third president of the United States. Recently a cousin informed me that we are distant relatives of Queen Victoria of England (1837-1901). Although that is fascinating, all of us have a famous Relative who has done something for us.

Boaz, the relative and kinsman-redeemer of Ruth, appears as a type of Christ. What was a kinsman-redeemer? He could prevent property from passing out of the family when it was to be sold because of indebtedness. The kinsman-redeemer had to pay the price of the debt, and he had to be a near relative, willing to marry the widow of the deceased relative.

The beautiful love story in the book of Ruth illustrates Christ's love for His people and His ministry as our Kinsman-Redeemer. In Ruth's case, Boaz was her relative (Ruth 2:1, 20). Christ is able to be the Kinsman-Redeemer of the human race because, in His humanity, He is a relative of us all (Luke 3:23-38).

The kinsman-redeemer also had to possess the purchase price to redeem his impoverished relative. Fortunately, Boaz was a man of great wealth, able to buy back the land belonging to Elimelech, Naomi's deceased husband (Ruth 2:1) and able to marry Ruth to raise up a posterity for the deceased. Because Christ was the sinless Son of God (1 John 3:5), He was able to redeem the fallen human race by dying as a substitute for all humanity (1 Peter 2:24).

Finally, the kinsman had to be willing to redeem his relative. Boaz willingly bought back the forfeited property and married Ruth (Ruth 4:9-10). And Christ willingly laid down His life to redeem the human race (Matthew 20:28).

Have you acknowledged your "near relative" who is your Kinsman-Redeemer? He has paid your spiritual indebtedness; it is stamped "Paid in Full," but you must accept the payment. It is of no value if you do not receive it. Have you received it?

LESSON: *Christ is our Kinsman-Redeemer who has paid our spiritual indebtedness.*

MELCHIZEDEK:
A TYPE OF CHRIST

Thou art a priest forever according
to the order of Melchizedek. (Psalm 110:4)

W hen Lot got into trouble and was captured by Chedorlaomer, Abram, his uncle, pursued the kings north of Damascus and rescued Lot. Upon his return, Abram was greeted by an unusual figure: Melchizedek, king of Salem and priest of God Most High (Genesis 14:18). Who was this unusual man, and why was he important?

Melchizedek was king of Salem, which was later known as Jerusalem, but he was also a priest, combining the two offices into one as a type of Christ. Melchizedek's name comes from *melek*, meaning "king," and *zedek* meaning "righteousness"; hence, he is "king of righteousness." That position points to Christ, who is the ultimate "King of Righteousness." And as king of Salem, Melchizedek is king of peace—a type of Christ.

When Abram met Melchizedek, Abram paid tithes to him, implying that Melchizedek was the greater (Hebrews 7:4, 7). Since Abram was the forefather of Moses and the levitical system, that means that the new covenant of Christ is superior to the Mosaic law (vv. 9-25).

As Melchizedek combined the offices of priest and king into one, so also does Christ. Christ is the heir to the throne of David (Matthew 1:1) and will one day rule in Israel as rightful King (Luke 1:31-33). Although Christ is not of the tribe of Levi, God appointed Him Priest forever according to the order of Melchizedek (Psalm 110:4; Hebrews 7:17).

Melchizedek is an enigmatic figure, appearing in Genesis 14 "without father, without mother, without genealogy, having neither beginning of days nor end of life" (Hebrews 7:3). Why is that significant? Nowhere does it state that Melchizedek was born or that he died. For that reason he is like Christ, who is eternal, having no beginning or ending. Christ provides security for us since as a Melchizedekian priest He forever lives to intercede for us (Hebrews 7:24-25). Christ is a permanent priest. That provides security. The only way we can lose our salvation is if Christ could fail as our High Priest. We rest secure!

LESSON: *Melchizedek is a type of Christ, representing Christ's combining both offices of priest and king into one office and offering an eternal priesthood.*

JOSEPH:
A TYPE OF CHRIST

And he set [Joseph] over all the land of Egypt. (Genesis 41:43)

A"type" is a divinely intended Old Testament illustration foreshadowing a biblical truth in the New Testament.

Joseph appears as a type of Christ in the Old Testament. Although Joseph was the object of the special love of his father (Genesis 37:3) like Christ (Matthew 3:17), he was hated by his brothers (v. 4) as Christ was also hated by His people (John 15:24). Because Joseph's brothers hated him, they plotted his death and finally threw him into a pit (Genesis 37:18, 24). Similarly, Christ's brethren, the Sanhedrin (rulers) "plotted together to seize Jesus by stealth, and kill Him" (Matthew 26:4).

Both Joseph and Christ were sold for pieces of silver. When the Midianite traders came in their caravan, Joseph's brothers sold him to them (Genesis 37:26). Judas Iscariot delivered Christ to the Romans, selling him for thirty pieces of silver (Matthew 26:14-15). As a result, both Joseph and Christ became slaves. Joseph became a servant in Pharaoh's house (Genesis 39:4), whereas Christ became a servant as a result of His humiliation in taking on humanity and going to the cross (Philippians 2:7). Yet both Joseph and Christ were innocent. Joseph was imprisoned because of the false accusation of Potiphar's wife (Genesis 39:11-20), and both Pilate's wife and Pilate himself admitted the innocence of Christ (Matthew 27:19, 24).

Joseph was elevated from his humiliation to a position of power when Pharaoh made him ruler of Egypt (Genesis 41:43). Similarly, Christ has been elevated from His humiliation to a position of power whereby He has been given a name that is above every name (Philippians 2:9), and His exalted position anticipates the future day when He will rule over Israel and the nations in the millennial kingdom (Matthew 25:31). But in the providence of God, Joseph's brothers repented, recognized him as a savior, and submitted to his authority (Genesis 42:6, 21). Similarly a glorious day is coming when Christ's brethren will repent and the millennial kingdom will be inaugurated (Zechariah 12:10-14).

LESSON: *Joseph is a type of Christ, illustrating His rejection, innocence, and ultimate rise to power.*

OLD TESTAMENT SACRIFICES: A TYPE OF CHRIST

Behold, the lamb of God who takes
away the sin of the world! (John 1:29)

C entral to Old Testament worship was the knowledge that "the life of the flesh is in the blood, and I have given it to you on the altar to make atonement for your souls" (Leviticus 17:11). Without sacrifices, blood, and death, there was no forgiveness of sin. That knowledge was emblazoned on the mind of every Israelite. Forgiveness requires blood—not blood flowing in the veins, but spilled blood—death. Thus the Old Testament sacrifices anticipated the death of Christ and the blood He shed to provide forgiveness for the human race.

That was a lesson learned early in human history. Abel brought an animal sacrifice to the Lord, and He looked favorably on it although He rejected Cain's fruit offering (Genesis 4:4). When Abraham and Isaac ascended Mount Moriah, even the teenager recognized the need for a blood sacrifice (22:7). Once the Mosaic law became a part of the Israelites' way of life, animal sacrifices were a daily occurrence. Morning and evening, day in, day out, year in, year out, Israel offered sacrifices (Exodus 29:38-39). God said the sacrifice was to be offered at the entrance to the Tabernacle, "and I will meet you there" (v. 42). What is the lesson? That God only meets the worshiper when he comes bringing a blood sacrifice. The point is penetrating: God will only meet with those who come on the merits of the blood of Christ. Not our good works, tithes, or church attendance—only the blood of Christ enables us to have fellowship with the Father.

But there were not only daily offerings; the Israelites also offered two male lambs every Sabbath as a burnt offering; bulls, lambs, and goats at the beginning of each month (Numbers 28:9-15); and the Passover offering each year. Think of how much blood there was! It would have been a continual reminder that blood atones for sin. John the Baptist had those offerings in mind when he called Christ "the lamb of God." Ultimately the animals could never atone for sin, but by His one offering, Christ has once and for all atoned for our sin (Hebrews 10:4, 12).

LESSON: *The animal sacrifices of the Old Testament were types of the death of Christ, pointing to Christ as the ultimate sacrifice for forgiveness of sin.*

FEASTS:
A TYPE OF CHRIST

*Christ our Passover also has
been sacrificed. (1 Corinthians 5:7b)*

Christmas and Easter are two important events on the Christian calendar. Every December 25 we celebrate the birth of Jesus Christ, the incarnate God-Man, and every Easter we celebrate His bodily resurrection. These annual events are important to our faith. In Israel's religious calendar were seven important annual feasts that typified Christ's redemption and anticipated His future kingdom on earth.

The first feast was Passover, celebrated in March or April, commemorating Israel's deliverance from bondage in Egypt. As families, the worshipers killed and ate a lamb in commemoration of their redemption. The sacrificed lamb was a type of Christ. Peter reminds us that our redemption was "with precious blood, as of a lamb unblemished and spotless, the blood of Christ" (1 Peter 1:19).

The feast of Unleavened Bread followed for one week during which the Israelites ate bread without yeast (Leviticus 23:6), which illustrated Christ as the Bread of life (John 6:35) and the believer's communion with Christ. The bread without yeast illustrated the believer's separation from the world as Israel separated from their old life in Egypt.

The feast of First Fruits was on the third day during the week of Unleavened Bread. First fruits celebrated the nation's new harvest upon entrance into the Promised Land and illustrated the resurrection of Christ: "Christ has been raised from the dead, the first fruits of those who are asleep" (1 Corinthians 15:20).

Fifty days after the feast of First Fruits was the feast of Pentecost, during which the worshipers presented two loaves of bread as a wave offering to the Lord (Leviticus 23:15-21). Pentecost, fulfilled in Acts 2, portrayed Jews and Gentiles in one body.

The feast of trumpets foreshadowed Christ's regathering Israel to the land (Leviticus 23:24; Matthew 24:31). The Day of Atonement was a day of repentance, typifying Israel's repentance (Zechariah 12:10-14), necessary and preparatory for her blessing in the millennial kingdom. Tabernacles, the climactic feast, anticipated Christ's glorious millennial rule (14:16-19). Israel's feasts are rich with lessons of all we have and all we anticipate in Christ.

LESSON: *The feasts of Israel typify Israel's redemption through the death of Christ and anticipate Christ's glorious kingdom reign.*

Part 4
The Holy Spirit

The Titles of the Holy Spirit

*The thoughts of God no one knows except
the Spirit of God. (1 Corinthians 2:11)*

N ames are important in identification. The name *Ludwig van Beethoven* identifies the great composer as belonging to the family of Beethoven. *Otto von Bismarck* identifies the prince as belonging to the house of Bismarck. *Samuel de Champlain* indicates that Samuel comes from the family of Champlain.

The titles of the Holy Spirit identify the Holy Spirit as belonging to God; they reveal the Holy Spirit as deity. In 1 Corinthians 2:11 Paul draws an analogy between man and God, showing that as the spirit of man knows the nature of man so the Spirit of God knows the nature of God. The point is important. Just as the spirit of man is human, so the Spirit of God is divine. Matthew 3:16 is illustrative in describing the Holy Spirit as "the Spirit of God" since the Holy Spirit descended from the Father in heaven.

There are many spirits, but not all are holy. To distinguish the third Person of the Trinity, He is given a unique title setting Him apart from all other spirits—He is the "Holy Spirit." Paul reminds believers that at the moment they believed the gospel, they "were sealed in Him with the Holy Spirit of promise" (Ephesians 1:13). Believers are sealed in Christ with the Holy Spirit. That phrase identifies the equality of Christ and the Holy Spirit. Both are God. Both are persons.

The Holy Spirit is also called the "Spirit of Jesus" (Acts 16:7). Just as a vision from God appeared to Paul, calling him to mission work in Europe, so the Spirit of Jesus called him in similar accord. The statement identifies the Holy Spirit with Jesus and the Father, showing their equality. He is also called the "Spirit of the Lord" as the One sent from the Father and coming upon the Son for ministry (Luke 4:18).

God did not leave us orphans when Christ left this world; He sent a substitute. He made wonderful provision for believers, allowing us to be indwelt by the Holy Spirit, who empowers, encourages, instructs, and monitors our steps that we might walk in conformity with God's will and Word.

LESSON: *The titles affirm that the Holy Spirit is God, the third Person of the Trinity.*

THE HOLY SPIRIT
IS CREATOR

The Spirit of God was moving over
the surface of the waters. (Genesis 1:2)

Evolutionists are constantly forced to rethink their position. Several years ago the jawbone of a previously unknown form of mammal was discovered in the Painted Desert of Arizona, defying the evolutionary view that all warm-blooded creatures descended from only two families of mammals. In another discovery, scientists detected a quasar (light) coming from near the edge of the universe, hence (to their thinking) near the beginning of time. That has forced scientists to reconsider the age of the universe. Evolution is an unproved hypothesis that stands in defiance of biblical truth and is logically impossible.

Genesis 1:2 describes the role of the Holy Spirit in creation. At the beginning of creation the Spirit of God hovered over the world as a mother hen hovers over her eggs, brooding, warming them, and infusing life into the young chicks that are hatched. That is also the picture of Deuteronomy 32:11: "Like an eagle that stirs up its nest, that hovers over its young." Similarly the Holy Spirit hovered over the creation, filling it with the breath of life. The Holy Spirit, as the third Person of the Trinity, was involved in creation.

Job agrees: "By his spirit he hath garnished the heavens" (26:13, KJV). The brilliance of the sunrise and the colorful rays of the setting sun are the creative work of the Holy Spirit. Through His participation in creation the Holy Spirit has beautified the heavens.

The psalmist says, "When you send your Spirit, they are created, and you renew the face of the earth" (Psalm 104:30, NIV). The psalmist also declares, "By the breath of His mouth all their host [was created]" (33:6). *Breath* is the same word as *Spirit* and refers to the Holy Spirit in creation.

Man, the apex of God's creation, is included in the Holy Spirit's creative work. Elihu said, "The Spirit of God has made me, and the breath of the Almighty gives me life" (Job 33:4). From clay, from the dust of the ground, the Spirit of God created man—with a beautiful body to function properly and with a mind to love and serve Him.

LESSON: *The Holy Spirit, the third Person of the Trinity, was active in the work of creation, thereby affirming His deity.*

THE HOLY SPIRIT
IS A HELPER LIKE CHRIST

And I will ask the Father, and He will give you another
Helper, that He may be with you forever. (John 14:16)

In the ancient East a person would carry a heavy burden with a wooden yoke over his shoulders and the objects, such as heavy pails of water or grain, suspended on either side of the yoke. The weight caused the person's shoulders to stoop as he struggled under the burden. He needed someone to help him bear his burden.

On the eve of His crucifixion the Lord gave comforting words to His disciples. They were sorrowing because He had told them He was departing, but He had good news for them. He promised them "another Helper." When Christ was on earth He could only be in one place at one time, but He promised to send a substitute who would remain with every believer for all time. Moreover, this replacement would not be inferior. Jesus promised to send "another of the same kind." He did not merely send a "force" or a "power"; He sent a Person like Himself.

Jesus referred to the Holy Spirit as a "helper" or "comforter." The transliterated word is *Paraclete* and literally means "one called alongside to help." Just as the person carrying a heavy burden needed someone to come alongside and help him, so the believer needs divine help in his daily walk. The divine Paraclete is a Comforter, Advocate, and Friend at the heavenly court, teaching us, bearing witness of Christ, and convicting the world. He is our legal helper.

Jesus has sent the divine help that we need. Since Pentecost the Holy Spirit permanently indwells every believer from the moment of salvation. The Holy Spirit is indeed a helper like Christ—He teaches us, consoles, comforts, exhorts, guides, illuminates our minds. Christ has made perfect provision for our spiritual life. He died to bring us salvation; then He sent His Holy Spirit to permanently indwell us that we might live for Him.

LESSON: *God the Holy Spirit, who permanently indwells believers, is another helper like Christ.*

THE HOLY SPIRIT
IS A DOWN PAYMENT

*[God] anointed us, set his seal of ownership on us,
and put his Spirit in our hearts as a deposit,
guaranteeing what is to come. (2 Corinthians 1:21-22, NIV)*

When a young couple gets married, one of the first things they dream of is getting their own house. They work hard, save their money, and the day arrives when they make application to buy. They meet with the bank officials, sign the documents, and hand them a check for the down payment. The down payment does not pay for the house; it only represents 5 or 10 percent of the actual price. But its payment indicates there are more payments to come— frequently, thirty years of them!

Upon believing in Christ every believer receives the gift of the Holy Spirit. The Holy Spirit represents God's down payment to us—a promise that He will make further payments to us. Those further payments represent the realities of heaven. The Holy Spirit is God's guarantee that we will arrive safely on heaven's shore.

Paul says that God has "put his Spirit in our hearts as a deposit." The word *deposit* means a pledge or a down payment, guaranteeing that the full amount will be paid. By giving us the Holy Spirit at salvation, God in effect promises that we will receive our completed salvation, which He has begun to work out in our hearts. God will complete the transaction.

For that reason, Paul could speak with confidence that he preferred "to be absent from the body and to be at home with the Lord" (2 Corinthians 5:8), knowing that since God has given us the Spirit as a down payment (v. 5), he could rest in absolute assurance that when he died, he would go home to glory.

The Holy Spirit is given to believers as a down payment of our inheritance (Ephesians 1:14). What is our full inheritance? It is the completed experience of our redemption—when we are glorified in the presence of God.

God has made a wonderful provision for His people. He gives us His Holy Spirit at the moment of salvation, enabling us to live a supernatural life that is pleasing to Him. But the Holy Spirit is also God's down payment guaranteeing our safe arrival in heaven.

LESSON: *The gift of the Holy Spirit at salvation is God's down payment to believers, promising the full payment of eternal life.*

May 19

THE HOLY SPIRIT
IS A SEAL

In Him, you also, after listening to the message of truth,
the gospel of your salvation—having also believed, you were
sealed in Him with the Holy Spirit of promise. (Ephesians 1:13)

Ranchers brand their cattle to show their ownership. The red-hot branding iron burns the owner's brand on the hide of the steer. The particular brand—"Lazy K," "Rocking W," or "Bar J"—identifies the owner. Cattle rustlers would sometimes superimpose their own brand on the steer, covering up the original brand. However, if the steer were skinned, on the inside the original brand would be evident.

God has also placed His mark of ownership on believers. At the precise moment of salvation—simultaneous with believing in Christ—God "branded us" with His Holy Spirit. He sent His Holy Spirit to permanently indwell us as a sign of His ownership. God is the one who seals us at salvation, and the Holy Spirit is the seal.

What is the significance of being sealed with the Spirit? First, it indicates God's ownership of us—He has put His sign on us, and we belong to Him. Second, it provides security. If God has sealed us, who can break the seal? No one. No one can "unseal" us from God. No one can superimpose his seal upon us. The inside will always reveal that we belong to Him. Third, it assures the legitimacy of the contents. If God has put His sign on us, that shows the genuineness of our rebirth. Fourth, it shows God's authority over the believer. It means we are subject to Him, and He has authority over us.

What a blessed truth is that! Many Christians wrestle with the fear of losing their salvation. The Holy Spirit's seal is assurance to those who are troubled by insecurity and fear. Nothing can ever separate us from God. He has put His sign on us, and nothing can remove His seal. We may grieve the indwelling Holy Spirit, but we will never be unsealed (Ephesians 4:30). God will fulfill in us what He has promised. Our salvation is secure.

LESSON: *The Holy Spirit is our seal, assuring God's ownership of us and our security in salvation.*

THE HOLY SPIRIT
IS A PERSON

*For to us God revealed them through the Spirit; for the Spirit
searches all things, even the depths of God. (1 Corinthians 2:10)*

The cults frequently confuse the teaching concerning the Holy Spirit. Jehovah's Witnesses, for example, deny the personality of the Holy Spirit and thereby also reject the Trinity. They state: "God's holy spirit is not a God, not a member of a trinity, not coequal, and is not even a person. . . . It is God's active force . . . his energy. . . . [It] may be likened to a radar beam."

Many people equate personality with a body, but in fact a body is unnecessary for personality. The Holy Spirit is a person because He possesses the qualities of personality—intellect, emotion, and will.

The Holy Spirit has intellect: He searches the depths of God and knows the thoughts of God (1 Corinthians 2:10-11). And because He indwells believers, He reveals the deep truths of God to them.

The Holy Spirit has emotion—He can be grieved (Ephesians 4:30). Paul exhorts believers to speak edifying words, not hurtful, angry words. When we speak damaging words, we grieve the Holy Spirit. If the Holy Spirit were only a force, like a radar beam, how could He be grieved? We cannot grieve a mere force, but we can grieve a person.

The Holy Spirit has a will: He sovereignly distributes spiritual gifts to believers (1 Corinthians 12:11). Paul stresses that all believers have been given spiritual gifts, but they are sovereignly given at conversion "just as He wills." Because the Holy Spirit is a person, He wills to give us spiritual gifts according to our personality and need.

God has sent the blessed Holy Spirit as "another Comforter" to dwell within us, to teach us the truths of God, and to monitor our steps when we stray from fellowship with God.

LESSON: *The Holy Spirit has the attributes of personality, exhibiting intellect, emotion, and will.*

THE HOLY SPIRIT
IS A TEACHER AND GUIDE

*The Helper, the Holy Spirit, whom the Father will send
in My name, He will teach you all things and bring to
your remembrance all that I said to you. (John 14:26)*

When we traveled to Israel, a man named Pitch Abraham was our guide. As Pitch took us up the coast he explained the ruins at Caesarea; he guided us inland and northward to the ancient site of Caesarea-Philippi, within yards of the Lebanese border. We toured beautiful Galilee, returning through the volatile Samaria where Pitch wisely instructed us concerning our behavior. Down into the desert we traveled, examining ancient Beersheba and then beautiful, memorable Jerusalem. Pitch wisely guided us in our trip while ably instructing us about that memorable land.

G God has given every believer a personal Guide and Teacher who daily and constantly directs our affairs. On the evening prior to the crucifixion the disciples grieved that Jesus was leaving them. Jesus promised that although He was departing, He and the Father would send them the indwelling Holy Spirit to teach them. Just as Jesus had been their teacher for three years, now the Holy Spirit would teach them individually (John 14:26). That promise extended beyond the apostles.

Since the Holy Spirit indwells every believer (Romans 8:9), He also teaches every believer. This is an important ministry, revealing that understanding the Scriptures is more than an academic matter; it is a spiritual matter. The Holy Spirit must give understanding concerning scriptural verities. Jesus also spoke of this as the Spirit's guiding the believer into truth just as a guide directs a traveler in unfamiliar territory (John 16:13).

What specifically does the Holy Spirit teach? Jesus explained that the Holy Spirit "will bear witness of Me" (John 15:26). The Spirit draws attention to Christ. He confirms the truth about Christ. Any religious system that denies the truth about Christ is not being taught by the Holy Spirit. The Holy Spirit teaches in concert with Christ. It is imperative that we rely upon the Holy Spirit to give us spiritual insight and understanding of biblical truth.

LESSON: *The Holy Spirit affirms His personality in His work of teaching and guiding the believer into spiritual truth.*

THE HOLY SPIRIT
IS A DIVINE PROSECUTOR

*And He, when He comes, will convict the world
concerning sin, and righteousness, and judgment. (John 16:8)*

In a court case the attorney is very important. He frequently is the difference between winning or losing the case. A defendant seeks a successful defense attorney, and the prosecution employs an effective prosecuting attorney. Following Jesus' ascension into heaven, God sent His divine attorney to earth to convict the world concerning Christ.

Although Jesus came as Israel's Messiah, He was rejected. However, following His resurrection and ascension into heaven, He promised to send the Holy Spirit, who would continue to confirm Christ's ministry on earth. The Holy Spirit has a ministry, not only to believers but also to unbelievers. He "convicts the world." "Convict" is a legal term, indicating that the Spirit serves as a divine prosecuting attorney. He also serves as a defense counsel for the believer. When the believer testifies to an unbeliever concerning Christ, the Holy Spirit verifies the witness by convincing the unbeliever of the truthfulness of the witness.

Jesus taught that the Holy Spirit would convict the world of sin. What sin? The sin of unbelief in Christ (John 16:9). The ultimate sin and the greatest rebellion is refusal to believe in Jesus Christ. The only one who can deliver a person from that sin is the Holy Spirit. When Peter preached at Pentecost the people were "pierced to the heart" because the Holy Spirit had convicted them of the sin of unbelief (Acts 2:37).

The Holy Spirit also convicts unbelievers of righteousness. The resurrection and ascension of Christ vindicated Him as the Son of God (John 16:10). Because Jesus is God's Anointed, the grave could not hold Him. The Holy Spirit witnesses to the world concerning Christ's resurrection and ascension (Acts 2:24, 33). The Holy Spirit also convicts the world of judgment because in Christ's descent to the earth Satan was judged and defeated (John 16:11).

The good news about Christ is indeed true! He has risen; He has ascended into heaven. Christ has destroyed sin, Satan, and death—man's greatest enemies. And we have a divine defense Attorney to witness with us concerning these blessed truths.

LESSON: *The Holy Spirit is a divine Prosecutor, convicting the world of the sin of unbelief, the righteousness of Christ, and that Satan has been judged.*

THE HOLY SPIRIT
KNOWS ALL THINGS

The Spirit searches all things, even
the depths of God. (1 Corinthians 2:10)

One of the most beloved Bible verses is Romans 8:28. But I wonder how many of us read it in the context. Romans 8:28 is possible only because of what precedes it. The context is suffering (Romans 8:18-39), and when we suffer we don't even know how to pray. We don't have all the facts about our dilemma, so we really don't know what to pray for (v. 26).

At that point the Holy Spirit intercedes for us. He takes our inept prayers and carries them to the throne of God. In fact, it is not even clear who does the groaning when it says, "The Spirit Himself intercedes for us with groanings too deep for words." He unites with our petitions, and knowing our frame He corrects our errant prayers and intercedes for us "according to the will of God." We may pray selfishly, outside of the will of God, but the Spirit corrects our prayers. Then the Father answers. Aren't you grateful for the divine Corrector?

So it is in response to the Spirit's corrected prayer that the Father "causes all things to work together for good" (v. 28). Why does God work all things together for good? Because the Holy Spirit, who knows all things, has corrected our feeble and errant prayers, and since He knows what we really need, He has interceded for us at the Father's throne. What a Comforter!

This selfsame Holy Spirit reveals divine truths to us—truths we could not possibly know through our mortal minds. I recall witnessing to an intelligent man whose ultimate response was, "I don't understand." Sadly that is true. The Spirit had not yet revealed God's truth to him. Man can only know the things of humanity (1 Corinthians 2:11). Similarly, only God can know the things about God. So how shall we learn the things about God? The Holy Spirit will teach us. It is He who takes the divine truths, opens our minds, and lets us see heavenly things! That is why the believer who never graduated from high school will know more spiritual truth than the unbeliever with a Ph.D. Believer, feast on the Word, and let the Holy Spirit enlighten your mind.

LESSON: *The Holy Spirit knows all things.*

THE HOLY SPIRIT
IS EVERYWHERE PRESENT

*Where can I go from Thy Spirit? Or where
can I flee from Thy presence? (Psalm 139:7)*

Although Joe was raised in a Christian home by a meticulous mother, he rebelled against his upbringing. His mother had been mannerly, but Joe was messy—ink-stained ties, half-eaten sandwiches, his pipe, and sweaters lay among his architectural drawings. But there was a bigger problem. Joe dabbled with the occult. Finally, to remove himself from his mother's influence, he moved to San Francisco. Although Joe could escape his parental home, he will never escape from the Holy Spirit.

As David contemplated the Holy Spirit's presence, he exclaimed, "Where can I go from thy Spirit? Or where can I flee from Thy presence?" Nowhere. Because the Spirit is everywhere present, David could not flee Him. Not that he wanted to; he simply said it would be impossible if he should try. It is like trying to escape paying taxes. It's impossible. The IRS will find you wherever you are.

The reason the Holy Spirit is everywhere present is because He is "Spirit," not "a spirit." If He were a spirit (like Satan), He would be localized and limited in His presence. Because His nature is Spirit, like God the Father, He is everywhere present, filling every place with His being.

David mentions the most extreme distances possible: "If I ascend to heaven, Thou art there; if I make my bed in Sheol, behold, Thou art there" (Psalm 139:8). Should David be able to enter heaven, the Holy Spirit would be there; if David could descend into Sheol—which is the netherworld, not hell—the Holy Spirit would be there as well. David could not escape the presence of the Holy Spirit.

A rebel cannot escape the convicting ministry of the Holy Spirit. That is a triumphant truth. No matter where David found himself, "even there Thy hand will lead me" (v. 10). Like a father taking a fearful child's hand, so the Holy Spirit is present to comfort us. And when the darkness of the world's worry would overwhelm us, we are mindful there is no darkness with God. Christian, take comfort! The Holy Spirit's presence is your protection and comfort.

LESSON: *Since the Holy Spirit is everywhere present, neither believer nor unbeliever can escape His presence.*

May 25

THE HOLY SPIRIT
IS EQUAL WITH FATHER AND SON

*The grace of the Lord Jesus Christ, and the
love of God, and the fellowship of the Holy
Spirit, be with you all. (2 Corinthians 13:14)*

An earmark of the cults is their distortion of the Holy Spirit. The Jehovah's Witnesses, for example, state the Holy Spirit is "not a God, not a member of a trinity, not coequal, and is not even a person." Christian Science suggests the Holy Spirit is "Divine Science." Parley Pratt, a Mormon theologian, regards the Holy Spirit as an impersonal substance, a spiritual fluid. Need we take issue with such strange teachings? In denying the third Person of the Trinity, those doctrinal perversions strike at the heart of our faith and must be answered.

In the Great Commission, Jesus commanded the apostles to "make disciples of all the nations, baptizing them in the name of the Father and the Son and the Holy Spirit" (Matthew 28:19). When Jesus' followers made disciples, it was on the authority of God's name—Father, Son, and Holy Spirit. Would it make sense that they baptize in the name of two who have authority and one that has lesser authority? Or to baptize in the name of two persons and one "thing"? The unity and equality of the triune God is also seen in the context of giving gifts (1 Corinthians 12:4-6). Although there are "varieties of gifts, . . . of ministries, . . . of effects," there is "the same Spirit," "the same Lord," and "the same God," suggesting the equality of the three.

Similarly, the apostolic benediction, invoking God's blessing upon believers, comes from all three members of the Godhead: "The grace of the Lord Jesus Christ, and the love of God, and the fellowship of the Holy Spirit, be with you all" (2 Corinthians 13:14). That benediction, calling for God's blessing and coming equally from the Father, Son, and Holy Spirit, surely suggests all three are equal.

When Ananias lied to the Holy Spirit, it was the same as lying to God (Acts 5:3-4). Paul also attributed to the Holy Spirit the words the Lord spoke to Isaiah, suggesting the equality of the Father and the Spirit (28:25).

The cults are in grave error when they deny the Holy Spirit's equality with the Father and the Son; He is equally worthy of our honor and worship.

LESSON: *The Holy Spirit is equal with the Father and Son in His person and in His authority.*

THE HOLY SPIRIT
EMPOWERS US FOR WITNESSING

*You shall receive power when the Holy Spirit has come
upon you; and you shall be My witnesses. (Acts 1:8)*

A Christian barber who was convicted that he should witness for Christ was determined that he would witness to his next customer. He grew nervous as he contemplated what he was going to say to the customer relaxing in the chair. As he began to hone his razor on the leather strap, he blurted out, "Are you ready to die?" The customer fled the chair, his face unshaven!

Witnessing doesn't come easy for most Christians. It seems that if we preplan our approach, we tend to get nervous. And yet God has made ample, divine preparation for us through the Holy Spirit. In fact, Jesus commanded the disciples to wait until He would send the Holy Spirit from heaven—then they would have divine power (Acts 1:4, 8). Previously Peter had been a coward, even fearful of a servant girl (Matthew 26:69), but when the Spirit empowered him he was brave enough to confront the supreme court of Israel (4:8). Even after being threatened by the judicial hierarchy, the apostles continued "to speak the word of God with boldness" (4:31) because they were filled with the Holy Spirit. Even amid the most hostile opposition the Holy Spirit can strengthen us to faithfully witness for Christ even as the Lord strengthened Stephen (6:10).

Perhaps we think, *But that was the apostle Peter or Paul. I can't possibly do what they did.* We need to realize that the apostles were men of clay feet and fearful hearts too. Paul acknowledged that he came to the Corinthians "in weakness and in fear and in much trembling," but the resolution to his weakness was that he could speak "in demonstration of the Spirit and of power" (1 Corinthians 2:4).

God sent His Holy Spirit for all believers, and every one of us can speak to others about Christ with confidence and power. That was the testimony of the Thessalonian believers, who, despite severe persecution, heralded the message of Christ to others because of the Spirit's strength (1 Thessalonians 1:5-7).

LESSON: *All believers have received the Holy Spirit to strengthen them to witness faithfully for Christ.*

THE HOLY SPIRIT
CAN BE REJECTED

Do not grieve the Holy Spirit of God, by whom you were
sealed for the day of redemption. (Ephesians 4:30)

The question of whether the Holy Spirit is a person can be answered by the fact that He can be resisted and rejected. In the much debated statement in Mark 3:29 Jesus says, "Whoever blasphemes against the Holy Spirit never has forgiveness, but is guilty of an eternal sin." That warning could only be made about a person. I can stand at an electrical outlet and vehemently ridicule it, but there are no repercussions because I am ridiculing an inanimate object. When I ridicule a person, there are repercussions. The unbelieving Jews were attributing to Satan what Christ had done through the power of the Holy Spirit—and that was unforgivable.

Rebellious children resist the admonitions of their parents. A lazy employee resists the exhortation of his employer. A student resists the assignments of the teacher. We resists persons. The Holy Spirit may be resisted because He is a person. Stephen chastened the unbelieving Jews, "You men who are stiffnecked and uncircumcised in heart and ears are always resisting the Holy Spirit" (Acts 7:51). The One who had worked in their history by granting grace and lending leaders to the nation was the very One the people rebelled against—the Holy Spirit.

The Holy Spirit can also be lied to. When Ananias and his wife, Sapphira, sold their land and deceptively kept back part of the money, Peter told them that they had lied to the Holy Spirit (Acts 5:3). We do not lie to inanimate things. I cannot lie to a radar beam. A spoken matter becomes a lie when someone has heard and received a false message.

The Holy Spirit can also be grieved (Ephesians 4:30). I may express my displeasure concerning a building when I do not appreciate the architecture. But I do not grieve the building. I grieve the person of the Holy Spirit when I sin by speaking unkind and uncharitable words (v. 29). God has graciously provided His Holy Spirit to direct the spiritual path of people. It behooves us to respond to the promptings of the Holy Spirit.

LESSON: *The Holy Spirit is a person, seen in that He can be blasphemed, resisted, lied to, and grieved.*

THE SIN AGAINST THE HOLY SPIRIT

Whoever shall speak against the Holy Spirit,
it shall not be forgiven him, either in this age,
or in the age to come. (Matthew 12:32)

A pastor was preaching on the sin against the Holy Spirit, warning the people not to commit it, but he did not explain what it was. It caused great anxiety in the congregation as they asked each other, "Have I committed the sin against the Holy Spirit?"

What is the sin against the Spirit? Can it be committed today? Jesus made this statement after revealing His messianic credentials through His words and works. After He taught the Sermon on the Mount (Matthew 5-7), the people recognized that He had an authority greater than the religious leaders (7:28-29). Then His miracles followed. He healed the lepers, the sick, the blind; He stilled the storm; He cast out demons. All those miracles proved Messiah was in their midst (Isaiah 35:5-6). But as the leaders investigated, they concluded, "This man casts out demons only by Beelzebul, the ruler of demons" (Matthew 12:24). They were acknowledging that Jesus performed miracles but that He did it by the power of Satan.

Mark explains that blasphemy against the Holy Spirit is unforgivable "because they were saying, 'He has an unclean spirit'" (3:30). God said, "Behold, My Servant whom I have chosen, My Beloved in whom My soul is well pleased, I will put My Spirit upon Him" (Matthew 12:18). But the religious leaders said that one who taught and performed miracles by the power of the Holy Spirit did His miracles by the power of Satan! That is the blasphemy. That is the sin against the Spirit. It was both a personal and a national sin. With that statement Israel rejected her Messiah and was destined to suffer great calamity for it (Matthew 23:37-39).

To commit the sin against the Holy Spirit today would demand the physical presence of Jesus, performing His miracles and being rejected by His onlookers. The sin is not the same as unbelief. It is a sin that can never be forgiven. Many people who initially reject the gospel later come to faith in Christ. That would not be possible were unbelief the sin against the Spirit. But we do have a spiritual lesson here. As Carl Laney said, "The decision we make today will determine our spiritual life tomorrow."

LESSON: *The sin against the Holy Spirit was a first-century sin in which the leaders attributed Christ's miracles to the power of Satan.*

THE HOLY SPIRIT
REGENERATES BELIEVERS

He saved us, not on the basis of deeds which we have done in righteousness, but according to His mercy, by the washing of regeneration and renewing by the Holy Spirit. (Titus 3:5)

What mother has not held her newborn infant and gazed with amazement at the tiny miracle in her arms? Through her own body she has given life to a beautiful, new baby. For nine months she nurtured that life and through her own body sustained it. And yet the mother is not the one who actually gives life; she passes on the life that is given to her. God is the originator of all life.

Just as a child is born physically and must receive physical life from its mother, so a person must be born spiritually in order to inherit the kingdom of heaven. The spiritual new birth is effected by the Holy Spirit. Simultaneous to someone believing the gospel of Christ, the Holy Spirit infuses eternal life to him, effecting the new birth. In this verse Paul explains it as "the washing of regeneration."

Regeneration means a new birth. The same word is used to describe the rebirth of the world after Noah's Flood. Jesus used the same word to describe the new birth of the world in Messiah's future kingdom when He restores the world to its condition before Adam fell (Matthew 19:28). The Holy Spirit causes the believer to be born again by imparting new life. Jesus spoke of this when He told Nicodemus, "Unless one is born of water and the Spirit, he cannot enter into the kingdom of God" (John 3:5). The new birth is pictured as a washing, not water baptism, but a washing produced by the Word of God (Ephesians 5:26).

As we struggle with the old nature, what a privilege to have a renewed nature, to be "new creations" in Jesus Christ (2 Corinthians 5:17). Through regeneration God has given us new life to live for Him now. We receive a new mind that we may think new thoughts, we have a new heart that we may love God fully, and we have a new will that we may obey Him implicitly. Through regeneration we are assured of eternal life with God forever.

LESSON: *The Holy Spirit imparts new life to the one believing the gospel.*

THE HOLY SPIRIT
INDWELLS BELIEVERS

And I will ask the Father, and He will give you another
Helper, that He may be with you forever. (John 14:16)

T hanksgiving and Christmas are special holidays when people like to be at home. Statistics tell us that on those holidays 97 percent of Americans head home. We like to be with loved ones—parents, brothers, sisters, children.

Although Jesus was leaving His disciples, He promised to send them a substitute like Himself—"another Helper" who would come to live at home in them forever (John 14:16). That promise anticipated the Holy Spirit's coming at Pentecost. Moreover, Jesus taught them that the Holy Spirit would begin a new ministry upon His coming. Jesus said, "He abides with you, and will be in you" (v. 17). The Holy Spirit had a particular ministry in the Old Testament but would have a greater ministry in the New. Prior to Pentecost the Holy Spirit was "with them" ("alongside them"), but after Pentecost He would dwell "in them."

This was not a promise to the "elite Twelve" but to every believer. Without exception, every child of God is permanently indwelt by God's Holy Spirit. Jesus promised that all believers would receive the Holy Spirit (John 7:37). Paul also reminded the legalistic Galatians that they had "begun by the Spirit"—they had all received the Holy Spirit at salvation (Galatians 3:3). Even the carnal Corinthians were reminded, "Do you not know that your body is a temple of the Holy Spirit who is in you?" (1 Corinthians 6:19). Despite their carnality, the Corinthians were indwelt by the Holy Spirit.

In John 14:17 Jesus promises the disciples that after Pentecost the Holy Spirit would come to permanently make His home within them. No longer need they grieve because Jesus had left them for heaven. One like Jesus would settle down and make His home in their hearts. Surely that was great consolation for the sorrowing disciples. No longer would they be alone. God the Holy Spirit would permanently "abide in them"—at home in their hearts.

LESSON: *Since Pentecost, all believers are permanently indwelt by the Holy Spirit.*

ARE ALL BELIEVERS INDWELT WITH THE SPIRIT?

*Having also believed, you were sealed in Him with
the Holy Spirit of promise. (Ephesians 1:13)*

It is important that we learn to take God at His Word. When He says something we can—we must!—believe it. Although numerous Scripture references teach that the Holy Spirit indwells all believers at the moment of salvation, some still doubt this truth. They struggle and agonize, seeking some second experience although God has already done for them what they so desperately seek.

Ephesians 1:13 teaches that the moment we believe in Christ He sends His Holy Spirit to indwell and seal us as His own. The grammar of this verse indicates that the believing and the sealing occur simultaneously. The sealing does not follow believing but occurs at the very same moment.

A little later, Paul instructs believers to avoid unwholesome language, stealing, lying, and anger. Yet when a Christian does sin, the Spirit does not leave him; rather, Paul tells us, "Do not grieve the Holy Spirit of God" (4:30). The Spirit is grieved when we sin, but He does not leave us.

An even more dramatic lesson is painted by Paul when he instructs the Corinthians about morality. Corinth was a city that boasted one thousand temple prostitutes, who committed immorality in the name of religion. That was the Corinthian believers' background. Paul warns them not to participate with prostitutes any more (1 Corinthians 6:15). He tells them why: "Your body is a temple of the Holy Spirit who is in you" (v. 19). The same Corinthians who had committed incest and initiated lawsuits against each other—those carnal believers were indwelt by the Holy Spirit. Putting it another way, Paul wrote the Romans, "If anyone does not have the Spirit of Christ, he does not belong to Him" (Romans 8:9). That's clear. Anyone who doesn't have the Holy Spirit isn't a Christian, so the corollary would be that anyone who is a Christian is indwelt by the Holy Spirit.

You may not feel anything, but that doesn't change the fact: if you have believed in Christ you are indwelt by the Holy Spirit. Believe God's Word, and rest in the truth.

LESSON: *All believers are indwelt by the Holy Spirit.*

GRIEVING
THE HOLY SPIRIT

Do not grieve the Holy Spirit of God, by whom you
were sealed for the day of redemption. (Ephesians 4:30)

A young widow with one son came to America after World War II, full of hope for herself and her son. But her son fell in with bad company and eventually was jailed for breaking the law. His widowed mother paid his fine, only to experience further sorrow when he was jailed again. That son deeply grieved his mother.

Believers grieve the Holy Spirit when they sin. How? We grieve the Holy Spirit when we engage in unwholesome talk (Ephesians 4:29). Paul admonishes us, "Let no unwholesome word proceed from your mouth." When we reach into the refrigerator for an apple and pick up a rotten one, we quickly toss it into the garbage. We wouldn't think of putting rotten fruit in our mouth. Yet we are willing to put rotten words into our mouths—gossip, criticism, harshness, profanity—and all of it grieves the Holy Spirit.

We also grieve the Holy Spirit when we tell lies about other believers (v. 25) or become angry, allowing our anger to simmer for days (v. 26). Our anger should cool before the sun sets at the end of the day; otherwise, we give the devil a foothold. Harboring bitterness, anger, and malice toward others also grieves the Spirit (v. 31). Think of the damage we do to ourselves and to others when we harbor ill will. Although bitterness, anger, and malice are inward, they don't remain inside—they result in external sin such as wrath, clamor, and slander. Fellow believers are injured, and the Holy Spirit is grieved.

What is the solution? Speaking words that build up fellow Christians (v. 29). Have you ever noticed how many discouraged Christians there are—people who need a kindly, encouraging word to lift their spirits? We are to build up other believers according to their needs—but we must notice those needs! Also critical is our need to be kindhearted, forgiving others because Christ has forgiven us. Then believers will benefit, be built up, and the Holy Spirit will not be grieved.

LESSON: *The Holy Spirit is grieved when believers sin by unwholesome, critical talk and harboring an unkind, unforgiving spirit.*

SPIRIT BAPTISM:
UNION WITH CHRIST

*Do you not know that all of us who have been baptized into
Christ Jesus have been baptized into His death? (Romans 6:3)*

There are many inequities in life. Most people cannot afford the
fees to join an elitist country club; women may be restricted
from attending all-male educational institutions; some may lack
educational, ethnic, or other social requirements to join a club. But all
those are temporary, physical restrictions.

Spiritually, there are no divisive distinctions. All who have been saved
by grace are also baptized into Christ. There are no exceptions (Romans
6:3). All believers have been "united with Him" (v. 5). The imagery of the
word *united* is "grown together"—we are grafted into Christ as a limb is
grafted into a tree. What beautiful imagery depicts the close union and fellowship we now enjoy in Christ! The Holy Spirit has placed us into permanent union with Christ just as a tree surgeon grafts a branch into a tree.

Paul amplifies the blessing: because we have been baptized into Christ
we now "live with Him" (v. 8); we are "alive . . . in Christ Jesus" (v. 11). By
being baptized into Christ we are identified with Him in His death and resurrection. The implication is that sin need not rule as dictator over us any
longer; we have been released from sin's power (though that does not mean
we are sinless); we may now live in the realm of our union with Christ.
Paul's statement thunders with emphasis: "You are alive—living in Christ!"
That is our new state in Christ.

Jesus anticipated this glorious event in John 14:20: "In that day you
shall know that I am in My Father, and you in Me, and I in you." Child of
God, do you recognize your wondrous position in Christ? The Holy Spirit
has placed you into union with Him—you have the closest connection possible with Christ. You belong to Him, and He belongs to you. There are no
dues to pay, and you have higher privileges than the most elite country club.
Rejoice in your inalterable position in Christ.

LESSON: *The baptizing work of the Holy Spirit places believers into
union with Christ.*

Spirit Baptism:
Union with One Another

*By one Spirit we were all baptized into one body, whether
Jews or Greeks, whether slaves or free, and we were all
made to drink of one Spirit. (1 Corinthians 12:13)*

What is the first thing that comes to your mind when you hear the word *baptism*? Probably water. Most people identify baptism with water, and that is not entirely wrong. There are times, however, when *baptism* does not mean water; it means Spirit baptism.

Spirit baptism. What does it mean? Surely it is a strange term. Baptism by the Spirit is a ministry that occurs only in the church age. In Acts 1:5 Jesus tells the apostles, "You shall be baptized with the Holy Spirit not many days from now," indicating that it had not occurred previously and that it would begin shortly afterward, specifically at Pentecost (Acts 2). All believers in the church age are included in this spiritual transaction. There are no national priorities—Gentiles are included as well as Jews (1 Corinthians 12:13). Nor are there economic or social distinctions; slaves are included with free people. In Galatians 3:27-28 Paul expands his comments. There is no gender distinction in the baptism by the Spirit—women as well as men are included.

"You are all one in Christ Jesus," says Paul. On a similar note Paul repeats: "There is one body and one Spirit, just as also you were called in one hope of your calling; one Lord, one faith, one baptism" (Ephesians 4:4-5). The Body of Christ is not divided; there is only one body of believers into which all believers are baptized.

Also, the fact that there is no command for one to be baptized indicates the baptism by the Spirit is not something to be sought. It happens automatically at the moment of conversion.

What is the significance of the baptism by the Spirit? One important blessing is our union with one another. Most of us have sensed this experientially in a church fellowship. We interact with other believers who may be of different economic strata, color, nationality, or gender—yet we are all one in Christ. Physically, we may have great distinctions, but spiritually we are the same. We are united to one another.

LESSON: *The baptizing work of the Holy Spirit places believers into union with one another.*

FILLING OF THE
HOLY SPIRIT DEFINED

*And do not get drunk with wine, for that is dissipation,
but be filled with the Spirit. (Ephesians 5:18)*

While I was serving on the pastoral staff in an inner city church, destitute people frequently approached the church for help. On one occasion a man lay prostrate at the church entrance, his knuckles bloodied from constant falling on the sidewalk in his drunken state. We took him into the church, bathed and bandaged his hands, and fed him. Then he and I began our unusual walk to his home nearby. Since he was unable to walk on his own I firmly grasped him by the arm to support him. Two steps forward, one step backward! We even struggled to locate his keys before I was able to deposit him in his home.

What was that man's problem? Control. He was entirely controlled—but by the wrong thing. His body and mind were controlled by alcohol. Paul uses a similar example as a negative illustration of the Holy Spirit's filling in this verse. Believers are warned not to be controlled by alcohol but rather by the Holy Spirit.

Whereas believers are never commanded to be indwelt, baptized, or sealed by the Spirit (those all occur simultaneously at conversion), they are commanded to be filled by the Spirit, suggesting there are conditions involved in the Spirit's filling.

The command to "be filled" is emphatic. Unlike the other ministries of the Holy Spirit, filling is not only conditional; it is repeated. The present tense reinforces that it is something to be done over and over: "Be continually being filled with the Spirit." Another interesting feature about this verse is that it is passive: "Let yourselves be constantly being filled with the Spirit." What is the significance of that? It means the filling is not something we can do ourselves—God must do it. He is the One who fills us with His Spirit.

God has made enormous provisions for us by enabling us to be filled with the Holy Spirit, thus allowing us to live to please to Him. God has provided everything necessary for our spiritual maturity and service. Are you appropriating what God has provided for you?

LESSON: *The filling of the Spirit is conditional and repeated, enabling the believer to be controlled by the Holy Spirit.*

FILLING OF THE
HOLY SPIRIT DISPLAYED

Walk by the Spirit, and you will not carry out
the desire of the flesh. (Galatians 5:16)

Several conditions must be met if the believer is to be filled with the Holy Spirit. Paul exhorts, "Do not quench the Spirit" (1 Thessalonians 5:19). How do we quench the Spirit? Since the filling of the Holy Spirit has to do with ministry, to quench the Spirit is to pour cold water on the fire of the Spirit's active ministry. In the context, some Christians in the Thessalonian assembly were disparaging the revelation given to the church (v. 20). By application, we quench the Spirit when we belittle the teachings given to the church. The Spirit ministers through the instruction of the Scriptures; we can hinder that ministry by ignoring or speaking against the faithful teaching of the Word in the church.

A second exhortation related to the Spirit's filling is "Do not grieve the Holy Spirit of God" (Ephesians 4:30). The context makes this quite clear. Paul warns believers not to allow their anger to smolder (v. 26); he admonishes them not to steal but rather to work (v. 28) and to speak edifying rather than rotten words (v. 29).

How then do we grieve the Holy Spirit? By sinning. The Holy Spirit is grieved when Christians sin. He cannot fill and thereby control the life of the Christian when foul words proceed out of the believer's mouth and inconsistent conduct issues from his or her life.

The third instructive word is positive: "Walk by the Spirit" (Galatians 5:16). "Walk" is a metaphor, meaning "conduct your life." The thought is: be continually conducting your life in the sphere and power of the Holy Spirit. It means that we live our lives under the Spirit's control rather than the control of the old nature. We are to walk under the Spirit's dependence and power.

Who controls my life? My old nature? My sharp tongue? My impulse to "get even"? Or the indwelling Holy Spirit? Only if the latter is true, can I be filled with the Spirit.

LESSON: *We can be filled with the Spirit when we do not quench or grieve Him and when we walk under His control.*

THE HOLY SPIRIT
INTERCEDES FOR BELIEVERS

*The Spirit also helps our weaknesses; for we do not know
how to pray as we should, but the Spirit Himself intercedes
for us with groanings too deep for words. (Romans 8:26)*

Alan Johnson writes, "When one of our preschoolers desires to write to Granny, my wife gives her a sheet of paper and a pencil, and she expresses her feelings in lines, circles, and zigzag marks. They are truly unintelligible signs. When Mother gets the paper back, she adds certain intelligible words to appropriate marks on the paper such as, 'Hello, Granny' with an arrow to the first few scribblings, 'We miss you' connected to other marks, and finally 'Come visit us soon. I love you, Lynn.' Mother truly has interceded for Lynn to Granny, even as the Spirit intercedes for us to the Father" (*Romans, Volume 2*).

Most of us would acknowledge that there are many times when, through frustration or anxiety, we are unable to pray correctly. We can't frame the right words; our emotions run ahead of our comprehension. At such times the Holy Spirit rescues us from our inadequacies and lifts our prayers to heaven. The Holy Spirit pleads our case before the Father, and the Father responds. The Holy Spirit helps us by sharing our burden; He comes to our aid in the weakness of our fallen nature—be it physical, emotional, or spiritual.

In our inability to articulate our requests, the Holy Spirit unites with our spirit and pleads our cause "with groanings too deep for words" (Romans 8:26). That means the Holy Spirit communes so closely with the child of God that He unites with our regenerate spirit and, amid our groanings, carries them to the Father and clarifies them. Our prayers are imperfect, but the Spirit's prayers are perfect. He intercedes for us "according to the will of God" (v. 27). We make foolish requests, but the Spirit makes wise ones.

The beautiful conclusion to the Holy Spirit's intercession is the statement of Romans 8:28. The Father responds to the Spirit's importunate prayer on our behalf by making all things work together for our good. What peace we should enjoy knowing this blessed truth!

LESSON: *The Holy Spirit intercedes for believers according to God's will, and God responds by making all things work together for our good.*

THE HOLY SPIRIT
INSPIRED SCRIPTURE

No prophecy was ever made by an act of human will,
but men moved by the Holy Spirit spoke from God. (2 Peter 1:21)

One of the modern miracles is the jet airplane. A person can board a plane in Los Angeles and eleven hours later be walking the streets of Copenhagen. How is that possible? A man cannot do it himself. He is carried to his destination by a power greater than himself. He boards the plane and is carried along by a power not his own to the desired destination.

Similarly, in the writing of Scripture, the ancient writers were the ones who took up the pen and parchment and wrote down the sacred writings; yet it was a writing not entirely their own. They were carried along supernaturally to the desired destination. Peter mentions that the Scriptures were not the result of a human decision. Paul did not take up the pen one day, saying, "Let's see. I think I'll write some Scripture today!" Peter is emphatic that the Scriptures resulted because the Holy Spirit supernaturally carried the men along while they wrote. Peter attributes the origin of Scripture to the Holy Spirit. Human writers were involved, but as they wrote, they were supernaturally carried along by the Holy Spirit. Just as an aircraft carries the passenger to the destination appointed by the pilot, so the Holy Spirit superintended their writing so that it was without defect or error. The Holy Spirit determined the spiritual destination of the writings.

There is an important analogy between the birth of Christ and the writing of Scripture. Just as the Holy Spirit effected Mary's conception, ensuring the sinless human nature of Christ, so He superintended the writers of Scripture, ensuring the Scriptures would be without error.

The Holy Spirit's ministry in guiding the writers of Scripture was important since it assured the accuracy and inerrancy of God's Word. The Bible we read is not the result of human speculation, nor is it filled with error. Because the Holy Spirit guided the writers, we can have confidence in the trustworthiness and complete accuracy of the Scriptures.

LESSON: *The Holy Spirit guided the writers of Scripture, ensuring the complete accuracy of the Scriptures.*

THE HOLY SPIRIT
CAUSED THE VIRGIN BIRTH

*The Holy Spirit will come upon you, and the power of
the Most High will overshadow you; and for that reason
the holy offspring shall be called the Son of God. (Luke 1:35)*

The Messiah had to be of human (Davidic) lineage to qualify as
Messiah, yet He also had to be sinless—a seemingly impossible
requirement. How was that dilemma solved? Through the virgin
birth.

While a graduate student at the University of Pennsylvania, Donald G.
Barnhouse presented a masterful argument for the necessity of the virgin
birth. He argued that since the Holy Spirit begat Christ's humanity in Mary's
womb, He caused the humanity of Christ, and when Joseph adopted Jesus
as his own son, Jesus became heir to the throne of David since Joseph's
was the royal line.

The angel explained that Mary's conception was due to the Holy Spirit:
"Joseph, son of David, do not be afraid to take Mary as your wife; for that
which has been conceived in her is of the Holy Spirit" (Matthew 1:20).

"Of" explains the origin of Christ's birth; Joseph had no part in it. The
Holy Spirit was responsible for Jesus' conception. Matthew makes the same
point: "When His mother Mary had been betrothed to Joseph, before they
came together she was found to be with child by the Holy Spirit" (1:18).
Matthew is careful to explain the conception was prior to Mary and Joseph's
living together as husband and wife.

What is the significance of the virgin birth? First, it produced the humanity of Christ. Whereas the Holy Spirit caused Mary's conception, the
Child was born of a human mother, bringing Christ's humanity into existence. As God, Christ has existed for all eternity, but at Bethlehem He took
on humanity (without laying aside His deity).

The Holy Spirit's ministry also effected the sinless humanity of Christ.
Had Jesus been born of Joseph and Mary He would have been stained with
the sin nature—and unable to redeem anyone. Through the Holy Spirit's
ministry in Christ's birth, we have a Savior who is truly human, and thus
able to represent us, yet since He is without the sin nature He is also able to
redeem us. O, the depth of the wisdom and knowledge of God! His ways are
unfathomable!

LESSON: *The Holy Spirit enabled Mary to conceive, producing the sinless humanity of Christ.*

June 9

THE HOLY SPIRIT
ANOINTED CHRIST

The Spirit of the Lord is upon Me, because He
anointed Me to preach the gospel to the poor. (Luke 4:18)

In 1953 Queen Elizabeth was crowned Queen of England and the British Commonwealth, successor to her deceased father, King George VI. The public coronation was a visible reminder that she was the legally appointed heir to the British throne. Similarly, John the Baptist introduced Jesus of Nazareth to the nation as Messiah, the rightful heir to the throne of David. Just as the Old Testament kings and priests were publicly anointed and inaugurated into office, so Christ, at His baptism, was publicly recognized as Israel's Messiah and King. Through His anointing by the Spirit and His baptism, Jesus was "manifested to Israel" (John 1:31).

But how did the nation know Jesus was the Messiah? Isaiah predicted the glorious messianic age, announcing that Messiah would be recognized because the Spirit of the Lord God would be upon Him (Isaiah 61:1). In the Holy Spirit's power the Messiah would preach the good news, bringing comfort to the brokenhearted and liberty to the captives. At Jesus' baptism, the heavens parted, and the Holy Spirit descended in the form of a dove, lighting upon Jesus (Matthew 3:16). The Holy Spirit anointed Christ with power, and He went forth, ministering in the Spirit's power.

Immediately after His anointing "Jesus was going about in all Galilee, teaching in their synagogues, and proclaiming the gospel of the kingdom, and healing every kind of disease and every kind of sickness among the people (4:23). The anointing inaugurated Jesus into His public ministry, and the people had the witness in His miracles, performed through the power of the Holy Spirit. (As God, Jesus had power in Himself to perform miracles, cf. John 10:18.)

But there was a final witness. As the Spirit descended on Christ, the Father authenticated the event with His words, "This is My beloved Son, in whom I am well pleased" (3:17). Because the Holy Spirit authenticated the ministry of Christ, there is no excuse to reject Christ. The Spirit bears witness to the impeccable life and ministry of Christ. Have you acknowledged it? Do you belong to Him?

LESSON: *At Jesus' baptism, the Holy Spirit anointed Christ, inducting Him to His office and empowering Him for public ministry.*

June 10

THE HOLY SPIRIT
GIVES SPIRITUAL GIFTS

One and the same Spirit works all these things, distributing to each one individually just as He wills. (1 Corinthians 12:11)

Christmas was an enchanting time when I was a child. My father loved to give gifts, and he would purchase additional gifts even when he had already finished his shopping. He would usually buy us things we had asked for—toboggan, sled, games—but he also gave us gifts that we had not anticipated, which also delighted us.

The Holy Spirit has sovereignly and supernaturally given spiritual gifts to all believers. He gave them to us "just as He wills"; it was not our decision. The Holy Spirit recognized which spiritual gifts we needed and gave them to us accordingly. They may work in accord with our natural talents, but not necessarily. Many times the gifts are other than what we would have expected, and yet we rejoice in serving according to them.

We do not have to beg or pray to receive these gifts. They are "grace gifts"—given to us sovereignly out of His grace. For that reason Paul emphasizes "according to the grace given to us" (Romans 12:6). And for that reason there is a variety of gifts, and not all have the same gifts (1 Corinthians 12:4).

What is the purpose of the gifts? Although gifts are given to individuals, they are also given for the church. The purpose is to build maturity in the Body of Christ. Particularly important are the foundational gifts: apostle, prophet, evangelist, pastor-teacher, given to train other believers who will do the work of the ministry (Ephesians 4:11-12). Although the gifts of apostle and prophet were restricted to the apostolic church, the gifts of evangelist and pastor-teacher are given "to prepare God's people for works of service" (v. 12, NIV).

It is vital that we realize that the Holy Spirit has given each of us spiritual gifts that we are to use in helping the Body of Christ to mature and dwell in unity. Indifference, carelessness, and refusal to use our gifts renders the Body of Christ sick and ineffective. How are you using your gifts?

LESSON: *The Holy Spirit sovereignly gives each believer spiritual gifts at the moment of salvation.*

ALL BELIEVERS
HAVE SPIRITUAL GIFTS

To each one is given the manifestation of the
Spirit for the common good. (1 Corinthians 12:7)

Ann Landers's column contained the following story: "This is a story about four people named Everybody, Somebody, Anybody and Nobody. There was an important job to be done and Everybody was sure that Somebody would do it. Anybody could have done it, but Nobody did it. Somebody got angry about that, because it was Everybody's job. Everybody thought Anybody could do it, but Nobody realized that Everybody wouldn't do it. It ended up that Everybody blamed Somebody when Nobody did what Anybody could have."

Sound familiar? That anecdote has undoubtedly been heard in most churches. The Body of Christ does not function as it ought because many members are weak, sick, and crippled. For the body to function properly, all parts must be healthy and functioning.

Many Christians do not realize that they have been given spiritual gifts to help build up the Body of Christ. All believers, without exception, have been gifted and are important. Paul is emphatic in this statement: "To each one is given the manifestation of the Spirit" (1 Corinthians 12:7). Every believer has been given spiritual gifts for the benefit of all believers.

Which is the most important member of the human body? The eye? ear? nose? tongue? arm? leg? Which body part would you give up? Probably none willingly. All members are important for the body to be healthy. If a person is blind or deaf or a paraplegic, the body does not function as it ought. That is the message of 1 Corinthians 12:7. God has gifted every believer for the benefit of all. For the church to function properly it is important that every believer exercise the gifts that he or she has been given. Only then will the Body be whole and healthy.

Which spiritual gifts have you been given? How are you using them? Is the Body of Christ more healthy because of your ministry?

LESSON: *All believers have been given spiritual gifts for the maturing of the entire Body of Christ.*

June 12

THE GIFT
OF APOSTLE

And He gave some as apostles. (Ephesians 4:11)

In 1793 the British shoemaker William Carey sailed for India, paving the way for modern missions. His motto was "Expect great things from God; attempt great things for God," and he implemented that philosophy by translating the Scriptures into several Indian languages. William Carey left the British Isles for India as a "sent one."

The word *apostle* means "sent one," and it may be used in a general or particular sense. In the latter, it is restricted to the twelve, since only they were qualified to be apostles. They held the office of apostle, meaning they had followed Christ from the time of John's baptism until Christ's ascension (Acts 1:21-22). Christ specially chose the twelve from His disciples and named them His apostles (Luke 9:1). They received special authority as apostles, enabling them to perform miracles, verifying their message that the King was coming (Matthew 10:1-8). Apart from the twelve only Paul held that position (2 Corinthians 12:12).

In addition to the office of apostle there is also the gift of apostle (Ephesians 4:11). The apostles themselves held both the office and the gift and in that sense formed the foundation of the church (Ephesians 2:20). A few others, such as Barnabas, held the gift (Acts 14:14). Since the foundation is laid but once there was no further need for the gift after the apostolic age.

In a general, nontechnical sense, an apostle is "one sent" as a modern missionary. Paul called Epaphroditus, whom he had sent to Philippi, an apostle (Philippians 2:25). Paul also talked about his brethren: "They are messengers [apostles] of the churches" (2 Corinthians 8:23). In that sense, every Christian is an "apostle." We commission missionaries by laying hands on them, identifying with them and their ministry when they go out to proclaim the gospel. In that sense, "apostles," or missionaries, are important in building the church, the Body of Christ.

LESSON: *Although the office of apostle may be limited to the apostolic age, all believers are "sent ones," commissioned by Christ to spread the gospel.*

THE GIFT
OF GIVING

He who gives [let him give] with liberality. (Romans 12:8)

A Bible college president was courting a Christian millionaire who had previously given a million dollars to a secular university, soliciting him to make a substantial donation to the college. The college president outlined the college's ministry and its pressing financial needs. Finally, the president asked, "Can I count on you to support the Bible college?"

"Yes," said the millionaire.

"How much can I put you down for?" asked the president.

"Fifteen dollars a month," responded the millionaire. You might say that Christian millionaire did not have the gift of giving.

The one with the gift of giving demonstrates it by giving with liberality. Actually, the exhortation is to give with sincerity or simplicity, without secondary motives. Giving must not be done to gain public recognition or acclaim. For example, after a Christian man had died it was discovered that he had anonymously helped needy widows in town. He had paid for winter fuel and ordered the coal dealer to send a load of coal to the widows. He also sent them sacks of flour and sugar. That man was exercising the gift of giving with sincerity and anonymity. He did not seek public recognition.

The churches in Macedonia gave with joyful liberality—even beyond their ability. They also gave without compulsion; it was voluntary. But the key to the Macedonians' giving was that they had first given themselves to the Lord (2 Corinthians 8:2-8).

One mistake many make is thinking that we must be rich before we can give. But the Macedonians gave liberally out of their poverty (v. 2). They gladly shared their material goods with Paul in his ministry (Philippians 4:10-16).

Although not all believers have the gift of giving, all are to give. How are you serving the Lord in your giving? How are you specifically ministering to the needs of other believers?

LESSON: *Those with the gift of giving should give with liberality and sincerity, not seeking public recognition.*

THE GIFT
OF SERVING

Let each exercise them accordingly . . .
if service, in his serving. (Romans 12:6-7)

W hen Mother Teresa was asked, "You feel you have no special qualities?" she answered, "I don't think so. I don't claim anything of the work. It is his work. I am like a little pencil in his hand. That is all. He does the thinking. He does the writing. The pencil has nothing to do with it. The pencil has only to be allowed to be used" (*Time*, December 4, 1989, p. 11).

The gift of serving is general helpfulness to others. We get our word *deacon* from this word, and it means service to others, particularly those in physical need. This gift is likely the same as the one called "helps" in 1 Corinthians 12:28. The same thought is also reflected in Paul's exhortation "You must help the weak" (Acts 20:35).

There are examples of this gift in Scripture. It is used of "serving tables" in Acts 6:2; hence, a mother could consider her work of preparing meals for her family a spiritual ministry. The people of Antioch ministered to the starving saints in Jerusalem by contributing financially (Acts 11:29). Christians who help other needy believers financially are involved in a spiritual ministry. When Paul was in prison, Onesimus and Onesiphorus ministered to him, perhaps bringing him food and clothing (Philemon 13; 2 Timothy 1:16-18). Phoebe was a servant of the church and a "helper of many" (Romans 16:1-2). And Peter exhorts us to serve one another, relating it to hospitality (1 Peter 4:9-11). When we help those who are persecuted or suffering we are involved in a spiritual work.

All Christians are to serve one another, even if they don't have the gift. How can you exercise the gift of service? When I was a college student my boss came to me and said, "Remember what the Lord said, 'The Son of Man did not come to be served, but to serve'? Here's a broom. Sweep the floor!" The Lord Jesus is our example and supreme model in serving others.

Let's look for opportunities to serve others. Are there lonely widows who should be visited or invited to dinner? Are there errands to run for older people, sick people to be visited, someone I can help who is in financial need? Could I mow the lawn or shovel the walk for a senior citizen? Let's be the "pencil in the hand of God," allowing God to use us to serve others.

LESSON: *The gift of service is a general ministry of helpfulness to others in an unobtrusive way.*

THE GIFT
OF PROPHET

And He gave some as prophets. (Ephesians 4:11)

The economic and political events of the world seem to change as regularly as the weather. Who could have prophesied that Poland, Hungary, Czechoslovakia, and other former Communist countries would become democratic? And who would have foretold Iraq's invasion of Kuwait and America's subsequent declaration of war?

The New Testament prophet was similar to the Old Testament prophet in that he received revelation directly from God and spoke it forth to the people. The signs of a genuine prophet were distinguishable in that he always spoke in accordance with the Bible (his prophecy never contradicted the Scriptures), and his prophecies *always* came true—they weren't just 50 or 75 or even 90 percent accurate. For example, Agabus foretold a great famine (Acts 11:28) and Paul's capture in Jerusalem (21:10-11).

The prophet understood all mysteries and knowledge (1 Corinthians 13:2), which were unattainable through human reason because he received them directly from the Lord. He was important in maintaining doctrinal purity in the church before the Scriptures were completed.

Prophecy was a foundational gift for the church (Ephesians 2:20) that was important for spiritual edification (1 Corinthians 14:3). However, as the foundation of a building is laid but once, so the gift was given only at that time. With the completion of the New Testament Scriptures the gift of prophecy terminated. No new revelation is being given today. The revelation recorded in the sixty-six books represents the completion of God's recorded revelation.

Our need is not for more revelation. Our need is to respond to the revelation that has already been given. Whatever our need is for spiritual direction, comfort, encouragement, and exhortation, it is not for new revelation. We need to respond in faith and obedience to the completed revelation that has been given.

LESSON: *The gift of prophecy was a temporary gift (until the completion of the Scriptures), providing direct revelation from God to man through the prophet.*

THE GIFT
OF EVANGELIST

And He gave some ... as evangelists. (Ephesians 4:11)

A seven-year-old Christian girl wanted to witness for Christ. She asked her friend, "Do you know how to swim?" Her friend answered, "No."

"Well, you better learn because there are going to be one thousand years of rain."

Although Christians generally acknowledge the biblical injunction to witness, many are fearful and do not know how to do it. A foundational gift that the Holy Spirit has sovereignly given to the church is the gift of evangelism. Whereas all Christians are to evangelize, some have been given this spiritual gift.

What is the gift of evangelism? One who is so gifted has an unusual burden or passion to see lost people come to faith in Christ. The evangelist also has a clear understanding of the gospel. He does not enshroud it with excess baggage. He can give a clear, simple, accurate presentation, and he actively proclaims it. The gospel is more than a theory to him—it is a passion, and he regularly presents it to unbelievers at opportune moments. Peter is an example of evangelist in the book of Acts (2:14-40; 3:12-26; 4:8-12, 19-21). The evangelist also has great joy in seeing men and women come to faith in Christ (McRae, *The Dynamics of Spiritual Gifts*, pp. 56-57).

It is the tragic truth that it takes one thousand laymen and six pastors an entire year to win one convert to faith in Christ (Flynn, *19 Gifts*, p. 61). Surely God has given more Christians the gift of evangelism than that statistic reveals. In fact, all Christians are exhorted to evangelize. Paul admonished Timothy, "Do the work of an evangelist" (2 Timothy 4:5). How are you fulfilling your responsibility in evangelism? Does your unsaved neighbor know the gospel? Has he or she heard it from you?

LESSON: *The gift of evangelism is reflected in the ability to explain the gospel clearly and simply and the willingness to do it.*

June 17

THE GIFT
OF PASTOR-TEACHER

And He gave some ... as pastors and teachers. (Ephesians 4:11)

I was called to serve as interim pastor in a church that had been destroyed by the previous pastor. During his tenure, attendance had dropped from two hundred to twenty. The people were discouraged and broken. The pastor had berated the people, chastising them if they were sick, telling them that sin in their lives was the cause of their sickness. It is unlikely that that man had the spiritual gift of pastor and teacher.

The gift of pastor and teacher is a foundational gift, given to the church to equip believers for the work of the ministry in order to produce maturity in the Body of Christ. The word *pastor* means "shepherd" and beautifully pictures the work of a pastor. The pastor is to his people what a shepherd is to his flock.

What is a shepherd, and what does he do? He guides the flock, providing nourishment for them; he nurses them to health when they are sick and wounded; he guards and protects them from wild animals and danger. A shepherd does not kick or beat his sheep. By analogy, the pastor must feed the people from the Scriptures, faithfully teaching them the truth of God's Word. When they are discouraged he is to encourage and comfort them. When they are assailed by false teaching he is to instruct them concerning the truth. A pastor is to exhort the people but not harangue them.

The phrase "pastor and teacher" really refers to one gift but identifies two functions. The leader is to function like a shepherd, guiding, guarding, and protecting the flock (Acts 20:28-30). He is also to minister as a teacher, instructing the people in sound doctrine. For that reason Paul exhorts Timothy, a young pastor, to faithfulness in teaching (1 Timothy 1:3, 5, 10; 4:6, 11; 5:17; 6:2, 17). The pastor must guard his preparation time in studying God's Word that he will be diligent in teaching the people.

Pastoral work today is complex, difficult, and discouraging. Encourage your pastor by submitting to his leadership and responding to his teaching.

LESSON: *The gift of pastor and teacher is a foundational gift emphasizing the ministry of shepherding and teaching the people to bring the church to maturity.*

June 18

THE GIFT
OF FAITH

To another [is given] faith by the
same Spirit. (1 Corinthians 12:9)

O ne one occasion Hudson Taylor was witnessing to a Chinese man as they walked along in the Chinese interior. The man had not responded, and Taylor finally remarked, "I do not know anyone in this area, and I have immediate need of food and lodging. Now you are going to see the reality of my God when you see how God will provide for me." They continued to talk, and toward evening they came to a river. A man on a boat called out to them, "Do you know a man named Hudson Taylor?"

"Yes, I am he," replied Hudson Taylor.

"I have heard of you," responded the man. "Do you need food and a place to sleep? If so, come and stay with me."

The faith of men such as Hudson Taylor and George Mueller is well known. But the gift of faith continues today as well. This gift is the ability to trust God in difficult circumstances and believe that He will resolve the difficulty. In 1966, Northwestern Schools in Minneapolis closed its doors. A man of faith, William B. Berntsen, was elected president and remained president during the years 1966-72, while the college had no students and offered no classes. In 1972 the college was resurrected, and President Berntsen's faith was vindicated. Even while the college was in remission for six long years he trusted God to do the impossible and raise it up again. Today Northwestern College has more than one thousand students.

All Christians have faith for salvation and must exercise faith to live the Christian life. We cannot please God without living by faith (Hebrews 11:6). But the gift of faith goes beyond faith for salvation and that daily-life faith. One with the gift of faith "has the capacity to see something that needs to be done and to believe God will do it through him even though it looks impossible" (McRae, *The Dynamics of Spiritual Gifts*, p. 66). The history of mission organizations, Bible colleges, and Christian institutions is rooted in leaders who believed God for the impossible. And God did the impossible through them.

God wants all of us to live by faith because that is pleasing to Him. What needs do you have for which you should totally trust God?

LESSON: *The gift of faith is seeing a need and believing God to do great things.*

THE GIFT
OF EXHORTATION

Let each exercise them accordingly...
he who exhorts, in his exhortation. (Romans 12:6, 8)

A number of years ago when Billy Graham addressed a pastors' luncheon he exhorted the gathering of hundreds, "Pastors, encourage your people. Our churches are filled with discouraged people. Don't beat them. Encourage them. They need it."

That was sound, biblical advice. Our world is complex, filled with problems that promote anxieties the likes of which the world has never seen. The problems of today were unknown and unforeseen thirty years ago. Christians need encouragement and guidance as perhaps never before.

Exhortation means "one called alongside to help." Again, the imagery is taken from the oriental world, where someone would carry a burden with a wooden yoke across the neck and perhaps pails of water, grain, or produce suspended from each side of the yoke. A friend would come alongside, get under the yoke, and help the person carry his weighty burden. He was "one called alongside to help."

This gift has two emphases. One is that of "comforting, encouraging, and cheering up" another person. God cheers our hearts when we suffer affliction so that we in turn may cheer others (2 Corinthians 1:4). He may comfort us by bringing other Christians to cheer our hearts (7:6). That, in fact, is an important feature to remember—God uses people to encourage other people (1 Thessalonians 3:2).

Another emphasis of the gift of exhortation is to admonish or appeal to fellow believers to pursue a certain course of conduct. Performed in a spirit of love and gentleness, this aspect is vital in helping Christians pursue the right road. In this sense Paul and Barnabas exhorted the new Christians in Asia Minor to continue in the faith (Acts 14:22). And in this sense Paul urged the Roman believers, "Present your bodies a living sacrifice. . . . Do not be conformed to this world" (Romans 12:1-2).

Ask yourself: "Who in my sphere of influence needs encouragement and exhortation?" Are you willing to put your arm around that person and encourage that needy one?

LESSON: *The gift of exhortation involves comforting believers and appealing to them to pursue a right course of conduct.*

THE GIFT
OF SHOWING MERCY

Let each exercise them accordingly . . .
he who shows mercy, with cheerfulness. (Romans 12:6, 8)

I have come to have new respect and admiration for those who work in nursing homes. When my mother entered a nursing home and I visited her in her new surroundings, I saw Christian nurses uniquely gifted in showing mercy, compassion, and love. They embraced the elderly patients, helping them to walk and eat. They comforted them when they needed comfort. And when my mother passed away I saw those same nurses weep. Truly, they had the gift of showing mercy.

Mercy means having pity and compassion for someone in distress. The gift is to be demonstrated "with cheerfulness." Mercy performed with a long face or sour disposition is difficult to interpret.

The word *mercy* is used almost exclusively of God and Christ. Hence, Christ is a model of mercy for us. The blind men sought and received mercy from Him when they regained their sight (Matthew 9:27-30); the Canaanite woman obtained mercy on behalf of her daughter (15:21-28); an epileptic son found mercy from Him (17:14-18); ten lepers were mercifully healed of their leprosy (Luke 17:11-14).

From those examples we learn the meaning of mercy. Showing mercy is having compassion on the less fortunate, the suffering, the sick, and the poor. It may mean bringing food to the needy in the slums, spending time with the mentally retarded, or visiting the sick in their home or hospital. Above all, it is done with cheerfulness.

Showing mercy is not a "limited" gift; all believers are to show mercy. It is the lifestyle of the mature believer who has received wisdom from God (James 3:17). The tragic truth is that we can be doctrinally correct (like the Pharisees) and yet fail miserably in ministering mercy to a fellow believer.

Jesus appeals to us to show mercy. Doing so is parallel to loving one's neighbor—the apex of love (Matthew 22:39). What opportunities do you have to show mercy? Neighbors in need? A depressed person in the office? A shut-in? Poor people who need help? What is your "mercy quotient"?

LESSON: *The gift of showing mercy is showing compassion and ministering to those in need.*

THE GIFT
OF ADMINISTRATION

Let each exercise them accordingly . . .
he who leads, with diligence. (Romans 12:6, 8)

Several years ago *Time* magazine ran an article lamenting, "Where are the leaders?" It is generally recognized that there is an absence of leadership today. That void was illustrated when Pope John Paul visited Philadelphia several years ago, and not only Catholics but Protestants lined the streets to cheer the Catholic ruler. When asked why he cheered a Catholic leader a Protestant replied, "Because he is a great leader." People long for leadership, and if they don't have it in their own sphere of belief they will look elsewhere for it.

Leadership is a gift. This gift may also be called administration or governing (1 Corinthians 12:28). The word *lead* means "to stand in front, to be at the head, to rule or preside." It describes those who "have charge over you" (1 Thessalonians 5:12). This gift also describes the leadership in the home: "One who manages his own household well" (1 Timothy 3:4-5, 12).

The gift of administration or leadership may be exercised in a variety of ways. It may be demonstrated by directing vacation Bible school, administrating a Christian day school, Bible institute, college, or church. One gifted in administration may also give direction and leadership on a host of committees and activities in the local church. The person with this gift is able to organize projects and ministries, taking responsibility and giving direction to the task. This gift should also be demonstrated by all Christian parents in the way they rule their children and home. What a need there is for the display of leadership!

It is our responsibility to honor those who provide leadership and administrative direction. Recognize them, assist them, honor them. Perhaps God has gifted you in administration. Are you utilizing your gift, or are you sitting on it?

LESSON: *The gift of administration is seen in one who is able to organize, take responsibility, and provide leadership in seeing a task to its completion.*

THE GIFT
OF MIRACLES

To another [is given] gifts of healing by the one Spirit,
and to another the effecting of miracles. (1 Corinthians 12:9-10)

I well recall Jerry, who sat near me in chapel during my seminary days. One day he developed a fever of 105 degrees. The doctors were puzzled. As they examined Jerry they could not determine what caused the fever. They packed him in ice and lowered the fever to 102 degrees, but when the ice was removed the fever shot up again. They had no answer. But the seminary students and faculty prayed. What the doctors were unable to resolve God could cure. Jerry became well and today serves the Lord as a pastor.

To those who were familiar with that incident, there was no doubt whatsoever that God miraculously healed Jerry. But was it a demonstration of the gift of healing? There is a distinction between God's healing someone directly and someone's having the gift of healing. Whereas God may still heal directly, the gift of healing was a temporary sign gift that terminated with the apostolic age and the completion of the Scriptures. The gift of healing was originally given to authenticate the message the apostles preached; with the completion of the Bible, that gift is no longer necessary.

A distinction is observed between the gift of healing and the gift of miracles. The gift of healing is curing illnesses (Acts 19:11-12), whereas the gift of miracles is broader, i.e., Peter's judging Ananias and Sapphira in death (5:9-11) or Paul's smiting Elymas with blindness (13:8-11). Healings by Christ and the apostles were unique. They were instantaneous (Mark 1:42), complete (Matthew 14:36), permanent (14:36), limited (constitutional diseases such as leprosy, not merely psychological illnesses, Mark 1:40), unconditional (including unbelievers who exercised no faith and didn't know who Jesus was, John 9:25), always successful (except where the disciples lacked faith, Matthew 17:20), and included raising the dead (John 11:44; Acts 9:40; McRae, *The Dynamics of Spiritual Gifts*, pp. 69-70).

It is not always God's will to heal (2 Corinthians 12:8-9; Philippians 2:26-27; 1 Timothy 5:23). It is not a lack of faith that prohibits healing; God may desire to glorify Himself through your illness. Trust God and His sovereign purpose in your life. His way is perfect—even in your suffering.

LESSON: *The gift of miracles was to authenticate the message of the apostles until the Scriptures were given.*

THE GIFT
OF TONGUES

*To another [was given] various kinds
of tongues. (1 Corinthians 12:10)*

Surely one of the most hotly debated biblical topics today is the
issue of speaking in tongues. Are they in operation today? Committed Christians stand on both sides of the argument, and both
claim to be right.

What are tongues? From Acts 2 we discover that biblical tongues are
known languages. The multitude that heard the apostles speaking in
tongues were astonished: "How is it that we each hear them in our own
language?" (Acts 2:8; cf. vv. 6, 11). Visitors from Europe, Asia, Africa, and
the islands were hearing the apostles speak in their own native languages.

What was the purpose of tongues? This gift was a sign to unbelieving
Jews that God was doing a work in their midst. When Jews heard the foreign
languages in the assemblies, it was a sign that God was at work just as He
had been in the days of Isaiah (Isaiah 28:11). Tongues were an evangelistic
tool for reaching unbelieving Jews who knew Isaiah 28:11; they were not for
Gentiles because they didn't know Isaiah's prophecy, and thus tongues
would be meaningless to them.

Many believe that since tongues were a sign gift given to verify the
apostles' message, the need for tongues ceased when the Bible was completed. Paul taught that tongues would "cease themselves" (1 Corinthians
13:8). Since the verb is in the middle voice it means that tongues would at
some point stop of themselves, prior to the return of Christ. The writer of
Hebrews also placed himself outside the age of miracles (including
tongues), reminding his readers that God bore witness with "them"—he did
not see the miracles or tongues (2:3-4).

Although tongues has sharply divided Christians, we need to remember that ultimately God wants us to be Christlike. Christ died to reproduce
Himself in us so that we would exhibit His likeness in a sin-stained world.
The world does not need to hear combative Christians; it needs to see
Christlike Christians who exhibit the fruit of the Spirit: love, joy, peace, patience, kindness, goodness, faithfulness, gentleness, and self-control. Does
the world hear you criticizing God, or does it see your kindness?

LESSON: *Tongues were known languages, spoken supernaturally as
an evangelistic tool to win Jews to faith in Christ.*

June 24

THE GIFT
OF TEACHING

*God has appointed in the church
... teachers. (1 Corinthians 12:28)*

A high school teacher was asked to teach the adult Sunday school class in his church. He consented, and as he taught the class over several months it became apparent that he was embarrassed and uncomfortable with his task. His teaching consisted of reading the lesson out of the denominational quarterly. When he lifted his eyes from the page he would glance at the ceiling, being careful not to make eye contact with his audience. There was no allowance for questions or discussion. Did that man have the gift of teaching? Probably not.

What is the gift of teaching? At the outset it should be mentioned that the gift of teaching is distinct from the gift of pastor-teacher. The one with the latter must be both a pastor and a teacher, but one with the gift of teaching need not have the gift of pastor.

The gift of teaching is an important, foundational gift. It is linked with apostles and prophets as a primary gift, laying the foundation of the church (1 Corinthians 12:28). The emphasis on "first . . . then" reinforces that these three are primary gifts; the ones following, although important, are secondary.

The teacher is one who diligently studies the Scriptures and related studies. Some pastors say, "I don't like to read," but it is impossible to fulfill the gift of teaching without study. One who has the gift of teacher or pastor-teacher is motivated to study. The apostle Paul, who certainly had this gift, asked for books while he was in a dungeon awaiting execution (2 Timothy 4:13).

The teacher is able to harmonize the Scriptures and clearly communicate them. He or she has the ability to unfold the profound truths of God's Word in a simple, precise manner that enables people to understand. "I see that!" will be their response.

The teacher not only communicates Bible doctrines (1 Timothy 1:3; 4:11, 13; 6:2) but applies the Scriptures as well (1:5; 6:17). Response to teaching is important. We need to be "Berean Christians," receiving the Word eagerly and examining it "to see whether these things were so" (Acts 17:11). Are you a Berean Christian?

LESSON: *The teacher diligently studies the Scriptures, teaching and applying them with clarity.*

June 25

DISCERNING
OF SPIRITS

*To another [is given] the distinguishing
of spirits. (1 Corinthians 12:10)*

The Mormon church teaches many doctrines contrary to historic Christianity. For example, Mormons believe in a plurality of gods. Mormons also believe that man may evolve into God over a process of time. They say, "As man is, God once was; as God is, man may become." In fact, Mormons believe that Adam has become God the Father even though he led the human race into sin. Brigham Young stated: "He [Adam] is our father and our God, and the only God with whom we have to do." Those are astonishing statements, and orthodox Christians categorically reject such teachings on the one basis of the Bible.

How did people judge false doctrine before they had the complete Bible? Through discerning of spirits. In the early church God spoke directly to prophets, who announced His revelation, but there were also imposters to whom God had not spoken and who gave false messages. How would people know who was a true prophet speaking true revelation from God? The gift of discerning of spirits was necessary to separate true revelation from the false.

John explains this gift: "Test the spirits to see whether they are from God; because many false prophets have gone out into the world" (1 John 4:1). The one possessing this gift was able to discern whether the person giving a revelation was speaking by the Holy Spirit or through evil spirits. It was necessary in the early church before the Scriptures (as our final authority) were completed.

The duration of discerning of spirits is tied to the duration of prophecy. If the gift of prophecy was temporary (and it appears it was), then the gift of discerning of spirits was also temporary.

However, all believers must "discern the spirits." There are many false messages heralded today in pulpits, literature, television, and radio. Who can determine what is true? All of us. We must use the Bible, our sole source of authority, to determine what is true or false. For that reason it is imperative that we search the Scriptures diligently "to see whether these things [are] so" (Acts 17:11).

LESSON: *Discerning of spirits is the ability to recognize whether a revelation someone gives is genuine or false.*

SALVATION IN
THE OLD TESTAMENT

I will give you a new heart.... And I will
put My Spirit within you. (Ezekiel 36:26-27)

How were people saved in the Old Testament? Were they born again? Was it different from the way people were saved in the New Testament age? Those questions have been discussed by many people on many occasions.

When Jesus explained the new birth to Nicodemus and he exclaimed, "How can a man be born when he is old?" (John 3:4), Jesus reminded him that as a teacher of Israel he ought to have known the answer: "Are you the teacher of Israel, and do not understand these things?" (v. 10). As a teacher of the law, Nicodemus ought to have understood the Holy Spirit's ministry in producing the new birth in the Old Testament. How should he have known that?

Ezekiel, the prophet who was taken into captivity in Babylon, explained to the people why the nation would be devastated by King Nebuchadnezzar. It was because of their stubbornness and refusal to live by the Lord's commandments. However, in Ezekiel 36:25-27 the prophet explains how the nation will come into future blessing and why they have not enjoyed those blessings previously. It was because of Israel's disobedience, and they had been disobedient because they were unregenerate. There is a day coming when they will be regenerated. They will no longer be rebellious and unrepentant because God will give them "a heart of flesh" (v. 26). Instead of rebellion, they will have "a new spirit" within them. In fact, God will put His Spirit within them, causing them to obey His injunctions (11:19; 36:27). But those were things they ought to have enjoyed and experienced in Ezekiel's day. Isaiah also promised spiritual blessing to the people through the Holy Spirit (Isaiah 44:3). Those who believed were regenerated by the Holy Spirit.

People were born again in the Old Testament just as they are in the New Testament. No one can get to heaven other than through belief in God, and the only way they can believe and receive eternal life is for the Holy Spirit to regenerate them. God is merciful in every age.

LESSON: *The Holy Spirit regenerated people in the Old Testament, effecting the new birth and giving them eternal life.*

THE HOLY SPIRIT
INDWELT OLD TESTAMENT BELIEVERS

Do not take Thy Holy Spirit from me. (Psalm 51:11)

D avid prayed this prayer after he had committed adultery, fearful that God would remove His Spirit from him. That reflects the Spirit's Old Testament ministry of selective and temporary indwelling. Although the Holy Spirit did indeed indwell believers in the Old Testament, it was for the purpose of ministry and it was temporary. The Holy Spirit came mightily upon Saul, changing his heart and enabling him to lead the Israelites as their king (1 Samuel 10:10), but He departed when Saul forsook the Lord (16:14).

The book of Judges is filled with examples of the Holy Spirit's indwelling selected leaders. When the king of Mesopotamia subjugated the Israelites, God raised up Othniel, "and the Spirit of the Lord came upon him" (Judges 3:10). Othniel led the Israelites to victory.

Even more fascinating is the story of fearful Gideon, who was hiding in a winepress from the Midianites. God took a timid, self-deprecating man, put His Spirit upon him (6:34), and Gideon led Israel to triumph over their oppressors.

The Holy Spirit not only indwelt mature believers, but He indwelt carnal believers, such as Samson, as well as people with unusual backgrounds, such as Jephthah. Several times the Scriptures say, "The Spirit came upon Samson mightily" (14:6, 19). I am confident the Lord was not pleased with Samson's philanderings, yet He used this man who catered to his physical appetites in ridding the Israelites of the Philistines. Jephthah, the son of a harlot, had been raised in an idolatrous background, yet the Spirit indwelt this strange man and used him in a mighty military victory over the Ammonites (11:29-33).

Unlike David, we never need to pray, "Do not take Thy Holy Spirit from me." Thanks be to God, He has sent His blessed Holy Spirit to indwell us, not for one task or one month but forever. What a privilege we have that the Comforter indwells us permanently (John 14:16-17).

LESSON: *The Holy Spirit indwelt believers selectively and temporarily in the Old Testament.*

THE HOLY SPIRIT
EQUIPPED OLD TESTAMENT BELIEVERS

*I have filled him with the Spirit of God
in wisdom, in understanding, in knowledge,
and in all kinds of craftsmanship. (Exodus 31:3)*

Have you ever been faced with a job that you were convinced was too big for you? How did you handle it? It is when we are faced with titanic tasks that we learn to trust in God and not in ourselves.

God had called the Israelites out of Egypt to worship Him in the land He had promised them. Where would they worship? Since God is worthy of preeminent honor, they needed to build a suitable place of worship. God took Bezalel son of Hur and filled him with His Spirit. What was the result? Bezalel received the wisdom and knowledge in craftsmanship to artistically design in gold, silver, bronze, stonework, and wood carving (Exodus 31:3-5). Where there was inability, God gave ability.

When Moses faced imminent death, Joshua faced the task of leading the rebellious Israelites. But God called and equipped Joshua. He told Moses: "Take Joshua the son of Nun, a man in whom is the Spirit, and lay your hand on him" (Numbers 27:18). God placed His Spirit in Joshua to empower him to lead the Israelites into battle for the land they had been promised, and they were victorious. What was the key? The Holy Spirit's indwelling and empowering Joshua.

Similarly, when David was called to be Israel's architect to design the glorious Temple where Israel would worship, he "gave his son Solomon the plans for the portico of the temple, its buildings . . . he gave him the plans of all that the Spirit had put in his mind for the courts of the temple" (1 Chronicles 28:11-12, NIV). Have you ever seen pictures of Solomon's magnificent Temple? Could a man have designed that by himself? No, the Holy Spirit put it in David's mind.

Saul faced the awesome task of uniting the twelve independent tribes of Israel as one nation. But God appointed him Israel's first king and empowered him with His Spirit (1 Samuel 10:10). God equipped him for the task.

Are you faced with a task you think you can't handle? You're probably right; you can't do it on your own, but look to the Holy Spirit to empower you. He will energize you and fill you with the wisdom you need.

LESSON: *In the Old Testament the Holy Spirit empowered and indwelt believers, usually for a temporary ministry.*

Part 5

Man and Sin

CREATION
OR EVOLUTION?

God made the beasts of the earth after their kind,
and the cattle after their kind, and every thing
that creeps on the ground after its kind. (Genesis 1:25)

How old is the world? Has it existed for billions of years, or was it created more recently? Were the days of creation twenty-four-hour days, or were they long ages? Christians disagree over the manner in which God created the world, but they agree on one important matter: that He did create it. The world is not a product of evolution.

One view of creation is the day-age theory, which suggests that the days referred to in Genesis are lengthy periods of time. This concept is derived from 2 Peter 3:8: "With the Lord one day is as a thousand years, and a thousand years as one day," and Psalm 90:4: "For a thousand years in Thy sight are like yesterday when it passes by, or as a watch in the night." Since there is no time with God, when He speaks of days, they may be lengthy periods of time. Thus the days of creation may be linked to geological ages.

The gap theory also attempts to reconcile modern science with the biblical account. According to this theory Genesis 1:1 describes the original creation in which the earth was populated with plants, animals, and perhaps even pre-Adamic man. When Satan rebelled against God and was judged, the earth became chaotic and uninhabitable—"formless and void." Geological ages followed. Genesis 1:2 describes the recent re-creation of a previously fallen world that existed billions of years ago.

Still other Christians believe the earth was created in six days of literal twenty-four hours and that therefore the earth is relatively young, perhaps no more than ten or twenty thousand years old. This belief is based on the phrase "evening and morning" (cf. Genesis 1:8), suggesting a twenty-four-hour cycle. Exodus 20:11 also appears to suggest twenty-four-hour days. Any scheme suggesting lengthy time period necessitates death before the Fall.

But regardless of our view, Christians agree on one thing: God created the universe, the world, and humans directly. Mankind is not the product of evolution but the result of the creative work of an all-wise God—and therefore accountable to the holy God who created us.

LESSON: *The universe, world, and humanity are not the product of chaotic, evolutionary beginnings but the direct creative act of God.*

ATHEISTIC EVOLUTION

In the beginning God created the
heavens and the earth. (Genesis 1:1)

In 1911 Professor Charles Dawson led a group of students in excavation work and "discovered" a skull that supposedly was a missing link between man and ape. But in 1953 the Royal Geological Society exposed the skull as a hoax. Apparently the students had scraped the skull of a modern ape to give it the appearance of age, successfully fooling scientists for several generations. In 1891, when Dr. Eugene Dubois found a small part of a skull, a thighbone, and two teeth in Java, it too was heralded as the missing link. But the bones were later discovered to be human. Time-Life books have illustrated missing links by their ingenious drawings of transitional beings from ape to man. But there is no fossil evidence for these transitional forms. They exist only in the minds of the evolutionists. (The Institute for Creation Research in San Diego, California, has done an invaluable work in encouraging study in creationism and defending the biblical record.)

The failure to find a missing link is a serious problem for evolutionists. There should be numerous transitional forms—not only between man and ape, but between and within the various species of animals. Charles Darwin himself asked, "Why, if species descended from other species by fine gradations, do we not everywhere see innumerable transitionary forms? . . . Why do we not find them imbedded in countless numbers in the crust of the earth?"

An even greater problem for evolutionists is the problem of life itself. Where did life come from? How can life come from nonlife? If that were possible, we should see evolution from nonlife to life today. But we don't.

Contrary to evolution, the second law of thermodynamics teaches that everything tends to run down, from order to disorder. If you leave a cup of coffee sitting by itself it doesn't get hotter—it gets cold. If evolution were true we should see progress toward complexity, but instead we see everything running "downhill." (See H. Morris, *Scientific Creationism*.)

Evolution is an attempt to answer the riddle of life apart from God. But the answer remains, "In the beginning God . . . "

LESSON: *There is no scientific evidence of missing links, nor can evolution answer life's beginning apart from God.*

July 1

PROBLEMS
WITH EVOLUTION

Then God said, "Let the earth bring forth living creatures
after their kind; cattle and creeping things and beasts of
the earth after their kind; and it was so." (Genesis 1:24)

Have you ever seen an animal with the ears of a rabbit, the mouth of a dog, the body of goat, and the tail of a pig? Or have you seen something that is part Siamese cat and part pine tree? Ludicrous as it may sound, those are legitimate questions to ask the evolutionist. If evolution is true, why are there only two distinct kinds of life—animal and vegetable? Why are there not different forms of life in "other" categories? Why are there no transitional forms between animal and vegetable? Why are there no transitional forms within the animal kingdom? We see only dogs, cats, cows, horses, goats, pigs—nothing in between. All are within their distinct species. If evolution is true, there should be thousands of transitional forms.

But a more basic question is, Where did life come from? Most would agree that something cannot come from nothing, and the other option—that the universe is eternal—is refuted by the second law of thermodynamics. Even Thomas Huxley admitted he could find no record of the beginning of life and was unable to come to a conclusion as to the conditions of its appearance. Life must come from preexisting life; it cannot come from nonliving matter. So where did it come from?

If evolution is true, what stopped the evolutionary process? Evolutionists suggest there has been no observable change in Homo sapiens in fifty thousand years. Yet if evolution were true, change should be immediately observable. If evolution isn't occurring, then what stopped it?

We must remember that evolution is an attempt to find an answer to life's origins *apart from God.* But the biblical record is clear: man, the world, and the universe are the creation of God. And it is to this God that we are accountable.

LESSON: *Evolution has insurmountable obstacles; it is biblically and scientifically indefensible.*

KING OF
THE EARTH

Thou dost make him to rule over the works of Thy hands;
Thou hast put all things under his feet. (Psalm 8:6)

K ing of the earth. That is the destiny of man. It was God's purpose for man to rule as king of the earth. In God's original creation, Adam was the apex of His creation. He was the epitome
of God's handiwork. Why? The rest of creation was for Adam's benefit. God
told Adam and Eve, "Be fruitful, multiply, and fill the earth, and subdue it;
and rule over the fish of the sea and over the birds of the sky, and over every
living thing that moves on the earth" (Genesis 1:28). That was man's destiny—to rule over the animal and vegetable kingdoms. It was not God's intention that man be bitten by spiders and snakes or frightened by mice and
mountain lions. Man was not intended to fight the locusts that destroy his
crops or grasshoppers that chew his vegetable garden or worms that eat his
flowers.

With the Fall, man temporarily forfeited much of his authority to rule.
Because of sin's entrance into the world, man wages war with the elements
and watches insects destroy his crops. But that is not the end of the story.
The last Adam will redeem what the first Adam lost. Milton was right. There
will be a paradise regained.

Although man, through his Fall, is temporarily lower than the angels
(Psalm 8:5), he is destined for glory. Through his identification with Christ
he will regain the authority over the world that God intended for him. But it
will be Christ who brings it about. Christ demonstrated this when He rode
the unbroken colt into Jerusalem at the triumphal entry (Matthew 21:7). The
"beasts of the field" were "put under his feet" (Psalm 8:6-7). That previews
the millennial kingdom, when Christ will subdue all nature to Himself. No
biting snakes or fearsome lions in that day (Isaiah 11:6-9). The last Adam
will restore the fallen earth. He will be king. And we will reign with Him as
joint heirs in that perfect paradise.

LESSON: *Man was destined to rule as king of the earth but forfeited*
that right through the Fall; Christ will recover man's destiny at His return.

July 3

MAN IS A
PHYSICAL CREATION

*Then the Lord God formed man of dust from the ground,
and breathed into his nostrils the breath of life;
and man became a living being. (Genesis 2:7)*

Have you ever considered the usefulness of your thumb? How could you pick up your morning coffee cup without it? And think of your facial features. The nose is an interesting instrument. If your nose were inverted, with your nostrils pointing upward, you could drown when walking in a rainstorm! The eyes have heavy bone structure surrounding them to protect the delicate members. The eardrums are recessed sufficiently to prevent curious children from damaging them.

Is all that an accident, a result of chance? No, a thousand times, no! The human body is the most beautiful, magnificent, and intricate creation by God. It is God's masterpiece.

Genesis 2:7 pictures the work of an artist. As a potter shapes an earthen vessel from clay, so the Lord God constructed man from clay. Because God Himself created man, man is truly a work of art—a wonder. There is a play on words in this verse: "God formed man [*adam*] of dust from the ground [*adamah*]." It is intended to remind us that our origin is the earth and that to the earth our bodies will one day return. The dust is not a clod of earth but "the finest part of the material of the earth" (Keil & Delitzsch, *Genesis*).

If we were only a product of evolution we would not have any moral responsibility to God. But since God created us He has authority over us— we are accountable to Him. What does He desire of us? To give back to Him a useful life in this very body that He has created. Since our bodies are the temple of the Holy Spirit and since we are bought with a costly price, we should "glorify God in [our] bodies" (1 Corinthians 6:20). What does that mean? It means we will live morally responsible lives—not giving our bodies to adultery or immorality, nor abusing them through improper use of food or drink.

LESSON: *Man is the direct creation of God, having received a physical body that he may honor God.*

PURPOSE
OF THE BODY

The body is not for immorality,
but for the Lord. (1 Corinthians 6:13)

I n a course on the family at a state university the professor asked the students, "How many of you have experienced premarital sexual relations?" Out of a large class, only five indicated they had not. "Are you ashamed that you haven't?" asked the professor.

That incident illustrates a prevalent view that the body is the only important part of a person. This view is called "hedonism," claiming that we should do whatever gratifies the physical desires. It says that pleasure is the source of happiness and chief good in life. If you enjoy eating, eat to your body's fulfillment, regardless whether you abuse your body! If you have sexual desires, express them without moral restraint.

But there is more to life than the body! Jesus said, "What will a man be profited, if he gains the whole world, and forfeits his soul?" (Matthew 16:26).

A contrary view espoused by Greek philosophers viewed the immaterial, or the soul, as good and the material, the body, as evil. Through the centuries adherents to this view have become hermits, attempting to refrain from sinful thoughts or physical deeds. They impose strict rules, seeking to stifle physical thought, contact, or expression—all the while suggesting that the body is evil. That also is an unbiblical view. (See the Song of Solomon, a beautiful book meant to be understood literally as God's blessing upon the physical love relationship between husband and wife.)

How are you treating your body? Are you caring for it by eating the right foods without overindulging? Do you have a wholesome view of the body? The Lord created you as a sexual being, to be responsible within the confines of marriage. Young person, are you willing to say no to the one tempting you to relinquish your moral standards? If you are married, are you remaining faithful to your spouse in thought as well as deed?

LESSON: *The body has been created by the Lord and is therefore good, to be cared for physically and kept sexually pure.*

MAN IS A
SPIRITUAL BEING

And God created man in His own image, in the image of God He created him; male and female He created them. (Genesis 1:27)

In Bait Vegan, a western suburb of Jerusalem, you can visit a replica of ancient Jerusalem, designed by the renowned scholar Michael Avi-Yonah. The beautiful model, constructed on a 1,196 square yard site, is built on a scale of 1 to 50. Consulting the Mishna Tracts and the writings of Josephus, the builders carefully constructed the city as it was in the days of Christ. Herod's magnificent Temple, David's tower, Herod's palace with its beautiful gardens, the massive Antonia Fortress, as well as ordinary houses—all are precise replicas of the ancient, glorious city.

The model city is made "in the image" of ancient Jerusalem. Looking at that model we can understand what the great city was like in the days of Christ. In a similar way, God created man in His own image. How is man made in the image of God? We know it cannot mean a physical likeness because God is spirit without physical form (John 4:24).

First, it must mean personality—which includes intellect. Having personality, man is conscious of his existence (unlike animals). He is able to make choices. Man has intelligence to carry out God's command to subdue the world (Genesis 1:28) and to cultivate the land (2:15, 19). Man is able to devise ways to adapt himself to his environment, whether it be the frigid north or the tropical south.

As God is spirit, so man has a human spirit with reason, conscience, and will. As spiritual beings, we are created with the capacity to know and love God. Man's sin marred his spirit, and it is only through salvation that his spirit is given new life (Ephesians 2:1, 5). Man was also made with a moral nature, which was lost through the Fall. In Christ we are restored to the "righteousness and holiness" that was previously lost (4:24).

What is the significance of man's creation in God's image? Man is a unique being—far above all other creation. We have the capacity to know, love, obey, enjoy, and fellowship with God forever.

LESSON: *Man is made in God's image, having personality, spirituality, and morality.*

MAN IS ACCOUNTABLE
TO THE CREATOR

Consecrate yourselves therefore, and
be holy; for I am holy. (Leviticus 11:44)

W hile on a trip to the Galapagos Islands, Charles Darwin constructed a theory of human origins that has influenced millions of people. Writing his conclusions in the *The Origin of Species*, he emphasized the "survival of the fittest." He taught that in the struggle for existence only the stronger living things survived long enough to reproduce, eventually resulting in creatures better able to tolerate their particular environment. In time, species came into being. Although Darwin's theory has been revised by evolutionary adherents, the central emphasis is still there: life evolved apart from any intervention by God.

Aldous Huxley acknowledged his reason for believing in evolution in his article "Confession of a Professed Atheist": "I had motives for not wanting the world to have meaning. . . . The liberation we desired was simultaneously liberation from a certain political and economic system and liberation from a certain system of morality. We objected to the morality because it interfered with our sexual freedom" (Culp, *Remember Thy Creator*, pp. 110-11).

Do you see what Huxley is saying? He is speaking to an important issue. If holy God created man, then man is accountable for his actions to holy God. But if man is the product of an evolutionary process in which no Supreme Being had any part, then man is not morally responsible to anyone. Whatever he decides is right. He can set up his own standards.

Obviously, whether we believe in evolution or creation has enormous implications for our daily living. It affects our moral standards—whether we believe in situation ethics and whether we believe murder, adultery, stealing, and lying are wrong. If man is the product of evolution, who sets the standards? Who determines what is right or wrong? The evolutionist would have us believe we can establish our own standards, but looking at the world today we can certainly say that man has not fared well in setting his own standards. The point is clear: the One who said, "Let us make man in our image" (Genesis 1:26) is also the One who said, "Consecrate yourselves therefore, and be holy; for I am holy" (Leviticus 11:44).

LESSON: *Evolution is an attempt to explain creation apart from God and to justify removal of moral constraints.*

MAN IS A
LIVING SOUL

Those who had received his word were baptized; and there were added that day about three thousand souls. (Acts 2:41)

I was unable to be at my mother's side at her homegoing, but my two sisters were there. They sat with her into the night as the end approached. Her breathing became slower and shallower and the breaths further apart until suddenly there was no more breath. Life was gone.

Life is a mystery. What is it that enables a person to live? The Old Testament word sometimes translated "soul" is *nephesh,* meaning "life" or "self"; it refers to the person in his or her entire composition—body as well as feelings and emotions. *Nephesh* means "to breathe" and suggests the "life principle" or "essence of life."

We tend to compartmentalize man, making a person body *and* soul, but *nephesh* suggests the entire person. When David said, "[The Lord] restores my soul" (Psalm 23:3), he meant the Lord restores his life, his personal existence with all that he was as a person—appetites, desires, drives, and will. In times of deprivation people search for food to sustain their "souls," or their lives (Lamentations 1:11).

In the New Testament, the word *soul (psuche)* normally means the entire person. Following Peter's sermon at Pentecost, three thousand "souls" were baptized and added to the church (Acts 2:41). "Souls" means people who met for fellowship and prayer. But *psuche* may also mean the immaterial part of man, distinct from the body. Thus, although the body may be killed, the *psuche* cannot be killed (Matthew 10:28).

Following the breaking of the sixth seal, John glimpsed into heaven, seeing "the souls of those who had been slain" (Revelation 6:9). Although those believers were devoid of their earthly bodies, they had identity and a conscious existence in God's presence as well as some "form" since they were capable of wearing white robes (v. 11). When Christ returns, the "souls" of those who have been martyred will come to life and reign with Him (20:4), and they will be reunited with their resurrected, glorified bodies. What hope! We will be reunited with believers who have gone before, and we will know them in the entirety of their persons.

LESSON: *The soul usually refers to the entire person—body and immaterial being—but also expresses the feelings and emotions.*

ORIGIN OF
THE SOUL

Behold, I was brought forth in iniquity, and
in sin my mother conceived me. (Psalm 51:5)

Where did the human soul come from? Does God create a new soul every time a child is born? Why do children sin at an early age? Do parents pass on the soul to each child?

Ancient teachers such as Plato, Philo, and Origen taught that the soul existed in a previous state and at some point enters the human body. Origen thought that explained why some people enter life in different conditions. Perhaps the disciples were thinking of that when they asked Jesus, "Rabbi, who sinned, this man, or his parents, that he should be born blind?" (John 9:2). Apparently they thought the blind man sinned in his previous existence—before birth.

Roman Catholics and many Reformed Christians believe that parents pass on the physical part—the body—and God immediately creates the spiritual part—the soul—every time a child is born. However, if God creates the individual soul, why does each person sin? This view would demand that each individual experience an "individual Fall" to explain why all people sin.

Other Christians believe that parents are responsible for both body and soul being transmitted to each child. That best explains the sinful actions of every person, which begin at such a young age. Parents pass on the sinful nature as well as the body. David recognized this when he said, "I was brought forth in iniquity" (Psalm 51:5). David was not suggesting that sexual relations in marriage is sin; rather, he was affirming that when his mother conceived him, his sin nature was immediately present.

Since parents pass on the sin nature to their children, it is imperative that we lead our children to Christ at an early age and teach them to walk in obedience to His Word—that is the only antidote to the inherited sin nature.

LESSON: *In procreation, the parents pass on the soul as well as the body.*

MAN HAS
A SPIRIT

The dust shall return to the earth as it was, and the
spirit will return to God who gave it. (Ecclesiastes 12:7)

W hen a man dies, he dies like an animal. It's all over—that's it." Have you ever heard someone say that? That is the thinking of many people, but it's not true.

Man has an eternal spirit. Although man *is* a living soul, he *has* a spirit. Moses and Aaron acknowledged the Lord as the "God of the spirits of all flesh" (Numbers 16:22), meaning that all people—not just believers —have a spirit. Man's human spirit, therefore, is distinct from the Holy Spirit, whom only believers receive at the moment of salvation (Ephesians 1:13).

Both the Hebrew word *ruach* and the Greek word *pneuma* mean "breath" or "wind," possibly suggesting the breath of life that God gives to all people. The God who created the heavens and the earth also "gives breath to the people on it, and spirit to those who walk in it" (Isaiah 42:5). The human spirit describes the life of the person: when he is sick, his spirit is broken (Job 17:1).

The "breath" of man, however, is different from animals; man's breath and life is the result of a special creative act of God (Genesis 2:7). *Ruach* defines the entire immaterial conscious nature of man, as the prophet Isaiah said: "My spirit within me seeks Thee diligently" (Isaiah 26:9). The spirit may also describe a person's disposition (Psalm 32:2), thoughts (Ezekiel 13:3), turmoil (John 13:21), pride (Proverbs 16:18), or humility (Matthew 5:3).

In the New Testament there is some overlap of the words *soul* and *spirit,* but there are also distinctions. The "spiritual" person has received God's Holy Spirit, enabling him to know God; the "soulish" person knows only the things pertaining to the world (1 Corinthians 2:11-13). The unbeliever's spirit is dead toward God, following the spirit of the evil one (Ephesians 2:1-2). At salvation, the believer not only receives the Holy Spirit, but his human spirit is also renewed (Ephesians 4:23).

In contrast to the soul, which identifies the entire person, the spirit is distinct from the body. At death the body "will return to the earth as it was, and the spirit will return to God who gave it" (Ecclesiastes 12:7). God has made us spiritual beings that we might have fellowship with Him.

LESSON: *Man has an eternal spirit, given by God for fellowship with Him and renewed to make fellowship possible through faith in Christ.*

MAN HAS
A MIND

Be renewed in the spirit of your mind. (Ephesians 4:23)

Barbara Moore performed on the piano from memory 1,852 songs at the Philadelphia Bourse Building from October 25 to November 13, 1988. In Harbin, China, Gou Yan-ling, twenty-six, memorized more than fifteen thousand telephone numbers. Mrs. Shakuntala Devi of India demonstrated in twenty-eight seconds the multiplication of 7,686,369,774,870 by 2,465,099,745,779, an equation picked at random by the computer department of Imperial College, London, on June 18, 1980 (Guinness, pp. 18-19).

The human mind is amazing. Man was given a mind superior to all creation for the purpose of knowing God. But his mind has been affected by the Fall. As a result, it is depraved, filled with unrighteousness and wickedness (Romans 1:28-29). How else can we explain "adult" literature shops, the abuse of children, and flagrant displays of homosexuality? The unbeliever's mind is constantly inclined toward evil (Genesis 6:5). He is at war with God and refuses to subject himself to God's rule (Romans 8:7). His mind is blinded by Satan; hence, he cannot comprehend the glorious gospel (2 Corinthians 4:4). His mind basks in futility and ignorance, devoid of understanding (Ephesians 4:17-18).

Thanks be to God, that is not the end of the story! Upon regeneration we receive the mind of Christ (1 Corinthians 2:16). Does your life reflect that? We are to reflect humility, viewing others as more important, having the attitude of Christ (Philippians 2:3-5). That is not easily accomplished. It is a battle. We must make a decision to transform our minds (Romans 12:2); we are to make them new again (Ephesians 4:23).

Believers must choose to think right thoughts that are true, honorable, right, pure, lovely, of good repute, and excellent (Philippians 4:8). We have the capacity to think thoughts of bitterness, hatred, jealousy—but we don't have to. We must choose to set our "mind on the things above, not on the things that are on earth" (Colossians 3:2). What do you think about?

LESSON: *Although the unsaved person has a degenerate mind, upon salvation God gives us a new mind with the capacity to think right thoughts.*

July 11

MAN HAS A HEART

*You shall love the Lord your God
with all your heart. (Mark 12:30)*

A pious but cranky lady was greatly annoyed because her neighbors forgot to ask her to go with them on a picnic. On the morning of the event they suddenly realized that they had neglected to invite her, so they sent one of the children to ask her to come along. "It's too late now," she snapped. "I've already prayed for rain!" (*Our Daily Bread*, March 21, 1964). That incident reflects the nature of the human heart.

"Heart" can refer to a number of things. The unbeliever's heart is deceitful, desperately sick (Jeremiah 17:9), and foolish, darkened in willful refusal to honor God (Romans 1:21). It may be dull, refusing to comprehend (Acts 28:27). In constantly ignoring God's wooing grace the unregenerate person's heart is stubborn and unrepentant, storing up judgment from God (Romans 2:5).

Heart also refers to moral decisions: the unbeliever's heart is trained to be greedy (2 Peter 2:14). Or it may reflect desire: the man who looks on a woman with adulterous thoughts has committed sin in his heart (Matthew 5:28).

The heart may also express the will—for good or evil (Matthew 6:21; 12:34). The Lord moves upon the will of the believer by "opening the heart" (Acts 16:14), and there is no distinction between Jews and Gentiles—God cleanses both their hearts by faith (15:9). The heart reflects moral decisions when believers love one another (1 Thessalonians 3:13). The regenerate heart shows emotion by rejoicing at the resurrection of Christ (John 16:22). But the apex of the regenerate heart is the ability to love God (Mark 12:30). That is the supreme service of the heart.

How can I have a heart that responds righteously? First by believing in Christ as an act of the will (Romans 10:10). Christ then comes to "settle down and be at home in my heart" (Ephesians 3:17). He not only takes up residence in my heart—He makes Himself at home. That means that in my thoughts, desires, moral decisions Christ is at the forefront. Above all else, my heart's desire is to please Him.

LESSON: *The unbeliever has a heart dominated by sin and the old nature, whereas the believer has a regenerate heart that desires to please God.*

July 12

MAN HAS
A WILL

The sinful nature desires what is contrary to the Spirit,
... so that you do not do what you want. (Galatians 5:17, NIV)

We prize freedom. Nineteen ninety will be remembered as a historically significant year because East Germany, Czechoslovakia, Poland, Hungary, Romania, and Bulgaria all gained freedoms unknown in more than forty years.

We also prize the freedom of the will. We say that man has a free will—after all, can we not choose to do as we please? I can choose whether I want a Ford or a Chevy, whether I want to live in Little Rock or Los Angeles, and whether I want to use Colgate or Crest toothpaste. However, that does not mean freedom of the will. The ability to make right moral choices relates to freedom of the will. Does man have the freedom to choose good? Does a sinful, unregenerate person have a free will?

Man's will was affected by the Fall. Sinful man must make moral decisions based on his nature—he cannot function contrary to it. His intellect, volition, and power of choice are all affected by a tendency toward transgression. "The sinful nature desires what is contrary to the Spirit . . . so that you do not do what you want" (Galatians 5:17, NIV). The unsaved person is propelled by the sinful nature, disabling him from living a life that pleases God. The unbeliever functions in the sphere of his depraved nature. Donald Grey Barnhouse used to say that a man has the freedom to jump from a fifteenth floor of a building, but he does not have the freedom to jump back up again. Similarly, sinful man is restricted by his sinful nature. Paul expressed this problem when he stated, "I am not practicing what I would like to do, but I am doing the very thing I hate" (Romans 7:15).

What is the solution? The believer is not under the same bondage as the unbeliever. Paul instructs us, "Do not let sin reign in your mortal body that you should obey its lusts" (6:12). Since the Holy Spirit has taken up residence in believers and the believer's spirit has been renewed, we have the ability to make choices that please God. We have been set free from the law of sin and death (8:2). We have been released from Satan's penitentiary to serve the Lord in the freedom of our new will.

LESSON: *The unregenerate will is bound by depravity and unable to please God, but the regenerate will has been set free to serve God.*

MAN HAS
A CONSCIENCE

*Pray for us, for we are sure that we have a
good conscience, desiring to conduct ourselves
honorably in all things. (Hebrews 13:18)*

A sixty-eight-year-old woman told police in New York that she killed her newborn baby thirty-eight years before and buried the baby's remains in her backyard. The police sergeant explained, "She finally had to tell somebody about it. She could see the grave site. It was only within a few feet from her window where she sat most every day. She said she had a guilty conscience. She said she hadn't slept in 38 years."

Everyone may not read the Bible and therefore know God's exact standards, but everyone has an inner voice, or a conscience. Everyone hears that inner voice, which protests immoral behavior and commends good behavior (Romans 2:15). That is not to say that the conscience is infallible. It may be culturally conditioned and may persuade people according to their cultures and customs.

A Christian may even have a weak and defiled conscience (1 Corinthians 8:7). Growing up in a culture where food was sacrificed to idols the Christian convert may have become a vegetarian because his conscience indicated the meat was actually offered to a deity. But his conscience misguided him. Paul lived "with a perfectly good conscience" even though he was persecuting Christians in the process (Acts 23:1). Unbelievers who constantly violate the prompting of the conscience become seared. It becomes insensitive to the truth. Deliberate rejection of God's truth may render the conscience insensitive or "cauterized" (1 Timothy 4:2).

Believers may have a "good conscience, desiring to conduct ourselves honorably in all things" (Hebrews 13:18). How is that possible? The Word of God, rather than culture or custom, must light our path. And we must be quick to obey the Word as we discover its truths. Nothing will render a conscience ineffective as quickly as neglect to obey the Scriptures. Let us read the Word of God and listen to His internal monitor.

LESSON: *The conscience is God's inner voice that condones or condemns our actions and is most effective when governed by the Word of God.*

July 14

MAN HAS
A SIN NATURE

*If I am doing the very thing I do not wish, I am no longer
the one doing it, but sin which dwells in me. (Romans 7:20)*

Post a sign in the library stating, "No talking," and watch the results. You will see people talking everywhere. Riding the train in
Disneyland in California, I noticed the sign: "Keep arms inside
the car." Immediately a teenager poked her arm out of the window in defiance of the warning. What is it in us that makes us want to defy the law?
Why do we want to walk on the grass when it says, "No walking on the
grass"?

The answer lies in our old nature. All members of the human family
have a fallen, sinful nature, a capacity to sin. It is sometimes called the
"flesh" (Romans 7:18). Flesh may mean our physical bodies, but it also
describes an immaterial part of us—our fallen sin nature. Paul describes his
struggle with the sin nature and inability to do right in Romans 7:14-25. As
children of the human race, we are also heirs of Adam's nature; we are
fallen, sinful creatures with a propensity toward sin. Even though our mind
may direct us toward the good, our old nature gives us an appetite toward
evil.

Some people deny that we have a sin nature once we become Christians, but call it what you will—a capacity to sin, a tendency toward evil—
something within all of us keeps us from walking in perfect harmony with
God's Word. If someone still denies that, I'd like to speak to his wife or
mother. I'm confident they would tell a different story!

But there is good news. In referring to our old nature as "our old man"
in Romans 8:6, Paul tells us that our old nature, or capacity, "was crucified
with [Christ]," rendering it ineffective. But why then do I still struggle? Historically, we died to sin's dominion over us when we were crucified with
Christ. We must now count on that as having happened—we must consider
ourselves dead to sin. Then sin will no longer have dominion over us (Romans 6:11).

LESSON: *All of us have an old nature, a capacity to sin, but when we
realize that we died together with Christ, sin need not have authority over
us.*

ORIGINAL
SIN

Through the one man's disobedience the
many were made sinners. (Romans 5:19)

One Saturday morning my wife, youngest son, and I were walking along the beach on the Atlantic looking for sharks' teeth when we noticed a man-of-war washed ashore. When we picked him up, the breeze blew the yard-long tentacles across my son's chest. As he screamed in pain, I quickly pulled the tentacles away. My hands and his chest felt as if they were ablaze. As we ran down the beach to the first aid station, my son cried out, "It's all Adam's fault!" It was a painful but good theology lesson.

All suffering and sin can be traced to our original parent, Adam. We call this "original sin" because it comes from our first parent, because it affects every human being from the time of birth, and because it is the inner basis of every sin we commit. Original sin means Adam—and thereby the entire human race—is guilty before God and deserving of punishment.

Paul paints a sordid picture of this, reminding us that through Adam's sin the entire human race died (Romans 5:15), came under God's judgment (v. 16) and condemnation (v. 18), and became sinners (v. 19). Adam's first sin brought sin, suffering, and death to the human race. Man violated God's standard and is culpable—he must satisfy the righteous justice of God's law.

Original sin also means that man is depraved. We speak of the "total depravity" of man, meaning that Adam's sin extends to all of man's nature and faculties—his mind, heart, and will, as well as his body. Therefore unbelievers are "darkened in their understanding" (Ephesians 4:18); their minds and conscience are defiled (Titus 1:15). We wonder about the immorality in society, the high crime rate, the lewd programs on television, the mockery of Christ—but it all comes from the corrupted heart of man. Adam's first sin brought corruption to all humanity.

But there is a solution. Original sin and guilt can be removed by a substitute. The perfect life and death of Christ provide that substitute, removing our guilt before God when we trust Jesus as our Sin Bearer. Just as the first Adam brought condemnation and death, so the last Adam, Christ, brought justification and life. Have you trusted in Him?

LESSON: *Adam's sin brought guilt, sin, and death to the entire human race, but Christ removes the guilt from all who trust Him.*

June...

THE
TEST

From any tree of the garden you may eat freely; but from the tree of the knowledge of good and evil you shall not eat, for in the day that you eat from it you shall surely die. (Genesis 2:16-17)

A wise mother tells her preschool child, "You may ride your tricycle on the sidewalk, but don't ride it in the street, or I won't let you play outside." A father may tell his teenaged son, "When you drive the car, make sure you obey the speed limits, and be home by eleven o'clock, or I'll not let you use the car anymore." Are those parents crippling their children's expression? Are they being unfair? No. They are wise parents who have placed constraints on their children to help them.

Loyalty is best seen when it has been put to the test. In the Garden of Eden God put Adam and Eve to the test, allowing them to freely eat the fruit of any tree—except from the tree of knowledge of good and evil. It did not seem a difficult test. After all, they could eat from all the other trees, and there must have been hundreds, probably thousands, of varieties.

The test was whether Adam would be obedient. Adam would come to a knowledge of good and evil either the right way or the wrong way. If he obeyed God by not eating the fruit, he could learn good and evil through obedience; if he disobeyed God, he would learn good and evil—as Satan had promised—but the wrong way. And he would indeed die, physically and spiritually (Genesis 2:17).

What is the purpose of testing? The purpose of a test is not always a solicitation to evil, to entice us to sin. A test may show our mettle, our character. Take courage when testing comes. The purpose is not to see you fail; it is to reveal the quality of your obedience to God, your loyalty and steadfastness amid adversity.

God desires our loyalty and our love. The best expression is our steadfastness in testing. Job said, "When He has tried me, I shall come forth as gold" (Job 23:10). As gold is purified through smelting, so our testing is designed not to destroy us but to show our loyal love for the Lord.

LESSON: *God tested Adam and Eve by enabling them to come to a knowledge of good and evil through obedience or disobedience.*

TEMPTATION

Indeed, has God said . . . ? (Genesis 3:1b)

A man who had been trained in one of the great educational institutions became an evangelist. He had a "golden tongue," able to move audiences to respond. But he left evangelism and entered the newspaper business. In an interview on television he explained, "I could not continue in something I no longer believed in." What happened? Doubt concerning the Word of God.

Doubt is the vehicle Satan uses to drive into the human heart. Eve, listening to the enticing voice of the tempter, doubted what God had said to her. The temptation came to her through a serpent—an unlikely source. Why would she submit to an ugly, repulsive snake? In reality, Satan was the tempter; the snake was only the vehicle—and in all probability the snake was a beautiful creature before the Fall.

Satan used the craftiest animal to tempt Eve. That is a reminder that temptation won't come to us in avenues where we are strong; it will come where we are weak. Satan's temptation began by causing Eve to doubt what God had said: "Indeed, has God said . . . ?" (Genesis 3:1). "Really now, did God actually say that?" It was a clever ruse, and that temptation continues today. Evangelicals battle issues among themselves because of this temptation to doubt God's Word.

Eve fell prey to the temptation to exaggerate God's command, claiming that God had said, "You shall not . . . touch it" (v. 3). Eve opened the gate to sin when she exaggerated God's command, and Satan took his next step: "You surely shall not die!" (v. 4). An outright lie. It is a small step from an exaggeration to a lie. Satan took the step and Eve followed. Finally, the deceiver promised a reward: "You will be like God" (v. 5). He did not need to entice her any further. It was almost too easy. Eve took the fruit and ate—and brought sin into a previously perfect world. The greatest temptation we face is accepting reason and abandoning a simple faith in the plain promises and warnings of Scripture.

LESSON: *Satan tempted Eve by casting doubt and lying about God's Word while making false promises. That is the nature of temptation.*

SUBMISSION TO
TEMPTATION

When the woman saw that the tree was good for food, and that
it was a delight to the eyes, and that the tree was desirable
to make one wise, she took from its fruit and ate; and she
gave also to her husband with her, and he ate. (Genesis 3:6)

Handyman James Wallaice of Hayes, England, said he was "overcome with temptation" when he saw a policeman leaning over the side of a swimming pool, and he gave in to it. He was fined $52 in court for shoving patrolman Thomas Clark into the pool.

Why do we give in to temptation? What is it that makes us think, say, and do things that are sin? Sin begins with the "lust of the flesh" (1 John 2:16); Eve "saw that the tree was good for food" (Genesis 3:6). The flesh is our fallen, sinful nature. All of us possess an inner capacity, an inclination, to sin. It is part of our nature as fallen men and women, and it inclines us to commit acts of sin. Thoughts of anger, venomous words, and adultery have their origin in our sinful nature.

A second reason we submit to temptation is the "lust of the eyes" (1 John 2:16). When Eve saw "that it was a delight to the eyes" (Genesis 3:6), she ate the fruit. The eyes are the windows through which outward temptation enters the body. The eyes see, and the body craves. The eyes lead the body to fulfill its physical gratification. They make us desire things we don't need and that don't belong to us.

The third temptation is "the boastful pride of life" (1 John 2:16). When Eve saw "that the tree was desirable to make one wise" (Genesis 3:6) she succumbed. That is boasting in what we have and do; it is self-reliance and independence from God. It is empty and futile, and it is sin.

What can we learn here? The temptations that came to Eve come to us in the same three ways. A wise professor told his students, "Stay away from the shopping centers. You will learn to covet things there." We must stay away from situations that lead us to sin. Where do you spend your spare time? Does it encourage you to sin? What should you change to lessen the temptations in your life?

LESSON: *We are tempted to sin through our old nature, through our eyes, and through pride.*

JUDGMENT
ON SATAN

I will put enmity between you and the woman, and between
your seed and her seed; He shall bruise you on the head,
and you shall bruise him on the heel. (Genesis 3:15)

M ost people don't like snakes. On the first day of her visit to our
Florida home, my mother-in-law came face to face (or toe to
toe) with a snake. She froze, and the snake slithered away.
Snakes are repulsive to us, and there is probably good reason—they
are identified with the curse. Following the sin of Adam and Eve, God first
judged the serpent. By forcing it to crawl on its belly, He ensured that the
snake would eat dust as it crawled along (Genesis 3:14). Apparently the
snake's appearance was altered considerably—in form, movement, and
shape.

In speaking to Satan, the power behind the snake, God announced
that there would be conflict between Satan and the woman—specifically,
between "Satan's seed" and the "seed of the woman" (Genesis 3:16). What
is the offspring of Satan and the woman? Satan's offspring probably refers to
demons or unbelievers, whereas the offspring of the woman is believers and
ultimately Christ. That means there will be a conflict between believers and
unbelievers, between demons and Christ. God foretold the results of the
conflict in the first announcement of the gospel: "He shall bruise you on the
head." Christ would have a major victory: He would deliver a death-blow to
Satan at the cross. Christ's death was a triumph over Satan, rendering him
powerless (Colossians 2:14-15; Hebrews 2:14). Satan would have a minor
victory: Christ would die, but through His death Satan was nonetheless
defeated.

We need not live in bondage to Satan. He is a defeated enemy.
Through the cross Christ has triumphed. Have you believed in Christ's victory? Have you trusted in Him to give you victory over Satan? We need not
live a mediocre, servile life—live in the victory that Christ has won.

LESSON: *Through His death on the cross, Christ judged Satan and*
triumphed over him.

July 20

JUDGMENT
ON THE WOMAN

*I will greatly multiply your pain in childbirth, in pain
you shall bring forth children; yet your desire shall be
for your husband, and he shall rule over you. (Genesis 3:16)*

A rabbinic saying states, "The man is restless while he misses the rib that was taken out of his side, and the woman is restless until she gets under the arm from whence she was taken." The divine intention for marriage was that husband and wife live in harmony in their divinely ordained spheres. But with the Fall conflicts began.

God announced that Eve would experience pain and sorrow in pregnancy and childbearing. The word *pain* that describes Eve's suffering in pregnancy is the same word as *toil*, used to describe the pain Adam would experience in farming (Genesis 3:17). Both man and woman would suffer because of sin. Eve's sorrow appears to be related to her independence from Adam. In listening to the serpent and plucking the fruit, Eve acted apart from Adam. So in the course of reproduction, Eve would experience pain, a constant reminder of sin. Eve sought sensual pleasure in taking the fruit, so she will reaped the fruit of that sin with sorrow.

Eve was also told, "Your desire shall be for your husband." What does that mean? It may mean sexual desire (Song of Solomon 7:10); it may reflect her desire to be under her husband's authority; or it may mean enticing him to sin, as in Genesis 4:7, thereby assuming leadership. Probably the last sense is correct. Because Eve enticed the man to eat—and thereby took the lead—God announced that Adam would have authority over her.

The third part of the judgment, "He shall rule over you," is not a prophecy of wife abuse; rather, it is God's design that the woman shall be subordinate to the man because she sought to rule over him.

The New Testament completes our understanding of the marital relationship. Husbands are to love their wives as Christ loved the church, and wives are to be submissive to their husbands. When both of those injunctions are followed, a loving, harmonious relationship may exist.

LESSON: *In judging Eve, God announced that she would bear children in pain and her husband would be in authority over her.*

July 21

JUDGMENT
ON THE MAN

*Cursed is the ground because of you; in toil you shall
eat of it all the days of your life. (Genesis 3:17)*

When I was a youngster, my mother would give me one cent for
every three dandelions I dug out of our lawn. I don't remember how much I earned, but I know there were a lot of dandelions. I don't dig up dandelions anymore; now I dig up dollar weeds. They
run their lengthy horizontal roots beneath the surface like a network of electrical wires and decorate the entire lawn as they pop up. Dollar weeds are a
yardworker's nightmare.

But dollar weeds are not our only nemesis. Our environment mirrors
the effects of the Fall: moles and blight destroy the farmer's crops; hail or
drought may ruin what is left.

Adam's sin not only affected humanity but the environment as well. In
His judgment on Adam, God announced that the ground was cursed (Genesis 3:17). The earth would no longer produce fruits and vegetables spontaneously, but man would be obliged to labor under hardship to bring forth
the produce of the land. Only with painful labor would Adam extract the
crops from the ground. He would fight thorns and thistles (and no doubt,
dollar weeds and dandelions). But nature would resist Adam's advances.

Another judgment was placed on Adam—death (Genesis 3:19). No
one had experienced death yet, and perhaps Adam didn't understand it. He
was created from the dust of the ground, and God announced that he would
return to the dust. He would die. The judgment of Adam includes every
member of the human race. Whether a peasant or the president, no one
escapes. It is the destiny of every human being.

But there is hope. Creation groans as a woman in childbirth, longing
for the day of delivery (Romans 8:22), and as believers, we also wait for the
redemption of our body at the return of Christ (v. 23). Jesus Christ has reversed the effects of Adam's sin, and we long for the day when the full effects
of that reversal will be realized at His return.

LESSON: *In judging Adam God cursed the ground, causing Adam to
labor for his produce until he died.*

JUDGMENT
ON HUMANITY

*Therefore, just as through one man sin entered
into the world, and death through sin, and so death
spread to all men, because all sinned. (Romans 5:12)*

The hearse on the neighbors' driveway told the story. Their teen-aged daughter had lost a battle with leukemia. Why this young girl? After all, she was a Christian, a dedicated one. Her parting words were, "Tell the kids Jesus is real." Stricken with grief, her parents thought their hearts would tear from their bodies. Death seems especially tragic when it tolls for the young. And yet it is inevitable—it awaits the young and old, rich and poor, saint and sinner.

The sin of our first parents, Adam and Eve, brought death to the entire human race. Adam is viewed as the head of the human race, and Romans 5:12 says that sin entered the world through him. The one act of disobedience, Adam's eating the forbidden fruit, plunged all humanity over the precipice into death—physical death, spiritual death, or separation from fellowship with God, and eternal death, final separation from God.

Why should we be responsible for Adam's sin? After all, if it was his sin why should we suffer? Romans 5:12 says that death spread to all mankind because "all sinned." How could all people have sinned? Hebrews 7:9-10 paints an analogy. Levi paid tithes to Melchizedek through Abraham. But Levi was born several hundred years after Melchizedek. Although Levi was not yet born, he was "seminally present" in Abraham. Similarly, the entire human race was "in the body of Adam"; all of us were seminally present in Adam, and in that respect all of us participated in Adam's sin. So we are all guilty.

However, that is not the end of the story. The last Adam, Jesus Christ, brought justification and life to those who believe. If you have never trusted Christ, do it now, and enter into life. Then eternal death will have no hold over you; instead, Jesus Christ will give you eternal life.

LESSON: *All humanity participated in Adam's sin and is therefore guilty and subject to death.*

MAN IS
DEPRAVED

*Being darkened in their understanding, excluded from the
life of God, because of the ignorance that is in them,
because of the hardness of their heart. (Ephesians 4:18)*

On a Los Angeles freeway, a car cut off a pickup truck. Infuriated, the truck driver followed the car until it exited the freeway. When the car came to a stop at a traffic light, the truck driver jumped out, and wielding a hammer, began to smash the windshield of the car. The man in the car responded by pulling out a handgun and shooting the trucker. "Dad, I've been hit!" screamed the man to his father sitting in the truck. The father got behind the driver's seat and began to smash the car with his truck until the police arrived.

That may be an extreme example but it portrays man's nature: man is depraved. What does that mean? It does not mean that every sinner commits every conceivable sin or that he is not capable of doing good. It does mean that he puts himself first—seen in the modern "me" generation, the "I deserve . . . " syndrome. He is primarily a "lover of self," putting himself and pleasure ahead of God and others (2 Timothy 3:2-4). The reason is that his mind is set on the flesh—he follows the impulses of his base nature. He does not curb his sinful appetites. For that reason he is at war with God (Romans 8:7). His life is governed by a mind-set that is futile, spent on vain things; he has no spiritual understanding. His heart—the place he makes decisions—is hardened toward God and truth (Ephesians 4:18). And since his mind and conscience are corrupted, nothing is pure to him. His mind is polluted, a cesspool of mental sewage (Titus 1:15).

Depravity means the unbeliever's mind, heart, will, emotion, intellect, and nature are all polluted as a result of original sin—Adam's sin in the Garden of Eden. His life, thoughts, and deeds are unacceptable to God. Furthermore, because of his basic nature, he is spiritually unable by himself to live a life that conforms to God's Word and will. Spiritually, he is dead (Ephesians 2:1). He needs God's help. But God is rich in mercy; His grace is limitless. As the Spirit of God convicts and calls, God enables him to respond and believe the gospel (Ephesians 2:4-9).

LESSON: *Man is polluted in mind, heart, and will, rendering him unacceptable to God and unable to respond to God on his own.*

CAUSES
OF SIN

Being darkened in their understanding, excluded from the
life of God, because of the ignorance that is in them,
because of the hardness of their heart. (Ephesians 4:18)

When the five young men from Wheaton and Northwestern colleges approached the Auca Indians in South America, attempting to bring them the gospel, they lost their lives—their speared bodies were found floating in the river. Why did the Auca Indians kill those devout young men? Because of ignorance. They had never heard the gospel; they had never read the Bible. They knew nothing of God's standard of righteousness.

Ignorance is one word that explains why people sin. When Paul came to Athens he found people worshiping idols, even erecting a statue "to an Unknown God" (Acts 17:23). He told the Athenians that God overlooked their sins, not by forgiving without a basis but by withholding judgment. God is patient. But when Paul brought them the gospel, he called on them to repent (v. 30).

Sometimes people are not responsible for their ignorance. They cannot help being born in Sri Lanka or North Korea, where the gospel is suppressed. They cannot help being born in a home where the parents are anti-Christian and refuse to allow their children to hear the gospel. Yet the Scripture indicates there is an ignorance for which people are responsible. Unbelievers indulge in futile thinking (4:17)—that appears to be by choice. And there may be a connection with the next statement: "Being darkened in their understanding." Who darkened their understanding? Their own thought processes. They are ignorant "because of the hardness of their heart" (v. 18). In this case they are responsible for their ignorance—they have hardened their hearts toward the truth.

What is the remedy? It is simply "But God . . . " (Ephesians 2:1). God gives light to the darkened mind; He brings knowledge to the ignorant—knowledge that can save and deliver from vanity and futility.

LESSON: *Some sins may be committed in ignorance, but man is still under judgment and accountable to God for his sin.*

SIN COMES
FROM THE HEART

*The heart is more deceitful than all else and is
desperately sick; who can understand it? (Jeremiah 17:9)*

I can remember the moment someone told me President John F.
Kennedy had been shot. I remember where I was standing and the
conversation that ensued. An upset office coworker exclaimed,
"That's entirely contrary to the nature of man to do something like that!"

Sadly, that notorious act was born in the heart of an unregenerate
man, and Jesus pointedly taught that "out of the heart come evil thoughts,
murders, adulteries, fornications, thefts, false witness, slanders" (Matthew
15:19). We noted earlier that the heart is the seat of the emotions and the
will, the place where decisions are made. We would like to think the heart
is pure, capable only of love, but that is not true. As a result of Adam's sin in
the Garden, the entire human race fell into sin and man's heart was corrupted. Consequently, man is deceitful, treacherous beyond all other things and
incurably wicked (Jeremiah 17:9). This is the Lord's evaluation: Man is not
good by nature.

Although natural man sees the evidence of God in creation, he refuses
to honor God because his foolish heart is darkened (Romans 1:21)—even
to the point of ignoring God (Psalm 14:1). Natural man has a stubborn and
unrepentant heart; he has only contempt for the rich kindness and patience
of God (Romans 2:4-5). The unsaved person is spiritually blind.

"Above all else, guard your heart, for it is the wellspring of life" (Proverbs 14:23, NIV). That is accomplished when God shines "in our hearts to
give the light of the knowledge of the glory of God in the face of Christ" (2 Corinthians 4:6). God must change our hearts. When we come to the end of
our pride, ego, and self-confidence, then through our faith God gives us a
new heart, and we enter a new dimension of thinking, believing, loving. We
have a capacity to love, but God must change our old heart into a new heart,
and we must desire that change.

LESSON: *The heart of an unbeliever is hardened and blind toward
God and must be changed to see and enjoy the beauty and blessing of God.*

SIN COMES
FROM THE WORLD

If you were of the world, the world would love its own;
but because you are not of the world, but I chose you out
of the world, therefore the world hates you. (John 15:19)

To pass the time, a pregnant mother began regularly watching soap operas on television. After the baby was born the mother made a startling discovery. When the mother had watched a familiar program and the theme song had ended, the baby began to fuss. A British researcher discovered such behavior common with unborn and newborn children. Peter Hepper of Queen's University in Belfast refers to it as "fetal soap addiction"—"behavior after birth indicating that a newborn has become familiar with a soap opera theme while still in the uterus." What was he saying? Some unborn and newborn children are addicted to television!

Television, of course, is a morally neutral medium. It is the programming that makes it either good or bad. When showing morally objectionable programs, TV becomes part of the world system that opposes God's people. A divorce attorney for thirty years said that TV is the leading cause for divorce. He suggested that people have obtained their morals from watching adultery in programs such as "Love Boat" and "Dynasty."

The world is in opposition to Christ. It hates Christ because He exposes its evil (John 7:7). The world's opposition is reflected in a ready rejection of God's moral standards—immorality displayed in movies and TV, discussed in literature, bellowed in modern music. The world also hates Christians because Christ has chosen them out of the world (15:19). The world loves its own. Christian friend, expect opposition. Do not attempt to befriend the world or live at peace with it. Although we live in the world (we do not withdraw from society), we are to keep away from its evil (17:15).

Christian, what is your relationship to the world? Are you on friendly terms? Are you at peace with it? Does your lifestyle indicate your absorption with the world? Or are you standing in opposition—living as a light amid the dark deeds of the world?

LESSON: *The world is controlled by Satan in opposition to Christ and His people.*

SIN COMES
FROM THE FLESH

*I know that nothing good dwells in me, that is,
in my flesh; for the wishing is present in me,
but the doing of the good is not. (Romans 7:18)*

According to the rabbis there are as many commandments and restraints in the law as the body has members and the 'Evil Impulse' is said to be king over 248 members and the two great passions which the 'Evil Inclination' plays the most upon are the passions of idolatry and adultery" (Rienecker and Rogers, *Linguistic Key,* p. 578).

We generally think of an enemy as someone or something outside of us. It is the other person, the outside circumstance. But we have an enemy "within the gate." Paul describes his conflict as a believer in Romans 7 (an unbeliever doesn't have a conflict—he has only the old nature): "I am of flesh" (v. 14); "sin which indwells me" (vv. 17, 20); "nothing good dwells in me, that is, in my flesh" (v. 18); "evil is present in me" (v. 21); "a different law in the members of my body, waging war against the law of my mind" (v. 23); "the body of this death" (v. 24). The point seems clear: believers have a conflict within that keeps them from living righteously. We have thoughts of anger, bitterness, jealousy, impurity—where do these thoughts come from? From within. Call it what you will—the old nature, the capacity to sin, a tendency toward evil, an ability to commit sin—we all have it. No Christian is devoid of this old nature.

What is the solution? "Walk by the Spirit, and you will not carry out the desire of the flesh" (Galatians 5:16). In our daily war with the sin nature we have a greater Power resident within us. When we believed in Him, God sent His blessed Holy Spirit to indwell us so that we may live in the realm of the Spirit, not the flesh (Romans 8:9). The flesh has been crucified (Galatians 5:24). We do not have to submit to the rule of the old nature; we may submit to the authority of the Holy Spirit, allowing "a new General" to direct our lives. A Christian Indian explained victory over the flesh: "I have two dogs living within me. Which one wins? The one to whom I say, 'sic em.'"

LESSON: *Believers have an old nature that entices them to sin, but the solution is found in living under the control of the indwelling Holy Spirit.*

SIN COMES
FROM THE DEVIL

Put on the full armor of God, that you may be able to
stand firm against the schemes of the devil. (Ephesians 6:11)

S ome years ago the expression "The devil made me do it" was popular. In a sense, that is true—though we cannot blame him for our sins as a cop-out. In the believer's struggle with sin, acts of sin may be due to the lure of the world, the enticement of his old nature, or solicitation by Satan. Any one of those reasons or a combination of all three may be the reason we commit acts of sin.

We are to stand firm against the "schemes of the devil" (Ephesians 6:11). *Schemes* is from the word *methodeia*, which is related to our word *method*. Satan has methods that suggest his scheming and craftiness. C. S. Lewis wrote a satire, *The Screwtape Letters*, showing how Satan attacks people. Satan deceives us into thinking biblical doctrines are incompatible with modern science, fosters dissatisfaction with the church, hinders prayer, and creates doubt. It is important to remember that Satan is the father of lies (John 8:44) and will seek to pervert the truth. Perhaps one avenue in which Satan is particularly successful today is fostering disunity in the church. If Satan can create disunity among Christians he will render the church ineffective. They will be too busy fighting with themselves.

How can we successfully wage war against the devil? If we submit to God's authority and draw near to Him, offering Him a pure life, Satan will flee from us (James 4:7-8). That necessitates aligning ourselves with God and separating ourselves from a world that is hostile toward Him. If we maintain friendship with the world we will not successfully resist the devil (vv. 4-10). We must stand firm in faith (1 Peter 5:9) because we are in a battle. We are to take a military stance against Satan, our strength being a firm faith in our great God. In our war with Satan we must "put on the full armor of God" (Ephesians 6:11). As Paul concludes his discussion of the Christian's armor, he presses the need for prayer (vv. 18-19). Perhaps prayer completes the Christian's armor. And perhaps it is prayer that we employ so little. And perhaps that is the reason we lose so many battles with Satan.

LESSON: *Sin comes from Satan, who discourages us and keeps us prayerless and doubting, thus rendering us ineffective.*

WHAT IS SIN?

Sin is lawlessness. (1 John 3:4)

M ary Baker Eddy, founder of Christian Science, denied the existence of sin. "Evil is but an illusion, and it has no real basis," she claimed. In contrast, other greats have acknowledged sin's existence. Seneca the philosopher said, "We have all sinned, some more, some less." Goethe, the poet, exclaimed, "I see no fault which I might not myself have committed." Coleridge remarked, "I am a fallen creature . . . an evil ground existed in my will previous to any given act." The Chinese refer to "two good men; one dead, the other unborn" (Bancroft, *Christian Theology*, p. 214). Most people will acknowledge sin, but what is it?

The Bible uses several words to describe sin. One is *transgression* (Galatians 3:19). Sin is transgressing God's law; it is "stepping over the boundary." God gave Israel the law to show Israel His standard. When an Israelite committed murder or adultery or stole something, he sinned because he had stepped over the boundary of God's law.

Sin also means to "miss the mark" or "fall short of the glory of God" (Romans 3:23). God has established a standard, and failure to keep that precise standard is to sin, or miss the mark of God's standard. Moreover, man deliberately chooses to miss God's moral mark—it is a voluntary choice.

Sin is rebellion against God (1 John 3:4). It is a frame of mind that results in lawless action. Why will a group of young men smash dozens of mailboxes with a baseball bat? Rebellion against constituted laws.

Sin is also a nature or principle within man (Romans 7:17). Paul lamented, "The good that I wish, I do not do; but I practice the very evil that I do not wish," concluding that it is "sin which dwells in me" (vv. 19, 20).

What a dilemma if there were no solution! But "Jesus Christ has set you free from the law of sin and of death" (Romans 8:2). Apart from Christ there is no solution to sin, but trusting Him resolves the dilemma.

LESSON: *Sin is rebellion against God, overstepping His boundary, and missing the mark of His standard.*

SIN IS
TRANSGRESSION

If you show partiality, you are committing sin,
and are convicted by the law as transgressors. (James 2:9)

When children are small, parents set boundaries on their activities for their own good. A parent tells the child, "You must
stay in the yard," or, "You may ride your tricycle down the
sidewalk on our side of the street, but don't cross the street," and, "Do not
talk to strangers." What is the purpose of such boundaries? To inhibit the
child? No, it is for his welfare and protection.

God has set boundaries in His Word for our good, but when we cross
them, we sin. When the spies brought a negative report to Israel, exhibiting
their unbelief, the Lord pronounced judgment on Israel for believing them —
the older generation would not enter the land. When some decided to attempt to take the land anyway, Moses warned them that they were transgressing God's commandment (Numbers 14:41-42). In the Old Testament
sin was transgressing God's covenant, the Mosaic law (Deuteronomy 17:2).
God had bound Himself to the nation by His covenant; violating the covenant meant they had "crossed over" God's law.

The New Testament also emphasizes the transgression of God's law.
The first transgressor, Adam, overstepped the boundary of God's commandment when he ate the forbidden fruit (Romans 5:14). Then when sin prolif-
erated, God gave the law to the nation to reveal the seriousness of their sin
(Galatians 3:19). James points his readers to the heart of the law when he
reminds them that when they show partiality, favoring the rich and scorning
the poor, they transgress the royal law that says, "You shall love your neighbor as yourself" (2:8-9).

Just as a parent disciplines an errant child, so God punishes transgressors of His law (Hebrews 2:2). That is why the salvation Christ provided is
so significant. We are transgressors, we cannot perfectly keep God's standard. But Christ kept God's righteous standard, and through faith we are
identified with Him. And we are reckoned righteous in Him. For that reason,
"how shall we escape if we neglect so great a salvation?" (Hebrews 2:3).

LESSON: *Sin is transgressing, or "crossing over," God's commandments.*

SIN IS
MISSING THE MARK

All have sinned and fall short of the glory of God. (Romans 3:23)

Suppose on a warm summer day you see a group of youthful swimmers on the beach in southern California. One of them remarks, "Let's jump to Catalina Island." In their hilarity they begin running out into the waves, seeing how far they can jump. Some jump only four feet, some five, some perhaps eight feet. But all fall far short of jumping to Catalina Island, which is some twenty miles off shore.

So it is with sin. Sin is falling short of God's mark. Some may "jump" further in life than others, but all fall very far short of God's standard. In the Old Testament the word *chata* means a willful decision to miss the mark; it is a voluntary decision rendering man responsible. Man does not merely miss God's target, he doesn't even shoot at it—he shoots at a different one. For example, Jehu willfully chose not to obey God's law; he willfully refused to reject Jeroboam's idolatry (2 Kings 10:31). "Missing the mark" can be very far from the target as the homosexual sins of Sodom demonstrated (Genesis 18:20). God reminded Israel that He withheld rain because of their sin, desiring to lead them to repentance (1 Kings 8:35).

In the New Testament the the most common word for sin, *hamartia,* also means "to miss the mark," or to fail to reach a goal. Paul looked at humanity, Jews and Gentiles, and concluded that none gets a passing grade (Romans 3:9-20). All humanity—Jews and Gentiles, black and white, rich and poor—have missed the mark of God's standard and fall short of His righteousness (Romans 3:23). Some in their serious opposition to the gospel, "fill up the measure of their sins" (1 Thessalonians 2:16).

But whatever sins we commit, there is forgiveness. It is for all our sins that Jesus came to be slaughtered as the Lamb of God who took away sin (John 1:29). He was our substitute for sin, suffering and dying in our place (Isaiah 53:12). He took our burden of sin upon Himself that we might be relieved of it (2 Corinthians 5:21).

LESSON: *Sin is willfully missing the mark of God's righteous standard.*

SIN RESULTS
IN GUILT

Whoever keeps the whole law and yet stumbles in
one point, he has become guilty of all. (James 2:10)

Ann Landers's column is filled with letters from guilt-ridden people. "I cheated on my spouse thirteen years ago. Should I tell her?" "I withheld information on additional income from the IRS. What should I do?" People are oppressed and burdened by sin committed many years ago. They carry it with them. They are not free. Their guilt haunts them like a shadow stalking their path.

When man violates God's standard, God views him as guilty. In the Old Testament it was a violation of the mosaic covenant (Leviticus 5-6). If a person cursed father and mother or committed adultery, incest, or homosexuality, he was guilty of death (20:6-13); It was a serious matter because the guilty person stood condemned to death before God.

In explaining righteousness, Jesus explained the true intention of the law. It was not merely external. The one who is angry with his brother is guilty before God (Matthew 5:21-22). Guilt is a serious matter, sufficient to assign the sinner to hell.

But surely one single sin could not be that serious, could it? James says, "For whoever keeps the whole law and yet stumbles on one point, he has become guilty of all" (2:10). One single sin is sufficient to incur guilt before God.

Jesus Christ offered the solution. Through His death, He rendered Satan powerless. By His death Jesus will "deliver those who through fear of death were subject to slavery all their lives" (Hebrews 2:15). The phrase "were subject to slavery" reinforces the guilt people are under. Satan holds us hostage in our guilt, and we cannot be set free except upon accepting the ransom that Jesus paid for us. Are you carrying an enormous burden of guilt today? You need be captive no longer. Jesus died to set you free.

LESSON: *Through sin man stands guilty before God, but Jesus Christ offers the payment for the guilt.*

SIN RESULTS
IN BAD THINGS

*The foreman of the sons of Israel saw that they were
in trouble [evil] because they were told, "You must
not reduce your daily amount of bricks." (Exodus 5:19)*

Twenty minutes after a British Airways plane had taken off for
Spain, the windscreen blew out, sucking the captain out of the
cockpit at twenty-three thousand feet. But he was saved by crew
members who clung to his ankles for fifteen minutes while the copilot landed the plane safely in England.

Life is filled with "bad things"—calamities that come our way. One
particular Hebrew word, *ra*, expresses this concept. *Ra* may mean misfortune, calamity, repulsiveness, or evil.

When Judah told his father, Israel, that if they were to receive grain
from Egypt, they would have to take Benjamin with them, the aged patriarch
grieved over his young son saying, "Why did you treat me so badly [evil]?"
(Genesis 43:6). Here the word *evil* means emotional suffering and grief.
Amid Israel's wandering in the wilderness the people complained to Moses,
"Who will give us meat to eat?" (Numbers 11:4)—and they lamented for
Egypt. With the burden of complaining people Moses accused the Lord of
bringing trouble (evil) on him (v. 11).

Evil may also mean suffering through loss of a loved one. When Naomi traveled to Moab with her husband and two sons and all three of her
loved ones died, Naomi lamented, "The Almighty has afflicted [dealt evil]
me." She saw the deaths of her husband and sons as misfortune, or evil.

Isaiah warned those who sought military alliances instead of trusting
in the Lord that God "will bring disaster" (Isaiah 31:2). Micah reminded
false leaders who mistreated the people that God would hide His face from
them "because they have practiced evil deeds" (Micah 3:2). Lot begged the
Sodomites, "Do not act wickedly" (Genesis 19:7). In those instances evil is a
moral problem, stemming from an evil heart.

Ultimately evil is due to sin. The first sin in the Garden caused all of
the calamities of life, but individually we are also responsible for moral
sins. We look to a future day when Messiah will return, heal us of our calamities, and dry our tears.

LESSON: *The calamities, misfortunes, and moral evils are the result
of the sin in the Garden as well as personal sins.*

August 3

SIN RESULTS
IN PHYSICAL DEATH

*Inasmuch as it is appointed for men to die once
and after this comes judgment. (Hebrews 9:27).*

As a young pastor I always dreaded the prospect of officiating at a funeral service. Then it happened. Julius and his wife were driving down the highway when she noticed that the car was veering toward the shoulder. She looked over at her husband, and his head had slumped. He was dead. I'll never forget that funeral. At the service, she threw herself on the casket and cried, "O Julius, Julius." Her words tore at my soul as I shared her grief.

Death is common to all. It is common because of Adam's initial sin; our first father, in his rebellion against God, drew all humanity into the bonds of death. What was true of Adam is now true of all of us: "Till you return to the ground, because from it you were taken; for you are dust, and to dust you shall return" (Genesis 3:19). God made our physical bodies from the dust of the ground, and because of Adam's sin these physical bodies will return to dust. As head of the human race, Adam represented us all, and with his sin death spread to all humanity (Romans 5:12). Death, the separation of soul from body (James 2:26) is both the consequence of and penalty for sin. Although the law condemns men, sin nonetheless existed before the law (Romans 5:14). Hence, "it is appointed for men to die once, and after this comes judgment" (Hebrews 9:27). Christian Science notwithstanding, all must pass this road.

Whereas Romans 5:12-21 gives devastating news, it also gives the triumphant solution: "If by the transgression of the one, death reigned through the one [Adam], much more those who receive the abundance of grace and of the gift of righteousness will reign in life through the One, Jesus Christ" (Romans 5:17). Although we face death, we face it triumphantly because Jesus Christ has removed its sting. We have the hope of life eternal through faith in Him.

LESSON: *Adam's sin in the Garden brought physical death to the entire human race.*

SIN RESULTS
IN SPIRITUAL DEATH

From the tree of the knowledge of good and evil
you shall not eat, for in the day that you eat
from it you shall surely die. (Genesis 2:17)

Walter L. Wilson tells of riding to the cemetery with the undertaker in a hearse. As they rode along, Dr. Wilson asked the undertaker, a young man in his thirties, "What do you suppose the Bible means by saying, 'Let the dead bury their dead'?" Replied the undertaker, "There isn't a verse like that in the Bible." When Dr. Wilson assured him there was, the young man commented, "How could a dead person bury a dead person?" Dr. Wilson explained the verse by pointing out to him, "You are a dead undertaker in front of the hearse driving out to bury the dead friend at the back of the hearse. That person is dead to her family, and you are dead to God" (Naismith, *Notes, Quotes*, p. 53).

Augustine said that sin is the punishment of sin—meaning that the condition into which man is born, dominated by the sin nature, is part of the penalty of sin. It also reflects man's spiritual death, which is his estrangement from God.

Spiritual death began in the Garden of Eden when man disobeyed God. When God tested Adam He warned him not to eat the forbidden fruit, "for in the day that you eat from it you shall surely die" (Genesis 2:17). The moment Adam bit into the fruit, he died spiritually (and he began to die physically). The fellowship he once enjoyed with God was broken, illustrated when he hid himself from God (3:10).

God cannot condone evil, nor can the evildoer have fellowship with Him (Psalm 5:4-5). Only the righteous can enter His presence (24:3-4). But a life spent in sin results in spiritual death and, if not averted, eternal death (Romans 6:16, 21, 23). Sin pays terrible wages. The ultimate payday is spiritual, physical, and eternal death (v. 23).

But there is a grand solution. Although the wages of sin is death, "the free gift of God is eternal life in Christ Jesus our Lord" (Romans 6:23). Spiritual death can be averted by accepting the free gift that God offers you in Christ Jesus. You cannot work for it or pay for it. It must only be received as a gift through faith—you stop trusting everything else, and you trust in the Lord Jesus Christ alone for salvation. By doing so you will forever avert spiritual death.

LESSON: *Spiritual death is separation from God.*

SIN RESULTS
IN ETERNAL DEATH

This is the second death, the lake of fire. And if anyone's name was not found written in the book of life, he was thrown into the lake of fire. (Revelation 20:14-15)

One morning two Jehovah's Witnesses knocked at my door. We had a lengthy discussion about a variety of doctrines, but I tried to bring them back to the crucial issue: Jesus is God. As I talked to them about Romans 10:9, 13, I implored them to believe that Jesus is God come in the flesh, that He died as a substitute for their sins, and that by believing in Him, they could be assured of eternal life. My heart was heavy as I saw them walk away, and I wondered how much they had really considered my words. The very thing they denied—eternal death— would be their lot should they refuse the gracious invitation of Christ.

Eternal death is the final death. The one who continues in spiritual death until physical death occurs will enter eternal death, which is irreversible. It is the permanent separation from God. It is not annihilation. Eternal death is not loss of consciousness—it is continued existence in the place prepared for the devil and his followers. John describes the second death: "If anyone's name was not found written in the book of life, he was thrown into the lake of fire" (Revelation 20:15). At the end of the Millennium, all unbelievers face Christ at the great white throne judgment and are reminded that their eternal judgment in hell in just. Christ taught that "these will go away into eternal punishment" (Matthew 25:46). Just as life is eternal, so is the punishment. Jesus revealed that they would "be cast out into the outer darkness; in that place there shall be weeping and gnashing of teeth" (8:12). The second death is not annihilation; it is continued suffering.

As long as there is physical life the second death can be averted. If you are living apart from Jesus Christ, you can avoid eternal death by placing your trust in Him. Then you will be an heir of life, not death, and you may look forward to living and reigning with Christ for all eternity.

LESSON: *The second death—conscious eternal suffering—occurs when a person continues in spiritual death until the time of physical death.*

PENALTIES FOR SIN

*If we walk in the light as He Himself is in the light,
we have fellowship with one another, and the blood
of Jesus His Son cleanses us from all sin. (1 John 1:7)*

A man from an affluent New England family deceived police, politicians, and press when he staged his pregnant wife's murder, then accused a habitual criminal from a police lineup. He immediately collected insurance money, expecting eventually to gain a sizable amount. It was the perfect crime—except for one thing. His brother knew what had happened, and he could not live with his conscience. He confessed to the police, implicating his brother, whereupon the murderer committed suicide. There is a payday for sin!

The unbeliever will suffer eternal punishment in the lake of fire (Revelation 20:11-15). When on that final day the books are opened, the recorded deeds of unbelievers will convict them, and their deeds will demand eternal punishment.

John wrote his first epistle to warn believers that sin disrupts fellowship with the Father. He explained that sin will direct believers into darkness (1 John 1:6). We are children of light, destined to walk in the light, but John indicates it is possible for believers to walk in darkness. We are privileged to have fellowship with the Father and the Son—sharing our very lives with God and fellow believers, but sin will hinder fellowship (1 John 1:6-7).

Sin also results in loss of joy (v. 4). Living in a turbulent world, Christians may enjoy the tranquil peace of God; they may know genuine joy. Sin will also misdirect a believer into loving the world rather than loving God and other believers (2:15-17). If we love the world, we will be devoid of God's love, crippled in our ability to love others. Sin also hinders our prayers. God will not hear us if we ignore His commandments (3:22). How important it is that we reject sin!

The consequences of sin are serious. If you have never trusted in Christ you await an endless tragedy of suffering. Do not procrastinate any longer. Come to Christ in faith, trusting His atoning death on your behalf.

LESSON: *Sin has a price tag: an unbeliever will suffer eternal punishment, whereas a believer will suffer loss of fellowship and blessings.*

WHEN A CHRISTIAN SINS

If we say that we have fellowship with Him and yet walk in the darkness, we lie and do not practice the truth. (1 John 1:6)

In a world filled with anxiety, tension, and pressure, a Christian can reflect joy and tranquillity, or the peace of Christ. That is a believer's privilege (John 15:11). But when a Christian sins there is a loss of joy. Perhaps it is true that no one is as miserable as a Christian living in sin. If we sin and remove ourselves from fellowship with Christ, we suffer serious loss—loss of joy.

The joy doesn't originate with us. Jesus said it is "My joy." When we avoid walking in fellowship with Christ, His joy is no longer our portion. Since joy is connected with fellowship, our downward trend begins with a loss of fellowship. John wrote to remind us that "our fellowship is with the Father, and with His Son Jesus Christ" (1 John 1:3). What a privilege! The eternal Father and Son have moved heaven and earth to have fellowship with us mortals. Fellowship means "sharing"—enjoying the closest possible union with Father and the Son. But sin ruins that close communion just as unfaithfulness can ruin an intimate marriage relationship. John says it is impossible to walk in darkness and have fellowship with Christ (v. 6)—it is only possible as we walk in the light (v. 7).

Sin also brings a loss of peace. Finding peace is like finding the pearl in an oyster—it is a treasure. Peace is the prerogative of the one who steadfastly trusts the Lord (Isaiah 26:3). But since peace is only ministered to the believer through the Holy Spirit, the sinning believer will only know turmoil and anxiety. The peace of God will escape him. When the sinning believer ruptures his fellowship with Christ, he forfeits His promises: "My peace I give to you" (John 14:27), "In Me you may have peace. In the world you have tribulation" (16:33). The sinning believer trades Christ's peace for the world's tribulation. A bad swap!

Are you walking in the darkness, away from the Light of the world? Are you anxious, devoid of peace, far away from home? Come back. The Savior is waiting for you and welcomes your return.

LESSON: *When the believer sins, there is a loss of joy, peace, and fellowship, until he turns homeward to Christ.*

August 8

PROVISION
AGAINST SIN

Thy word I have treasured in my heart,
that I may not sin against Thee. (Psalm 119:11)

Although the believer faces a formidable foe in sin, God has made abundant provision for victory by providing us with His Word. "Thy word I have treasured in my heart, that I may not sin against Thee," proclaimed the psalmist (Psalm 119:11). With all his heart the psalmist sought to keep God's precepts (v. 10). As an act of the will, with all his conscious being he sought to obey God's revealed will in His Word. That is the antidote to sin. The inspired Scriptures were given "for teaching, for reproof, for correction, for training in righteousness" (2 Timothy 3:16). The Word of God sanctifies believers in the truth (John 17:17).

In a court case a strong defense attorney is very important to win the case. Christians have the strongest defense attorney in Christ, who pleads our case before the Father. "If anybody does sin, we have one who speaks to the Father in our defense—Jesus Christ, the Righteous One" (1 John 2:1, NIV). We need not worry whether we can afford His services. "He always lives to make intercession" for us (Hebrews 7:25). His defense on our behalf never stops. For that reason, sin will never prevail over us.

If we looked to ourselves to try to overcome sin we would surely be dismayed. But God has provided the Holy Spirit. In detailing the sins that emanate from the old nature—immorality, strife, jealousy, anger, envy— Paul says, "Walk by the Spirit" (Galatians 5:16). We can achieve victory over sin not in our own strength but in God's provision—the indwelling Holy Spirit. We are to walk in His power.

When we are "filled with the Spirit" (Ephesians 5:18) we can carry out the commands of Scripture. We can live a life that is pleasing to God. How specifically does the Spirit help us? He teaches us God's Word (1 Corinthians 2:10-13), enabling us to understand and apply it to daily living. Let's not give in to the enemy. God has made provision for us to win the war against sin.

LESSON: *God has provided victory over sin for us through His Word, the intercession of Christ, and the indwelling Holy Spirit.*

Part 6
Salvation

WHAT IS SALVATION?

Believe in the Lord Jesus, and you shall be saved. (Acts 16:31)

How can a person be saved and assured of heaven? If we were to ask bystanders in the street that question, we undoubtedly would hear a variety of answers. As one man confided: "I have never been unfaithful to my wife; I'm a good, moral man. I've taught my children to recite the Lord's Prayer and the Beatitudes. I think I'll make it." Is a person saved by his works? As J. Vernon McGee commented, "Salvation by works? That's like jumping out of an airplane clutching a sack of cement instead of a parachute!" Or as George Whitefield said, "Heaven by works? I'd just as soon climb to the moon on a rope of sand."

Years ago my cousin explained John 3:16 to me, and as I read it, I believed it: "Whoever believes in [Christ] should not perish but have eternal life." It does not say, "Whoever believes and gives a tithe," or, "Whoever believes and does good works daily," or, "Whoever is baptized and joins a church." We should do those things, but they have no part in salvation. Jesus said, "Whoever believes . . . may have eternal life." It is faith in Christ that saves . . . plus nothing.

Don't works have a part in salvation? Titus 3:5 tells us, "He saved us, not because of righteous things we have done, but because of his mercy" (NIV). Works should be the *result* of salvation, not part of salvation. Paul reminded the Ephesians that salvation is "not as a result of works, that no one should boast" (2:9). If works played a part in salvation then we could boast because we would have something to do with achieving it. But God effects salvation, not man.

Whereas faith is the channel by which we are saved, ultimately it is God's grace that saves us: "For by grace you have been saved through faith" (Ephesians 2:8). Grace is God's undeserving favor whereby He accepts the death of Christ on our behalf and applies the benefits of His death to our spiritual bank account. Faith simply lays hold of God's grace. Isn't it amazing? There is nothing that you or I can do to merit salvation. Absolutely nothing. In that way God gets the honor, not us. Have you stopped trusting in your works and come to Christ by faith alone?

LESSON: *What a wonder that God receives us into His heaven, not through any works we could offer Him, but by faith in Christ alone!*

WHAT IS FAITH?

If you confess with your mouth Jesus as Lord,
and believe in your heart that God raised Him
from the dead, you shall be saved. (Romans 10:9)

I n Tzeltal, a language in south Mexico, faith is "hanging onto God with the heart." In Valiente, a Panamanian language, one says, "To lean on God." In the Sudan, the Anuaks say, "Putting oneself in God's hands." The nearby Uduks in the north say faith is "joining God's word to one's body."

What is faith? Is it simply believing some facts? Is it a feeling? Although most would agree that the Bible teaches salvation is by faith, not all agree on the nature of faith.

Saving faith involves three things. It involves knowledge or intellect. Certain facts must be believed. Paul instructed the Philippian jailer, "Believe in the Lord Jesus, and you shall be saved" (Acts 16:31). That is the same as believing that Jesus is Lord (Romans 10:9).

What is the meaning of "Lord"? After the resurrection it is always used to describe the deity of Christ. Jesus is God. There is no salvation without believing that. Saving faith is also believing that He died as the substitute for my sins and was raised bodily (1 Corinthians 15:3-4). That is the heart of the gospel.

Faith also involves conviction, or the emotions. Believing facts alone will not make one a Christian. H. G. Wells devoted considerable space to Jesus in his *Outline of History*. He believed in Jesus as a historical figure but made no claim to being a Christian. In saving faith the Holy Spirit convicts me of my need of a Savior. I sense my sinfulness and my great need for Christ to rescue me from sin's penalty (John 16:8; Acts 2:37).

But even knowledge and conviction are not enough. Saving faith also involves trust. "Believe in your heart" is an act of the will (Romans 10:9), trusting that Jesus died to pay for your sins. Saving faith, then, is knowledge of the facts about Christ in His person, a conviction that He died for me, and a trust in Him (to the exclusion of all else) for my eternal salvation.

Have you ventured down that road? Has your will been moved so that you have stopped trusting everything else and you now hope in Him alone for your salvation?

LESSON: *Saving faith involves knowledge about Christ, conviction that He died to save me, and trust in Him for that salvation.*

August 11

THE WORD OF GOD
IN SALVATION

So faith comes from hearing, and hearing
by the word of Christ. (Romans 10:17)

I attended a church service in which a visiting evangelist brought the message. He began by giving a lengthy account of his life and ministry. I waited, with closed Bible on my lap, for him to open the Bible and begin to expound the Scriptures. It never happened. In fact, he never even explained the gospel. When he concluded his talk, he gave an invitation, and more than a dozen people walked forward. I turned to my wife and asked, "Why are those people going forward?" They had not received the basic information essential for making a spiritual decision.

That raises the question, What part does the Bible have in effecting salvation? It is true that "whoever will call upon the name of the Lord will be saved" (Romans 10:13), but Paul asks, "How then shall they call upon Him in whom they have not believed?" (v. 14). In a series of questions and responses, Paul logically explains that people do not believe the gospel unless they hear it—and that requires someone's proclaiming it to them. "So faith comes from hearing, and hearing by the word of Christ" (v. 17).

To believe something a person must hear it. Ultimately, he is not saved by meditating, praying, or enjoying an experience; he is saved through hearing and believing the Word of God. His Word is therefore instrumental in bringing men and women to faith.

What must they hear? The basic gospel. Paul explains it: "Christ died for our sins according to the Scriptures, and that He was buried, and that He was raised on the third day" (1 Corinthians 15:3-4). Since the Word of God is living, it penetrates our innermost being, bringing conviction (Hebrews 4:12). Then it brings forth the new birth (James 1:18; 1 Peter 1:23).

It is impossible to be saved apart from the Word of God. For that reason it is important that you and I speak a specific word to our hearers that enables them to be saved. The "Roman Road" is helpful: Romans 3:23; 6:23; 5:8.

LESSON: *The Word of God is instrumental in effecting the new birth.*

IS SURRENDER A PART
OF THE GOSPEL?

Believe in the Lord Jesus, and you shall be saved. (Acts 16:31)

Must Christ be Lord or Master of one's life before he can be saved? Must a person surrender every part of his life to Christ in order to be saved? The word *Lord* (*kurios*) can variously mean "sir," "master," or "Lord," but the crucial issue was Christ's claim of deity. The Jews sought to stone Him to death because He claimed equality with God (John 5:18).

To be saved one had to acknowledge Jesus as God by referring to Him as "Lord," a term equivalent to the Old Testament "Yahweh," or "Jehovah." Although such a claim incurred the wrath of the Jewish people, that is precisely what Paul emphasized: "If you confess with your mouth Jesus as Lord . . . you shall be saved" (Romans 10:9). That did not simply mean master —that would not have been a critical issue. There were many masters, but there is only one God. Acknowledging Jesus as God was necessary for salvation, and that evoked opposition. J. Gresham Machen, the great Princeton and Westminster professor, stated, "When the early Christian missionaries called Jesus 'Lord,' it was perfectly plain to their pagan hearers everywhere that they meant to ascribe divinity to Him."

What about passages where Jesus calls His hearers to be His disciples? For example, He demanded that they put Him ahead of family. He called on them to count the cost, concluding, "No one of you can be My disciple who does not give up all his own possessions" (Luke 14:33). If that were a criterion for salvation, then who would be saved? Who has given away all his possessions? The answer lies in the meaning of *disciple*. The word means "learner" and has no bearing on salvation. Some "disciples" were even unsaved (John 6:66). Jesus was calling on people to follow Him as learners. Further, if discipleship is necessary for salvation, then so is baptism because making disciples and baptizing are linked in Matthew 28:19.

Of course, if every new Christian made Christ Lord of his or her life, there would be no carnal Christians. That is a wonderful ideal, but it is not reality (1 Corinthians 3:1, 3). Believers *should* make Christ the Master of their lives. He is Lord in fact, and He should be our Lord in practice. But that is a message for Christians; it is not part of the gospel.

LESSON: *Acknowledging Jesus as Lord is to recognize Him as God, a requisite for salvation.*

IS REPENTANCE A PART
OF THE GOSPEL?

God is now declaring to men that all
everywhere should repent. (Acts 17:30)

I s repentance necessary for salvation? Didn't Paul preach "repentance toward God and faith in our Lord Jesus Christ" (Acts 20:21)? Most everyone will agree that repentance is a part of the gospel. The Scriptures clearly indicate that. But there is a difference of opinion on the meaning of repentance. Just what is it? One writer suggests, "Surely it is required for salvation that a man repent and turn away from his sins. How can one turn from and forsake his sins without forsaking his will for God's will?" That statement confuses the meaning of repentance. Repentance (*metanoia*) means "change of mind." Change of mind about what? (1) God. Where He has been ignored, He is recognized as sovereign Judge. (2) Christ. No longer is He the object of profanity; He is seen as the Savior. (3) Self. Pride is gone; sin looms oppressive and heavy.

Repentance does not mean to turn from sin or a change of conduct. That should naturally follow when one believes. But if repentance means a change of conduct, then we are requiring an unsaved person to change his life before he comes to Christ. As Donald Grey Barnhouse said, "Then we are asking an ungodly person to perform a godly act," which is impossible. An unsaved person cannot clean up his life before he comes to Christ. Repentance as a change of mind is part of believing and should not be understood as a separate "work." One cannot change the mind without believing and cannot believe without a change of mind (Acts 20:21).

Repentance should result in a change of conduct, but the change of conduct is not part of the gospel. Change of conduct comes through teaching, fellowship, and reading the Word. It cannot be preliminary to faith; it follows faith. It is vital to a pure gospel that we do not add anything—however good our intentions—to its terms.

LESSON: *Repentance as a change of mind (not conduct) is part of the gospel.*

IS BAPTISM A PART
OF THE GOSPEL?

Believe in the Lord Jesus, and you shall be saved,
you and your household. (Acts 16:31)

Some churches and denominations teach that in order to be saved one must not only believe in Christ but also be baptized. Is that correct? What is the scriptural basis for this belief?

Some point to Acts 2:38: "Repent, and let each of you be baptized in the name of Jesus Christ for the forgiveness of your sins." There are several explanations here: First, the word *for* (*eis*) means "because of," that is, Peter commands them to be baptized *because* their sins are forgiven—not to bring about forgiveness of sins.

Second, the historical context is important. Peter is addressing a nation under judgment. They are guilty of having rejected and crucified their Messiah, and for that reason judgment is coming upon the nation (Matthew 23:37-39). The remedy? Disassociate themselves from the nation under judgment. By baptism they would publicly declare that disassociation. Josephus writes that prior to the destruction of Jerusalem in A.D. 70 the Jewish Christians fled the city and saved their lives. That is Peter's appeal in Acts 2:38.

What about Mark 16:16, which says, "He who has believed and has been baptized shall be saved"? The latter half of that verse says, "He who has disbelieved shall be condemned." It doesn't say, "He who has disbelieved and has not been baptized shall be condemned." A person is lost for not having believed, not because he has not been baptized. There is an additional problem with Mark 16:16. The ending of Mark, verses 9-20, is not found in the oldest manuscripts and is probably not a part of the original text.

One further problem. If baptism is essential to salvation what shall we do with the many verses that tell us salvation is only by believing in Christ? For example, John 3:16; Acts 16:31; Romans 4:5; 10:9. We must always let the clear verses of Scripture interpret the more difficult verses. To believe in Christ for salvation is a clear teaching of Scripture.

One final note. If baptism is necessary for salvation, then we are implying that Christ's work alone was inadequate to save. Are we willing to make that claim?

LESSON: *Baptism is not a requirement for salvation.*

August 15

SECURITY
OF SALVATION

*I give eternal life to them; and they shall never perish,
and no one shall snatch them out of My hand. (John 10:28)*

Are you a cat Christian or a monkey Christian? There is a big difference. Notice how a mother cat carries her kittens—she grasps them by the neck with her teeth. On what does the kitten's security depend? The mother. By contrast, the baby monkey grasps its mother with its tiny paws—and hangs on for dear life. On whom does the baby monkey's security depend? Itself!

Does our security in salvation rest upon our ability "to hang onto God," or does it depend on God's ability to keep us? Our security in salvation rests in the work of the Father, Son, and Holy Spirit. The very ones God chose in eternity past are the same ones He has justified and will ultimately glorify (Romans 8:29-30). None is lost is the process.

We are also kept secure in our salvation by the power of God because we are hidden in the hollow of Christ's hand (John 10:28-29). The Father gave us to the Son, and no one (including ourselves) can snatch us out of His hand. Could we be any more secure than that? Is anyone stronger than Christ? Enter into rest, dear friend, if you are a believer. No one can rob you of your security in Christ.

Christ's work has also secured our eternal destiny. He has fully paid the price for our sins—nothing more is owing (Ephesians 1:7). God's wrath has been removed from us; He is fully satisfied with Christ's payment (Romans 3:25). Our sins have been removed and will not be called into question again (Colossians 2:13). Moreover, Christ continues His work on our behalf by constantly praying for us (Hebrews 7:25). If we could be lost again, then Christ would be ineffective in His work of intercession. Is that possible?

At salvation God sealed us with His Holy Spirit—He put His brand mark on us, indicating He owns us (2 Corinthians 1:22). The Holy Spirit is God's down payment to us that we will arrive safely on heaven's shore.

Dear Christian, do not fret and worry about your eternal destiny. Rest in God's promise: "No one shall snatch them out of my hand." God's Word is reliable.

LESSON: *Our salvation is eternally secure because of the work of the Father, Son, and Holy Spirit.*

COMMON
GRACE

He did not leave Himself without witness
in that He did good and gave you rains
from heaven and fruitful seasons. (Acts 14:17)

Years ago the Canadian government introduced "Family Allowance" to all Canadian households, in which the parents receive a regular monthly check based on the number and ages of the children. There are no strings attached. Parents receive a check for every child each month. Formerly it was $5, later it increased to $20 per month. The child may be French or English, rich or poor—parents receive an allotment for every Canadian child.

Common grace is like that. God extends common grace to every member of the human race—American or Chinese, educated or uneducated—everyone is a recipient. No strings are attached. What is common grace? It involves several things, including general blessings such as sunshine and rainfall, enabling both believing and atheist farmers to harvest their crops (Matthew 5:45). Paul reminded the people of Lystra that God had witnessed to them by "giving you rain from heaven and crops in their seasons; he provides you with plenty of food and fills your hearts with joy" (Acts 14:17, NIV).

The purpose of common grace is clear: it should lead the unbeliever to faith in Christ. In common grace God also restrains sin. He may do so through the Holy Spirit as in the days of Noah (Genesis 6:3), or through prophets (Isaiah 1:16-20), or through human government (Romans 13:1-4). A corollary aspect of common grace is convicting people of sin. The Holy Spirit does that by convincing people of the sin of rejecting Christ, His righteousness, and the certainty of judgment (John 16:8-11).

Common grace is essential because it is preliminary to saving grace. Through common grace people receive a witness from God; they come to recognize His existence and that He is a God of grace but also a God of judgment. Common grace renders men inexcusable; they have God's witness. Then, as the Holy Spirit bears witness of Christ (John 16:8-11—a somewhat narrower aspect of common grace), their hearts have been prepared to respond to the gospel. Have you seen God's goodness operative in your life? Have you responded to it?

LESSON: *Common grace is extended to everyone, revealing God's existence, kindness, convicting work, and judgment.*

SAVING
GRACE

*No one can come to Me, unless the Father
who sent Me draws him. (John 6:44)*

Amazing grace! How sweet the sound, that saved a wretch like me! I once was lost, but now am found, was blind, but now I see." Those beautiful, well-known words were penned by John Newton two centuries ago. They extol the marvelous grace of God.

What is grace? Are there different kinds of grace? We speak of two distinct kinds—common grace and effective, or saving, grace. Everyone, believer and unbeliever alike, is the recipient of common grace, but only believers receive saving grace. Special or effective grace is exactly that—it is effective in those that receive it. They respond to it. Effective grace is necessary for salvation because unbelievers' hearts are hardened (Ephesians 4:18) and their spirits are dead (2:1). How can we respond when our spirits are dead and our hearts as hard as stone? We can't. God must move upon our sin-scarred hearts to make us willing to do His will and believe the gospel.

How is special grace seen in the Scriptures? We recognize it by the word *call.* God called Paul to be an apostle (Romans 1:1); Paul didn't choose God—he was too busy hauling Christians to jail. He reminded the Roman Christians that they were "the called of Jesus Christ" (v. 6). God called some of them out from among the Gentiles (v. 5). All believers were called into the family of God because of God's sovereign purpose when He chose us in eternity past (8:28-29). No one is able to come to God apart from His special "inviting" grace (John 6:44). And the Holy Spirit makes it effective as He gives life to the believing sinner.

There is another side to this coin. Effective grace doesn't eliminate responsibility. You can't sit back and say, "Well, if I'm not one of the called ones I can't come anyway." That isn't true. People are lost because they refuse the gracious gospel invitation, not because they aren't called. The invitation is for everyone. If you haven't yet responded to the invitation, come home today. The Lord's banquet table awaits you.

LESSON: *Saving, or effective, grace is necessary because people are dead in sin, and it is effective to all to whom it is extended, effecting their salvation.*

August 18

CHOSEN

He chose us in Him before the foundation of the world, that we should be holy and blameless before Him. (Ephesians 1:4)

The mere preaching of the gospel does not save an individual. The message must be activated by the election and calling of God for an individual to be drawn to Him. It would be as if one had thrown a rope to a drowning man. The throwing of that rope could not save the man unless someone were at the other end drawing him in to shore.

"That is what God has done. By his election, God draws to himself the one who has heard the message. The man may have the rope, but he still needs the efficient force of God drawing him in. Who, therefore, deserves the praise for salvation, the man who grabbed the rope? No— the God who draws him in!" (Green, *Illustrations*, p. 115).

What is election? Election is God's choosing some people from among the masses to be saved. It is His free choice because He is a sovereign God. He has chosen the foolish and the weak to bring honor to His name (1 Corinthians 1:26-29). Election is individual; for example, individual Thessalonian believers were chosen (2 Thessalonians 2:13).

When did election take place? It was "before the foundation of the world" (Ephesians 1:4). Spurgeon said, "God certainly must have chosen me before I came into the world or He never would have done so afterwards!" When God chose us in eternity past it was not because of any goodness on our part. It was because of His sovereign choice and love.

Why did God elect us? He chose us for Himself. The verb is in the middle voice, emphasizing God chose us for fellowship with Himself.

What should be our response? Awe, wonder, and praise. Do not try to understand this teaching—you cannot. The Bible teaches it, and we should praise God that He chose us, enabling us to believe the gospel. If you are an unbeliever, the issue is not election; it is, "Believe in the Lord Jesus, and you shall be saved." Man cannot say, "Maybe I'm not one of the elect." God is responsible for election. People are responsible to believe. If you have never believed, will you believe in Christ now?

LESSON: *Before the foundation of the world, God chose believers for fellowship with Himself.*

August 19

MARKED OUT BEFOREHAND

*In love He predestined us to adoption as sons
through Jesus Christ to Himself, according to
the kind intention of His will. (Ephesians 1:4-5)*

While living in the desert city of Moreno Valley, California, I watched the surveyors invade the tumbleweed field across the street. They spent days marking off streets and establishing property boundaries. Not long afterward the builders rolled in, poured cement slabs, and began to construct houses. Within months, dozens of ranch houses had been erected, all with properly established yards and streets. How did the builders know where to build? Where the surveyors had marked out the boundaries for each yard.

As the surveyors established street and yard boundaries, so God has established the boundaries of all things: He predestined (to predestine means "to mark out beforehand") the death of Christ (Acts 4:28), that believers be conformed to the image of Christ (Romans 8:29), our adoption as sons (Ephesians 1:5), and ultimately, all things that happen (Ephesians 1:11). That is not to suggest, however, that the non-elect are predestined to damnation. That is not taught in Scripture. People are lost because they refuse to believe the gospel.

In eternity past, God marked us out for salvation to be adopted into His family. Did any merit on our part cause Him to predestine us? No. It was "in accordance with his pleasure and will" (Ephesians 1:5, NIV). Why? Martin Luther correctly said, "God's will has no why." We ask the impossible when we ask why. We cannot know—the reason for God's predestination is locked up in the vault of God's mystery. Nor is it necessary that we know.

What is the purpose of predestination? It is "to the praise of his glorious grace" (Ephesians 1:6, NIV). Some colleges have showcases displaying the trophies won through exemplary performances in basketball, football, and other endeavors. Our lives are to be like trophies to God's glorious grace. That is the purpose of predestination. Is your life a beautiful trophy of God's glorious grace?

LESSON: *In eternity past, God marked us out for salvation, that our lives should be to the praise of God's glorious grace.*

FOREKNOWN

*For whom He foreknew, He also predestined to become
conformed to the image of His Son, that He might be
the first-born among many brethren. (Romans 8:29)*

W hat does it mean to say God foreknew us? Does it mean He knew beforehand who would believe and that He chose people for salvation based on that knowledge?

Actually, the word *knowledge* is similar in meaning to *choose*. This is seen in the Lord's statement to Israel: "You only have I known of all the families of the earth" (Amos 3:2, KJV). Keil says foreknowledge is "not merely taking notice, but is energetic, embracing man in his inmost being, embracing and penetrating with divine love." When the Lord "knew" the Israelites in the wilderness, He lovingly cared for them (Hosea 13:5).

Foreknowledge is virtually equivalent to election as seen in Genesis 18:19, where it signifies the Lord's gracious fellowship with Abraham: "For I have chosen [known] him, in order that he may command his children and his household after him to keep the way of the Lord." Similarly, John writes, "We know that we have come to know Him, if we keep His commandments" (1 John 2:3). Here also "to know" involves a loving relationship; it is more than intellectual awareness. A clear example of the means of foreknowledge is Romans 11:2: "God has not rejected His people whom He foreknew." Clearly, that means more than knowing beforehand; it means God has not rejected His people whom He chose. Furthermore, foreknowledge involves people—it is not just seeing beforehand who would believe. God foreknew certain people whom He predestined (Romans 8:29-30).

Peter says Christ "was foreknown before the foundation of the world" (1 Peter 1:20). In eternity past God chose Christ to be the Redeemer. In that sense, we understand 1 Peter 1:1-2: "Aliens . . . who are chosen according to the foreknowledge of God." In eternity past God foreknew; He chose believers to belong to Him and inherit all the riches in Christ. Who can fathom the mysteries of God? When we attempt to understand this, we walk where angels fear to tread. Let us rejoice in the wonder of God's foreknowledge, expressing praise through the sacrifice of our lips and lives.

LESSON: *Foreknowledge, which is basically synonymous with election, means God's decision to enter into a relationship with His people.*

August 21

CHRIST'S DEATH IS
A SUBSTITUTIONARY ATONEMENT

[Christ] gave Himself as a ransom for all. (1 Timothy 2:6)

During the Korean War a truck loaded with American soldiers sat at the roadside when suddenly a hand grenade was hurled out of the bushes. Stunned, the men stared in disbelief at the hand grenade lying beside the truck about to explode. Without hesitation one of the soldiers jumped down and hurled his body onto the grenade as it exploded, ripping his body apart. The soldier had sacrificed his life that the men in the truck could live.

Jesus' death was not simply the death of a martyr or an example of bravery. He died as a substitute for sinners. There are two Greek prepositions translated "for" that indicate Jesus' death was substitutionary. In the phrase "His life a ransom for many" (Matthew 20:28), the word *for* is the preposition *anti* and means "instead of" or "in place of." Jesus told the disciples He was giving His life as a payment price in the place of sinners. He died in our stead.

That the preposition *for* means substitution can also be seen from its usage in Luke 11:11, where Jesus asks, "Now suppose one of you fathers is asked by his son for a fish; he will not give him a snake instead of a fish, will he?" The word *instead* is *anti*, here clearly showing the meaning of substitution as the snake is substituted for a fish.

In 1 Timothy 2:6 Paul declares that Jesus "gave Himself as a ransom for all." *For* here is the preposition *huper*, also meaning "on behalf of" and emphasizing substitution. The same preposition is used in Philemon 13, where it is translated "in your behalf." Paul was reminding Philemon that the runaway slave Onesimus was minister to Paul as a substitute on behalf of Philemon.

The doctrine of the substitutionary death is immensely important. For us to be released from the guilt and bondage of our sins so that we might have eternal life, it was important that One die in our place. Have you put your trust in the One who died as your substitute? His death was of infinite value to completely pay the price for your salvation. But you must believe in Him as your substitute. Will you?

LESSON: *Jesus Christ died as a substitute for all humanity, paying the price for all sins.*

CHRIST'S DEATH
PROVIDED REDEMPTION

*In Him we have redemption through His blood,
the forgiveness of our trespasses, according
to the riches of His grace. (Ephesians 1:7)*

My father was a jeweler, and I recall seeing customers come into his jewelry shop bringing watches to be repaired. When someone brought a watch in, my father would write the customer's name on a tag, tear off a stub, and hand it to him. When the watch was repaired the customer would return, pay for the repair work, and receive the repaired watch. The customer was redeeming his watch. The watch had once been new, but it became defective and needed to be repaired.

Jesus Christ has redeemed us to Himself through His death (Ephesians 1:7). The word *redemption* means "to buy back by the payment of a price." It is taken from its usage in the Roman world. In Paul's day there were far more slaves than free people. When the Romans conquered their enemies, they would capture many of their defeated foe and return them to Rome. The captives would become slaves, and they would be traded and sold at public auctions in the marketplaces. It would be possible to purchase a slave in the marketplace and set the slave free once the purchase price had been paid.

Jesus Christ provided redemption for believers by paying the price for us all—with His death. Paul said, "We have redemption through His blood" (Ephesians 1:7). Blood emphasizes death. When enough blood is shed, death takes place. Our redemption necessitated the death of God's Son.

The human race was created in innocence, but man was marred through sin in the Garden. Through His death, Christ paid the price necessary to release us from slavery to sin. We were set free from slavery through the death of Christ when we trusted in Him. If you are a believer, Christ's death released you from the snare of sin, giving you freedom and victory (Romans 6:6). You need no longer live in bondage to the old master of sin. You have received your declaration of emancipation. You have been set free from sin's slavery.

LESSON: *Jesus Christ bought us back to God by paying the price of redemption and setting us free from slavery to sin.*

CHRIST'S DEATH
PROVIDED FORGIVENESS

*He made you alive together with Him, having
forgiven us all our transgressions. (Colossians 2:13)*

Joe Louis, who reigned as the world's heavyweight boxing champion for nearly thirteen years, may well have been the greatest heavyweight boxer of all time. Not only did he reign the longest of any heavyweight boxer, but he defended his title twenty-five times, which remains a record. At one point in his championship Louis went on a "bum of the month" campaign, defending his title seven times in seven months, easily defeating his opponent each time. During his brilliant career Louis earned more than four million dollars—a staggering amount for his day. But when his career was over, Louis was broke—and he owed the IRS more than one million dollars. Louis took a menial job but was still unable to pay his debt; in fact, the interest accumulating on his debt was more than the wage he was earning. Eventually, the U.S. government canceled Louis's debt since it recognized there was no way he could repay it.

One of the marvelous results of the death of Jesus Christ is the forgiveness that He has provided for believers. Ephesians 1:7 declares that in Christ we have "the forgiveness of sins." The word *forgiveness* means a pardon, or cancellation, of a debt that cannot be paid. What the U.S. government did for Joe Louis materially, Jesus Christ has done for all believers spiritually. All of us were in a spiritual debt that we could not pay. No amount of self effort, tithing, or good works could pay the necessary price. But Jesus Christ canceled our debt—at a very expensive price. It cost Him His life. His death was the necessary price for the payment of our sins (Hebrews 9:22).

The result is that the believer's sins have been removed as far as the east is from the west (Psalm 103:12). God will never call his or her sins into account again. The believer stands in a perpetual state of forgiveness. Rejoice, Christian, you have been forgiven! God has written "paid in full" across your indebtedness of sin. Let God's peace pervade your soul as you contemplate the richness of His forgiveness.

LESSON: *Through the death of Christ the believer has been totally forgiven and may therefore enjoy peace.*

CHRIST'S DEATH
PROVIDED SATISFACTION FOR SIN

*And He Himself is the propitiation for our sins, and not for
ours only, but also for those of the whole world. (1 John 2:2)*

In 1741 the eloquent, educated Jonathan Edwards preached what may be the most famous sermon ever, "Sinners in the Hands of an Angry God." It was an eloquent exposition of Deuteronomy 32:35, and although the nearsighted Edwards read his sermon, he was interrupted by people clinging to the pews and crying out for God to spare them from hell. Such was the impact of his sermon. The people caught the import of his words: God hates sin and must punish it.

The wrath of God is a neglected subject today. Yet the Old and New Testaments alike are rife with discussion of His wrath. There are more than twenty different words used 580 times in the Old Testament to describe God's wrath. It burns like fire against sin (Jeremiah 21:12) and against those committing idolatry (Joshua 23:16). God will pour out His wrath in judgment when His people forsake Him (Ezekiel 5:13-17).

How then can the wrath of God be averted? In the Old Testament that was only possible when the high priest entered the Holy of Holies on the Day of Atonement, asking for a deferral of the payment for sin for another year. Man cannot, however, offer anything that will assuage God's wrath. How then is the problem solved? God must provide the remedy for sin.

Romans 3:25 explains that, through His death, Christ was publicly displayed as a satisfaction for sin. ("Satisfaction" is a suitable synonym for "propitiation.") The wrath of God was covered and appeased through Christ's making full, complete, and satisfactory atonement for sin. God's holiness and righteous standard was upheld and satisfied through the death of Christ. So we can say, "God is propitiated," or, "God is satisfied."

That is of enormous significance for us. We were helpless. We were sinners, and there was nothing we could do to avert God's wrath. We were worthy of eternal punishment because of our sin. Yet in His mercy God provided the solution to our dilemma in sending Christ to make satisfactory atonement for our sin. Have you responded in faith to God's offer of reconciliation?

LESSON: *The wrath of God has been averted and His righteousness satisfied through the death of Christ for sin.*

August 25

CHRIST'S DEATH PROVIDED RECONCILIATION

God was in Christ reconciling the world to Himself. (2 Corinthians 5:19)

When William Tyndale was translating the New Testament into English he encountered great difficulty in finding a satisfactory word to convey the meaning of the work of Christ in reconciling man to God. Finding no adequate word, Tyndale joined two simple words: "at" and "onement," making "atonement," thus giving in its etymology a clue to the Bible's teaching of reconciliation.

Reconciliation brings together two parties that were formerly hostile to each other. In Christ's death on the cross, God and man, who had been separated through sin, were brought together. Who moved away from fellowship? Man did through his sin in the Garden of Eden, by turning his back in rebellion and moving away from fellowship with God. Hence, it was man who needed to be reconciled to God. In our unsaved state, we were at war, enemies of God. We were in need of reconciliation (Romans 5:10).

How could reconciliation be established? When a husband and wife are separated, one party needs to initiate the peace process. In man's estrangement from God it was God Himself who initiated the reconciliation: "God was in Christ reconciling the world to Himself" (2 Corinthians 5:19). How did Christ accomplish reconciliation? Through His death (Romans 5:10). Since Christ is God, His death was of infinite value, providing reconciliation for the world. That is significant since Christ's death rendered the world "savable." However, the whole world is not saved; the reconciliation only becomes reality when it is accepted by faith. It is effective only for those who believe.

What a monumental truth! We all appreciate peace. V-E day and V-J day were important in 1945, signaling an end to hostilities with Germany and Japan. An even greater peace has been effected through the death of Christ. By acknowledging your sin and believing in Christ's death as your substitute, the hostility between you and God is removed. You can live at peace with God.

LESSON: *Through the death of Christ, God reconciled the world to Himself; man enters into the benefits of reconciliation by believing in Christ.*

CHRIST'S DEATH
PROVIDED JUSTIFICATION

Therefore having been justified by faith, we have
peace with God through our Lord Jesus Christ. (Romans 5:1)

W hen Gerald Ford became president of the United States in
1974, he pardoned former President Richard Nixon of any
charges that could be leveled against him. It became legally
impossible to charge Mr. Nixon with any of the criminal activities he had
supposedly been involved in. How was that possible? By a legal act, President Gerald Ford pardoned Richard Nixon.

That illustration, however, only features the negative aspect of justification. Justification, meaning "to declare righteous," is a legal act whereby
God the righteous Judge, pardons us, removing all our sins and the basis of
our separation from Him. God has legally acquitted us of our sins.

How can He do so? The reason God can pardon us from our sins is the
death of Christ—justification is "in his blood" (Romans 3:25). Payment
must be made for sin—something we could never do. But Christ made sufficient payment for our sins (5:9).

However, the application of the benefits of Christ's death comes only
through belief (v. 1). Whereas Christ's death was sufficient for the sins of
the world, His death is efficient only in those who believe. Faith is necessary; it is the channel through which we are saved.

Justification is even more. On the positive side, it involves the bestow-
al of Christ's righteousness on the believing sinner. He is declared righteous. In a courtroom setting, God the righteous Judge deposits to our
account the righteousness of Christ. The elderly seminary president Lewis
Sperry Chafer, with tears streaming down his face, told his students, "Gentlemen, I have never gotten over what it means to be declared righteous."
May we never get over the wonder of our justification.

LESSON: *Justification is a legal act of removing the believer's sins*
and declaring the believing sinner righteous.

OUR
INHERITANCE

We are children of God, and if children, heirs also,
heirs of God and fellow-heirs with Christ. (Romans 8:16-17)

I n Los Angeles a seventy-two-year-old man who lived a life of poverty died in a back alley with only three dollars in his pocket—and more than $200,000 in the bank. Pushing a shopping cart, he spent his latter years roaming southern California streets, sleeping in alleys at night. When it was cold or rainy, he slept in an old car. He was heir to his father's estate but scorned his inheritance, preferring instead to live a life of poverty. State officials as well as relatives tried to force the money on the recluse, but he refused it. He was heir to an inheritance that would have enabled him to live a comfortable life, but he refused it.

In Christ believers have received a great spiritual inheritance. God Himself has made us His heirs. And since we are children of God, He has also made us fellow-heirs with Christ (Romans 8:17). Moreover, this inheritance is so certain, so secure, despite our suffering on this earth, that we will one day receive our inheritance.

What will that inheritance entail? We will be "glorified with Him." This truth is designed to encourage us amid our sufferings. The hardships we experience are no comparison with the wonder of the glorified body we shall receive at the Lord's return. Do not dismay, dear Christian, at your trials. You have an inheritance reserved for you in heaven—and you will joyfully claim it.

Through Christ, God has lifted us out of bondage to the law and set us free. We are no longer slaves under the jurisdiction of the law; rather, we have been purchased out of slavery and adopted into sonship. As sons we are heirs of God (Galatians 4:7). We are "heirs of the promise," assured that we will ultimately obtain the inheritance (Hebrews 6:17). In this hope we have "strong encouragement . . . an anchor of the soul, a hope both sure and steadfast" (vv. 18-19).

Are you living in a spiritual back alley, scavenging garbage cans for food? God has given you a great spiritual inheritance. Rejoice! Lift up your head! Despite difficult circumstances today you will have a glorious tomorrow when you claim your heavenly inheritance.

LESSON: *In Christ believers have received a spiritual inheritance that is reserved in heaven for them.*

THE NEW
BIRTH

Truly, truly, I say to you, unless one is born again,
he cannot see the kingdom of God. (John 3:3)

Several years ago William Sumner, editor of the *St. Paul Dispatch*, wrote a heated editorial blasting a prominent political figure for his public conversion. Wrote Sumner, "One wishes, that _____ had endured a long hermitage, fasting and wearing uncomfortable clothing out on the desert somewhere, perhaps flogging himself, before becoming so oppressively Born Again. . . . Why does such a fellow have to come bellowing out to the world that he is Born Again!"

That column, as much as any perhaps, reveals the misunderstanding so many folks have about being "born again." The words "You must be born again" (John 3:7) are not arbitrary. They come from none other than the lips of our Lord. It wasn't a suggestion or a committee recommendation. It was Christ's command. The necessity of the new birth is clear. One "cannot see the kingdom of God" without it.

What is it? Even Nicodemus, member of the esteemed Sanhedrin, Israel's supreme court, wanted an explanation. The "second" birth is contrasted with the first. The first birth occurred through sinful parents; the new birth has its origin in God. These are born "not of natural descent, nor of human decision or a husband's will, but born of God" (John 1:13, NIV). John 3:3 confirms this thought since "born again" may read "born from above"—from God. The first birth occurs through the corruptible seed of the parents, but the second birth is effected through incorruptible seed, God's Word (1 Peter 1:23). The first birth is a product of the flesh; the second birth is a product of the Spirit, as He regenerates the believing sinner, giving Him life (Titus 3:5).

The new birth and regeneration are the same, that is, the Holy Spirit gives life to the believing sinner. Just as the mother gives life to her newborn infant, so the Holy Spirit gives life to the one trusting in Christ. This, then, is the most critical issue each of us will ever face: "You must be born again." There is no alternative; there is no other way.

LESSON: *The new birth is produced by the Holy Spirit through the Word of God as the repentant sinner trusts in Christ.*

THE NEW
NATURE

Put on the new self, which in the likeness of God has been created
in righteousness and holiness of the truth. (Ephesians 4:24)

People who knew Cy said he was an entirely new man. "I knew him before, and he's entirely different now," exclaimed a co-worker. "For one thing, he lost most of his vocabulary now that he 'got religious'! Now he's kind and gentle; he wasn't that way before." What made Cy change?

The change was not part of Cy's basic nature. He received a "new nature," which enabled him to live an extraordinary life. As a new creation (2 Corinthians 5:17), believers receive a new, divine nature (2 Peter 1:4). That does not mean we are in any sense "divine" or "little gods" as some teach. It means we receive a new, incorrupt nature that is able to govern and direct our lives. We receive this new nature, this new capacity for good, because we have been born anew as children of God (John 1:11-13). Our new nature will be controlled by the Holy Spirit (Galatians 5:25), enabling us to produce the fruit of the Spirit rather than the deeds of the flesh.

The unsaved person has only one nature—his unregenerate nature that directs him into rebellion against God—but the believer has two natures, which are in conflict. Paul describes the conflict in Romans 7. There is warfare within the believer, and who wins the war? Whichever nature we allow to act as "commander-in-chief." If we submit to the old nature, we will indulge in sin; if we allow the Holy Spirit to control our new nature, we will walk in obedience (Romans 7:15–8:4). The image of God is renewed in the believer through his new nature. Adam lost fellowship with God, but through the new nature we regain fellowship with God.

The miracle of the new nature involves several new capacities. We have a new mind, so we have the "mind of Christ" (1 Corinthians 2:16), with the ability to appraise spiritual things. We have a new heart, the center of our will, with the ability to choose to obey God (Romans 6:17). God has also given us a new will, that we may dedicate our bodies to Him (12:1). Children of God must "put on the new self" for the new nature to be at work in us. Then we will be conformed to the image of Christ.

LESSON: *Believers have received a new nature, involving a new mind, heart, will, and spirit, that we may obey God.*

SANCTIFIED

*By this will we have been sanctified through the offering
of the body of Jesus Christ once for all. (Hebrews 10:10)*

A little boy was about to begin eating a sucker when he saw his sister coming toward him. Thinking she would probably want part of his sucker, he quickly made a swipe of the sucker on both sides with his tongue, making the sucker his. Then he sat down and began to lick the sucker—that's practical sanctification. Finally, he finished the sucker and threw away the stick. That's completed sanctification.

There are three parts to sanctification. First, there is positional sanctification, our standing and position before God based on Christ's death. Because we are in Christ, God looks on us through Christ and reckons us sanctified and holy. That is why Paul could write believers in different cities and call them "saints"; they were "holy ones," set apart for God. Just as Paul could address saints in Rome and Corinth, so today there are saints in Riverside and Cleveland. This is our position because of the death of Christ—we are sanctified. Positionally we are "set apart," saints of God.

Our practical, or experiential, sanctification may or may not measure up to our positional sanctification. A man may be an architect because he is licensed as one, but his work may or may not measure up to his position. He may develop good designs or poor ones—but that does not change his position. He is an architect. Paul's prayer for believers is that they be sanctified entirely (1 Thessalonians 5:23). Similarly, Peter admonishes, "You shall be holy" (1 Peter 1:16). Believers are to mature, to progress in their walk. Believers are mature spiritually. That is positional sanctification.

Completed or ultimate sanctification is future and will occur when our bodies are transformed into the image of Christ (Ephesians 5:26-27).

What a blessed truth that we stand completed, holy, sanctified before God! We could not achieve that on our own. Yet the exhortation is still there: "You shall be holy, for I am holy." We are to live lives that are set apart from sin and set apart to Christ. What do you need to consider in your life to bring it into conformity with God's standard of holiness?

LESSON: *We are sanctified because of Christ's death; we are to pursue sanctification daily, and we will be completely sanctified at Christ's coming.*

SET FREE
FROM SIN'S AUTHORITY

Even so consider yourselves to be dead to sin,
but alive to God in Christ Jesus. (Romans 6:11)

One day D. L. Moody met a boy who was clutching something in his hand. "What do you have in your hand?" asked Mr. Moody. "I have a bird," exclaimed the boy, "and I'm not going to let him go." "I'll give you a quarter for him," offered Mr. Moody. The boy took the quarter and gave Mr. Moody the bird, whereupon the famed evangelist opened his hand. The bird hesitated momentarily and then quickly flew away. It was free.

Sin once held us firmly in its grasp, and we were unable to escape. But by identifying with Christ in His death, we have been released from bondage. We have been set free from sin's oppression. We did not free ourselves; we have been set free because we are identified with our spiritual Liberator, Jesus Christ. In His atoning death, Christ died for sin, and those who believe in Christ are identified and united with Him (Romans 6:2-4). Since death means separation, believers have been separated from sin through Christ's death. That does not mean sin no longer exists, but that it need not rule over us any longer.

Our identification with Christ has united us with His new resurrection life. Just as Princess Diana partakes of all the privileges of royalty through her union with Prince Charles, so believers partake of the new life through their union with Christ. Just as the "common" life no longer has authority over Diana, so our old life in its unregenerate state no longer has authority over us. Our old unregenerate self has been crucified with Christ that the old way of life may no longer operate in us: "He who has died is freed from sin" (Romans 6:7).

Does that mean we naturally live perfect, sinless lives? No. The key to daily triumph over sin is to count on our union with Christ and our death to sin (Romans 6:11). Offer your body to God as an instrument of righteousness. Satan and sin have been rendered powerless through the cross (Hebrews 2:14). It is the prerogative of a child of God to live triumphantly, not under sin's domination.

LESSON: *Believers have been united with Christ in His death and resurrection and are set free from sin's domination.*

RELEASED
FROM THE LAW

*Christ is the end of the law for righteousness
to everyone who believes. (Romans 10:4)*

At Mount Sinai God inscribed His law on tablets of stone as Israel's constitution. They were to live by that law, and there were three features to it. The moral law, encoded in the Ten Commandments and other passages, invoked God's moral standard for the people. That was the moral principles governing man's relationship to man and man's relationship to God. The civil law detailed man's civil duties to his neighbor: how to treat husband, wife, children, slaves, and poor people. The ceremonial law described how Israel was to worship, detailing the five offerings (Leviticus 1-7) and the seven feasts (Leviticus 23).

Christ was born under the law and lived under the law (Galatians 4:4). He was the only one to perfectly fulfill it in order that He might rescue us from its jurisdiction and oppression (Matthew 5:17; Galatians 4:5). Christ terminated the law (Romans 10:4). The civil and ceremonial law has been terminated (nor is it possible to fulfill the ceremonial aspects of the law since there is no Temple in Israel).

We are no longer under law but under grace (Romans 6:14). Christ fulfilled the law and died to it so that in our union with Him we are joined to Him (Romans 7:4). The law no longer has jurisdiction over us. Christ has delivered our emancipation proclamation. That does not mean we ignore the Old Testament or the Ten Commandments. All the Ten Commandments (except the Sabbath law) are repeated in the New Testament and are therefore obligatory. But we have been released from legalistic bondage that we might serve God "in the new way of the Spirit, and not in the old way of the written code" (Romans 7:6, NIV).

What was the purpose of the law? To intensify sin, to mirror men in their sinful estate before a holy God (Galatians 3:22). That should force us to faith in Christ in whom we can fulfill the law and be freed from it (Galatians 3:24-26).

Dear reader, what are you basing your hope on? Are you trying to keep the Ten Commandments, all the while recognizing that you are not succeeding? Are you putting yourself under a legalistic system to gain merit before God? Christ has rescued us from the foolishness and futility of any legalistic system. He has fulfilled the law for you and me. What we could not do—He did. He has brought us into the realm of grace. He is now our righteousness, not through the law but through faith.

LESSON: *Christ fulfilled and terminated the law that we might be rescued from the law and justified by faith.*

UNION
WITH CHRIST

In Him you have been made complete. (Colossians 2:10)

Marriage is a God-blessed ordinance that takes two people and, defying the laws of mathematics, makes one out of two. An even greater union makes us one with Christ. At salvation the Holy Spirit baptized us into Christ, joining us to Him forever (1 Corinthians 12:13). He placed us "in Christ." The meaning and magnitude of this truth surely escapes all of us. In Christ! That is our position. Do you know the riches of your inheritance in Christ? It means He chose us (Ephesians 1:4) and adopted us into His family (v. 5). It means we were joined to Him in His crucifixion, burial, and resurrection (Romans 6:2-5). As He was raised to a new and glorious life, so we too may "walk in newness of life" (v. 4). We no longer have to give in to bad temper and impatience toward wife, husband, or children. We can live a new life because we are united to Christ.

Christ constantly indwells us, enabling us to constantly enjoy fellowship with Him (1 Corinthians 1:9). Do you enjoy the fellowship with your best friend? Now you may enjoy constant fellowship with a closer Friend. Fellowship means sharing; Jesus Christ now shares our lives because we are "in Christ." We have died to the world's desires and affections; Jesus Christ now lives His life through us (2:20). Because we are in Christ, we experience His faithfulness, strength, and protection, giving us confidence in Him (2 Thessalonians 3:4).

In this relationship we look forward with faith to the future because He will keep us from the day of wrath that is to come upon the earth (Romans 5:9). In Christ Jesus we will obtain the salvation He has promised us (2 Timothy 2:10). We look forward to the day this earthen vessel will appropriate immortality as we are "glorified with Him" (Romans 8:17). In that day we will realize our position as "fellow heirs with Christ." Nothing, absolutely nothing, can sever us from His love and this union. Our blessedness and joy in this union is linked to our "walk in Him" (Colossians 2:6).

LESSON: *Our position in Christ means we are positionally united to Him to enjoy His fellowship and blessings forever.*

SIN NATURE
HAS BEEN JUDGED

Knowing this, that our old self was crucified with Him,
that our body of sin might be done away with, that we
should no longer be slaves to sin. (Romans 6:6)

Rasputin, the Russian monk who held emotional control over Czar Nicholas's wife, taught that in order to exalt the grace of God it was necessary to sin greatly. Only in that way could one comprehend the greatness of God's forgiveness and grace. Paul answers that perversion in Romans 6:1-2: "Are we to continue in sin that grace might increase? May it never be!" The believer no longer needs to live in slavery to sin because through His death Christ judged the believer's sin nature. We have been set free from slavery to our harsh slavemaster.

All who have been united to Christ have died to sin (Romans 6:3). How is that significant? Death means separation; it separates the one who died from those that previously had authority over him. While we are alive, civil laws have authority over us. When death takes place that authority ends. When a husband dies, he no longer has authority over the widow. Similarly, since we died with Christ, we died with respect to sin; it no longer has authority over us, although that does not mean we no longer commit sin.

We have been raised together with Christ to walk in newness of life. "Our old self was crucified with [Christ], that our body of sin might be done away with" (v. 6). Upon our union with Christ, He judged our sin nature from the cross, robbing it of its power over us. Its power has been broken.

Is victory over the old nature automatic? No, it must be appropriated. We are commanded, "Consider yourselves to be dead to sin, but alive to God in Christ Jesus" (v. 11). Our death is positional, and we only realize its reality as by faith we count on it as having happened. It is like claiming an inheritance. If we leave the money sitting in the bank, it does us no good. By faith we must count on our death and resurrection with Christ. Then we may walk in newness of life, victorious over the sin nature.

LESSON: *Through our union with Christ we have died with respect to the old sin nature, rendering it inoperative in our lives.*

RICHES
OF GRACE

*Blessed be the God and Father of our Lord Jesus Christ,
who has blessed us with every spiritual blessing in the
heavenly places in Christ. (Ephesians 1:3)*

I n 1917, Lewis Sperry Chafer, who became the first president of Dallas Theological Seminary, wrote a fascinating book, *Salvation,* in which he outlined thirty-three things that happen to a believer at the moment of salvation. (1) In the eternal plan of God the believer has been foreknown (Romans 8:29), elected (1 Thessalonians 1:4), predestinated (Ephesians 1:11), chosen (Matthew 22:14), called (1 Thessalonians 5:24), (2) reconciled to God through Christ (2 Corinthians 5:18), (3) redeemed from condemnation by Christ's blood (1 Peter 1:18), (4) related to God through propitiation (1 John 2:2), (5) his sins covered by atoning blood (1 Peter 2:24), (6) vitally conjoined to Christ for judgment of the "old man" unto a new walk (Romans 6:6), (7) freed from the law (Romans 7:4), (8) born again as children of God (John 1:12), (9) adopted as adult sons (Romans 8:15), (10) acceptable to God by Jesus Christ through sanctification (3:22), (11) justified through faith (5:1), (12) forgiven all his trespasses (Colossians 2:13), (13) made right by the blood of Christ (Ephesians 2:13), (14) delivered from the powers of darkness, (15) translated into the kingdom of His dear Son (Colossians 1:13), (16) built upon the rock Christ Jesus (1 Corinthians 3:11), (17) made a gift from God to Christ (John 17:6), (18) circumcised in Christ (Colossians 2:11), (19) made a partaker of the holy and royal priesthood (1 Peter 2:5), (20) made a chosen generation and a peculiar people (1 Peter 2:9), (21) given access to God (Ephesians 1:18), (22) placed within the "much more" care of God (Romans 5:9), (23) given his inheritance (Ephesians 1:18) and (24) our inheritance (1 Peter 1:4), (25) blessed by a heavenly association (Ephesians 2:6), (26) granted heavenly citizenship (Philippians 3:20), (27) made part of the family and household of God (Ephesians 2:19), (28) changed to light in the Lord (Ephesians 5:8), (29) vitally united to the Father, Son, and Spirit (1 Thessalonians 1:1; John 14:20; Romans 8:9), (30) blessed with the "first fruits" and the "earnest" of the Spirit (2 Corinthians 1:22), (31) glorified (Romans 8:30), (32) made complete in Him (Colossians 2:10), and (33) blessed with every spiritual blessing (Ephesians 1:3).

Can we begin to fathom the Father's love for us in Christ? Can we comprehend the riches of our inheritance in Christ?

LESSON: *The believer has untold spiritual riches and blessing in his standing with God through the death of Christ.*

ADOPTION

You have received a spirit of adoption as sons
by which we cry out, "Abba! Father!" (Romans 8:15)

In Roman culture when a son was adopted into a family he came under the *patria potestas*—the father's absolute power over the family. When adopted, the new son lost all rights in the old family and gained all the benefits of a legitimate son in his new family—in a legal sense, he had a new father. He also became an heir to his new father's estate. Blood sons who were born later did not affect his inheritance. The adopted son's old life was wiped out, his debts canceled as though they never had existed. In the eyes of the law the adopted person was literally and absolutely the son of his new father (Barclay, *Romans,* pp. 110-11).

That is the background Paul has in mind as he reminds us of one of the benefits of Christ's death—Christ has brought us into God's family. We are adopted sons. That is our new position in Christ, and it means we enjoy full privileges as adult members of God's family. We have not the status of children, under tutors and without benefits, but the full benefits of adulthood in God's family.

What are these benefits? We have been released from slavery under the law—which produced fear. Since we have been adopted as sons, fear is gone; we have freedom and intimacy in the family wherein we call God, "Abba! Father!" (Romans 8:15). *Abba* is an Aramaic word for father that suggests intimacy; some have suggested it could be translated "papa" or "daddy." Because of our adoption we are no longer slaves but sons, and as sons we are heirs of God (Galatians 4:4-7).

But our adoption was expensive—it required the death of Christ to set us free from slavery (Galatians 4:5). Our adoption will be fully realized when Christ returns and transforms our mortal bodies into that which is immortal (Romans 8:23).

Perhaps you have never had a happy family relationship. Believers have the best, most intimate family relationship possible. You have a loving Father, and you have all the privileges of an adult child.

LESSON: *Adoption is placing the believer into God's family.*

FAMILY
FELLOWSHIP

What we have seen and heard we proclaim to you also, that you also may have fellowship with us; and indeed our fellowship is with the Father, and with His Son Jesus Christ. (1 John 1:3)

I well recall my early days as a Christian. How important the fellowship with other believers was to me! Discussing biblical truths on the steps of the church building until 11:00 P.M., laboring together in feeding the hungry with food and the gospel at the rescue mission, traveling together to rural areas to minister the gospel—fellowship was vital to me then and still is.

We have been called into a greater fellowship—with the Father, Son, and Holy Spirit. Fellowship (*koinonia*) means "association," "communion," "a close relationship," and "sharing." God made our heavenly fellowship possible when He called us into fellowship with Christ (1 Corinthians 1:9). Even though we have divisions on earth, God is faithful in bringing us into fellowship with Christ. At the Communion table, where we remember Christ's death, we fellowship with Him (1 Corinthians 10:16). Since the Holy Spirit is "another Comforter" like Christ, we are also brought into fellowship with Him (2 Corinthians 13:14; Philippians 2:1).

What shall we do to foster fellowship with the Father, Son, and Holy Spirit? We cannot have intimate fellowship with unbelievers who loathe the Christ we love (2 Corinthians 6:14). Light and darkness are not compatible. We may also need to suffer. Paul desired to know Christ intimately through the power of His resurrection but also through fellowship with Christ's sufferings, "becoming like him in his death" (Philippians 3:10). This may mean ostracism and rejection for the cause of Christ. It means walking in the light and confessing our sins (1 John 1:6, 9).

Christ has made our heavenly fellowship possible. He brought us eternal life and revealed the Father, that we might have fellowship with God the Father and the Son. John saw and heard the eternal Life, proclaiming it that we may have fellowship with Him. This fellowship is our destiny, and in it our joy becomes complete.

LESSON: *Through Christ, believers have been brought into fellowship with the Father, Son, and Holy Spirit.*

Part 7
The Church

WHAT IS
THE CHURCH?

*Gentiles are fellow-heirs and fellow members
of the body, and fellow-partakers of the promise
in Christ Jesus through the gospel. (Ephesians 3:6)*

W hat is the church? There are as many ideas about the nature of the church as there are traditions. For some the church is a traditional 11:00 A.M. Sunday service; to others it is a building ("I'll meet you at church"); some consider using only a certain version of the Bible or a particular form of the service as essential; to others it is an ecclesiastical hierarchy of bishops and archbishops. What is the church?

The church is not Israel. Although some people refer to the church as the "new Israel," that is an incorrect designation. The word *Israel* always refers to the physical descendants of Jacob. Israel means the Jewish people, hence, calling the church "the new Israel" is a misnomer.

Nor is the church the kingdom. People sometimes say, "We are building God's kingdom." The kingdom refers to the future age of righteousness when Christ will rule on earth. Christ must build that kingdom; we cannot. The church is distinct from the kingdom; the church exists in this present age from the Day of Pentecost until the rapture. The kingdom is the future reign of Christ following His return to earth.

A church is not a building; the building is a place for the church to meet. Believers may meet in an ornate cathedral or in a storefront in a shopping center. The Greek word for church means "a called out group" whereas the English word *church* means "belonging to the Lord." A church is therefore a special group of people bought by the blood of Christ that meets together in worship.

Indeed, the church is people, but what kind of people? It is composed of people from all ethnic backgrounds—Jews and Gentiles. God's grace has extended to the four corners of the globe, calling out Jews and Gentiles, black and white, rich and poor, educated and uneducated, progressive and primitive to be heirs of God and joint heirs with Christ. O the richness of God's grace! It extends to every tribe, tongue, and nation, that we may magnify the God of all grace.

LESSON: *The church is a believing body of people, composed of Jews and Gentiles, redeemed by the blood of Christ.*

September 8

WHEN DID
THE CHURCH BEGIN?

*I will build My church; and the gates of Hades
shall not overpower it. (Matthew 16:18)*

Birthdays are important. Every February we observe Presidents' Day in honor of Abraham Lincoln, who was born on February 12, and George Washington, who was born the same month. When our children are young we give them birthday parties to celebrate the day of their birth. Even in our adult years, we recognize one another's birthdays by sending cards, flowers, and gifts.

The church also has a birthday. What is the date of its birth? There are differences of opinion, some suggesting it existed in the Old Testament. But when Jesus responded to Peter's great declaration of faith, He told Peter, "I will build My church" (Matthew 16:18). Jesus declared that the church was still future; He had not yet begun to build it. Since the church is one body of believers through the unique operation of the Holy Spirit—placing believers into the Body of Christ that special baptizing work of the Spirit identifies the beginning of the church (1 Corinthians 12:13).

When did the baptizing work of the Spirit begin? Immediately prior to His ascension to heaven Jesus told the apostles that the baptizing work had not yet begun, but it would in "not many days" (Acts 1:5). Later, when Peter was in Jerusalem, he explained that Gentiles had received the Spirit just as the Jews had "at the beginning" (11:15). "At the beginning" points to the initial baptizing work of the Holy Spirit and looks back to the descent of the Spirit at Pentecost in Acts 2. The Feast of Pentecost in Acts 2 marks the birthday of the church. The church began at Pentecost.

The birthday of the church is indeed a cause for celebration. God sent the Holy Spirit to indwell all believers, unifying them as one in the Body of Christ. The Holy Spirit permanently joined us to Christ for life and fellowship. He distributed spiritual gifts to all believers, enabling us to minister to one another. And He empowered us for service supernaturally. We indeed have great cause for a birthday celebration.

LESSON: *The church began at Pentecost (Acts 2) by the baptizing work of the Spirit, placing believers in union with Christ and one another.*

THE CHURCH
AND ISRAEL

I am not ashamed of the gospel, for it is the power
of God for salvation to every one who believes,
to the Jew first and also to the Greek. (Romans 1:16)

How many "people of God" are there? Some suggest there is only one people of God—Israel. They say God entered into covenant blessings with Israel in the Old Testament, but the nation forfeited those privileges through disobedience and apostasy. So Israel has been set aside, and God is now working through the church—the "new Israel." The blessings that God formerly bestowed on Israel have supposedly been transferred to the church. Is that true?

A careful study of biblical teaching reveals that there are two people of God—Israel and the church—and they are distinct. The word *Israel* always refers to the physical descendants of Jacob—the Jewish people. "Israel" never refers to the church as a spiritual entity. Even after Israel rejected the Messiah and the church had been born, Israel still describes the Jewish people.

Peter addressed the "men of Israel" (Acts 2:22; 3:12) and "the people of Israel" (4:10). Throughout the book of Acts the nation Israel remains distinct from the church. Paul also recognized the distinction between Israel and the church. He prayed for Israel (Romans 10:1), all the while recognizing that God had not abandoned them because they remained His people (11:1-2). Because Israel rejected her Messiah, the nation has been judicially blinded in this present age (although some still become believers). But a great future awaits the nation when the blindness will be removed. God will bring not only individual salvation to Israel but national blessings as well (vv. 25-26).

While preaching the gospel, Paul brought the good news to both Jews and Gentiles, recognizing the unique place Israel holds in history. He affirmed that the gospel "is the power of God for salvation to every one who believes, to the Jew first" (1:16). Israel continues to hold a prominent place in God's plan—she has a priority in hearing the gospel. Do you have Paul's burden for the Jewish people? We are under an obligation to bring them the good news of their Messiah.

LESSON: *Although Israel remains distinct from the church, it has not been abandoned but will come into future blessing at Christ's second coming.*

September 10

THE CHURCH
AND THE KINGDOM

*To you it has been granted to know the
mysteries of the kingdom of heaven. (Matthew 13:11).*

The twentieth century has witnessed spectacular progress. The United States has given out about $200 billion in foreign aid since World War II, providing food and medicine to suffering people. Enormous advances have been made in medicine, cancer cures have been discovered, organ transplants are being made, and the average life expectancy is lengthened. Technological progress is staggering. One computer disc can contain the equivalent of one-fourth of a million pages, including several Bible translations, Greek and Hebrew texts, commentaries and dictionaries. Portions of the Bible are available to 98 percent of the world. More than 1.5 billion people claim to be Christians. The gospel is broadcast over radio and television, and with the collapse of Communism, the gospel is penetrating eastern Europe.

What does all that mean? Will the church usher in Messiah's kingdom? When Jesus preached, "Repent, for the kingdom of heaven is at hand" (Matthew 4:17), to what was He referring? Long ago, God told David that one of his descendants would rule on earth in a kingdom age (2 Samuel 7:16). Jesus offered that kingdom to the nation Israel. There was but one condition—repentance. If the nation would repent and acknowledge Jesus as the Messiah, the kingdom age would be inaugurated. But Israel rejected Jesus as the Messiah, so the offer was withdrawn and the kingdom withheld until Christ's second coming.

Jesus announced there would be an intervening church age, which would be a secret form of the kingdom, prior to the establishment of the kingdom (Matthew 13:11). Although all Christians become members of the spiritual aspect of the kingdom (Colossians 1:13), in a future, physical kingdom Messiah will personally reign on earth. It is distinct from the church. The church will not usher in the kingdom; Messiah alone will do that. We look forward to the day when Messiah's glory will fill the earth and all will have a knowledge of God. In the meantime we labor, spreading the gospel, bringing men and women to faith in Christ.

LESSON: *The church age is an intervening age, distinct from the future kingdom that will be established at Christ's second coming.*

September 11

THE LOCAL CHURCH

*They were continually devoting themselves
to the apostles' teaching and to fellowship,
to the breaking of bread and to prayer. (Acts 2:42)*

He had been a member for years; he was familiar with the ritual, the hymns. Although he didn't know Christ as his personal Savior, he was faithful in attendance, going through the motions encouraged by formal religion. Then he fulfilled a boyhood dream. He bought a farm. In the rural community he attended a small chapel—and heard the gospel for the first time. As his tractor lumbered along the rows on his acreage, he had ample time to reflect on the Bible studies. While sitting on the tractor, meditating, he came to faith in Jesus Christ. He had been confronted with the simple gospel in a local church.

The Bible uses the word *church* in two different ways. The most common meaning of *church* is to describe a local group of believers; hence, Paul writes "to the church of God which is at Corinth" (1 Corinthians 1:2) and "to the church of the Thessalonians" (1 Thessalonians 1:1). Writing today, Paul might have written "to the church in Sao Paulo," "to the church at Hong Kong," and "to the church which is at Oklahoma City."

A building is not essential to a local church (although good facilities are certainly helpful in carrying on the ministry). The early church did not have buildings; they met in homes. Writing to Philemon, Paul addressed "the church in your house" (Philemon 2). A church also met in the home of Prisca and Aquila (Romans 16:4). There could also be more than one local church in a city or region, as Paul addressed "the churches of Galatia" (Galatians 1:2).

But a local church is more than just a group of people meeting together—they meet together for a purpose. A local church gathers to worship God because they have come to faith in Christ, for fellowship and building up one another, for instruction in God's Word that they may grow spiritually, to observe the ordinances of baptism and the Lord's Supper, and for ministry, including evangelism.

A local church depends on people. Have you identified yourself with a local body of believers? Are you involved in the biblically ordained purposes of the church?

LESSON: *A local church is a group of believers in Christ, gathering for worship, instruction, fellowship, and ministry.*

THE UNIVERSAL CHURCH

And He put all things in subjection under
His feet and gave Him as head over all things
to the church, which is His body. (Ephesians 1:22-23)

ed and yellow, black and white; all are precious in His sight.
Jesus loves the little children of the world." That song, which
many of us sang in our childhood, contains an important truth.
Believers from around the world—whether black or white, rich or poor,
Easterner or Westerner—all belong to one another. We are one body in
Christ. Patrick Johnstone, writing in *Operation World,* estimated that
1,563,000,000 or 32.4 percent of the world's people call themselves Christians (1986). Christians are found in 215 countries around the world—even
in countries where they are severely oppressed, such as Albania, Mauri-
tania, and Mongolia.

This is a picture of the universal church. All believers in Jesus Christ,
from all nations—the Western world and the Third World, from the Day of
Pentecost (Acts 2) until the rapture—are members of one body called the
universal church. We all become members of this body at the moment of
our salvation (1 Corinthians 12:13). There is no division; there are no denominational differences, doctrinal hobbyhorses, or hierarchical, gender,
or economic distinctives. We are all one body in Christ. This is the one
church that Jesus promised to build (Matthew 16:18). Jesus is not building a
denomination or exclusive club of Christians. He is building the one true
church composed of everyone who has faith in Him as Savior.

In this universal church Jesus is the Head, controlling and exercising
authority over it. There is unity, "one body" (Ephesians 4:4) and no human
distinctions (Galatians 3:28). Therefore when we say, "I am of Paul," "I am
of Apollos," we sin against Christ and against each other by hurting the
unity of the body to which we belong. While remaining faithful to the funda-
mentals of the faith, let us fulfill practically the unity that we have positionally, "being of the same mind, maintaining the same love, united in spirit,
intent on one purpose" (Philippians 2:2).

LESSON: *The universal church is composed of all believers from*
Pentecost until the rapture.

THE CHURCH IS PICTURED AS A BUILDING

You are God's household, having been built upon the foundation of the apostles and prophets, Christ Jesus Himself being the cornerstone, in whom the whole building, being fitted together is growing into a holy temple in the Lord. (Ephesians 2:19-21)

Several years ago we decided to build a new home. We stopped at the empty lot and walked among the weeds, anticipating what the house and yard would look like. Then one day as we drove by the lot the slab was poured. The most important part of the house had been built. The slab had a proper foundation with steel reinforcement to ensure the house could be built on the foundation. Then the walls went up, the rafters, the sheathing—finally the house was finished. The landscapers sodded a lawn, planted some shrubs, and we moved in.

Although the church is not a building, the figure of a building is used to illustrate the church. The church has an entirely solid foundation—it is built on the apostles and prophets—and the cornerstone, the most important building block, is Jesus Christ (Ephesians 2:20). There will be no cracks in this foundation; the walls will not crumble. The church will remain intact. That means the apostles and prophets, along with evangelists, pastors, and teachers, are gifted leaders who have been given to the church for the purpose of bringing it to spiritual maturity. This strong foundation ensures that a strong superstructure will be built (Ephesians 4:11-13).

This building "being fitted together is growing into a holy temple in the Lord" (Ephesians 2:21). The stones, which represent believers, are carefully fitted together by cutting and rubbing them, preparing the dowels and dowel holes, and fitting the stones together. What is the result? We are "being built together into a dwelling of God in the Spirit" (Ephesians 2:22). The church is a figurative building, a temple wherein the Holy Spirit dwells for the purpose of bringing glory to God.

LESSON: *The church is pictured as a building, built on the foundation of Christ and the apostles and growing into a holy temple for God.*

THE BRIDEGROOM
AND THE BRIDE

*Husbands, love your wives, just as Christ also loved
the church and gave Himself up for her. (Ephesians 5:25)*

He was only nineteen, and she was eighteen, but it was evident to all that they were in love. The day arrived when I was able to publicly present them as husband and wife. In anticipation of that important day he had made preparations to provide a suitable home for them. When I later visited them, I was astonished at the beautiful house he had built for her as a symbol of his love.

Christ is pictured as the Bridegroom, preparing for the day when He will call His bride, the church, to be with Him. He has gone "to prepare a place" for her (John 14:2). In ancient times the bridegroom would prepare a place for his bride by adding an apartment to his father's home; so also Christ has gone to the Father's house to prepare a place for His bride. When He returns for her, He will bring her to live with Him in the heavenly home He has prepared (John 14:3). What a glorious wedding day to look forward to!

What does the bride do in preparation for her wedding day? She buys the most beautiful gown she has ever worn and beautifies herself so that she will be attractive in the eyes of the one she loves. Similarly, the church is being prepared for her wedding day. Christ is sanctifying her, cleansing her in preparation for the great day. To sanctify means to set apart; the church is being set apart and cleansed through the Word. That means there is growth, maturity, and increasing godliness in believers' lives. It is all for a singular purpose—"that He might present to Himself the church in all her glory, having no spot or wrinkle" (Ephesians 5:27). When the Bridegroom comes, He doesn't want His bride to appear in a dirty, wrinkled wedding dress. He is looking for a pure bride.

How will I be prepared to hear the call of the Bridegroom? Arno Gaebelein said, "Heaven is a prepared place for a prepared people." The Bridegroom gave Himself up for the church—He died for her that she should live with Him in heaven. I will hear the Bridegroom's call if I trust Him as the One who has prepared me for heaven by dying in my place.

LESSON: *Christ has prepared His bride by dying for her, and He is beautifying her for her wedding day by sanctifying her.*

September 15

THE CHURCH IS
PICTURED AS A FLOCK

And I have other sheep, which are not of this fold;
I must bring them also, and they shall hear My voice; and
they shall become one flock with one Shepherd. (John 10:16)

One evening, while H. R. P. Dickson was visiting desert Arabs, "shortly after dark, an Arab shepherd began to call out one by one the names of his fifty-one mother sheep, and was able to pick out each one's lamb, and restore it to its mother to suckle. To do this in the light would be a feat for many shepherds, but this was done in complete darkness, and in the midst of the noise coming from the ewes crying for their lambs, and the lambs crying for their mothers" (Wight, *Manners and Customs*, p. 159).

The shepherd and his flock illustrate the relationship of Christ and the church. Whereas we make distinctions in life—French, Russian, Chinese, black, white, male, female—in the church of Jesus Christ there is unity. There is one flock, not two or two hundred. It is one flock composed of all believers. Jesus promised to bring Gentiles, who were despised in His day, and unite them with Jewish believers into one flock (John 10:16).

The flock also illustrates ownership—it belongs to the Shepherd. It has but one Shepherd—Christ. Just as the shepherd's voice is familiar to the sheep, so believers hear the voice of Christ and follow Him (John 10:27). There are many false shepherds who would lead the sheep astray, but the sheep do not follow the deceptive voices. They know the Shepherd.

What does the Shepherd do? He nourishes the sheep, leading them to food and water. Christ provides spiritual nourishment for His own, feeding them with the living Bread (John 6:35). Likewise, His undershepherds are commissioned to tend the lambs (21:15-17). The shepherd also protects the flock from savage animals that would devour it. Undershepherds guard the flock against spiritual wolves who would destroy it through false teaching (Acts 20:28-30).

Are you listening to the voice of the Shepherd? Are you resting in His intimacy and security and trusting in His guidance?

LESSON: *The church is pictured as a flock of sheep, nourished, protected, and unified by Christ the Shepherd.*

September 17

THE CHURCH IS
PICTURED AS BRANCHES

*I am the vine, you are the branches; he who
abides in Me, and I in him, he bears much fruit;
for apart from Me you can do nothing. (John 15:5)*

The wind howled all night, and in the morning we saw a branch from our tree, hanging bent and broken. It didn't take long for the leaves to wither. Although the rest of the tree was green and healthy, the branch had dried up—it was dead. We had to cut it off and throw it away.

In John 15 Jesus illustrates His relationship with church age believers as a vine and its branches. He declared, "I am the true vine" (v. 1). The vine is rooted to the soil and is the source of nourishment that enables the branches to grow and produce fruit. The ability to grow lies not with the branches but in the vine.

Jesus promised believers that by abiding in Him they will bear much fruit. What is "abiding"? It is a simple word, *meno*, meaning to remain, stay, or live. When Jesus calls us to "abide in Me," He is calling us to continue believing in Him. Although some give Him a casual hearing and go their way, He calls us to stay with Him and live in fellowship with Him. This intimate union is graphically illustrated in the vine and the branches. A branch by itself is useless—it dries up. But attached to the vine it draws life and nourishment from the vine and bears fruit. That is how we are to live in fellowship with Jesus.

Sometimes branches don't bear fruit; what then? Then the gardener prunes them in order that they bear more fruit. Pruning is painful, but sometimes the surgery is necessary to bring health to a sick limb. Do not rebel at God's surgery; He is pruning you that you will produce fruit. Though the process is painful, a bountiful harvest of fruit will be the result.

What kind of fruit should we produce? In the context of John 15 the fruit is joy: "These things I have spoken to you, that My joy may be in you, and that your joy may be made full" (v. 11). Joy is a fruit of the Spirit; additional fruit of the Spirit is, "Love . . . peace, patience, kindness, goodness, faithfulness, gentleness, self-control" (Galatians 5:22). As we live in union with Christ our lives will be fruitful, reflecting the reality of our union with Christ.

LESSON: *Believers are united to Christ as the branch is to the vine, drawing life from the Vine and producing fruit.*

THE CHURCH IS
PICTURED AS A PRIESTHOOD

*You are a chosen race, a royal priesthood, a holy nation,
a people for God's own possession, that you may proclaim
the excellencies of Him who has called you out of darkness
into His marvelous light. (1 Peter 2:9)*

In ancient Israel there were twelve distinct tribes, but not all were equal, nor did all have the same responsibility and authority. The tribe of Levi stood distinct because they mediated God's truth to the people. Only descendants of Levi were permitted to serve as priests. When King Saul intruded into the priestly function he was punished severely (1 Samuel 13:9-14).

In the church there are no special "priestly" classifications. The Reformers uncovered the great biblical doctrine of "the priesthood of all believers." Peter identifies all Christians as "a royal priesthood" (1 Peter 2:9). Every believer is to mediate God's truth, functioning as a priest in dispensing it to a needy world. Whereas only the priest could approach God in the Old Testament economy, in the New Testament every believer may "draw near with confidence to the throne of grace" (Hebrews 4:16). All New Testament believers may enter the holy place, as it were, by the blood of Jesus (10:19).

How can we serve as "New Testament priests"? In contrast to Old Testament priests, church age believers do not offer dead animals; we offer ourselves as living sacrifices to God (Romans 12:1). As members of the church all believers are priests, offering intercessory prayer for government leaders (1 Timothy 2:1-2), missionaries (Acts 13:3), the sick (James 5:15), those that are suffering (Acts 12:5), and those that are ministering (Ephesians 6:19). We also offer sacrifices, praising God with our lips (Hebrews 13:15). But praise is not devoid of deeds; the kindnesses of the Philippians were "a fragrant aroma" to God (Philippians 4:18). As priests we declare God's excellencies for having delivered us out of darkness into His light (1 Peter 2:9).

If you are a child of God, you are a New Testament priest. Are you fulfilling your priestly duties?

LESSON: *In the church all believers are priests, offering themselves as living sacrifices and mediating God's truth to the world.*

THE CHURCH
GATHERS TO WORSHIP

Let the word of Christ richly dwell within you;
with all wisdom teaching and admonishing one another
with psalms and hymns and spiritual songs, singing
with thankfulness in your hearts to God. (Colossians 3:16)

For what purpose do Christians gather together on Sunday? Some might say, "To evangelize unbelievers," or, "To hear a sermon," or, "To meet with other Christians." There are a variety of reasons that Christians gather on the Lord's Day—many of them good ones—but there is an overriding reason that Christians meet: to worship God. Unfortunately much of our preaching, prayer, and singing today is man-centered. Worship is a largely lost expression of the church today, yet it must be at the core of our meetings.

Worship is a confusing word. How do we worship God? Worship is first of all not mechanical; it is spiritual: "God is spirit; and those who worship Him must worship in spirit and truth" (John 4:24). Nor is worship restricted to one day a week; it is a continual expression of the believer as he presents his body as a spiritual service of worship (Romans 12:1). Further, since worship is "in truth" it must also involve God's Word. Paul told Timothy to "give attention to the public reading of Scripture, to exhortation and teaching" (1 Timothy 4:13).

Early church worship was patterned after synagogue worship, where the Scriptures were read consecutively. The Psalms are important in worship since they focus attention on God, extolling His majesty, sovereignty, and greatness. Prayer is also a vital element in worship as it expresses dependence upon God and trust in Him. Through prayer the church unleashes His power (Acts 4:31; 12:5, 12; 13:3). Singing is important in worship, lifting the heart to God in praise and adoration (16:25) and creating thankful hearts (Colossians 3:16). Giving is an act of worship (1 Corinthians 16:2; 2 Corinthians 8:1-8).

Worship is not relegated to one hour a week—it involves 168 hours a week. It is both corporate and private; we meet with other believers to praise God and praise Him privately through song and prayer.

LESSON: *Worship focuses on God, praising Him through the exposition of the Scriptures, singing, and prayer.*

September 19

THE CHURCH WORSHIPS
ON THE LORD'S DAY

*On the first day of the week, when we were gathered together
to break bread, Paul began talking to them. (Acts 20:7)*

On which day of the week should Christians gather for worship? Ellen White, founder of the Seventh Day Adventists, wrote, "In the last days the Sabbath test will be made plain. When this time comes, anyone who does not keep the Sabbath will receive the mark of the beast and will be kept from heaven" (*The Great Controversy,* p. 449). Apparently in a vision Mrs. White had seen a halo of glory around the fourth commandment. Thereafter, keeping the Sabbath (Saturday) became the test of obedience, and, according to Mrs. White, in the last days people will not be saved unless they keep it.

To whom was the Sabbath given? The Sabbath law is the fourth commandment (Exodus 20:8), given to the nation Israel, not the church (19:1–20:2). Nine of the ten commandments are repeated in the New Testament and are incumbent on the church. But the fourth commandment, the Sabbath law, is not repeated in the New Testament. If we demand keeping the law, including the Sabbath, then we must keep all 613 commandments. We cannot arbitrarily select those we wish to keep. But the majority of Christians recognize that the law—with its 613 commandments—was given to Israel, not the church. We are not prohibited from eating pork or from wearing shirts made of two different materials. We are not obligated to give 28 percent (the actual tithe), nor are we required to keep the Sabbath.

Christians meet for corporate worship on the Lord's Day—the first day of the week. That is the day believers first met to commemorate our Lord's resurrection (John 20:19, 26). All Christ's postresurrection appearances were on Sunday; even Pentecost—the descent of the Holy Spirit—was on Sunday. Early church believers gathered to break bread on the Lord's Day (Acts 20:7), and on that day they set aside their offerings for missions (1 Corinthians 16:2). Sunday is an important, distinct day in which we gather to worship the resurrected Christ who has given us everlasting hope.

LESSON: *The Sabbath was part of the law, given to Israel; the church observes Sunday to remember the Lord's resurrection.*

September 20

THE CHURCH GATHERS
FOR INSTRUCTION

*Until I come, give attention to the public reading of
Scripture, to exhortation and teaching. (1 Timothy 4:13)*

The early Christians continually devoted themselves to the apostles' teaching—as well as other Christian doctrines (Acts 2:42). The results were quickly noticeable: they saturated Jerusalem with teachings about Jesus (5:28). Even amid persecution, the apostles continued to teach the facts about Christ—His deity, atonement, bodily resurrection, ascension, and second coming (v. 42).

Where did they teach? In public places and in private homes—a valuable pattern for us to emulate. The effect of instruction is observed: when Paul taught the believers in Antioch they were called "Christians," or "little Christs" (11:26). The believers so adhered to the instruction that their lives were changed; they became like "little Christs." What a compliment!

Is teaching that important? The last record of Paul in Acts is that he devoted himself to teaching about Christ (28:31). In Paul's letters to Timothy we see that instruction prevents the spread of false doctrine (1 Timothy 1:3), produces love from a pure heart (v. 5), produces spiritual nourishment (v. 6), and is the spiritual vitamin that every Christian needs for growth.

Godliness, our ultimate goal, is possible only through instruction (4:7-11). As a leader, Timothy was to be absorbed in teaching and persevere in it (vv. 13, 16). Teaching also solves labor-management problems—it teaches submission to authority (6:2). In fact, the Scriptures were inspired by God for the very purpose of being profitable for teaching (2 Timothy 3:16).

How can I learn the teachings of Scripture? Begin a daily pattern of systematic Bible reading, jotting down insights, promises, blessings, and instructions. Get involved in a home Bible study. Read books on Bible doctrine. Attend evening classes taught on a lay level at a Bible college or seminary. Instruction is vital to a Christian's growth. It is no more possible to grow spiritually without instruction than to grow physically without food.

LESSON: *Instruction is a vital function of the local church, necessary for spiritual growth.*

September 21

THE CHURCH GATHERS
FOR FELLOWSHIP

*We, who are many, are one body in Christ, and
individually members one of another. (Romans 12:5)*

My wife and I befriended a young widow whose backyard adjoined ours. She had immigrated from Paraguay, and her husband, a contractor, had left her financially well provided for. Yet in conversation she exclaimed, "I appreciate the good things I am able to enjoy here, but I miss the close fellowship we had in Paraguay." Perhaps our material blessings have made us too independent of one another.

What is fellowship? Is it talking about sports with fellow Christians? Is it sharing a meal and talking politics? The word *fellowship* (*koinonia*) means "sharing," but sharing what? It is sharing the new life in Christ with fellow believers. Early Christians devoted themselves to the fellowship of breaking bread and prayer (Acts 2:42). They ate a fellowship meal called a love feast, followed by the Lord's Supper wherein they remembered His death. Believers frequently had prayer fellowship. When persecuted or suffering they shared the suffering together in prayer (4:23-31; 12:5, 12). They also shared in missionary ventures through prayer (13:3); when they needed guidance in decision making they shared in a life of prayer (1:24; 14:23).

Fellowship is vital for a vibrant, spiritual life. Note Paul's instructive statements on "one another" in Romans illustrating fellowship: "[We are] members one of another" (12:5); "be devoted to one another in brotherly love" (v. 10); "be of the same mind toward one another" (12:16); "love one another" (13:8); "let us not judge one another" (14:13); "let us [build] up one another" (v. 19); "be of the same mind with one another" (15:5); "accept one another" (v. 7); "admonish one another" (v. 14). These exhortations are definitive statements expressing fellowship.

How can we foster fellowship? Meet with other believers for serious prayer; help widows, the needy, the downhearted; encourage and exhort those who need it; visit with other believers in their homes and develop both fellowship and accountability toward each other. We belong to each other. We cannot live alone.

LESSON: *Fellowship is sharing the new life in Christ with fellow believers through prayer, love, admonition, encouragement, and unity.*

THE CHURCH SCATTERS FOR EVANGELISM

*Those who had been scattered went about
preaching the word. (Acts 8:4)*

As two Christians drove their boat out into the lake to fish, one of the men proceeded to cast his line inside the boat. "Whatever are you doing?" exclaimed his friend. "I'm fishing the way a lot of Christians do evangelism—in the church building. This is no more peculiar than Christians who fail to fish in the world but want to fish inside the church building."

Where is evangelism to take place? Christ commanded us to go into the world and make disciples (Matthew 28:19; Mark 16:15; Luke 24:47; John 17:18). Early Christians preached in public places with remarkable results—in a short time five thousand men were saved (Acts 4:4). Christ sent us to proclaim the message not in a monastery but in the world, the marketplace, homes, businesses —places where people live and work and congregate.

Who is to evangelize? Must it be done by a professional evangelist or at least the pastor? Following Stephen's death the church was persecuted and forced to scatter, and "those who had been scattered went about preaching the word" (8:4). That refers to common, ordinary Christians. They were not trained in seminaries but were ordinary Christians who had been rescued from eternal punishment and had a heartfelt message to proclaim to the world. Our mission will never be fulfilled if we wait for the professional evangelist. The mission to evangelize is everyone's mission.

What is the message we are to proclaim? Philip went to Samaria "proclaiming Christ" (8:5); he preached "the good news about the kingdom of God and the name of Jesus Christ" (v. 12); Philip "preached Jesus" (v. 35); Paul and missionaries preached the Lord Jesus (9:20). A simple message—Jesus Christ!

Who cannot proclaim that message? If Jesus Christ has touched your life you can be the bearer of good news. All believers are responsible to carry this news to the world. It is not optional. God has no other plan, no other means—He is depending on you and me to carry it to the world.

LESSON: *Christians scatter in the world to proclaim the good news about Jesus Christ.*

THE CHURCH
ADMINISTERS DISCIPLINE

Do you not judge those who are
within the church? (1 Corinthians 5:12)

During the Reformation the followers of Menno Simons determined that the Scriptures demanded a high standard of godliness and doctrinal purity, concluding that church discipline was necessary to achieve that standard. These Anabaptists practiced the ban—expulsion from fellowship—for those who held aberrant beliefs. When members married unbelievers or committed moral sins, the Anabaptists practiced avoidance—withdrawing all religious, social, and business contact. In some cases where a professing Christian mistreated his wife, Menno Simon's followers went to the man's home, gave him a thrashing, and even drove him from his own home to bring about repentance.

Church discipline seems strange today because it is practiced so infrequently, yet it is a biblical doctrine. Church discipline should be practiced in cases of immorality. When the man in the Corinthian church committed incest by living with his stepmother, Paul commanded the Corinthians, "Remove the wicked man from among yourselves" (1 Corinthians 5:13). They were not to associate with him. For what purpose? To produce repentance (1 Corinthians 5:5).

Discipline extends beyond immorality. Doctrinal error is also to be judged. John warned that those who denied the true humanity of Christ were not to be received into fellowship (2 John 7-10). Paul cautioned Timothy concerning false teachers who taught "strange doctrines" (1 Timothy 1:3-11).

The church must begin to take seriously the biblical injunctions to discipline. We cannot allow false views of the atonement of Christ, for example, to be taught in our churches. We must deal with moral and other sinful practices committed by Christians. However, our attitude is important. How shall discipline be rendered? "In a spirit of gentleness," knowing we are also capable of the same sins (Galatians 6:1).

LESSON: *Believers are to exercise church discipline in doctrinal and moral matters.*

WHO CAN BE AN ELDER?

An overseer, then, must be above reproach,
the husband of one wife, temperate, prudent,
respectable, hospitable, able to teach. (1 Timothy 3:2)

In a day when pastors are being ordained in their teens, married three times, and seeking salaries of more than $100,000 a year, we need to return to the biblical qualifications for church leaders as set forth in 1 Timothy 3:1-7.

These qualifications impinge on elders and pastors, depending on how a church is organized. They are not optional but obligatory. The text testifies, "An overseer [elder or pastor] must be . . . " We ought not to take casually what God takes seriously. An elder must be "above reproach." He is one who can't be censured. Opponents are unable to bring a charge against him.

He is the "husband of one wife." He has proved himself a model of faithfulness in marriage. Infidelity disqualifies a man from the pastorate just as cutting off a finger would disqualify the Old Testament priest from functioning as a priest.

He is "temperate," meaning sober in judgment. He is also "prudent," namely, discreet. He doesn't act unwisely. He is "respectable," suggesting a well-balanced behavior in his habits. (He doesn't spend four days a week on the golf course.) Like Will Rogers, he knows no strangers; he is "hospitable."

He has skill in "teaching," being able to lead new believers from milk to the meat of the Word. He is "not addicted to wine." Nor is he a fighter; he is "not pugnacious." Instead, he is "gentle," a reasonable person. He is "uncontentious," refusing to insist on his rights. He is not moved by "money" (he isn't constantly being "called" to a higher salaried church).

He has an exemplary family, reflecting his ability to rule four hundred in the church because he can rule four at home. He is not a "new convert"; he is mature and has developed in maturity over a period of time. He even has a "good reputation with unbelievers." His testimony extends beyond the church yard.

For the church to be effective, it is imperative that leaders follow the qualifications set forth in 1 Timothy 3:1-7 and that believers in the church demand those qualifications from their leaders.

LESSON: *For the church to be pure, mature, and effective, it is imperative that its leaders reflect the qualifications of 1 Timothy 3:1-7.*

September 25

ELDERS GUIDE
THE CHURCH

Let the elders who rule well be considered worthy
of double honor, especially those who work hard
at preaching and teaching. (1 Timothy 5:17)

K nock. Knock. You open the door, and two handsome young men in their early twenties are standing at your door to spread their cultic beliefs. You glance at a name tag attached to the jacket, and it reads: "Elder John Smith." Is this a biblical elder?

What is an elder? *Elder (presbuteros)* is a normal word (as the English word itself indicates) meaning an older man or woman (1 Timothy 5:1-2). In technical usage the word identifies a leader in the church who is an older man and spiritually mature. He is older chronologically, and he is not a spiritual neophyte. That's why it's peculiar to have a young man in his early twenties announcing himself as "Elder John Smith." A "younger" can't be an "elder"!

Who qualifies to be an elder? Their qualifications are enumerated in 1 Timothy 3:1-7. They are men who are faithful in marriage, having model homes and believing, obedient children, and are gentle, uncontentious, mature leaders.

What do elders do? They give spiritual leadership to the church (Acts 14:23; 15:2, 4, 6), rendering decisions over doctrinal matters (15:22). They have the serious responsibility of guarding the flock of God from the wolves that infiltrate the assembly, bringing their false doctrines (20:17-30). They must protect believers from doctrinal error by teaching the true doctrines of the faith. They must be capable of teaching—that is a fundamental requirement (1 Timothy 3:2; 5:17). When believers are discouraged, the elders are to visit them, praying with them for restoration (James 5:14).

How are elders to serve? Positions of authority bring the temptation to lord over other people. Peter warns elders to serve with humility, being examples of Christ to their flocks (1 Peter 5:1-5). Moreover, elders are to serve without mercenary motives (v. 2).

LESSON: *Elders are older men who are also spiritually mature, set in authority over the church.*

DEACONS SERVE
THE CHURCH

*Deacons likewise must be men of dignity, not double-tongued,
or addicted to much wine or fond of sordid gain. (1 Timothy 3:8)*

Mr. Lange was a reliable servant. You could depend on him. He set up Sunday school rooms, moved furniture when necessary, polished the benches, repaired broken windows, cared for the grounds, and organized help for the needy. But that wasn't all. In talking to this humble, unassuming man one quickly sensed his deep devotion to Christ. Tears trickled down his face as he talked of His Savior. He was a "Barnabas" who encouraged fellow believers. He fulfilled his ministry as a deacon.

Although it is not specifically mentioned, it appears the office of deacon began with the election of the seven men in Acts 6:1-6. The word *deacon*, a general word meaning service, is used in Acts 6:2, referring to "serve tables."

What are the responsibilities of deacons? From Acts 6 it is evident that deacons are to look after the poor in the congregation so that those charged with the responsibility of teaching the people will not be sidetracked. Since they are not to be "double-tongued" (1 Timothy 3:8) they may be involved in visitation and counseling but are careful to keep confidences. Although deacons should know the Word well, their qualifications do not call for ability to teach. In summary, deacons are responsible for a variety of general ministries in the church fellowship.

Qualifications of deacons are similar to elders' qualifications (1 Timothy 3:8-13). They must be dignified, sincere, not addicted to much wine, not mercenary, having a good track record, faithful in marriage, and having an exemplary family.

What are we doing to minister to the widows, the needy, and the poor in our churches? Are we fulfilling our obligations? Many widows lead difficult lives because they do not receive the help they should from fellow believers. Some churches use their resources wisely, as deacons organize those who have mechanical, electrical, and plumbing abilities to help others. All of us must have a "deacon's heart," ready to serve others.

LESSON: *Deacons are set apart to their office to serve the church in many general areas of need—physical and financial as well as spiritual.*

September 27

WOMEN SERVE
THE CHURCH

*I commend to you our sister Phoebe, who is a servant
of the church which is at Cenchrea. (Romans 16:1)*

Susanna Wesley, mother of nineteen children, including the famed
hymnwriters and evangelists John and Charles, is well known.
She took her ministry as a mother seriously, inculcating Christian
truth to her children and nurturing and disciplining them in godliness. Who
can estimate her influence in the life of John Wesley, who led England in a
revival and saved the nation from a revolution? What was her influence that
guided Charles to write such glorious hymns?

Women are called to serve the church in many ways. It is unclear,
however, whether there is a specific office of deaconess in the New Testament. Whereas Phoebe is called a servant (the same word can be translated
"deaconess"), that may simply be a general term for servant since the word
is used more often in a nontechnical way. Actually, it makes little difference, since women are called to serve either officially as deaconesses or
informally.

What are women to do in the church? Those who have successful
marriages are to train younger women concerning their relationships to
their husbands and children (Titus 2:3-5). What a significant ministry that is!
Many a pastor's family would have been preserved had the pastor delegated
the responsibility of counseling to spiritual women instead of counseling
married women himself. Who knows the needs of women better than a spiritually discerning woman?

In 1 Timothy 5:8-13 older widows are set apart for ministry in the
church. (Note the similar qualifications to elders and deacons.) The older
widows apparently are not seeking remarriage but service in the church.
Some have suggested that women officially serve the church as "director of
women's ministries" in which they would counsel women, organize women's Bible classes, and teach other women. They are also to teach children
(2 Timothy 3:15). As day-care centers mushroom, there are many opportunities to teach children the truths of Scripture.

Women have a very important place in the ministry of the church, and
we must provide biblically patterned opportunities for women to serve.

LESSON: *Spiritually mature women are set apart to serve the church
through training other women and teaching children.*

MINISTRY
TO WIDOWS

*This is pure and undefiled religion in the
sight of our God and Father, to visit orphans
and widows in their distress. (James 1:27)*

My father died at the age of forty-eight, leaving my mother a widow at forty-six years of age. We lived in a small, friendly town, and my parents had a circle of five families that belonged to the same church and visited one another regularly. The five families usually spent Sunday afternoons visiting together at one of their homes. But when my father died, everything changed. The other four families continued to visit with each other but excluded my mother. I well remember her spending Sunday afternoons crying.

Does the church have a responsibility to widows? What is it? James exhorts his readers to visit widows and orphans—the helpless and needy—amid their affliction because that is pure and pious worship. "Visit" implies comfort in sorrow, financial help, and other forms of assistance.

Indeed, the church has a responsibility to widows materially, emotionally, and spiritually. But the responsibility falls first of all on their families. If a widow has children or grandchildren, they have an obligation to support her (1 Timothy 5:4). In so doing, they show genuine reverence for their family member, fulfilling their spiritual obligations. And in that way the church is able to assist those who are "widows indeed," that is, widows who are alone in the world with no relatives (v. 16). In those cases the church not only has a spiritual obligation but a material obligation as well. The church has a genuine obligation to visit, comfort, and materially support widows who have no family members (v. 3).

When I was the guest speaker in a church I prayed for widows in the pastoral prayer. After the service a widow thanked me profusely. "I can't remember when I ever heard someone in the church pray for widows," she said. What an indictment! Have we forgotten our primary obligation to those with desperate physical and emotional needs? Look around you. Do you know any widows? Do not neglect them.

LESSON: *The church has an obligation to visit, comfort, and encourage widows, especially those who have no family members.*

MEANING OF
THE LORD'S SUPPER

*The Lord Jesus in the night in which He was betrayed
took bread; and when He had given thanks, He broke it,
and said, "This is My body, which is for you;
do this in remembrance of Me." (1 Corinthians 11:23-24)*

The Lord's Supper is referred to by several different names. It is the "Lord's Supper" (1 Corinthians 11:20) because He is the host, and it is in remembrance of Him. It is also called "Communion" because it is a fellowship or "communion of the blood of Christ" (1 Corinthians 10:16). It is also called the "Eucharist," meaning "thanks" since Christ "took a cup and gave thanks" (Matthew 26:27). In Acts 2:42 it is called "Breaking of Bread," but this probably also includes the Agape Feast, or fellowship meal, which early Christians ate together before the Lord's Supper. The same would be true of "the Lord's Table" (1 Corinthians 10:21).

The Lord's Supper was instituted by Christ the evening before His crucifixion when He met with His disciples in the Upper Room (Matthew 26:26-29). The entire event could properly be called "the last Passover and the first Lord's Supper" since Christ first ate the Passover with His disciples in commemoration of Israel's deliverance from Egypt—but also in anticipation of His impending crucifixion as the Lamb of God, slain for the sins of the world.

Following the Passover, Christ instituted the Lord's Supper. The bread they ate symbolized His body, given for the sins of the world. (The word *broken* is not in the oldest manuscripts. In fulfillment of prophecy, Christ's body was not broken, [Psalm 34:20; John 19:33, 36]). The cup followed, symbolizing the blood Jesus shed for the remission of sins. When blood is shed, death takes place; hence, the cup symbolized Jesus' death (Matthew 26:27-28).

Jesus instituted a new covenant, in contrast to the old, which could never take away sins since the offerings were the blood of bulls and goats. But Christ's death provided "forgiveness of sins" (Matthew 26:28). The Lord's Supper, then, is a memorial in remembrance of Christ (Luke 22:19; 1 Corinthians 11:25). The memorial is a proclamation of the Lord's death (1 Corinthians 11:26) but also looks forward to Christ's return. And in the Lord's Supper believers have fellowship with Him (10:16). Its solemnity is seen by the need for self-examination (11:28-31).

LESSON: *The Lord's Supper is a memorial of fellowship with Christ, looking back to His death and looking forward to His second coming.*

WHAT IS BAPTISM?

Those who had received his word were baptized. (Acts 2:41)

J B. Lightfoot describes Jewish proselyte baptism: "As soon as he grows whole of the wound of circumcision, they bring him to baptism, and being in the water they again instruct him in some weightier and in some lighter commands of the Law. Which being heard, he plunges himself and comes up, and, behold, he is an Israelite in all things" (*International Standard Bible Encyclopedia*, 1:386).

What is the meaning of baptism? Unfortunately, the English word has never been translated and is simply a transliteration of the Greek word *baptizo*. *Baptizo* comes from *bapto*, meaning "to dip," and was used of dipping a garment into dye or dipping one vessel into another. For example, Jewish proselyte baptism was self-immersion. In secular writings *baptizo* was used of a sinking ship, sinking in the mud, or drowning. Through the centuries Christians have understood baptism to mean either immersion, pouring, or sprinkling.

Baptism first of all means identification with Christ. Peter exhorted his hearers to "be baptized in the name of Jesus Christ" (Acts 2:38), meaning they were submitting to Christ's authority over them. In Greek writings "into the name" meant "into the account" of someone, suggesting ownership.

Baptism also means the rebellion is over. The participant makes "his final surrender" to Christ's lordship and authority. The sequence in the New Testament is always belief followed by baptism. At Pentecost, those who believed the Word were baptized (Acts 2:41).

Water baptism illustrates what happens to believers. It illustrates they have been joined to Christ in His death, burial, and resurrection (cf. Colossians 2:12). It is a symbol that the baptized person is a new creation walking along a new path. Whereas baptism itself does not save us, it illustrates our rescue even as Noah and his family were rescued in the ark (1 Peter 3:18-21).

Baptism also means identification with the church. Those that had been baptized identified themselves with the other believers in teaching and fellowship (Acts 2:41-42). Converts in the early church quickly identified with the church in baptism and fellowship.

Baptism is an important initiatory rite, a visible sign to the church fellowship and the world that we serve a new Master.

LESSON: *Baptism is a symbol to the church and the world that we have been redeemed and united to Jesus Christ.*

HOW ARE
PEOPLE BAPTIZED?

*And they both went down into the water, Philip as
well as the eunuch; and he baptized him. (Acts 8:38)*

The mode of baptism frequently evokes controversial discussion. One man had been sprinkled when he was young, but later in life he was immersed. When someone asked him, "How were you baptized?" he would respond, "How were *you* baptized?" "By sprinkling." "Oh, so was I!" he'd exclaim. When another would answer, "By immersion," his rejoinder was, "Oh, so was I!" He kept the unity of the faith with his friends!

In pouring, the person kneels while the pastor pours water over his or her head three times in the name of the Trinity. It is suggested that pouring best fits the Holy Spirit's coming upon the person (Acts 2:17-18). The *Didache*, written in the second century, allowed for pouring.

Sprinkling, originally used for sick people who were unable to be immersed publicly, did not become popular until the third century. Support is garnered from the Levites who had water sprinkled on them (Numbers 8:5-7; 19:8-13). Sprinkling also illustrates the Spirit's ministry in Ezekiel 36:25.

In immersion the person is entirely submerged in the water. It is generally agreed that the early church practiced immersion. The word *baptizo* suggests immersion. Thayer translates it "to dip repeatedly, to immerge, submerge." The phrases "in the Jordan" and "coming up out of the water" suggest immersion (Mark 1:9-10). Its secular usage of drowning or sinking a ship also suggests this meaning. It is unfortunate that the word was never translated into an equivalent English word; perhaps that would have avoided much of the controversy about the subject.

Evidence indicates the word *baptizo* means immersion, the method the early church practiced. Pouring was not used until the second century and sprinkling not until the third. Although each of us undoubtedly has an opinion about which mode of baptism is correct, we ought never to make this an issue of fellowship. There are cardinal doctrines over which we must take issue, but the mode of baptism is not one of them—salvation does not depend on it.

LESSON: *The word* baptizo *means immersion, the mode of baptism practiced by the early church.*

Part 8
Angels, Satan, and Demons

CREATION OF ANGELS

Praise Him, all His angels; Praise Him, all His hosts! Praise Him, sun and moon; Praise Him, all stars of light! (Psalm 148:2-3)

Where did angels come from, and why were they created? Apparently angels were present at the creation of the earth because Job says they "sang together" and "shouted for joy" (Job 38:7). God had heavenly spectators as He fashioned the heavens and the earth, the solar systems, the stars and planets. The angels applauded as He created the sea, birds, fish, and finally man. They were at the foundation of the earth to applaud God's handiwork.

Angels also had a beginning. God alone is eternal. Since the Scriptures indicate the angels existed at the time of earth's creation we conclude that God created them prior to the earth.

We also know that Jesus Christ created all things "both in the heavens and on earth, visible and invisible, whether thrones or dominions or rulers or authorities—all things have been created through Him and for Him" (Colossians 1:16). Since He created the invisible as well as visible, the "thrones, dominions, rulers, and authorities," we know He created the angels in their different rankings.

No doubt God created each angel directly and simultaneously. Since angels do not procreate (Matthew 22:30), God had to create each one directly. Being the direct creation of God, angels have a high status (temporarily higher than man; Hebrews 2:9), and for that reason they are called "sons of God" (Job 1:6).

Why were angels created? What is their purpose? They were created to attend to the majesty of God. Just as the guards at Buckingham Palace decked out in splendid, colorful uniforms attend to Queen Elizabeth II, giving honor and dignity to her regal position, so angels give honor to God as they attend to the Lord of heaven and earth. Perhaps the creation of the angels gives us some insight into the majesty of God and the honor and adoration that is due Him—not only from angels but from you and me as well.

LESSON: *All angels were created directly by God, prior to the creation of the world and universe.*

EXISTENCE
OF ANGELS

Bless the Lord, you His angels. Mighty in strength, who perform His word obeying the voice of His word! (Psalm 103:20)

During World War II, Capt. Eddie Rickenbacker was shot down over the Pacific Ocean. For weeks nothing was heard of him while thousands across the nation prayed for him. Then he returned. Rickenbacker recounted his ordeal: "And this part I would hesitate to tell, except that there were six witnesses who saw it with me. A gull came out of nowhere, and lighted on my head—I reached up my hand very gently—I killed him and then we divided him equally among us. We ate every bit, even the little bones. Nothing ever tasted so good." The gull saved the lives of Rickenbacker and his friends. Through that experience Rickenbacker came to faith in Christ and later confided to Billy Graham: "I have no explanation except that God sent one of His angels to rescue us" (Graham, *Angels*, p. 16).

Do angels exist? Indeed, they do! How do we know? We acknowledge the validity of stories such as Rickenbacker's, yet our authority for knowing that angels exist is the Bible. Thirty-four books of the Bible refer to angels, seventeen in the Old Testament and seventeen in the New. The word *angel* is used 103 times in the Old Testament and about 165 times in the New. Angels are discussed in Genesis and in Revelation. If we believe the Bible, we certainly believe in angels. They are part of God's revealed truth in the His Word.

Angels appear in tangible form in the Bible: Moses conversed and ate with angels (Genesis 18); they rescued Lot and his family from Sodom (Genesis 18-19); an angel punished the Israelites when David sinned in taking a census (2 Samuel 24); one directed Joseph to Egypt (Matthew 2:13) and back to Israel (vv. 19-20); an angel rescued Peter from prison (Acts 12); they ministered to Christ following His temptation (Matthew 4:11). Ultimately, the testimony of Christ is at stake because Christ spoke frequently about angels, acknowledging their existence (Matthew 22:29-30; 24:31; 25:31-32, 41). And Christ's Word is reliable.

LESSON: *The Old and New Testaments both affirm the existence of angels.*

ANGELS ARE
SPIRIT BEINGS

Are they not all ministering spirits? (Hebrews 1:14)

Hang gliders are fascinating to watch. I remember taking the chair lift up Mount Norquay at Banff National Park in western Canada; the view was spectacular—snowcapped mountain peaks and lush valleys entranced the eye. The people at the bottom of the chair lift looked like ants. Suddenly I watched a young man with a hang glider run to the edge of the cliff and dive out into space. My hands were moist just watching him leap. Off he sailed, gliding lazily along until he landed at the bottom of the mountain. I supposed many have desired the freedom to jump into space unrestricted.

Angels are spirit beings, unhindered by the confines and some of the restrictions of a human body. They are identified as "ministering spirits" sent to serve believers (Hebrews 1:14). Similarly, demons, who are identified as fallen angels, are called evil spirits (Luke 8:2).

Do angels have bodies? Some believe that angels have bodies because they are subject to space limitations—they must move from one place to another. It is possible that angels have bodies that are different from ours. We know, for example, that the resurrection body will be different from our present body—yet it is a body nonetheless (1 Corinthians 15:44).

Do angels have gender? Whereas we know that angels do not marry or procreate (Matthew 22:30), they nonetheless appear as men in the Scriptures. When three angels appeared to Abraham they appeared as men (Genesis 18:2); when an angel brought a message to Samson's mother, he was called "a man of God" (Judges 13:6). We conclude that angels appear as men in the Scriptures, and although they are spirit beings, they are not necessarily sexless.

Because angels are spirit beings they are immortal; they are not subject to the corruption and decay of a human body. They do not die (Luke 20:36). Believers, though temporarily made lower than the angels (Psalm 8:5), have a greater destiny than angels.

LESSON: *Whereas they frequently appear as men, angels are spirit beings and therefore immortal.*

SPIRITUAL CONDITION
OF ANGELS

There was war in heaven, Michael and his angels
waging war with the dragon. And the dragon
and his angels waged war. (Revelation 12:7)

Two classes of angels exist: "the angels of God" (John 1:51) and "the devil and his angels" (Matthew 25:41). The angels that belong to God are "holy," divine attendants set apart to serve Him and adorn His holiness. They are set aside to attend the heavenly Groom when He returns for the marriage banquet (Mark 8:38). They are also "chosen," or elect, chosen by God to administrate His heavenly rule (1 Timothy 5:21). The devil's angels are fallen since they rebelled with Lucifer against God and in their restless estate serve their evil master by afflicting people (Luke 8:2; 11:24-26).

Why are some angels holy and some evil? Lucifer, the highest created angel rebelled against God, seeking to exalt himself above the throne of God and rule the other angels. He wanted to be like God Himself (Isaiah 14:12-14). But God judged him, casting him down from his lofty position (vv. 12-15). When he fell, Lucifer (also known as Satan), took a host of angels with him who became "fallen angels," or demons.

What about the angels that didn't fall? It was their choice to remain loyal to their Creator. Apparently the angels were under a period of testing during which Lucifer and his followers fell. Lucifer enticed the angels through his "many sins and dishonest trade" (Ezekiel 28:18). After some angels chose to follow Lucifer and others chose to remain loyal to God, God confirmed the devil and his angels in their fallen estate and His godly angels in their holiness. The angels that followed Satan cannot be redeemed; they are consigned to the eternal fire prepared for them, and they cannot escape it (Matthew 25:41). Christ did not take on the nature of angels to redeem them; He took on the nature of man to redeem fallen humanity (Hebrews 2:14-18). There is a continuing conflict between the holy and fallen angels, to culminate when Michael and his angels battle the devil and his angels (Revelation 12:7-9).

The fallen angels are believers' opponents (Ephesians 6:11-12), but God has made provision for us by enveloping us with spiritual armor to rescue us from Satan's assaults (Ephesians 6:10-18).

LESSON: *God tested the angels; some chose to remain loyal to Him, but some followed Satan and fell into an irremediable state of rejection.*

PERSONALITY
OF ANGELS

*There is joy in the presence of the angels of God
over one sinner who repents. (Luke 15:10)*

W hat is an angel like? Does he have a will, or is he merely an automaton without thoughts or emotion? Do angels have personality?

We readily identify God and humans as having personality, and we define personality as someone's having intelligence, emotions, or feeling, and a will. Do angels possess those attributes?

Angels have intelligence. When the angel Gabriel approached Mary, he knew her unique blessing as a mother among mothers when he pro-claimed, "Hail, favored one!" (Luke 1:28). When she was disturbed by the statement, Gabriel recognized that and sought to allay her fear: "Do not be afraid, Mary, for you have found favor with God" (v. 30). Gabriel explained the blessing that would come to her in bearing the Messiah. Angels also seek to acquire greater knowledge by understanding what the prophets wrote (1 Peter 1:12).

Angels have emotion. When God created the world they expressed their emotion by shouting for joy at the beauty of His creation (Job 38:7). Angels express emotion by rejoicing. In the majestic, heavenly scene surrounding the throne of God, tens of thousands of angels sing, "Worthy is the Lamb" (Revelation 5:12). Is it possible to sing praises to God without emotion? Hardly!

Angels have a will. Some obey God by an act of the will, and some disobey God the same way. Lucifer, the highest ranking angel, exercised his will when he said, "I will make myself like the Most High" (Isaiah 14:14b). Many angels followed Lucifer in that rebellion against God. Those angels who didn't follow Lucifer remained loyal to God by an act of their will.

The personality of angels further adorns the grandeur of God; there are other beings besides humans that worship God by an act of the will.

LESSON: *Angels have personality, possessing intelligence, emotion, and will.*

October 7

POWER
OF ANGELS

Bless the Lord, you His angels, mighty in strength, who perform His word, obeying the voice of His word! (Psalm 103:20)

During the early years of Communist rule in China, one missionary family elected to remain and minister in that land. Inflamed by Communist leaders, a mob gathered in a planned assault on the missionary house. Seeing the mob, the missionaries knelt on the floor, invoking God's protection. When they arose from prayer they noticed the mob quietly dispersing. Puzzled by the turn of events, the missionary met a friend the next day and inquired what happened to the mob. "Haven't you heard?" exclaimed his friend. "There were angels with swords standing at each corner of the house, frightening the mob from attacking your house."

What kind of power do angels have? Because they are the creation of God and their power is sanctioned by God, angels have enormous power; they are "greater in might and power" than humans (2 Peter 2:10-11). They are "mighty in strength" and able to obey God's bidding (Psalm 103:20).

Angels have the power to appear as men. When the three angels visited Abraham, he saw them as three men who talked and ate with him (Genesis 18:2, 8, 9). They also have power over men. The two angels God sent to Sodom struck the homosexuals of Sodom with blindness, preventing their immoral advances (19:1-11) and destroyed the city (vv. 19:13, 24-25). On the night prior to Peter's impending execution, angels broke his chains and unlocked the prison gates (and kept the guards asleep), setting the apostle free (Acts 12:7-11).

Angels have power over the elements. Four angels control the entire earth by holding back the winds (Revelation 7:1). During the Tribulation, angels unleash the trumpet and bowl judgments on earth (Revelation 8:6–9:21; 16). Near the end of the Tribulation angels will scour the entire earth, bringing the Hebrew people back to the land of Israel (Matthew 24:31).

Angelic power is limited by God's control; He determines its boundaries. Satan was entirely limited in what he could initiate against Job (Job 1:12; 2:6). Further, holy angels resist and limit the attacks of fallen angels (Revelation 12:7-9). Praise Him for His unseen messengers who protect us and carry out His holy will!

LESSON: *Angels have greater power than humans, reflected in helping believers and judging sin.*

ANGELS
WORSHIP GOD

And one [angel] called out to another and said,
"Holy, Holy, Holy, is the Lord of hosts,
the whole earth is full of His glory." (Isaiah 6:3)

L ittle Joan asked, "What do the angels do in heaven, Mummy?" "They sing and play harps," answered her mother. "Haven't they any radios?" questioned little Joan (Prochnow, *Speaker's*, p. 205). Some people think that is all angels do. But angels have a great variety of ministries and functions. Undoubtedly, the most important thing they do is worship and praise God. Isaiah saw one group of angels called seraphim (meaning "burning ones," probably suggesting their devotion to God) worshiping God. In their triple cry, "Holy, Holy, Holy," they proclaimed the infinite holiness of God. They saw the brilliance of God's glory flooding the whole earth.

John saw four angels, called "living creatures" (similar to the ones Ezekiel saw in chapter 1), surrounding the throne and similarly proclaiming, "Holy, Holy, Holy, is the Lord God, the Almighty, who was and who is and who is to come" (Revelation 4:8). These angels continuously surround God's throne in praise day and night. What is their function? They praise God for His holiness, power, and eternal existence. In Revelation 5:8-13 the four angels sing a new song in worshiping God. They praise God for providing redemption for all tribes and people through the death of Christ. They praise Him for the glorious status of the redeemed children of God. Their ultimate adoration is for Christ: "Worthy is the Lamb that was slain to receive power and riches and wisdom and might and honor and glory and blessing."

Surely one of the lost elements in modern worship is the lack of worship. One Christian leader said, "I wouldn't be surprised to see someone selling popcorn in the aisles of our churches." He was lamenting the lack of proper worship in our churches. If angels who know God much more intimately than we do see the need to worship, how much more should we! Does your life express your worship of God? How can you learn to worship God in a more genuine way?

LESSON: *Angels worship God because He is worthy.*

ANGELS ADMINISTRATE
GOD'S GOVERNMENT

*I saw four angels standing at the four corners of the earth,
holding back the four winds of the earth. (Revelation 7:1)*

E ach day we read our newspapers with considerable interest as
we see the political changes taking place. Poland, Hungary, and
the other eastern European countries have overthrown oppressive regimes. Democracy is restored in Panama. Are there unseen forces at
work in current events?

Angels administrate God's kingdom rule. Although men establish themselves as kings, presidents, and prime ministers, only one really rules—
God. His sovereign kingdom extends beyond national boundaries. He rules
from His throne in heaven, and "His sovereignty rules over all" (Psalm
103:19). How does He administrate His kingdom? One means God uses is
angels. The psalmist mentions angels who administrate God's rule: "Bless
the Lord, you His angels, mighty in strength, who perform His word, obeying the voice of His word!" In what do they obey His Word? In carrying out
the details of governing His kingdom.

In carrying out God's rule, Michael, the archangel, came to Daniel's
rescue when Daniel was opposed by "the prince of the kingdom of Persia"
(an evil angel). Michael also stands guard over the nation Israel, protecting
and preserving her (Daniel 12:1). Surely, one of the modern miracles is the
existence of the Jewish people and the modern state of Israel. God has preserved Israel through angelic protection.

Angels will be particularly active during the Tribulation carrying out
God's administrative rule. There will be a great battle between Michael and
his angels and Satan and his evil angels (Revelation 12:7-9). Satan will attempt to destroy the Jewish people, but angels will preserve them. (Michael
and Satan even fought over the body of Moses [Jude 9].) Angels will sound
the trumpets, announcing God's judgment upon a disobedient and unbelieving world (3:6). In fact, angels hold back the elements, or destructive
agents, in order to protect the people of God (7:1). What a comfort to know
that God has His unseen messengers, actively at work, controlling the nations, preserving His people, and guarding His own!

LESSON: *Angels administrate God's government, protect Israel, and
guard His people.*

ANGELS
SERVE CHRIST

Angels came and began to minister to Him. (Matthew 4:11)

W hen the president of the United States moves about the country, he is constantly surrounded by attendants. Some are secret service agents who protect him from physical harm; others take care of scheduling details. It was said of President Reagan that he never carried any cash. When he needed to make the smallest purchase, an attendant would pick up the tab.

From the beginning of His earthly sojourn to His ascension to heaven, Jesus Christ was attended by angels. Even before His birth, angels told both Mary and Joseph of the impending event (Matthew 1:20; Luke 1:26-38). And when Jesus was born, a throng of angels chorused the announcement of His birth (Luke 2:13-14). An angel also guarded His infant life by warning the family to flee to Egypt to escape the murderous Herod (Matthew 2:13). And when the danger was past, an angel instructed the holy family to return to the land of Israel (vv. 19-20).

When Satan's temptations ended, angels came and ministered to Christ (4:11). How did they minister to Him? Perhaps by bringing Him food. He had fasted forty days and nights and needed food to strengthen Him. In the Garden of Gethsemane when Christ agonized over the prospect of bearing the sins of the world, an angel came and ministered to Him (Luke 22:43). And when the Temple police came with lanterns and clubs to arrest Him and Peter tried vainly to defend Him, the Lord reminded Peter that He could call tens of thousands of angels to defend Him (Matthew 26:53).

On resurrection day, an angel removed the stone from the entrance of the tomb to let the people see that the resurrection had occurred (Matthew 28:2). Angels also attended Christ's triumphant ascension into heaven (Acts 1:10-11). When He comes again, Jesus will return as King of kings with a host of angels attending to Him (Matthew 25:31). Indeed, we worship the Lord of lords whose honor is reflected in the angels that constantly attend Him.

LESSON: *Angels ministered to Christ for the duration of His earthly life.*

NUMBER
OF ANGELS

And suddenly there appeared with the angel a multitude
of the heavenly host praising God. (Luke 2:13)

Ancient Jews believed there was a vast number of angels, illustrated in this ancient account: "There were 12 Mazzaloth [sign of the Zodiac], each having 30 chiefs of armies, each chief with 30 legions, each legion with 30 leaders, each leader with 30 captains, each captain with 30 under him, and each of these with 365,000 starts—and all were created for the sake of Israel!" (Edersheim, *Life and Times of Jesus the Messiah*, 2:749).

Such statements, which date back to Israel's captivity in Babylon, demonstrate Israel's belief in innumerable angels and their rankings. The Bible itself teaches that there is a host of angels—innumerable in number. At the birth of Christ a "multitude" of angels chorused His birth announcement (Luke 2:13). That describes a large, indefinable number.

Angels are also described as "hosts," meaning armies: "The Lord of hosts is with us" (Psalm 46:7, 11). That means innumerable angels of God, pictured as a victorious army with God as their head, are with believers. In Gethsemene Jesus reminded Peter, "Do you think that I cannot appeal to My Father, and He will at once put at My disposal more than twelve legions of angels?" (Matthew 26:53). A Roman legion consisted of six thousand soldiers, so Jesus was saying He could have appealed to more than seventy-two thousand angels to defend Him. That is a significant number, but even that is merely a portion of the existing angels.

Perhaps the most interesting biblical statement about the number of angels is Revelation 5:11 (NIV): "I looked and heard the voice of many angels, numbering thousands upon thousands, and ten thousand times ten thousand." John's statement reinforces the concept that angels number beyond tens of millions—they cannot be counted.

Countless numbers of angels adorn the throne and presence of God. They reflect and reveal His majesty, power, and wisdom in creation—their vast number draws attention to the greatness of our God.

LESSON: *Angels are innumerable.*

ORGANIZATION
OF ANGELS

*I saw the Lord sitting on His throne, and all the host of heaven
standing by Him on His right and on His left. (1 Kings 22:19)*

Are angels organized? Many examples in Scripture suggest this.
The prophet Micaiah presents a picture of God enthroned in
heaven, with the armies of angels arrayed on His right and left
(1 Kings 22:19). Job tells us that angels had a regular accountability before
God (Job 1:6; 2:1). Apparently, "they came as members of the heavenly
council who stand in the presence of God" (NIVSB*). Scripture also suggests there are rankings of good angels: "rulers and authorities" (Ephesians
3:10), and evil angels: "rulers," "powers," "world forces of darkness," "spiritual forces of wickedness" (6:12).

Michael, who is also called "great prince" (Daniel 12:1), is the only
one called "archangel" (Jude 9). There were other "chief princes" (Daniel
10:13), but apparently Michael was the foremost. Michael serves as protector of Israel, particularly in the future Great Tribulation (Revelation 12:7-9).

Another prominent angel is Gabriel, who appears as God's special
messenger, announcing the new kingdom program at different epochs of
history. Gabriel explained the coming world powers of Medo-Persia and
Greece to Daniel (Daniel 8:15-21). His climactic ministry was announcing
the birth of Christ (Luke 1:26-38). Lucifer, the "shining one," was undoubtedly once one of God's highest angelic creations, but he sinned and became Satan (Isaiah 14:12-17).

The cherubim are a high ranking order of angels that are guardians of
God's holiness. They prevented Adam and Eve from returning to the Garden
(Genesis 3:24) and surround the throne of God (Ezekiel 1). Satan originally
was a cherub (Ezekiel 28:14). The seraphim, similar in rank to the cheru-
bim, surround the throne of God, praising and adoring His majestic name
(Isaiah 6:2). They proclaim the absolute holiness of God.

Angelic organization shows us that God is a God of order; His kingdom is not haphazard. It also teaches us the majesty of God. With His tens
of thousands of attendants of differing ranks, our God is clearly the Lord of
lords. He is worthy of adoration.

LESSON: *There is organizational ranking in the angelic realm.*

*New International Version Study Bible.

October 13

Names
of Angels

*And suddenly there appeared with the angel a multitude
of the heavenly host praising God. (Luke 2:13)*

Angel means "messenger," which describes angels' activities. As messengers angels herald important news to man from the throne of God. Gabriel appeared to Zacharias, announcing the birth of his son, John the Baptist, who, as a latter-day Elijah, would introduce the Messiah to the world (Luke 1:11-23). Angels are also messengers of judgment, God's divine agents sent to execute punishment on sin. They sound the seven trumpets (Revelation 8:6–9:21) and pour out God's judgment on earth from the seven bowls (Revelation 16).

Angels are called "holy ones." As created beings set apart for God they praise His faithfulness (Psalm 89:5) and honor His matchless name (v. 7). As holy ones, angels are jealous for God's righteousness and accompany Christ, their commander-in-chief, in judging the rebel nations (Zechariah 14:5).

Since they have unusual strength, angels are called "sons of the mighty" (Psalm 89:6). When God issues a command, angels have the power to carry it out (103:20). And because they are the creation of God, they are also called "sons of God" (Job 1:6; 2:1). On rare occasions angels are called "God" (*Elohim*), not to indicate deity but because they are a supernatural class.

Angels are also "watchers," supervisors of God's kingdom. An angelic watcher announced Nebuchadnezzar's humiliation to Daniel (Daniel 4:13). They are "hosts," an innumerable mighty, heavenly army surrounding their divine Commander (Psalm 89:8). The heavenly host carries out God's divine will (103:21). Young David fearlessly faced Goliath in the name of Lord and the angelic armies (1 Samuel 17:45). At Christ's birth a host of angels sang the praises of Messiah's birth (Luke 2:13-14).

Angels are also called "stars," describing their heavenly station. The stars sang for joy at creation (Job 38:7). The ministry of the divine messengers reveals the holiness of God. The Sovereign Lord is attended by innumerable angels to carry out His will. That should remind us of the greatness of our God and the certainty of the execution of His divine will.

LESSON: *The names of angels illustrate their mission as messengers of God, heralding news from God and carrying out His divine will.*

CHERUBIM
AND SERAPHIM

*Seraphim stood above Him . . . and one called out to another
and said, "Holy, Holy, Holy, is the Lord of hosts,
the whole earth is full of His glory." (Isaiah 6:2-3)*

When God expelled Adam and Eve from the Garden of Eden, He stationed cherubim, angels of the highest order, with flaming swords at the entrance, prohibiting the first parents from reentering the Garden (Genesis 3:24).

The prominent post of the cherubim is illustrated in their position above the mercy seat (Exodus 25:17-22). Cherubim were carved of gold, stationed at opposite ends of the mercy seat with outstretched wings covering it and their faces toward it. It was at the mercy seat, which covered the Ark, that God met man. The cherubim attend God in the administration of mercy to man. Ezekiel identified the cherubim as "four living beings" having human form, four faces (a man, a lion, a bull, and an eagle), four wings, and feet like calves' hooves (1:5-7). Under their wings they had the hands of a man (v. 8). Their appearance was "like burning coals of fire or like torches. Fire moved back and forth among the creatures; it was bright, and lightning flashed out of it" (vv. 13-14, NIV). Their brilliance suggests they radiate God's glory (v. 28).

What do cherubim do? "They are proclaimers and protectors of God's glorious presence, His sovereignty, and His holiness" (Dickason, *Angels*, p. 63). Remaining in God's presence, cherubim are identified with God's glory.

Seraphim, meaning "burning ones," hover above the Lord's throne and call out, "Holy, Holy, Holy is the Lord of hosts," causing even the doorposts and thresholds to shake (Isaiah 6:3-4). Their name identifies them as being on fire in devotion to God. By bringing a burning coal for cleansing to Isaiah, they revealed man's need for cleansing before he can approach God (vv. 6-7).

Perhaps that is a message we have lost in the twentieth century; nothing seems holy anymore. When George Burns plays the role of God in a Hollywood movie we know something has gone awry. But God is still holy. And He still meets us on His terms, not ours. We know very little of God if we fail to recognize and revere His holiness.

LESSON: *The cherubim and seraphim adorn the holiness of God and reveal man's inability in his sinfulness to approach a holy God.*

MICHAEL
AND GABRIEL

And there was war in heaven, Michael and
his angels waging war with the dragon....
And the dragon was thrown down. (Revelation 12:7, 9)

Only two good angels, Michael and Gabriel, are mentioned by name in the Scriptures; Michael, designated "the archangel," may be the highest ranking angel (Jude 9). Whereas the apocryphal book Enoch names seven archangels, the Bible only mentions Michael and refers to him as "the archangel" (cf. 1 Thessalonians 4:16). Michael means "Who is like God?" calling attention to God's peerless person. As an archangel, Michael is a chief or principal ruling angel. Perhaps Lucifer was also an archangel before he fell, because he desired to dominate God (Isaiah 14:13-14). Michael is also identified as "one of the chief princes" whose ministry is the protection of Israel (Daniel 12:1), just as other angels are appointed over other nations by God or Satan. In his protection of Israel, Michael waged war with "the prince of the kingdom of Persia" (an evil angel) for twenty-one days (Daniel 10:13). During the Tribulation Michael and his angels will battle Satan and his hordes of demons, who will be defeated and expelled from heaven (Revelation 12:7-9).

Gabriel, whose name means "mighty one of God" or "God's hero," stands in the presence of God (Luke 1:19). It is his responsibility to explain God's new kingdom to the people. When Daniel was perplexed about his vision, Gabriel explained the prophecy concerning Alexander the Great as well as the prophecy about Antichrist (Daniel 8:15-26). Gabriel also told Daniel about the "seventy sevens," the prophetic 490 years, culminating in the rise of the Antichrist during the seven-year Tribulation period (9:20-27). Gabriel was also privileged to announce to Zacharias the birth of his son, John the Baptist (Luke 1:19), and the miraculous conception of the Messiah and His future reign to the virgin Mary (vv. 26-38).

It is evident that God is a God of order, employing angels to defend His beloved people and announce the advent of a new era. But to Michael belongs the privilege of giving the trumpet blast, calling the "dead in Christ" out of their graves to be reunited with living believers to be "caught up together with them in the clouds to meet the Lord in the air" (1 Thessalonians 4:17). Are you listening for Gabriel's trumpet call?

LESSON: *Michael is an archangel, a protector of Israel, whereas Gabriel announces God's unique message of a new program in history.*

WHERE DO ANGELS LIVE?

The living creatures give glory and honor
and thanks to Him who sits on the throne,
to Him who lives forever and ever. (Revelation 4:9)

Where do angels live? Why, in heaven of course! Actually some do live in heaven, but with the fall of Lucifer they have other dwelling places. For some, heaven is their permanent home. Since the seraphim hover over the throne of God, they appear permanently in heaven (Isaiah 6:2) as do the cherubim, who also adorn God's throne (Ezekiel 1:4-14; cf. Revelation 4:6-9). Gabriel also stands in the presence of God (Luke 1:19), and a host of other angels dwell in His presence as well (Mark 12:25).

It appears that some angels also live in the "second heaven," the celestial heaven—realm of sun, moon, and stars. How do we know that? Christ is seated in heaven "after angels and authorities and powers had been subjected to Him" (1 Peter 3:22), meaning they are "beneath" Him. "Authorities and powers" refers to all spirit beings—including fallen angels. They do not have access to the third heaven. The angels' association with the stars also suggests their dwelling place in the celestial heavens (Job 38:6-7; Revelation 9:1).

It appears that both good and evil angels have access to "the heavenly places," which must include the atmospheric heaven and the realm of human life on earth. Although God has blessed us in this sphere (Ephesians 1:3) and "rulers and authorities" dwell here (3:10), so do the "forces of this darkness" and "spiritual forces of wickedness," or Satan's emissaries, demons (6:12).

Although some demons freely roam in their destructive work, some live in the abyss, a temporary imprisonment (Revelation 9:1-11). When Satan unlocks the abyss in the Tribulation hordes of demons will emerge, having been imprisoned because of their wickedness. Satan will be bound and thrown into the abyss for the duration of the millennial kingdom (20:2-3). Other angels are "kept in darkness, bound with everlasting chains" (Jude 6, NIV), probably the same angels as those who are cast into hell (Tartarus; 2 Peter 2:4), only to be released and thrown into the lake of fire (Matthew 25:41). What a difference in their dwelling places! The glorious presence of God because of a willful choice, or a destiny of darkness in the abyss because of rebellion. Choices are important—and sometimes eternal.

LESSON: *Good angels dwell in the atmospheric, celestial, and third heavens, whereas some evil angels are free and others are bound in hell.*

ORIGINAL STATE
OF ANGELS

The Son of Man . . . comes in the glory of
His Father with the holy angels. (Mark 8:38)

One spring morning, the cleaning maid at a motel in Daytona Beach found a young man dead in his room, overdosed on drugs. The death was all the more tragic because he came from a prominent New England family that had great aspirations for him. Many in the family had excelled to national prominence. But that young man never would. He had great privileges and opportunities, but he rejected them for a self-inflicted sentence of death.

All of God's creation was originally termed good (Genesis 1:31), so we know that angels too were created good; in fact, angels are called holy (Mark 8:38). God originally created angels for something special and partic-ular- -to serve Him. For that reason they originally enjoyed the glory of His presence continually. Angels had access to God (Job 1:6). Enjoying the splendor of heaven's beauty, brimming with the effulgence of God's glory —that was the privilege of all angels originally.

But angels were also created with limitations. Although angels are spirit beings, they are not able to be everywhere present at the same time. When the angel Gabriel appeared to Mary in Nazareth, he could be nowhere else at that moment. He was limited to being in Nazareth. Angels are also limited in intellect—they do not know all things. They are unaware of the time of Christ's return (Matthew 24:36). They are also unaware of the details of prophecy. The Old Testament Scriptures predict the sufferings of Christ and the future glory of His earthly reign. Angels have longed to obtain a clear glimpse of these future events—but have been unable (1 Peter 1:10-12).

Although their original state was holy, some angels rebelled against God and took a host of angels with them in their fall. That resulted in two classes of angels: the elect (1 Timothy 5:21) and the evil (Matthew 25:41). Whereas their original state was holy and blessed with God's presence, the fall of some is a reminder of man's own Fall.

LESSON: *Angels were originally created holy, yet with limitations, for the purpose of bringing glory to God.*

October 18

ANGELS' MINISTRY TO NATIONS

*The prince of the kingdom of Persia was with-
standing me . . . then behold, Michael, one of
the chief princes, came to help me. (Daniel 10:13)*

One of the strangest stories ever told is that of Rasputin, the Russian monk. Rasputin belonged to a strange religious sect called
the Khlysty, which taught that one should sin that one could
repent and receive salvation. Rasputin taught, "Sin in order that you may
obtain forgiveness," and, "Only through me you can hope to be saved; and
the manner of your salvation is this: you must be united with me in soul and
body." That claim led him and others to great immorality. Tragically, he
made a deep impression on Czarina Alexandra, wife of Czar Nicholas of
Russia, whereby he influenced government policy at a crucial time in Russia's history. He hindered possible reforms that otherwise might have averted the Russian revolution and the death of the czar and his family. Did
Rasputin act on his own? Or was there a supernatural power behind him,
influencing him and the destiny of the nation?

In Daniel's weakness, God sent an angel to assist him, yet the angel
was delayed for twenty-one days (Daniel 10:13). Why? Because the "prince
of the Persian kingdom" was resisting the angel sent to help him. Who is the
"prince of the Persian kingdom"? "Apparently a demon exercising influence
over the Persian realm in the interest of Satan" (NIVSB). The demon was
exercising evil influence and authority over a political nation. Even though
Michael, the archangel, assisted in the battle, it was not over. The angel told
Daniel he must return to fight the prince of Persia (v. 20). The high ranking
demon and Satan were influencing government policy in Persia against
God's people.

When we see moral setbacks in national policy in our own nation, and
in others, we must realize the reason is more than poor legislation by ill-
advised leaders. We are in a spiritual battle. We struggle "against the world-
forces of this darkness, against the spiritual forces of wickedness in the
heavenly places" (Ephesians 6:12). How shall we do battle? By putting on
the full armor of God (vv. 10-20). Stand firm therefore!

LESSON: *Angels and demons influence the nations of the world for
good and for evil.*

ANGELS' MINISTRY
TO UNBELIEVERS

*The Son of Man will send forth His angels, and they
will gather out of His kingdom all stumbling-blocks,
and those who commit lawlessness. (Matthew 13:41)*

When President Bush ordered the invasion of Panama, he did not personally go to Panama, rifle in hand, and attack the Noriega regime. He ordered twenty-four thousand American troops to invade Panama and rid the Panamanian people of the dictator and drug smuggler.

In the same way God uses His emissaries to carry out His judgments. In that sense, angels have a ministry to unbelievers. Angels came to Lot in Sodom, pleading with him to abandon the city because "the Lord has sent us to destroy it" (Genesis 9:13). Near the end of the Tribulation, and prior to the horror of the bowl judgments, an angel announces the impending judgment (Revelation 14:6-7), another angel announces the fall of Babylon (v. 8), and another announces judgment upon those who worship the Beast (vv. 9-10).

Angels are particularly used by God in His judgment of the world at the end of the age. They are compared to reapers, who, sickle in hand, cut down the grain. Similarly, at the end of the age, they will be God's divine agents, sent to gather evildoers and throw them into the fiery furnace (Matthew 13:39-42). John also pictures angels as harvesting the earth. Using a sharp sickle, an angel reaps the ripe grape clusters and throws them into God's winepress, where they are crushed (Revelation 14:14-20). All that is symbolic of the judgment of the earth.

The climactic judgment upon the earth is the series of bowl judgments at the end of the Tribulation, just prior to Christ's return. As God's instruments, angels pour out the judgments upon an unrepentant and unbelieving world (Revelation 16).

Angels also have the prestigious privilege of announcing the triumphant return of Christ in judgment (19:17-21). That is a stark reminder of the righteousness that God demands. He will punish sin. Those who refuse his grace, offered through the meritorious death of the Lord Jesus, will face God's angelic messengers—not as friends, but as foes.

LESSON: *Angels are God's divine agents, sent to carry out His judgments upon unbelievers and an unbelieving world.*

October 20

RELATIONSHIP OF
ANGELS TO PEOPLE

What is man that you are mindful of him? . . . You
made him a little lower than the heavenly beings and
crowned him with glory and honor. (Psalm 8:4-5, NIV)

What is the relationship of angels to human beings? There are some similarities between men and angels. Both are limited by time and space, both are dependent on God, and both are accountable to God. Angels are "sons of God" by creation (Job 1:6), whereas believers are "sons of God" by redemption (John 1:12).

Men and angels also have differences. They have different destinies. In the original realm of creation, man was created lower than the angels (Psalm 8:5). From our study we have noticed the great power of angels. But man's station is not fixed. His destiny is higher. One rendering of Psalm 8:5 reads, "Thou has made him a little while lower than the angels," suggesting man's subordination to angels is temporary. Man's created destiny was to subdue the earth and rule the world (Genesis 1:28). Through sin, man forfeited that rule, but through Christ he will regain his intended position in the future (Psalm 8:5-8). Even the carnal Corinthians were told, "Do you not know that we shall judge angels?" (1 Corinthians 6:3).

Angels and men also have differences in God's service. Angels are "ministering spirits" sent to protect and help believers (Hebrews 1:14). Men, on the contrary, are given the command to communicate the gospel, a privilege not granted to angels (Matthew 28:18-20). Men and angels also differ in their constitution. Although angels may appear as men, they are spirit beings (Hebrews 1:14) and are normally invisible (Psalm 34:7). But human beings are both spirit and body (Genesis 2:7) and have the power to procreate. Since angels do not procreate, they are fixed in number (Matthew 22:30), having been individually created by God. Angels are greater "in might and power" than people, suggesting they are greater in intelligence and strength. Angels are not subject to death (Luke 20:36), unlike human beings. But human beings are the object of redemption; Christ died for men, not angels (Hebrews 2:14-18). He loved and died for fallen men and women, for you and me.

LESSON: *Men are a little lower than the angels, but in union with Christ, believers have a more exalted position than angels.*

ANGELS PROTECT BELIEVERS

He will give His angels charge concerning you,
to guard you in all your ways. (Psalm 91:11)

John G. Paton, well-known missionary to the New Hebrides Islands, recounted an occasion when angry natives attempted to storm his residence. The Patons prostrated themselves in prayer to God throughout the fearful night. When daybreak came, Paton and his wife peered out and in astonishment watched the natives slowly depart. When the tribal chief was converted a year later, Paton asked him why they had not attacked. Astonished, the chief responded, "Who were all those men you had there with you?" Paton replied, "There were no men there; just my wife and I." The chief argued that he and his men had seen hundreds of big men in shining garments with drawn swords, encircling and guarding the Paton home. Then Paton understood that God had sent His angels to protect him and his family (Green, *Illustrations*, p. 19).

That illustration beautifully portrays one purpose of angels: they are "sent out to render service for the sake of those who will inherit salvation" (Hebrews 1:14). Angels have been commissioned by God to render official service to believers. How do they help believers? Probably by means of physical preservation, among other things. The hope of the Scriptures is the ultimate deliverance of God's people from their enemies. In the interim, God uses angels to preserve and physically rescue His people that they may be heirs of His kingdom. A continuing theme in the Scriptures is that God will deliver His people from trouble: "The Lord is my rock and my fortress and my deliverer" (Psalm 18:2); "The angel of the Lord encamps around those who fear Him, and rescues them" (34:7); "He is their strength in time of trouble. And the Lord helps them, and delivers them" (37:39-40).

Little do we realize how God guards His own as we drive the freeways or as we experience opposition in the Lord's work. The Lord frustrates the plans of our enemies. How marvelous are the unseen attendants God has given to guard, protect, and keep us!

LESSON: *One of the ministries of angels is to protect believers.*

October 22

ANGELS ARE SUPERNATURAL FRIENDS

An angel said, "Do not be afraid." (Acts 27:24)

The *Shelby* (Ala.) *Democrat* reported about a man who ran for the office of sheriff and was resoundingly defeated. He only received fifty-five of a possible thirty-five hundred votes. Next day the man was seen strolling down Main Street wearing two guns. "You were not elected, and you have no right to carry guns," some citizens admonished him. "Listen, folks," he responded, "a man with no more friends than I've got in this country needs to carry guns" (Prochnow and Prochnow, *The Public Speaker's Treasure Chest*, p. 183).

Friends are extremely important. Believers have supernatural friends in angels. Angels have been instrumental in guiding people to spread the gospel. An angel directed Philip to proclaim the gospel to an important Egyptian official. The angel instructed Philip to go south to the road leading to Egypt (Acts 8:26). There he met the Ethiopian who, as a result, came to faith in Christ. An angel also instructed Cornelius, a Gentile, to invite Peter to his home (Acts 10:3-6). Peter came and preached the gospel to the Gentiles in Cornelius's home, with the result that the gospel began to spread to the Gentiles.

Angels have also delivered believers from harm. When the apostles were arrested and placed in a common jail for preaching the gospel, an angel came during the night, opened the prison gates, and released them (Acts 5:19). When Peter was arrested and imprisoned, the night prior to his planned execution an angel removed the chains from Peter's wrists, sprung open the prison doors, and accompanied him out of the prison (12:7-10)!

Angels encourage believers. When the angel had released the apostles from prison he encouraged them to continue proclaiming the gospel (5:19-20). During the trip to Rome, their lives were imperiled, but an angel comforted and strengthened Paul and his friends (27:23-24).

Surely we are unaware of God's constant guidance as He dispenses His supernatural friends—angels—to guide us, protect us, and even lead us in conversation with unbelievers.

LESSON: *Angels protect, guide, and encourage believers.*

ANGELS ATTEND
BELIEVERS AT DEATH

The poor man died and he was carried away
by the angels to Abraham's bosom. (Luke 16:22)

The parsonage was next door to the home of a grieving widow. Her beloved Harry had passed on to glory in their bedroom, and that bedroom became a sacred shrine to her. Whenever the pastor visited her, she would invariably lead him to the hallowed bedroom and exclaim, "Just think, pastor. Angels came into this room, and from this room they carried Harry to heaven!"

One of the most fascinating stories our Lord told was that of Lazarus and the rich man. As in life, so also in death their lives stood in complete contrast. In life the rich man had much and Lazarus little; in death Lazarus had much and the rich man little.

The statement regarding their deaths is poignant: "The rich man also died and was buried" (Luke 16:22b). It is a harsh, abrupt statement. Although he must have been surrounded with many friends in life, in death he was entirely alone. He entered the eternity of Hades by himself. But not so with Lazarus! When Lazarus died, "he was carried away by the angels to Abraham's bosom" (v. 22a). Undoubtedly Lazarus had few friends in life, but at the critical moment of death he was surrounded by heavenly friends. The angels of God came to carry the poor beggar home to glory. Lazarus entered the bliss of heaven in the royal accompaniment of God's angelic messengers.

Perhaps you are reading this and living with your entire focus on this world. If you have never given any thought to death, God, and eternity, you will fare no better than that rich man. You may live well in this life, but you will not die well. You will die alone. What should you do? The answer lies in Jesus Christ. He came to this earth, lived an entirely righteous life, allowed vile men to spit on Him, hit Him, ridicule Him. And in the end He died—the righteous One for an unrighteous world. Jesus solved the dilemma of death. By trusting in His death on your behalf, you, like Lazarus, can look forward to a royal entrance into heaven.

LESSON: *Angels carry believers into the presence of God at death.*

October 24

CREATION
OF SATAN

You were the anointed cherub who covers.
... You were blameless in your ways from
the day you were created. (Ezekiel 28:14-15)

Where did Satan come from? In Ezekiel 28:12-19 the prophet gives us an unusual picture. In discussing the pride of the king of Tyre, Ezekiel describes not only the king of Tyre but also the power behind the king of Tyre—Satan. The language of the passage surpasses anything that could relate only to a human leader.

Ezekiel describes Satan and his origin. Initially, Satan is seen in his exalted position before his fall (vv. 12-15). Satan was "full of wisdom and perfect in beauty" (v. 12). He lived in Eden, the presence of God. This may have been a pre-creation Eden; certainly it was before the Fall of man in the Garden. The dazzling display of brilliant stones in the eternal city of God was seen in him (v. 13)—stones that also adorned the high priest's garment (28:17-20) and beauty that will also be seen in the eternal city (Revelation 21:19-20). God created him as the "anointed cherub," signifying his prominent place as one of the privileged guardians of God's holiness (v. 14). He was the "anointed cherub who covers," having the profound privilege of attending the throne of God. His original state was blameless—he was created without sin (v. 15). Since God creates all things good, we know Satan was created an exalted being of moral integrity, in beauty and perfection, to guard and adorn the holiness of God.

In his original state Satan was called the "star of the morning," meaning the "shining one," probably suggesting he radiated the Shekinah glory of God (Isaiah 14:12).

What a privilege Satan had, to enjoy God's presence, having been created righteous and beautiful. But he willfully abandoned that privileged state. Perhaps that teaches us the importance of the will—that our wills *must* be submitted to His. How utterly futile to exert our wills contrary to God's! It is possible to walk away from the privileges of fellowship with God—but spiritual shipwreck will result, and we will be dashed to pieces on the rocks on sinful self-indulgence.

LESSON: *Satan was originally created an innocent and beautiful high-ranking angel to guard and adorn God's holiness.*

REALITY
OF SATAN

*Jesus was led up by the Spirit into the
wilderness to be tempted by the devil. (Matthew 4:1)*

A t the mention of the word "devil" most people probably conjure up thoughts of a man in a red suit, with horns, forked tail, and a pitchfork. And many laugh at the idea. Of course, Satan has gained a great victory if he can fool people into believing that image. He is much more dangerous than a man in a red suit. Stories of satanic influence from around the world and over the centuries can be documented. But our belief in the reality of Satan comes first of all because the Scriptures teach his existence.

Satan, whose name means "adversary," is initially seen in Genesis 3:15, although he is not mentioned by name. Having pronounced judgment upon the serpent, the Lord pronounces another judgment—upon Satan, the power behind the serpent that led Adam and Eve to sin. The statement indicates there will be an ongoing battle between Satan and believers. He is also mentioned in Job 2, where he gives account to God (2:1). Satan is seen as responsible for David's taking a census of the people (1 Chronicles 21:1), and he is observed in his primary role as accuser of Israel (Zechariah 3:1-2).

The New Testament evidence for Satan's reality is overwhelming: every New Testament writer mentions him; nineteen New Testament books refer to him. Particularly important in teaching the reality of Satan is the temptation of Christ (Matthew 4:1-11). That historical event involves real people: Jesus and the devil; in real places: the wilderness, the holy city, pinnacle of the Temple, a high mountain; discussing real things: stones, bread, and nations. The conclusion is important. Everything about that story is historical, tangible, and real. A natural understanding of the story demands that the devil be real as well. It is inconceivable that every part of the story be historical and real except the devil. If the devil is not real then the temptation of Christ was not real. But we know that the Scriptures are reliable and since they mention Satan, we know that he is real. And the first lesson in the fight with our adversary is to know that he exists.

LESSON: *The devil is real, mentioned numerous times in both the Old and New Testaments.*

THE FALL
OF SATAN

How you have fallen from heaven, O star of the morning, son of the dawn! You have been cut down to the earth. (Isaiah 14:12)

Where did sin come from? Surely that is one of the most difficult questions we can ask. We know that God alone is eternal; there was a time when God was alone, and there was no sin. But sin did not come from the nature of God. Nor did He create it. We must conclude that within His eternal decree God allowed for sin. The creature is responsible for sin, not the Creator. God created all things perfect, but He must have created Lucifer with the freedom to sin. Satan is responsible for the origination of sin in the universe.

We can pinpoint the beginning of sin in the universe. Lucifer, who became Satan, was one of God's highest ranking angels, but at some point—probably prior to the creation of the world—He rebelled against God (Ezekiel 28:15). He was created innocent, blameless, but he sinned. That indicates the beginning of sin in the universe; Satan rebelled against God.

Isaiah describes the nature of Satan's sin: "I will ascend to heaven, I will raise my throne above the stars of God, and I will sit on the mount of assembly in the recesses of the north. I will ascend above the heights of the clouds; I will make myself like the Most high" (Isaiah 14:13-14). The five "I wills" are clear. Satan attempted to position himself in authority above God. His sin was pride. Satan sought equality with God in heaven (v. 13). He wanted to establish his rule over all the other angels, to sit on the mount and rule as king. He wanted to make himself equal with God (v. 14).

The reason for Satan's sinful pride was his beauty and splendor (Ezekiel 28:17). And so God cast him down from his lofty position as a high-ranking angel in heaven. Though it is not be wise to rank sins, pride is a particularly heinous sin before God. God looks for the opposite. God wants to see a broken and contrite heart in us—not pride (Psalm 51:17).

LESSON: *Because of his pride, Satan, as a high-ranking angel, rebelled against God and brought sin into the universe.*

Domain
of Satan

The ruler of this world has been judged. (John 16:11)

I f you walk along the beach at the Atlantic Ocean in Florida you may come across a warning, stating that if you are found guilty of harming turtles' eggs during hatching time in the spring you are liable to six months' imprisonment and a large fine. It is astonishing that our world is a place where unborn turtles are protected but unborn children are murdered. Why this reversal of values?

The answer lies in the nature of the world. Who rules the earth? It is the domain of Satan; he is called "the ruler of this world" (John 12:31). He controls it, governing its thinking, even affecting legislation. This world of unbelievers, its philosophy, and system lie in the control of Satan (1 John 5:19). They follow his dictates and standards—that is why the value system of this world is perverted (Ephesians 2:2).

What is Satan's purpose as ruler of this world? His purpose is to create a counterfeit kingdom in opposition to Christ. He will entice people to love the world, giving it their allegiance, thus subverting their allegiance to God (1 John 2:15-17). Satan will cause people to love their deeds of darkness rather than believing in the Light (John 3:19). Satan entices people to glory in self and carnal desires, so immoral materials are allowed in schools, whereas the Bible is banned.

The world system is hostile toward God—there can be no coexistence. Friendship with the world means being an enemy of God (James 4:4). The world loves unbelievers but hates followers of Christ (John 15:18-19).

What is the believer's relationship to the world? Having identified with Christ in His death, the believer has died to the world (Galatians 6:14). Just as his surroundings have no effect on a dead person, so the world should have no effect on the believer. Therefore, we are warned, "Do not conform any longer to the pattern of this world" (Romans 12:2, NIV). God has made provision for us to escape the world's pollution (2 Peter 1:4).

LESSON: *As ruler of this world, Satan has perverted God's intended value system, creating an environment that is hostile toward God.*

PERSONALITY
OF SATAN

Stand firm against the schemes of the devil. (Ephesians 6:11)

B lessed are the strong, for they shall possess the earth. If a man smite you on one cheek, smash him on the other!" This is the perverted message in the Satanic Bible, by Anton LaVey, founder of the First Church of Satan in San Francisco. In Spotswood, New Jersey, a former model leads members of the Satanist Lilith Grotto in satanic rituals, while in Chicago witchcraft is practiced at The Pagan Way.

Is Satan real? Is he a person? Or is he merely an influence or a tendency toward evil? The Bible pictures Satan as a person, having all the traits of personality: intelligence, emotion, and will. Believers are warned to "stand firm" against his scheming, which indicates his intelligence (Ephesians 6:11). By his craftiness he is able to deceive people (2 Corinthians 11:3). His unusual intelligence is also reflected in his use of Scripture; he even challenged Christ with it, although he misinterpreted it (Matthew 4:6). Although he is not all-knowing, his unusual intelligence is evident in his deception of the entire world (Revelation 12:9).

Satan also has emotions. In a display of emotional self-will, Satan sought to displace God from His rightful place of honor as he exclaimed, "I will ascend to heaven; I will raise my throne above the stars of God" (Isaiah 14:13). Satan also exhibits emotion in condemning people (1 Timothy 3:6). In the final Tribulation on earth Satan will display great wrath, knowing his time is short (Revelation 12:12). Satan's will is aptly displayed in his rebellion against God (Isaiah 14:13-14).

Is Satan a person? Indeed he is. Jesus even acknowledged him as a person (John 8:44). What then shall we do? Do not be dismayed, dear Christian. Although Satan is a real enemy, "greater is He who is in you than he who is in the world" (1 John 4:4). The indwelling Holy Spirit is stronger than external dwelling Satan. God has given you and me the spiritual resources to be victorious. Moreover, Satan is a defeated enemy (Hebrews 2:14). "Submit therefore to God. Resist the devil and he will flee from you" (James 4:7).

LESSON: *Satan is a real person, having the attributes of intelligence, emotion, and will.*

NAMES
OF SATAN

*Now judgment is upon this world; now the ruler
of this world shall be cast out. (John 12:31)*

Aname tells something about an individual. Today most parents
do not usually consider the actual meaning of the name they
give their child. But in the past that was common. Abraham
called his son "Isaac," meaning "he laughs," as a reminder that Sarah
laughed when God told her that she would have a son. Hosea named his
son Jezreel, meaning "God sows," to remind the sinful nation that God was
sowing judgment against them.

The names of Satan tell us a great deal about him. He is called the
devil, meaning "an accuser," "a slanderer." It is an apt name because he
slanders believers; he is an "accuser of the brethren" (Revelation 12:10). In
his access to God, Satan libels believers. Where would you and I be without
the effective intercessory work of Christ?

Our spiritual opponent is also called "Satan," meaning "adversary."
He is both the adversary of God and of the people of God. When the Word of
God is proclaimed, Satan comes and takes it away (Mark 4:15). Similarly, he
is specifically called our adversary (1 Peter 5:8), meaning "a legal adversary
in a lawsuit." That, too, pictures Satan accusing us to God.

As the "god of this world" (2 Corinthians 4:4), Satan is the ruler of this
present, evil world system. He blinds people's minds to the truth of God,
persuading them to reject the saving gospel of Christ. A similar term is
"prince of the power of the air" (Ephesians 2:2), but that does not suggest
the evils of radio as some people once believed; instead it denotes the earth
and the realm surrounding it.

He is also called the "evil one," who has control over the entire world
(1 John 5:19). Jesus referred to him as "ruler of this world" (John 12:31)—
but a ruler whom Jesus defeated. Through Christ's substitutionary death for
sinners, He defeated Satan and his power over people. Although Satan is
"ruler of this world," Christ dethroned him at the cross (John 16:11).

Although we recognize Satan as a fierce foe, he is a defeated foe. In
Christ we are safe. Are you resting in the finished work of Christ for your
victory over Satan?

LESSON: *Satan is the ruler of this evil, world system, but he has been
defeated through the substitutionary death of Christ.*

SATAN'S
POSITION

The ruler of this world has been judged. (John 16:11)

W hat is Satan's position? How much authority does he have? Perhaps this is best illustrated in Jude 9, where Jude discusses the false teachers' refusal to respect authority. Jude mentions Michael, the archangel, as one who respected authority. When he argued with Satan about the body of Moses, Michael did not dare bring an accusation against Satan. He left that to God. Considering that Michael is the highest ranking angel, his caution clearly reminds us of Satan's original exalted position.

Satan has a position of authority over the fallen angels (Matthew 25:41). How many angels are under him? We don't know, but it is a significant number, perhaps a third of all the angels. One man alone, the Gerasene demoniac, was indwelt by "Legion," a number that described a contingent of six thousand Roman soldiers. That suggests there must be a very large number of fallen angels. It is so large that the "eternal fire" has been especially prepared for the devil and his angels.

The number is also so large that organization and rank are mentioned. There are four levels: rulers (chief rulers), powers (those having significant power), world forces of this darkness (those that serve over regions of gospel ignorance), spiritual forces of wickedness (serving over regions of sin; Ephesians 6:12).

As the "ruler of this world" Satan has authority over this world's system (John 12:31). What does that mean? He blinds people's eyes, inhibiting their understanding of the glorious gospel of Christ (2 Corinthians 4:4). The media ridicules people who believe the Bible literally. Who encourages such disparaging remarks? Satan. He has blinded their minds with a lie because he is a liar (John 8:44). Knowingly or not, unbelievers live under the influence and authority of Satan (Ephesians 2:2); in fact, the whole world lies under his influence.

But there is good news. At the cross Jesus judged the "ruler of this world" (John 16:11). Our archenemy has been defeated. Have you aligned yourself with the victorious side?

LESSON: *Satan is the authoritative leader of innumerable fallen angels, who influence unbelievers and the entire world system.*

SATAN'S ACTIVITY
AGAINST GOD

*Satan disguises himself as an angel
of light. (2 Corinthians 11:14)*

S atanism is a counterfeit of Christianity. In Satan's opposition to God, he mocks the truth. For that reason, satanists and witches are organized into local covens, consisting of thirteen members (to ridicule Christ and the twelve apostles). They meet on Friday evenings, in monthly meetings called the esbat, or in larger meetings called sabbats (probably a parody of the Sabbath). At their night meetings they stand inside a large circle, attired in black robes or naked, chanting, "Yod He Vav He," meaning "blessed be," but mocking God by using the four Hebrew letters YHVH, from which the majestic name Jehovah, or Yahweh (translated Lord in our Bibles), is derived. In mockery they renounce good deeds they have committed. A feast follows, preceded by a blasphemous grace. At the sabbat meeting a dog or cat is killed and offered to Satan—again a ridicule of Christ's death.

Usually Satan is more deceptive than overt, blasphemous satanic meetings. He has counterfeit teachers and counterfeit doctrines. He disguises himself as an angel of light, employing false workers who parade as servants of righteousness (2 Corinthians 11:13-15). Some churches and pastors minister Sunday after Sunday while denying the deity and humanity of Christ, His substitutionary atonement, and His bodily resurrection. They are antichrists (1 John 2:22; 4:3), who teach false doctrines (1 Timothy 4:1-3).

Satan has, from the beginning, opposed God's rule. He solicited Eve to sin and disobey God (Genesis 3:1-7). Presently, he motivates unbelievers to disobey God (Ephesians 2:2). Satan employs "counterfeit christs" to oppose God's rule and deceive people (Matthew 24:11, 24; 1 John 4:3). He will also be the supernatural force behind the Antichrist, who will perform miracles in counterfeit opposition to Christ's rule (2 Thessalonians 2:9-10).

How shall we respond? Remember, God is rich in mercy (Ephesians 2:4). Put your trust in the Lord Jesus, and He will deliver you from Satan's domain. You may then have confidence that "greater is He who is in you than he who is in the world" (1 John 5:4).

LESSON: *Satan seeks to counterfeit the work of God, teaching false doctrine and using false teachers.*

November 1

SATAN'S ACTIVITY AGAINST BELIEVERS

Stand firm against the schemes of the devil. (Ephesians 6:11)

A Christian teacher was popular in teaching the Bible in a prominent Christian institution. He faithfully taught in the Bible department for a number of years—but during that time spent the weekends in another city with a woman other than his wife. How could he teach the Bible during the week and commit adultery on the weekends?

After discussing a variety of areas pertaining to the Christian life, Paul warns believers "to stand firm against the schemes of the devil" (Ephesians 6:11). Paul warns us against the crafty methods and strategy of the devil. He is deceitful and clever.

What are some of his crafty methods? He deceives Christians into lying, deceitfulness, and selfishness (Acts 5:1-11). Ananias and Sapphira wanted the acclaim of giving up all their material possessions, but at the same time they wanted to retain some of them. Recognizing their sin of deception, Peter pronounced judgment on Ananias, "Why has Satan filled your heart to lie to the Holy Spirit?" (Acts 5:3). Satan influenced Ananias to lying and deception.

Satan also lures Christians into sexual sins. Married couples are warned not to deprive one another sexually except on agreement and for a limited time—"lest Satan tempt you because of your lack of self-control" (1 Corinthians 7:5). God gave humans a sexual drive, and sexual activity is proper within the confines of marriage. Depriving a marriage partner sexually may lead the deprived one to sin. The widespread sexual perversion of our society—adultery, fornication, and homosexuality—suggests Satan has been successful.

Satan tempts believers into discouragement and worry in the midst of trials. Paul feared for the Thessalonians, lest amid their persecution Satan might lead them astray (1 Thessalonians 3:5). Peter warned believers to cast their worries on the Lord, standing firm in faith, lest they be devoured by Satan (1 Peter 5:7-8).

We are in a war. And we'd better be prepared for the battle. How? We must put on God's armor: living truthfully and righteously in the world, spreading the gospel, dispelling doubts through a robust faith, and aggressively spreading the Word of God (Ephesians 6:10-20).

LESSON: *Satan attacks believers, enticing them to sin.*

Satan's Activity Against Unbelievers

*The devil comes and takes away the word from their heart,
so that they may not believe and be saved. (Luke 8:12)*

A pastor had faithfully explained the gospel to a wealthy businessman in a small farming town. Having heard the word on a number of occasions, the businessman had come under conviction of sin and his need to trust in Jesus Christ for his salvation. One day he decided to resolve the matter. He went to the pastor and announced, "Pastor, I've made my decision. I've decided not to believe in Jesus Christ." It was a serious decision, and the businessman eventually died without Christ.

What happened? How could someone hear the glorious good news about Jesus and not believe in Him? Jesus Himself answered the question. He explained the varying responses when the Word of God is sown. One response is compared to trying to sow seed on hard ground. It's impossible—the seed can't penetrate the earth. Similarly, when some people hear the Word of God, the devil comes and snatches it away before they believe (Luke 8:12).

How does Satan do that? After all, the gospel means "good news"—why don't people believe it? Satan's work is "the great cover up." Satan hides—"covers up"—the good news so that unbelievers do not understand what it is (2 Corinthians 4:3-4). They are deceived into believing bad news. He blinds their minds, causing them to remain in darkness, disallowing them from seeing the light of Christ's gospel. He may do that by ridiculing the story of creation or causing doubt about the miracles of Christ or His bodily resurrection.

Satan may also deceive unbelievers into believing they can attain salvation through works or human effort (Colossians 1:18; 1 Timothy 4:1-3). He may also create an attachment to the world and its system, enticing the person into slavery to sin and away from God's love (1 John 2:15-17).

Listening and responding becomes imperative. Do you listen? Do you respond to the Scriptures? Jesus said, "Take care how you listen" (Luke 8:18). How we listen and respond has eternal significance.

LESSON: *Satan blinds the minds of unbelievers to God's truth, hindering them from believing the gospel.*

November 3

REALITY OF DEMONS

If I cast out demons by the Spirit of God, then the kingdom of God has come upon you. (Matthew 12:28)

A mother told police that she heard strange voices, one male and one female, telling her to bite off her four-year-old daughter's ear. Grasping the child's head with her hands, the mother poked her daughter in the eye and then proceeded to bite off her ear. What made the mother do it? "Strange voices."

Were those voices demons? How can we know whether demons exist? Cultures from around the world—Babylonian, Egyptian, Greek, Roman, and many others—have all acknowledged a belief in demons, and many pagan cultures worshiped them. More important, the Bible affirms that demons exist.

Christ encountered demons on a number of occasions. When a demon-possessed man, both blind and dumb, was brought to Jesus, He healed him by expelling the demon (Matthew 12:22-29; Luke 11:14). When a Canaanite woman cried to Christ to help her daughter, He healed her by casting out the demon (Mark 7:24-30). Two violent, demon-possessed men approached Christ, and He expelled the demons into a herd of swine (Matthew 8:28-34). And when Christ sent out the apostles He gave them authority over demons, enabling them to cast them out (Matthew 10:1).

Paul taught that idolatrous sacrificial worship was actually offering sacrifices to demons (1 Corinthians 10:20-21). To those who make an empty profession of faith, James warned, "The demons also believe, and shudder" (James 2:19).

Demons exist. They cannot be explained away by trickery, mental illness, or psychological problems. A serious warning is in order—people should refrain from activities that lead to involvement with demons: the Dungeons and Dragons® "game," ouija boards, horoscopes, fortune tellers, and many more serious "adventures." Tragedy has resulted for many who have ventured into Satan's backyard to play. "Beloved, do not believe every spirit, but test the spirits to see whether they are from God" (1 John 4:1).

LESSON: *Christ taught the existence of demons.*

ORIGIN
OF DEMONS

*And [Satan's] tail swept away a third of the stars of
heaven and threw them to the earth. (Revelation 12:4)*

Where did demons come from? Since God alone is eternal, they cannot have had an eternal existence; they must have had a beginning. When and how did they come into being? Over the centuries people have had differing ideas about the origin of demons. A popular ancient Greek idea was that demons are the spirits of evil people who have died. However, that cannot be true since the Bible teaches that evil people are confined in conscious torment after death, as taught in the story of Lazarus and the rich man (Luke 16:19-31).

Another suggestion is that they are the spirits of people who lived before Adam. Satan supposedly ruled over a race of people on earth, but God judged him, and the race over which he ruled became demons—spirits without bodies. All angels, both good and evil, are distinguished from demons, since angels apparently have spiritual bodies. For that reason, demons seek to indwell a body. However, this theory is also unbiblical since Scripture teaches that Adam was the first man created (Matthew 19:4), and Adam was the one through whom sin entered the world (Romans 5:12-21). There was no sin on earth prior to Adam.

Some believe that demons came into existence when angels cohabited with women (Genesis 6:1-4). But that is unlikely since Genesis 6 refers to marriage, and there is no evidence of demonic offspring.

In all probability, demons are fallen angels. When Satan fell, he led a host of angels with him in his rebellion (Revelation 12:4). The Bible calls them his fallen angels (Matthew 25:41), but they are also called demons since he is the prince of demons (Matthew 12:24). Since demons are called spirits and angels are spirit beings, it follows that demons are fallen angels (Luke 10:17-20).

We should remember the words of the disciples: "Lord, even the demons are subject to us in Your name" (Luke 10:17). Satan and his demons are a defeated enemy. In Christ we stand secure and protected. Our lives are "hidden with Christ in God" (Colossians 3:3).

LESSON: *Demons are fallen angels who came into existence when, together with Satan, they rebelled against God.*

NATURE
OF DEMONS

*[The demons] cried out, saying, "What do we
have to do with You, Son of God? Have you come
here to torment us before the time?" (Matthew 8:29)*

Ena Twigg, a prominent medium from suburban London, "rid a
mansion of a supposedly noisy ghost by ascertaining from the
ghost that he was annoyed because the new owners of his house
had ripped out a bookcase he had built with his own hands. Ena told the
aggrieved ghost in effect to mind his own business and the troublemaker
sulked off into the netherworld" (*Southwest Scene,* June 4, 1972).

What is the nature of demons? Since demons are fallen angels, they
have the characteristics of angels. We can learn a lot about the nature of
demons by studying Christ's encounters with them. For one thing, demons
have personality. They have great intelligence, and they know who Jesus is.
They recognized Him as "the Holy One of God" (Mark 1:24) and as the Son
of God (Luke 8:28). They also know His authority over them (Mark 1:24) and
their ultimate judgment (Matthew 8:29). One evil spirit even knew the apostle Paul (Acts 19:15).

They also have emotion: they cried out to Jesus, begging Him not to
torment them (Luke 8:28). In fear of their future judgment they shudder (James
2:19). They have a will: they asked Jesus for permission to enter the swine
(Luke 8:32). They also have names. When Jesus asked the demon his name
he replied, "Legion," because many demons had entered the man (v. 30).
Personal pronouns ("I," "me") are used to describe them (vv. 27-30).

Like angels, demons are spirit beings, not having bodies of flesh and
blood (Ephesians 6:12). But, although they are spirit beings, they are localized in time and space. Demons will continue to exist for all eternity in the
eternal fire that has been prepared for them (Matthew 25:41).

Jesus not only has power over demons, but He also brings healing and
wholeness to troubled souls. The man who had been possessed by demons
lacked control over himself, but when Jesus healed him he sought fellowship with Christ. He no longer wanted the old, troublesome, tormented
path—he sought the peace and tranquillity that fellowship with Jesus
brings.

LESSON: *Like angels, demons are spirit beings with personality, reflecting intellect, emotion, and will.*

MORAL NATURE
OF DEMONS

*Where you have envy and selfish
ambition, there you find disorder
and every evil practice. (James 3:16, NIV)*

I n Clearwater, Florida, a woman was imprisoned for robbing two St. Petersburg banks. She claimed she was innocent, however, charging that it was "Wanda"—one of her seven "personalities"—that had robbed the bank. The woman did not remember robbing the bank—it was Wanda. Nearly ten years earlier the same woman had been charged with murdering an elderly person, but then too she claimed Wanda had committed the crime.

What is the influence of demons over people? Do they instigate people to commit crimes? Demons are called "unclean spirits" (Matthew 10:1) and "evil spirits" (Luke 7:21). Since demons can indwell unbelievers and since they are evil, it follows that they will influence people toward evil. Their aggression is evident—they are called "powers of this dark world . . . spirit forces of evil" (Ephesians 6:12, NIV).

The nudity of the demon-possessed man suggests the demon led the man into immorality (Luke 8:27). Nudity had become a way of life for that man, for he "had not put on any clothing for a long time." The false teachers with their "shameful ways" were similar—their "open, extreme immorality not held in check by any sense of shame" (2 Peter 2:2, NIV).

But demons may influence people in far more subtle ways as well. Demons are responsible for "bitter envy," "jealousy," and "selfish ambition" (James 3:14, 16). How else can we explain a major church split that resulted when an elder became jealous because a child was served a larger portion of meat at a church dinner? Demons bring "disorder and every evil practice" (James 3:16, NIV).

The Christian is not possessed and need not be oppressed by demons. Whereas demons bring jealousy and strife, the Spirit of God brings wisdom from above: "pure, then peaceable, gentle, reasonable, full of mercy, and good fruits" (James 3:17). How do we attain that? We must nourish ourselves regularly on God's Word and appropriate His promises. Believe and obey what you read—then you need not fear.

LESSON: *Demons will lead people into immorality as well as sinful attitudes.*

DEMONIC ACTIVITY AGAINST GOD

*The Spirit explicitly says that in later
times some will [pay] attention to deceitful
spirits and doctrines of demons. (1 Timothy 4:1)*

A study conducted by University of Pennsylvania and University of Delaware researchers confirmed that television violence increased on children's shows in the 1980s. In each of three successive seasons, children's weekend daytime programs contained more than twenty-five acts of violence per hour, much of it committed in a "humorous" context (*Tampa Tribune,* January 26, 1990).

Perhaps we do not think of television as a sphere of demonic activity —certainly not children's programs! But what does the research cited above tell us? People are subtly taught to rebel against God's precepts. Whereas God commands us to abhor adultery, television teaches viewers to laugh at it or at least accept it as "normal."

It was Satan who originally taught people to question God's commands (Genesis 3:1). Demons lead people into false religious systems (Deuteronomy 32:17), which may also involve immorality (Leviticus 17:7) and great tragedy (Psalm 106:36-38)—all of which are opposed to God's Word.

The Holy Spirit warned that in later times some will pay attention to "doctrines of demons" (1 Timothy 4:1). What is that? The context suggests it is a religious system that corrupts the gospel of God's grace. Any system that exalts man's works as merit for salvation is the work of demons. John also warns us of false doctrine regarding the Person of Christ—belief in His true humanity and deity is essential (1 John 4:1-4). Evil spirits teach false doctrine about the Person of Christ. Demons have promoted the teachings of the cults—with their perversions of the gospel and the Person of Christ.

What can we learn from this? The beliefs that we hold are not incidental; they are crucial. John said, "Test the spirits to see whether they are from God" (1 John 4:1). What we believe about Christ is important. What we believe about salvation is important. Let us endeavor to learn the basic truths of the Christian faith and thereby resist demonic delusion.

LESSON: *In their rebellion against God, demons oppose God's Word, promoting counterfeit and false religions.*

November 8

DEMONIC ACTIVITY AGAINST BELIEVERS

Taking up the shield of faith with which you will be able to extinguish all the flaming missiles of the evil one. (Ephesians 6:16)

A young man with a keen mind committed his life to Christ and entered seminary for training. He married, but his home life developed problems. Upon graduating from seminary he became a pastor, eager to serve Christ. But it was not long until his wife left him, taking their children with her. She renounced the church and moved in with another man. Discouraged and depressed, the young man resigned the pastorate. He struggled to find a solution, but filled with depression he committed suicide.

What led him to commit suicide? How could that tragedy happen? Apart from the human circumstances, there was a spiritual factor. The forces of evil are arrayed against the believer, for we are in a battle (Ephesians 6:12). For that reason we are exhorted to put on the full armor of God. It appears the enemy will strike us where we fail to cover ourselves. Therefore, Satan and his demons will attack believers, tempting them to lies and untruthfulness, to deception and unrighteousness (v. 14), to turmoil, causing them to fall in battle (v. 15), to doubt, bringing about failure in life (v. 16), to vulnerability, and to ignorance of and failure to proclaim the Word (v. 17).

Believers may be physically afflicted by demons; Paul received a "thorn in the flesh, a messenger of Satan [brought by a demon]" (2 Corinthians 12:7). Job's affliction may similarly have come through demons as Satan attacked him, taking his material goods, his children, and his health (Job 1:13–2:10). Since the world is Satan's sphere, demons may lure believers away from the love of God to a love of the world (1 John 2:15-17).

Has God not made adequate provision for us? Must we live in fear and depression? No, indeed! The grace of God that was sufficient for Paul's thorn is more than adequate for the bushel of thorns with which we may be afflicted. Troubles come, but it is forever true that God's "grace is sufficient for you" (2 Corinthians 12:10). Do not allow your sufferings to lure you away from faith in the Lord. He is entirely sufficient.

LESSON: *Demons may afflict believers physically, emotionally, or spiritually, tempting them away from fellowship with God.*

DEMON POSSESSION

He was casting out a demon, and it was dumb; and it came about that when the demon had gone out, the dumb man spoke; and the multitudes marveled. (Luke 11:14)

I n 1964, when Rosemary Brown was playing the piano in her home in suburban London, she suddenly lost control of her hands. Looking up she saw Franz Liszt, with hawk nose and white hair, guiding her fingers over the keys. "Liszt controls my hands for a few bars at a time and then I write the music down. Chopin tells me the notes at the piano and pushes my hands onto the right keys; if it is a song, Schubert tries to sing it," claims Brown. Philips Records has recorded her music—which she claims is written by the old masters. Rosemary had little musical training or ability, but she acknowledges she has had psychic experiences (*Time*, July 6, 1970).

Are spirits working through Rosemary Brown? We cannot say for certain, but that raises the question, "What, in fact, do demons do?" Demons seek to possess or dominate people by inhabiting their bodies and controlling them. This is referred to as demon possession or "to be demonized." Demons may inflict suffering, causing blindness and dumbness (Matthew 12:22); they may lead a person to self-destruction and suicide, as in the case of the man who cut himself in Mark 5:3-5; but they may also give occult powers through fortune telling or other means (Acts 16:16). In the case of the man from the Gerasenes, a spirit indwelt him, gave him supernatural strength, sent him into a rage, brought him grief and oppression, exercised control over his own body and mind, and even changed his voice (Mark 5:2-9).

How does demon possession or oppression come about? Undoubtedly, by yielding to sin. Perhaps a family history of activity (such as involvement with the occult) leads to demonization. But there may also be voluntary engaging in sin, which is Satan's domain.

What is the solution? Walk in obedience to God's Word. Fill your mind with His Word (Philippians 4:8). Nothing will bring peace, blessing, and victory besides living in harmony with God's Word and will (1 Peter 5:6-9).

LESSON: *Demons seek to indwell a body and exercise control over the person.*

DEMONIC ACTIVITY
AGAINST UNBELIEVERS

*[The unclean spirit] has often thrown him both into
the fire and into the water to destroy him. (Mark 9:22)*

A man assumed to be retarded was picked up at Daytona Beach
and treated in the hospital. As psychologists evaluated the Texas drifter, twenty-seven personalities in the man began to unfold—personalities ranging from a legal scholar to a lesbian. There was
Mark, "a growling, angry tough. Pete spoke Spanish. Cye was a religious
mystic. Michael was a rock 'n roll lover who disconnected a stereo in anger
over Eric's classical music. Philip spoke in legal terminology; Max, a librari-
an, would speak in guttural German. Female personalities also appeared.
Sometimes, the former shipping-and-receiving worker would become Maria,
a middle-age housekeeper" (*Florida Times-Union,* October 23, 1982).

It is possible that that man was possessed by evil spirits. Demons can
alter a person's thinking. The demon-possessed man of the Gerasenes refused to wear any clothing or live in a house as the demons drove him into
the desert. They had afflicted his mind (Luke 8:27-29). Demons also alter a
person's thinking through "cravings of our sinful nature and following its
desires and thoughts" (Ephesians 2:3, NIV). Thus people may be led into
immoral thoughts and acts. The ultimate result is a complete abandonment
to immoral corruption (Romans 1:18-32). Demons may lead people to suicide. Before Jesus expelled the demon from the boy, he threw the boy into
fire and water, attempting to destroy him (Mark 9:22).

Our thinking is important in repelling demonic influence. If we allow
sinful thoughts into our minds through sinful literature and activities, we
open the door to demonic oppression in our lives. And that includes
thoughts of discouragement and self-pity. What are you doing to develop a
wholesome mind? Are you reading the right literature? Are you careful in
your television viewing? In addition to feeding your mind daily on God's
Word, read Christian classics such as Oswald Chambers's *My Utmost for His
Highest.* As we constantly renew our minds in fellowship with Christ we shut
the door to demonic influence.

LESSON: *Demons seek to control the body and mind, leading a person to depraved thoughts and activities, including suicide.*

THE
OCCULT

There shall not be found among you anyone who uses
divination, who practices witchcraft, who interprets omens,
or a sorcerer, who casts a spell, or a medium, a spiritist,
or one who calls up the dead. (Deuteronomy 18:10-11)

A Christian shop owner was approached by another Christian who asked him, "Do you sell ouija boards?" "Why, yes, I do." He was unaware that ouija boards are part of occult paraphernalia. Other Christians play Dungeons and Dragons®. Is that harmless? No! It is definitely dangerous.

The occult ("mysterious") deals with the demonic supernatural and is manifested in various ways—some *seemingly* innocent. Astrology is the belief that our lives are influenced by the position of the stars (one evangelical pastor plants his garden based on astrology); horoscope columns consider the position of the planets at the time of a person's birth, which supposedly influence his or her destiny. Horoscope information is sometimes written by spiritist means.

Fortune-telling, both fraudulent and occultic, seeks to tell a person's future, an act that is condemned by God. Palmistry, reading the markings of a person's hands, is one example; tarot cards, which are highly illustrated, enticing cards, really have no power, but they distract people from the Bible, the true knowledge of God.

Magic is the attempt to control others through casting spells, using demonic forces. "White" and "black" magic both are satanic in nature.

A ouija board is a game of supposedly communicating with the spirits of dead people. It is *not* harmless; some people have become demon possessed after playing with the ouija board.

Extrasensory perception is knowing something without the aid of the senses, whereas clairvoyance is the ability to see objects without being present. It is dangerous to meddle with these unknown entities.

There is one common denominator in all occult practices: they attempt to give a person knowledge apart from the Word of God. They seek to supplant the Bible. Our source of knowledge is the Bible; to seek knowledge in the occult is risking demonic attack and influence.

LESSON: *Many seemingly innocent games and experiences may lead a person deep into the occult and demonic bondage.*

CONFINEMENT
OF DEMONS

---

*God did not spare angels when they sinned, but
cast them into hell and committed them to pits
of darkness, reserved for judgment. (2 Peter 2:4)*

In Southfield, Michigan, a Cherokee medicine woman claims she exorcised the spirits of seven Native Americans from two homes near an ancient Indian burial ground. The spirits apparently were "confused," and the medicine woman showed them "how not to be earthbound." She claimed they were "misguided" because the nearby Indian burial ground may have been disturbed. This raises the question, What is the future of demons? What is their destiny?

Of the evil angels, or demons, that rebelled against God, some are free, but others are bound. Scripture also implies that there are two classes of evil angels that are bound. One class is confined permanently, awaiting the final judgment. When they sinned, God "cast them into hell and committed them to pits of darkness, reserved for judgment" (2 Peter 2:4). This hell is a placed called Tartarus, considered by Greeks to be a subterranean abyss, a terrible place of punishment, lower than hades (the normal word for hell). In Greek mythology this was where the Titans and Giants who rebelled against Zeus were cast. Why were some angels cast into Tartarus, and what was the terrible sin that they committed? We are not told.

Other demons are bound in the abyss, having been expelled there by Christ when He cast demons out of people (Luke 8:31). This is a temporary place of confinement since the demons emerge from the abyss during the Tribulation to torment people (Revelation 9:1-11). A very deep or bottomless place, the abyss is also the place where Satan will be bound for a thousand years (20:1-3).

The confinement of demons is an important reminder (and encouragement) to believers that our enemy is indeed defeated and his judgment is assured. Whereas Satan and his hordes will ultimately be cast into the abyss, believers will live and reign with Christ for a thousand years in a perfect environment and a demon-free world (Revelation 20:4).

LESSON: *Some fallen angels remain free as demons, whereas others are confined, some temporarily and others permanently.*

DEFEAT
OF SATAN

*Through death He might render powerless him who had
the power of death, that is, the devil. (Hebrews 2:14)*

V-E Day, Victory in Europe, will long be remembered as a day when freedom triumphed over oppression. With the Allied forces advancing on Berlin from the west and the Russian forces coming from the east, Hitler's millennial dream was about to explode. On April 30, 1945, Hitler had his favorite Alsatian dog poisoned; at 3:15 P.M. his mistress, Eva Braun, took poison, and at 3:30, sitting at a table near her, Adolf Hitler shot himself in the mouth with a pistol. The Third Reich had collapsed.

We have an even greater enemy than Adolf Hitler, but he too is a defeated foe. His defeat was anticipated when, in the Garden of Eden, the Lord pronounced it. The Lord announced that a descendant from the woman will "bruise you on the head" (Genesis 3:15). What is a bruise on the head? A skull-crushing blow! It was a presage of Satan's ultimate defeat.

That prophetic statement looked forward to the cross where Satan's defeat would occur. Until then Satan held all of humanity in the bondage of sin. But Jesus Christ partook of humanity, that as representative of mankind He could live a perfectly righteous life and go to the cross, offering Himself in death as a perfect sacrifice for sin (Hebrews 2:14). Through Jesus' death the full price for sin's penalty was paid. Sin and Satan were conquered. Christ removed Satan's power over sin in this life and his authority over death in the life to come. Satan has been defeated.

At a future day, Satan will be cast out of God's presence (Revelation 12:10), and when Christ returns, Satan will be thrown into the abyss where he will be bound for a thousand years (20:2).

Where are you in your struggle with sin? Have you ever solely trusted in Jesus' death as the complete payment for your sins? If not, you are still struggling with Satan—a formidable foe. Come join the victory celebration. Put your confidence entirely in the death of Christ, and you will have life and liberty—and victory over Satan.

LESSON: *Through His death on the cross, Jesus Christ defeated Satan, depriving him of his authority in this life and in the life to come.*

Part 9
Last Things

PHYSICAL
DEATH

*It is appointed for men to die once and
after this comes judgment. (Hebrews 9:27)*

I n Aurora, Indiana, a woman was buried in the back of her beloved red Cadillac convertible. Ten years earlier, she had told her husband that she wanted to be buried with her 1976 Cadillac, so her husband bought fourteen plots at the cemetery. "The casket is going to be placed on the back of the car. The top's down, so it will just be placed on that, across the back," said the funeral home spokesman.

No matter how attached people are to this world, the day comes when each one will become detached from it. Physical death is a certainty, a reality. God promised Adam, the father of the human race, that should he disobey and eat of the forbidden fruit in the Garden, "You will surely die" (Genesis 2:17). Adam ate it anyway and brought death, not only to himself but to the entire human race. God told Adam, "By the sweat of your face you shall eat bread, till you return to the ground, because from it you were taken; for you are dust, and to dust you shall return" (3:19). Sin brought death, and "death spread to all men" (Romans 5:12). It is inescapable, unavoidable. Oh, we can deny its existence. Mary Baker Eddy, founder of Christian Science, said death is "an illusion, the lie of life in matter; the unreal and untrue," but that didn't change the fact of death. As a prominent Bible teacher pointed out, "One day Mary Baker Eddy stopped talking, she didn't see or hear anything anymore, she didn't even breathe anymore. I'd just as soon be dead as in a fix like that!"

But that is not the end of the story. Man is not like an animal that ceases to exist at death. The body dies, goes into the ground, and turns to dust, but not the soul. Jesus Christ has conquered death. Believers in Jesus Christ will receive new resurrection bodies. Christ has taken the sting out of death. You too can face the future with faith; through Christ you can say, "O death, where is your sting? . . . Thanks be to God, who gives us the victory through our Lord Jesus Christ" (1 Corinthians 15:55, 57).

LESSON: *Death is a reality for every human being, but believers in Jesus Christ will be resurrected in their physical bodies.*

SPIRITUAL DEATH

And you were dead in your trespasses and sins. (Ephesians 2:1)

Norm was one of the nicest people I'd ever met. He was never seen idling; he was always striding about, faithful and diligent in his work. While puffing on his pipe he attended to his duties seriously. His fellow workers could always count on him; he was reliable and would go out of his way to help his fellow workers. "Lazy" was not in his vocabulary. But there was one thing wrong with Norm. He ignored Jesus Christ. Norm was spiritually dead.

Spiritual death is alienation from God and precedes physical death. It does not mean a person lives a thoroughly wicked life; one can be moral, honest, and upright but spiritually dead. That means a life of futility, ignoring God's remedy for sin through His Son; it means living in spiritual darkness, devoid of understanding (Ephesians 4:17-19). Man's highest priority is to love God with all his heart, soul, mind, and strength (Deuteronomy 6:5; Matthew 22:37), so one who is spiritually dead has misdirected his purpose.

Because we are children of Adam, we were born spiritually dead. Adam died spiritually the moment he bit into the forbidden fruit (Genesis 2:17). God is holy and cannot have fellowship with sin. Apart from tearing down the sin barrier through trusting in the atoning death of Christ, man remains spiritually dead and cannot have fellowship with God. The unbeliever exists in a state of spiritual death (Ephesians 2:1, 5; Colossians 2:13). Spiritual death has spread to the entire human race, separating humanity from fellowship with God (Romans 5:12).

What is the remedy? It is stated in two beautiful words: "But God . . ." A dead man cannot help himself. God had to act—and He did. "God, being rich in mercy, because of His great love with which He loved us, even when we were dead in our transgressions, made us alive together with Christ [by grace you have been saved]" (Ephesians 2:4-5). Jesus Christ is the only cure for terminal spiritual illness. One who refuses the remedy will eventually suffer eternal death—eternal separation from God.

LESSON: *Spiritual death is separation from God and, apart from faith in Christ, will result in eternal death.*

ETERNAL
DEATH

*Then He will also say to those on His left, "Depart from
Me, accursed ones, into the eternal fire which has been
prepared for the devil and his angels." (Matthew 25:41)*

In February, 1987, a group of theologians and philosophers gathered at Claremont to discuss "death and the afterlife." One man argued that eternal life is implausible and the existence of God defies rational belief. Others argued that modern Christianity had moved away from hope for an afterlife and toward improving conditions here and now. One professor rejected the notion of an enduring soul or a personal identity after death. Only one professor suggested that the afterlife "might possibly be true."

Although men may cloud the issue, the Bible is clear. Eternal death follows physical and spiritual death. Whereas spiritual death is reversible, eternal death is not. It is fixed. It is separation from God forever. The issue must be resolved during this life. Where we will be for eternity is established in the present. The issue centers on Jesus Christ. He said, "Unless you believe that I am He, you shall die in your sins" (John 8:24). Refusal to believe that Jesus is God in the flesh and that He died as our substitute for sin is to suffer God's eternal wrath (v. 36). On the final day of judgment all these will be consigned to the "lake that burns with fire and brimstone" (Revelation 21:8). That is called the second death. It, of course, does not mean annihilation. Existence continues forever in the place of torment. But it is permanent separation from God.

Jesus taught the reality of eternal death, warning His hearers to fear God, "who is able to destroy both soul and body in hell" (Matthew 10:28). In His parable of the sheep and the goats, Jesus taught the reality of eternal death. Twice He referred to "eternal fire" (25:41) and "eternal punishment" (25:46), setting the duration of the punishment in contrast to the duration of "eternal life." Just as heaven will be eternal so punishment will be continually ongoing. But it can be averted. The concluding invitation is "Come. And let the one who is thirsty come; let the one who wishes take of the water of life without cost" (Revelation 22:17). Come to Christ, and you will avert eternal death.

LESSON: *Eternal death is separation from God for all eternity and is irreversible.*

WHAT ABOUT SOUL-SLEEP?

We prefer rather to be absent from the body and to be at home with the Lord. (2 Corinthians 5:8)

T wo teenagers leaped to their deaths from a fourteenth-floor hotel room. They left suicide notes saying they loved each other and wanted to spend eternity together. She was going into the Air Force, and since he was younger they couldn't be together. But it was a foolish and tragic choice because it didn't solve their separation.

Some teach the doctrine of "soul-sleep," suggesting that in death a person is in an unconscious state—the soul, as well as the body, is "asleep." That is an unbiblical teaching. The Bible is clear that there is conscious existence after death. The believer does not need to fear death; in fact he prefers "rather to be absent from the body and to be at home with the Lord" (2 Corinthians 5:8). The implication is that immediately upon death the believer is at home in heaven with the Lord.

The same thought is expressed in Philippians 1:23, where Paul says he has a "desire to depart and be with Christ." Departure from earth means being with Christ immediately. The Old Testament, although less specific, also teaches continued consciousness after death when the body "will return to the earth as it was, and the spirit will return to God who gave it" (Ecclesiastes 12:7). The repeated Old Testament phrase "and he was gathered to his people" (Genesis 25:8) suggests continued, conscious existence and fellowship with believers who have gone before.

But for the unbeliever there is eternal death, continued conscious existence in eternal separation from God. Physical and eternal death are the "wages" of sin (Romans 6:23; James 1:15). For the unbeliever there is conscious suffering for eternity (Matthew 25:41); there will be "weeping and gnashing of teeth," suggesting continued suffering (Matthew 8:12). The most graphic portrayal of continued existence immediately after death—and the denial of soul-sleep—is the story of Lazarus and the rich man (Luke 16:19-31).

The body sleeps at death, but the soul and spirit continue, either in joyful bliss in heaven's glories, or, as a result of ignoring the gospel, in tragic eternal separation from the Father.

LESSON: *The soul is not unconscious after death but continues in conscious existence, either in heaven or in hell.*

WHAT ABOUT PURGATORY?

If any man's work is burned up, he shall suffer loss; but he himself shall be saved, yet so as through fire. (1 Corinthians 3:15)

Roman Catholicism teaches that souls that are pure at death go to heaven, but those that are not pure must go to purgatory for cleansing and purification from venial or temporal sins that have not been paid for. The soul must be cleansed, purged, and readied for heaven in purgatory.

What is purgatory? It is both physical suffering and separation from God and is necessary because the person has not made complete satisfaction for sins. In this state the person is not ready to see God. Suffering in purgatory, which may last for centuries, is determined by the degree of sinfulness.

Is purgatory biblical? Where does the idea of purgatory come from? First Corinthians 3:13-15 is cited as defense for purgatory, but what does this passage teach? The context is dealing with rewards, not salvation (vv. 8, 14). Paul warns the readers that if they build upon a faulty foundation, they will lose their reward. On the judgment day their works will be evaluated; if their foundation was of wood, hay, and straw, their works will be burned up. What is the result? "He shall suffer loss"—of reward. What is burned up? The works.

But the fire does not touch the believer. Paul refers to the Corinthians as "those who have been sanctified in Christ Jesus" (1:2). One who is sanctified is surely fitted for heaven. Many passages also tell us that believing in Jesus readies us for heaven (John 3:16; 5:24). And the one who believes does not come into condemnation (Romans 8:1), meaning there could be no purgatory.

Dear friend, Jesus paid it all. He did not provide a 50 or 75 percent salvation. His atoning death provided 100 percent of our salvation. He Himself said, "It is finished!" (John 19:30). There is absolutely nothing that you or I can contribute to our salvation—not baptism, not tithing, not church membership, not suffering in purgatory. To suggest we can contribute something to our salvation is an insult to God. He has provided salvation as a free gift of His grace (Romans 3:24). You don't pay for a gift; you accept it. Don't trust in anything that you can supposedly offer God. Trust in Jesus alone. There is no other way.

LESSON: *A believer does not atone for any sins in purgatory; Jesus made complete payment for our sins, fitting us for heaven.*

ARE UNBELIEVERS ANNIHILATED?

At the end of the age the angels shall ... take out the wicked ... and cast them into the furnace of fire; there shall be weeping and gnashing of teeth. (Matthew 13:49-50)

A wealthy man built a house of twenty-two thousand square feet, with nine bedrooms, eighteen bathrooms, a wine-tasting room, indoor racquetball court, gymnasium, servants' quarters, garages for two stretch limos and six cars, an outdoor tennis court, children's wading pool, Jacuzzi, water volleyball court, and fifty-meter pool. The house also has a twelve hundred-square-foot room for model trains. "Call it your own little Disney World. It's self-contained. There's not even a reason to go to the country club," said a worker.

Some people believe that this life is all there is. "Eat, drink, and be merry, for tomorrow we die" is their philosophy. Death ends all, they claim. Some believe that at death everyone ceases to exist, whereas others believe that only Christians have eternal life, but unbelievers are annihilated. That is sometimes called "conditional immortality"; the one who believes the gospel receives eternal life at that point, but the unbeliever "sinks into nothingness" at death. According to this teaching, "death" (Revelation 20:14) and "perish" (John 3:16) are understood to mean destruction, or "deprived of existence."

Many Scriptures teach that the unsaved continue to exist forever. The word *eternal* that is used to describe continually existing life is also used to describe punishment (Matthew 25:46). If life continues eternally, so does punishment. Jesus taught that at the end of the age unbelievers will be thrown into the furnace of fire: "There shall be weeping and gnashing of teeth" (Matthew 13:50). John taught that unbelievers "have no rest day or night" (Revelation 14:11). Solomon taught that at death there is a separation of body and spirit, with the body returning to dust but the spirit continuing to exist (Ecclesiastes 12:7).

A serious problem with the teaching of annihilation is the fact that the Bible teaches degrees of punishment (Luke 12:48; Romans 2:12; Revelation 20:12). Annihilation would be the same for everyone; there could be no distinction in punishment. Death does not end all. There is a heaven to gain and a hell to shun. And he who believes in Christ shall not come into condemnation.

LESSON: *Unbelievers do not cease to exist at death but continue an eternal existence in torment.*

MUST WE INTERPRET PROPHECY LITERALLY?

As for you, Bethlehem Ephrathah, . . . from you One
will go forth for Me to be ruler in Israel. (Micah 5:2)

When my wife says, "Honey, would you please take out the garbage?" what does she mean? I could stop and reflect, *Hmm, maybe I've been acting like a bear lately. Maybe she wants me to clean up my act.* If she asks me, "Would you please bring home a loaf of bread today?" what is my response? Do I say to myself, *Things have been tough financially. She probably wants me to ask the boss for a raise?* Of course not. I take the sack of garbage and deposit it in the garbage can; I go to the store and buy a loaf of bread. Why? Because normal use of language is to communicate literally. Why should our study of prophecy be any different?

The Bible is understood very well when we interpret it literally, but what is literal interpretation? It is understanding words in their normal meaning. Reading about Adam and Eve and understanding words in their normal meaning, we realize they were historical people who sinned against God and plunged the human race into sin. Paul compares and contrasts Christ and Adam in Romans 5, understanding both to be literal, historical men. If Adam was not a literal, historical person, then we have no basis for saying Christ was either—a serious point indeed. In Exodus we read how Jacob's family grew into a nation of two million, was brought out of Egypt, and given the law. It makes good sense to understand that literally. Old Testament prophecies have been fulfilled literally: the prophecy of Christ's birth in Bethlehem (Micah 5:2), His virgin birth (Isaiah 7:14), His suffering on the cross (Psalm 22; Isaiah 53), and His resurrection (Psalm 16:10). Even figures of speech must be understood in their literal meaning first (e.g., mustard seed, tree, bird, and branches in Matthew 13:31-32).

Doesn't it make good sense to interpret prophecy literally if that is how the Bible as a whole is understood and if that is how other prophecies have been fulfilled? This is a crucial matter since it determines whether we will interpret the Bible consistently or not.

LESSON: *The literal method of interpreting the Bible is the way the Bible is normally understood and the way we should also interpret prophecy.*

How Do We
Interpret Literally?

*The mountains and the hills will break forth
into shouts of joy before you, and all the trees
of the field will clap their hands. (Isaiah 55:12)*

Just as a mechanic follows certain procedures in taking a motor apart, repairing it, and assembling it again, so when we interpret the Bible do we follow basic rules to help us interpret correctly. What are some of those rules?

When a word makes sense in its literal or normal meaning, we accept that meaning. For example, the Lord said, "I will return to Zion and will dwell in the midst of Jerusalem" (Zechariah 8:3). What does this mean? Some may say it means the Lord will come to the church and prosper the church. But what does the word *Zion* mean? Zion is a hill in the southwest corner of the old city of Jerusalem. Can Zion mean the church? No, because it means Jerusalem. It would be confusion (and error) to interpret Zion to mean the church.

Isaiah wrote, "The wolf will dwell with the lamb, and the leopard will lie down with the kid, and the calf and the young lion and the fatling together; and a little boy will lead them" (Isaiah 11:6). Can we interpret that literally? Yes, because we have precedence for it. Remember the Garden of Eden? These were conditions in the Garden before the Fall, and Isaiah anticipates the restoration of that world following Christ's return.

When Jesus said, "I will come again" (John 14:3), was that fulfilled at Pentecost when the Holy Spirit came? If that is our response then we have confused Christ with the Holy Spirit. Jesus said, "*I* will come again." He is distinct from the Holy Spirit; Jesus was promising that He personally would come again.

We recognize figures of speech. The psalmist said, "Under His wings you may seek refuge" (Psalm 91:4). Isaiah wrote, "The mountains and the hills will break forth into shouts of joy before you, and all the trees of the field will clap their hands" (Isaiah 55:12). Those are figures of speech. God does not have wings; He is spirit. The hills cannot shout nor can trees clap their hands. The Bible can be readily understood in its normal meaning. Read it with an open mind, and let God's Spirit give you insight.

LESSON: *When a word makes sense in its normal meaning we accept it that way; when it doesn't make sense, we recognize it as a figure of speech.*

THE UNCONDITIONAL COVENANTS

*I will establish My covenant between Me and you
and your descendants after you throughout their
generations for an everlasting covenant. (Genesis 17:7)*

God made four important covenants with His people that we call
"unconditional covenants"—there were no strings attached.
The four covenants are: the Abrahamic (Genesis 12:1-3), the
Palestinian (Deuteronomy 30:1-10), the Davidic (2 Samuel 7:12-16), and the
New (Jeremiah 31:31-34).

What is the nature of these covenants? They were literal. They were
not given in symbolic language to be decoded. In describing the covenant
with Abraham, God gave the dimensions of the land He was promising: "To
your descendants I have given this land, from the river of Egypt as far as the
great river, the river Euphrates" (Genesis 15:18). God promised a piece of
real estate to the Hebrew people that extended from the eastern border to
Egypt to the mighty Euphrates River.

These covenants were eternal. In reaffirming the covenant with Abraham, God promised the aged patriarch, "I will establish My covenant between Me and you and your descendants after you throughout their
generations for an everlasting covenant . . . I will give to you and to your
descendants after you. . . . all the land of Canaan, for an everlasting possession" (Genesis 17:7-8). The covenant did not promise land to one generation and then annul it. Nor did sin annul the covenant, because God
reaffirmed the covenant to Abraham after he sinned. The land was given to
Israel for an "everlasting" possession.

They were unconditional covenants. God did not demand that Israel
meet any conditions in order for the covenants to be fulfilled. The covenants
are punctuated with "I will . . . I will . . . I will," or, "God will . . . God will"
(Genesis 17:2-8; Deuteronomy 30:3-9). There are no conditions to met, no
"if" clauses.

They were made with a covenant people. The covenants were made
with Abraham, Isaac, Jacob, and the descendants of Jacob's twelve sons
(Genesis 35:9-12).

God is faithful and reliable. What He has said will surely come to
pass. He has made great promises to Israel, and the promises will be
fulfilled.

LESSON: *God made four important covenants with Israel that are literal, eternal, and unconditional.*

THE COVENANT
WITH ABRAHAM

Now the Lord said to Abram, "Go forth from your country, and from your relatives and from your father's house, to the land which I will show you; and I will make you a great nation, and I will bless you, and make your name great; And so you shall be a blessing; And I will bless those who bless you, and the one who curses you I will curse. And in you all the families of the earth shall be blessed." (Genesis 12:1-3)

There are three important features of the covenant with Abraham. First, God promised Abraham the land (Genesis 12:1). He called Abraham out of Ur to the new land that He would give him and his descendants as an everlasting possession. There were no conditions to be met—Abraham simply had to leave Ur (v. 4). The promise of the land is expanded in the Palestinian covenant, showing that the land belongs to Israel (Deuteronomy 30:1-10).

Second, God promised Abraham posterity, that He would make a great nation out of his descendants (Genesis 12:2). Abraham's grandson Jacob moved to Egypt with his family of seventy but emerged as a nation of two million four centuries later. Abraham became the father of the Hebrew nation. In addition to a great nation, God promised that Abraham's descendants would include kings (Genesis 17:6), specifically Messiah. That is further developed in the covenant with David (2 Samuel 7:12-16).

Third, God promised Abraham a blessing (Genesis 12:3). That reveals that the Abrahamic covenant had both physical and spiritual aspects. This is the basis by which God will bless Israel in the future; it is through the atonement of Christ, which provides forgiveness for Israel and all people. This is further discussed in the New Covenant (Jeremiah 31:31-34).

As the song suggests, "A great day is coming . . ." The Abrahamic covenant has never been fulfilled; Israel has not fulfilled it nor has the church. It awaits a future fulfillment when Israel will repent and recognize the Messiah, and He will return to establish the promised kingdom blessings with Israel and the Gentiles.

LESSON: *God made an unconditional covenant with Abraham, promising him a land, descendants, and a spiritual blessing for Jews and Gentiles.*

THE COVENANT WITH ABRAHAM RATIFIED

And it came about when the sun had set, that it was very dark, and behold, there appeared a smoking oven and a flaming torch which passed between these pieces. On that day the Lord made a covenant with Abram. (Genesis 15:17-18)

I n business transactions we frequently make official agreements ratifying a deal. Our business agreements are normally bilateral, that is, they are binding on two parties. When we purchase a house and assume a mortgage, the bank agrees to lend us money, and we agree to make monthly payments. Both have a responsibility in fulfilling the agreement.

The unconditional covenants God made with Israel are not bilateral; they are unilateral—binding on one party alone—God.

In Genesis 15:12-21 God ratifies His covenant with Abraham through a blood covenant. Normally in a blood covenant two parties entered into an agreement. They killed an animal, split it in half, and laid the halves open. Then the covenant parties would walk together between the halves, indicating the covenant was binding on them both. Should one party break the covenant, it meant forfeiting his life. It was a solemn covenant because blood was spilled to enact it.

When God ratified His covenant with Abraham, God alone passed between the halves of the slain animal, indicating that God alone is responsible for the fulfillment of the covenant. Abraham was asleep (Genesis 15:12) when God passed between the pieces. God is pictured as "a smoking oven and a flaming torch," language that describes Him as the brilliant light, the Shekinah. Since God is faithful, the covenant will be fulfilled.

On that day God made an unconditional covenant with Abraham, promising his descendants the land from eastern Egypt to the Euphrates River. But Israel has never received this land. Is God faithful? Indeed He is! His promises can be trusted. When Israel repents she will inherit the land and enjoy Messiah's blessings on earth.

LESSON: *God enacted the covenant with Abraham unconditionally; it is binding on God alone, and, since He is faithful, it will be fulfilled.*

THE PALESTINIAN COVENANT

*The Lord your God will restore you from captivity,
and have compassion on you, and will gather you
again from all the peoples where the Lord your God
has scattered you. (Deuteronomy 30:3)*

Forty-five minutes south of Beersheba in the Negev Desert of Israel, near an oasis of peach, fig, and olive trees, is the grave of the founding father of modern Israel. The inscription simply reads: "David Ben-Gurion, 1886-1973, *Aliya* 1906." *Aliya* means to ascend or "go up," and 1906 was the year Ben-Gurion "made *aliya*"—he emigrated to Israel from Poland. Although he was Israel's first prime minister, although he befriended Churchill, Adenauer, DeGaulle, Einstein, Truman, and Kennedy, although he proclaimed Israel's independence in 1948 and became a living legend in his day, the most important day in Ben-Gurion's life was the day he made *aliya*—the day he set foot in Israel!

For Jews to set foot in Israel is entirely biblical. The land belongs to them, and it is waiting to be filled with Jewish people. This small, though important, piece of real estate at the "navel" of the world, belongs to Israel. The Palestinian covenant is Israel's title deed to the land. God has promised that He will bring the Jewish people from captivity into this land promised as an eternal inheritance. Every Jew that sets foot in Israel is a harbinger of things to come. Deuteronomy 30 describes Israel's title deed, the Palestinian covenant. Six time God promises, "God will restore you from captivity" (v. 3), "God will gather you" (v. 4), "God will bring you into the land" (v. 5), "God will circumcise your heart" (v. 6), "God will inflict these curses on your enemies" (v. 7), "God will prosper you abundantly" (v. 9). God has promised to bring them into the land—and He will.

One day they will come: from Russia, from New York, from Germany, from Miami, from Poland, they will come; by boat, by plane, by land, they will come and live in *ha aretz*, The Land. When will this happen? One condition must be met: they must repent and acknowledge Jesus as the Messiah. In that glorious day, Messiah will return, the Jews will return, and the land of Israel will blossom and rejoice.

LESSON: *The Palestinian covenant is God's unconditional promise that the land belongs to Israel and that He will bring them back to it.*

November 26

THE PROVISIONS OF THE PALESTINIAN COVENANT

The Lord will scatter you among all peoples, from one end of the earth to the other end of the earth. (Deuteronomy 28:64)

The largest synagogue in the world is not in Israel; it is in New York City. Built in 1929, Temple Emanu-El on Fifth Avenue at 65th Street accommodates twenty-five hundred people in its chapel and more than six thousand in its facilities. That reflects the large number of Jewish people outside the land of Israel. Nearly six million Jews live in the United States, two million more than in the land of Israel. Many more live in the Soviet Union, Europe, and other nations.

Why are Jews scattered in Gentile countries around the world? Because God promised that should the people disobey Him, "the Lord will scatter you among all peoples, from one end of the earth to the other end of the earth." That has been fulfilled. Beginning in 722 B.C. the ten northern tribes were carried away captive into Assyria; in 586 B.C. Nebuchadnezzar invaded Judah and took the remaining tribes captive into Babylon. When Titus, the Roman general, destroyed Jerusalem in A.D. 70, the Jewish people were scattered around the world. Although there are sixteen million Jews in the world, only about four million live in Israel. The others are scattered in Gentile countries. In fact, there will be a fourth scattering. In the middle of the Tribulation, when many Jews have returned to Israel, the Antichrist will persecute them, and they will be scattered once more (Revelation 12:13-17).

Near the end of the Great Tribulation, Israel will meet the condition that will bring the people back to the land—they will repent. The priestly line and the kingly line will repent (Zechariah 12:10-14). Then God will act on their behalf. He will whistle for them, and they will respond and come back to the land—only this time they will come in faith. Their blindness will be removed (Romans 11:25-26); God will give them a new heart (Deuteronomy 30:6), and He will prosper them in the land. No longer will there be an Adolf Hitler or a Joseph Stalin to persecute the Jewish people. God will judge Israel's enemies (Joel 3:2-3), and the Jewish people will live in the land in the millennial kingdom; Messiah will prosper them spiritually and materially (Deuteronomy 30:9). Israel will come home.

LESSON: *God scattered Israel because of disobedience, but when Israel repents God will restore the Jewish people to the land.*

THE NATURE OF THE COVENANT WITH DAVID

When the Son of Man comes in His glory, and all the angels with Him, then He will sit on His glorious throne. (Matthew 25:31)

One of the legendary figures in history was Charlemagne, "Charles the Great," who became King of the Franks in A.D. 768. In a series of wars, Charlemagne extended his empire into Germany, Italy, Spain, and other European countries. On Christmas Day, A.D. 800, Pope Leo III crowned Charlemagne emperor of the Romans, marking the beginning of the Holy Roman Empire. Although Charlemagne saw himself as a spiritual as well as political deliverer and although he was a great ruler, his kingdom did not endure. He did not produce a "holy" empire.

To show the certainty of the fulfillment of His covenant with David, God swore by an oath that He would fulfill it (Psalm 89:3). Can God's word be counted on? Indeed it can! If God said it, it will certainly come to pass. God further promised David, "I will establish your line forever and make your throne firm through all generations" (v. 4). The covenant was unconditional.

In Gabriel's announcement to Mary the angel repeated the Davidic covenant from 2 Samuel 7:16, promising Mary that her Son "will reign over the house of Jacob forever; and His kingdom will have no end" (Luke 1:33). The same four words are used in verses 32-33: *house, throne, kingdom, forever.* The covenant will be fulfilled literally.

The covenant with David has not yet been fulfilled; it awaits a future fulfillment. The covenant will be fulfilled at the second coming of Jesus Christ to earth when the Lord returns to Jerusalem, conquers Israel's enemies, delivers the repentant nation, and establishes His throne in Jerusalem. The rightful heir to the throne of David will be established in that day (Matthew 25:31). He will not be crowned by a pope or as an heir to the House of Windsor in England. He will be crowned as a rightful successor to David (Matthew 1:1), "the greater David." He will inaugurate the only righteous rule this world has seen. The covenant will be fulfilled in the future—at Christ's return. The King is coming—He will inaugurate a holy empire that will stretch to the four corners of the world.

LESSON: *The covenant with David is unconditional and will be fulfilled literally at the second coming of Christ.*

THE PROVISIONS OF THE COVENANT WITH DAVID

And your house and your kingdom shall endure before Me forever; your throne shall be established forever. (2 Samuel 7:16)

There are four important words in God's covenant with David—*house, kingdom, throne,* and *forever.* What is the meaning of those words, and why are they important? God promised David that his "house" would endure forever. House stands for the dynasty or lineage of David. It was God's promise that David's line would continue—it would not become extinct.

That was an important promise since a qualified ruler in Israel would have to be David's descendant. An heir to the throne of England must be a descendant of Queen Elizabeth II; similarly, Israel's ruler has to be a descendant of David. Significantly, the opening words in the New Testament remind us "of Jesus Christ, the son of David" (Matthew 1:1). Jesus Christ has a rightful claim to David's throne because He is a descendant of David.

God also promised David that a future descendant would have an everlasting throne. A king's throne heralds the dignity and power of the kingship and his right to rule. When Gabriel announced this promise to Mary, he reminded her that God "will give Him the throne of His father David" (Luke 1:32). What kind of a throne did David have? A heavenly throne? No, an actual, earthly throne, a rule on earth, and that is the kind of throne from which Messiah will rule during the Millennium.

God also promised a kingdom to Messiah, David's descendant. A kingdom is a political, physical entity. It requires a land and a people over whom the king will rule. Moreover, the people must be willing to accept the king. When the Iranian people rejected the Shah, he could no longer rule. In the future the Jewish people will respond to Messiah, and He will rule over them in the Millennium.

Messiah's rule will be forever. It will never be destroyed; no earthly kingdom will supersede it (Daniel 2:44). The United States, Russia, and China will no longer exist; Messiah's kingdom will be all in all. His kingdom will be the final kingdom on earth. God's great promise to David will find fulfillment in the future kingdom age when Christ will establish His righteous rule on earth.

LESSON: *God promised David that one of his descendants, Messiah, would rule over an earthly kingdom forever.*

The Nature of
the New Covenant

*"Behold, days are coming," declares the Lord, "when I will make
a new covenant with the house of Israel and with the house of
Judah. . . . I will put My law within them, and on their heart
I will write it; and I will be their God, and they shall be My
people. And . . . they shall all know Me, from the least of them
to the greatest of them, . . . for I will forgive their iniquity,
and their sin I will remember no more. (Jeremiah 31:31-34)*

In 586 B.C., Nebuchadnezzar, the Babylonian, destroyed Solomon's magnificent temple, ending temple worship and sacrificial offerings. Through the sacrifices Israel received temporal forgiveness. How would the people now make atonement for their sins? Rabbi Yochanan ben Zakkai spiritualized the meaning of the sacrifices, teaching that penitence toward God and personal devotion to one's neighbor brought reconciliation to God (Fishbane, *Judaism*, p. 47). But on what basis does God forgive?

God promised Israel that He would enact a "new covenant," in contrast to the old Mosaic covenant, which could not provide permanent forgiveness of sins. This would be an unconditional covenant. Seven times God said, "I will . . . I will . . . ," a reminder that man cannot achieve forgiveness through self-effort. Forgiveness is not a cooperative venture between man and God. God must provide forgiveness.

But how? Forgiveness is not external, through works; it is internal. God said, "I will put My law within them, and on their heart I will write it" (Jeremiah 31:33). A new heart is necessary. That is a promise that God will regenerate the believing sinner. On what basis? He will forgive on the basis of Christ's atoning death. Jesus told His disciples, "This is My blood of the covenant, which is to be shed on behalf of many for forgiveness of sins" (Matthew 26:28). Christ's atoning death was the provision of the New Covenant providing forgiveness—impossible through prayer, penitence, or any other works.

Is the New Covenant through Christ's death lasting? Is it permanent? God told Jeremiah the New Covenant was as certain and permanent as the continuation of the sun, moon, and stars, as immeasurable as the heavens (Jeremiah 31:35-37). God's forgiveness through Christ is trustworthy.

LESSON: *The New Covenant is unconditional; it is based on Christ's death, which provides forgiveness to the believing sinner.*

THE FULFILLMENT OF
THE NEW COVENANT

*I will take you from the nations . . . and bring you into your own
land. . . . and I will put My Spirit within you (Ezekiel 36:24, 27)*

Not far from the Garden tomb in Jerusalem sits a small chapel.
Every Sabbath, Jewish worshipers—and visitors from around
the world—gather there to worship Jesus as the promised Messiah. As I sang in English with my Jewish brothers singing in Hebrew, tears
of joy streamed down my face. I was worshiping in Jerusalem with Jewish
believers! That small assembly of Jewish saints is a portent of things to
come. It anticipates the day when the New Covenant will be fulfilled with
Israel, and not just a few but the entire nation will turn in faith to Jesus as
the long awaited Messiah.

God enacted the New Covenant with "the house of Israel and with the
house of Judah" (Jeremiah 31:31; Hebrews 8:8). Although the church receives the blessings of forgiveness provided through the New Covenant, the
church does not displace Israel as the recipient of it. God made the covenant with Israel.

When will it be fulfilled? When the Jewish people are back in the land
of Israel. God promised, "I will gather them out of all the lands . . . and I will
bring them back to this place" (Jeremiah 32:37). Israel must first be restored
to the land. But they will not be in the land in unbelief. God will convert
them; their blindness will turn to sight as they recognize Jesus as their Messiah. Israel will be regenerated; God will put His Holy Spirit within them,
and they will obey Him (Ezekiel 36:24-27).

How does the church enter into the blessings? Although the New Covenant was made with Israel and will be fulfilled nationally with Israel when
the nation turns to the Lord in faith (Romans 11:26-27), the church also
enters into the blessings of the New Covenant. Christ's death, enacting the
New Covenant, made provision for Gentiles also (1 Corinthians 11:25). This
covenant will be fulfilled nationally with Israel at the end of the age; as a
blood covenant, the benefits accrue to individual Jews and Gentiles.
Through the New Covenant, Gentiles have been brought near and made "fel-
low-citizens" (Ephesians 2:19); they have been grafted in to partake of the
fruit of Israel's blessings (Romans 11:17).

LESSON: *The New Covenant will be fulfilled with Israel when the nation is regathered to the land and converted.*

THE "ANY MOMENT" RETURN OF CHRIST

Our citizenship is in heaven, from which also we eagerly
wait for a Savior, the Lord Jesus Christ. (Philippians 3:20)

When my wife flew to Canada to celebrate her parents' fiftieth wedding anniversary, my two sons and I remained at home. None of us was particularly adept at household things, proved by our initial meal of pizza and ice cream floats. There was one particular problem—we didn't know when my wife would return home. We divided the household responsibilities: preparing meals, doing the dishes, and washing the laundry. As we anticipated when she might be coming, we cleaned the house in earnest; we even decorated the living room with colorful streamers. She was coming at any time, and we wanted to be ready.

The teaching that Christ can come at anytime is called the "imminent" return of Christ. It does not say He is coming soon, but rather that He may come at any moment. What is the significance? Does that affect the way we live?

Reflecting on the trials and sufferings in this present age, Paul said we are "waiting eagerly" for the completion of our redemption (Romans 8:23, 25). As a pregnant mother anticipates the birth of her child, so all creation is groaning with labor pains, waiting for release. Paul exhorted the Philippians not to center their attention on earthly things because "our citizenship is in heaven, from which also we eagerly wait for a Savior, the Lord Jesus Christ" (Philippians 3:20).

We eagerly wait for our Savior because He can come at any moment. If we know His coming is far off, we don't wait eagerly. As we look for Him, we want to be pleasing to Him when He returns; therefore we are instructed to "deny ungodliness and worldly desires and to live sensibly, righteously and godly in this present age" (Titus 2:12-13). The Thessalonian believers left their idolatry to serve the true God and "to wait for His Son from heaven" (1 Thessalonians 1:10). What a simple, beautiful statement. Are you waiting for your Savior each day? As G. Campbell Morgan said, "I never begin my work in the morning without thinking that perhaps He may interrupt my work and begin His own. I am not looking for death—I am looking for Him." He may come today—what a glorious hope! Are you looking for Him today?

LESSON: *Jesus Christ may return at any moment for His church.*

WHAT IS
THE RAPTURE?

*The Lord Himself will descend from heaven with a shout,
with the voice of the archangel, and with the trumpet of
God; and the dead in Christ shall rise first. Then we who
are alive and remain shall be caught up together with them
in the clouds to meet the Lord in the air, and thus we
shall always be with the Lord. (1 Thessalonians 4:16-17)*

On October 14, 1944, General Douglas MacArthur led his troops back to the Philippines to liberate them from Japanese oppression. When he had been forced to flee from the island of Corregidor three years earlier, Gen. MacArthur had declared, "I shall return." And he did. He came to rescue the people from oppression. Just so, Jesus Christ will return for His bride, the church, because He promised, "I will come again" (John 14:3).

The rapture is the sudden, secret coming of Christ for His bride to catch us away to be with Himself (John 14:1-3). At the rapture (which may occur at any moment), all who died believing in Jesus will be raised to join living believers in ascending into glory with Jesus (1 Thessalonians 4:13-15). That is a great hope, because even death does not separate believers from Jesus; they remain "in Christ" (v. 16).

Some believers will not see death; they will be alive when Christ comes. In fact, believers are not to look for death; we are to look for Christ (Philippians 3:20)—that will change our perspective in living. At the rapture both living and resurrected believers will receive new, glorified bodies: "We shall all be changed, in a moment, in the twinkling of an eye, at the last trumpet . . . the dead will be raised imperishable, and we shall be changed" (1 Corinthians 15:51-52). As swiftly as an eye can cast a glance, we will all be transformed, receiving a new body just like Christ's (1 John 3:2). No more weariness, gray hair, slow reflexes, baggy bodies—we will be new physically and spiritually. The old nature will be gone; no more wrong thoughts or unkind words. "We shall be like Him" (1 John 3:2). Are you sorrowing because of a departed loved one? Are you troubled? Jesus is coming again to receive us to be with Him forever! It could be today! "Therefore comfort one another with these words" (1 Thessalonians 4:18).

LESSON: *The rapture is the sudden catching up of living believers, reuniting them with departed believers as both receive glorified bodies.*

December 3

THE JUDGMENT SEAT OF CHRIST

We must all appear before the judgment seat of Christ, that each one may be recompensed for his deeds in the body, according to what he has done, whether good or bad. (2 Corinthians 5:10)

In the Olympic games the three winning contestants mount individual platforms to receive awards from the judges and the accolades of the people. The judge places gold, silver, and bronze medals around the necks of the winners, rewarding them for competing faithfully and winning the contest.

Following the rapture of the church, Christ will evaluate the believers' works (1 Thessalonians 4:17). During this time church age believers will be rewarded for faithfulness. Paul's imagery of the judgment seat (*bema*) is taken from the raised platform in the Grecian games in Athens where the president sat. There he rewarded the contestants, crowning the winners with garland wreaths.

Christ will be the Judge at the *bema*, examining and evaluating our works. It is not a judgment concerning salvation; that was established the moment we trusted Christ. This is a judgment regarding rewards. Believers will be rewarded for deeds done in the body, whether good or worthless (2 Corinthians 5:10).

The temporary life we live on earth is important. We are exhorted to build into our lives gold, silver, and precious stones, which represent pure motives; those building with wood, hay, and straw build with impure motives and will have their works burned up. They will not receive a reward, though they will be saved (1 Corinthians 3:15). On that day the Lord will expose the motives of our hearts (4:5). Those who built on a faulty foundation will experience a loss of reward.

Take courage, Christian friend; "abide in Him, so that when He appears, we may have confidence and not shrink away from Him in shame at His coming" (1 John 2:28). Be faithful amid trials and difficulties. Our temporary affliction cannot be compared with the glory that will be revealed when He says, "Well done."

LESSON: *The judgment seat of Christ does not pertain to salvation; it is Christ rewarding believers for deeds done in this life.*

THE WRATH
OF GOD

Whoever rejects the Son will not see life, for
God's wrath remains on him. (John 3:36, NIV)

I never questioned my father's love for me. He spent time with us, taking us fishing or on picnics. He loved to play jokes on us, and he lavished gifts on us. Yet, in reflection (certainly not at the time) I realize he loved me because he disciplined me. He had a sense of justice, and when it was violated, retribution was forthcoming.

More Scriptures speak of God's wrath than His love. Although it is not a pleasant subject, it is nonetheless true—and essential as a corollary to His love and justice. If He is a God of love and if He is just, that love and justice must be reflected in a standard. And when God's standard is violated and when His patience has terminated, He displays His wrath.

What *is* wrath? Wrath is described as God's "anger and hot displeasure" against sin as, for example, when Israel indulged in idolatry in the desert (Deuteronomy 9:19). It is pictured as "kindling a fire" against those who transgress His commandments (see Lamentations 4:11). In the New Testament God's anger is directed toward people who refuse His gracious gospel. God's wrath already rests on those who have spurned His Son: "He who does not obey [believe] the Son shall not see life, but the wrath of God abides on him" (John 3:36).

Why does God display wrath? His wrath is necessary because of sin. Perhaps the fact that we ask the question means we don't have a proper regard for the holiness of God and the hideousness of sin. God's wrath is already revealed "against all ungodliness and unrighteousness of men" (Romans 1:18). Because God gave His Son as the supreme sacrifice for sin, to scorn Christ reflects the greatest sin and affront to God and can only bring God's wrath (Ephesians 5:6).

But God has made a provision for us to shield us from His wrath. The Lord Jesus made the supreme sacrifice for sin, satisfying the holiness of God. Those who respond and trust in Christ are no longer under God's wrath; rather, they are reunited in friendship to God. Are you in friendship with God?

LESSON: *Because He is holy, God displays His wrath against sin but receives into friendship the one who trusts in Christ.*

WHAT IS
THE TRIBULATION?

*And I heard a loud voice from the temple, saying to
the seven angels, "Go and pour out the seven bowls
of the wrath of God into the earth." (Revelation 16:1)*

When Jesus instructed His disciples before His impending departure, He warned them that they would experience tribulation in the world (John 16:33); in fact, He told them that the world would hate them (15:18). Paul wrote to the Romans, reminding them to rejoice in their tribulations (Romans 5:3). Christians should expect suffering in this world.

However, there is a future Tribulation, quite unlike any sufferings we experience now, coming upon the earth. What is it? It is the outpouring of God's wrath. That is the difference. Any tribulation we experience today may be due to our sins, the sins of others, or Satan's attacks. But the Tribulation will be different. It will be the unleashing of God's holy wrath upon a world that has scorned His name and repudiated His Son. Unbelievers will cry out, "Fall on us and hide us from the presence of Him who sits on the throne, and from the wrath of the Lamb; for the great day of their wrath has come" (Revelation 6:16-17a).

In the Tribulation God's wrath will be poured out upon the nations that have despised His Word and His witnesses (11:18). It is God's wrath upon Babylon, the epitome of rebellion against God (14:10; 16:19); it is His wrath upon an unrepentant, unbelieving world (9:20-21; 14:19). The Tribulation will climax with God's pouring out the seven bowls of His wrath upon a world that has gone awry (15:1, 7; 16:1). It is also a time of God's judgment aimed at unbelievers (14:7; 15:4), when the earth reels like a drunkard and totters like a shack (Isaiah 24:20-22).

The Tribulation is a time when God's patience is exhausted. Because He is just and holy He must ultimately punish sinners who scorn His grace. Thankfully, the Lord Jesus took the punishment that we deserved so that we might not face the wrath of God (Romans 5:8-9). While we endure sufferings in this world, we "wait for His son from heaven . . . Jesus, who delivers us from the wrath to come" (1 Thessalonians 1:10).

LESSON: *The Tribulation is the outpouring of God's wrath, judgment, and punishment upon an unbelieving world.*

WILL THE CHURCH
BE IN THE TRIBULATION?

*Much more then, having now been justified
by His blood, we shall be saved from the
wrath of God through Him. (Romans 5:9)*

Will the church be on earth during the Tribulation? Good people on either side have debated the issue, and we are mindful that this should not be a basis for disrupting Christian fellowship. Some interesting passages in the Bible speak to the subject.

Some statements in the Bible appear to promise that the church will be removed before the Tribulation. Romans 5:9 promises, "We shall be saved from the wrath of God through Him." "The wrath" refers to a specific wrath—God's wrath in the Tribulation (Revelation 6:16-17). Paul's logic is that if God did the greater thing for us (Christ died for us while we were sinners), then He will do the lesser—save us from the Tribulation (vv. 8-9). As D. L. Moody said, "If my friend Mr. Tiffany gave me a large diamond, I would not be afraid to ask him for some brown paper to wrap it in."

First Thessalonians 5:9 promises, "God has not destined us for wrath, but for obtaining salvation through our Lord Jesus Christ." The Thessalonians are worried that they are in the Tribulation; Paul instructs them that they are not destined for the Tribulation but for deliverance from it. God's purpose in rescuing the church from the Tribulation appears to be reconfirmed in 2 Thessalonians 2:13, which follows a discussion of the Antichrist and the Tribulation. Paul concludes that we should give thanks "because God has chosen you from the beginning for salvation."

Christians should not look for the Antichrist and the Tribulation events; they should look for deliverance from the Tribulation. A similar promise is given to the church in Revelation 3:10: "I also will keep you from the hour of testing, that hour which is about to come upon the whole world." The preposition "from" (Gk., *ek*) can simply be read, "out of." This is a promise not to deliver believers through the Tribulation, but from the Tribulation.

If God has done the greater for us by saving us when we were sinners, He will do the lesser by keeping us out of the Tribulation. We do not look for the Antichrist and suffering in the Tribulation; we look for Christ and deliverance from the Tribulation. *Maranatha*—O Lord come!

LESSON: *The Scriptures promise that the church will be kept out of the Tribulation.*

December 7

FALSE CHRISTS
IN THE TRIBULATION

*See to it that no one misleads you. For many
will come in My name, saying, "I am the Christ,"
and will mislead many. (Matthew 24:4-5)*

Sun Myung Moon, founder of the Unification Church, claims that Christ appeared to him in a vision on a Korean mountainside, asking him to carry on the mission that Christ Himself failed to achieve. Moon has said, "With the fulness of time, God has sent his messenger to resolve the fundamental questions of life and the universe. His name is Sun Myung Moon. . . . He fought alone against myriads of satanic forces in both the spiritual and physical worlds, and finally triumphed over them all. In this way, he came in contact with many saints in paradise and with Jesus, and thus brought into Light all the heavenly secrets through his communion with God" (*Divine Principle*, p. 16).

Moon is but one example of the many false prophets that have gone out into the world. He is a foreshadowing of *the* false prophet, the Antichrist, who will manifest himself in the Tribulation. The Antichrist, as a pseudo-messiah, will deceive many as he goes forth conquering (Revelation 6:2).

Jesus explained to His disciples what would happen during the Tribulation. He told of "wars and rumors of wars" and said that "nation will rise against nation, and kingdom against kingdom" (Matthew 24:6-7). This is precipitated by Antichrist to whom "it was granted to take peace from the earth" (Revelation 6:4). The Antichrist will invade Israel, having broken the covenant he made with Israel guaranteeing peace (Daniel 9:27). The Tribulation will climax with the campaign of Armageddon, the four world powers converging on tiny Israel (Daniel 11:40-45). As a result, Israel will suffer immensely.

Famines and earthquakes will result in food shortages and untold suffering (Matthew 24:7). A quart of wheat will cost a day's wages (Revelation 6:5-6). Many people will be unable to buy food and will die of starvation. The skyscrapers of the nations will tumble because of the earthquakes (Revelation 16:18-19). Death will be commonplace; one-fourth of the world's population will die because of hunger, war, and pestilence (Revelation 6:7-8).

LESSON: *False messiahs, wars, famines, and earthquakes will cause great suffering for Israel and the nations during the Tribulation.*

ISRAEL PERSECUTED
BY ANTICHRIST

Then they will deliver you up to tribulation,
and will kill you, and you will be hated by all
nations on account of My name. (Matthew 24:9)

One of the great modern tragedies is Israel's suffering under Naziism. Adolf Hitler was guilty of murdering 5,700,000 Jewish people and about the same number of Gentiles. The extermination camps at Buchenwald, Dachau, Auschwitz, and Bergen-Belsen horrified the world when the atrocities became known.

During the Tribulation another "Hitler"—the Antichrist—will arise. He will be deceptive, having lured Israel into his lair through a peace treaty (Daniel 9:27). For three and a half years he will pretend to be the benevolent friend and protector of Israel, enabling Israel to live in peace, in "unwalled villages" (Ezekiel 38:11). Then, during the middle of the Tribulation, he will violate his treaty, renege on his promises, and turn against God's covenanted people. He will terminate Israel's worship in the Tribulation temple (Daniel 9:27).

Antichrist will be supernaturally empowered by Satan to vent his fury on God's people Israel (Revelation 12:13). To escape extermination Israel will flee from the land, seeking refuge in the Gentile nations, where they remain until the end of the Tribulation (v. 14). The Antichrist will dog the Israelites into the Gentile nations, seeking to exterminate the people, but the Israelites will be harbored by Gentiles—many "Anne Franks" will be saved.

Christ warned those in Israel to flee Jerusalem immediately. Those on rooftops should not even come down; they should escape by running across the rooftops. Those in the fields shouldn't go back to get a coat (Matthew 24:17-18) because it would be a "Great Tribulation" unparalleled in the annals of human history (v. 21). Fortunately, those days will be shortened, that is, they will come to an end. They will last for three and a half years and no longer; otherwise no one would be left alive at the end of the Tribulation (Matthew 24:22). Even though these fearsome days are coming, it is good to know that God is sovereign and has the world in control. He will rescue His people Israel and bring the world to a conclusion just as He has planned.

LESSON: *In the middle of the Tribulation, the Antichrist will break the covenant with Israel and will persecute the nation.*

December 9

THE REMNANT
IN THE TRIBULATION

*And the dragon was enraged with the woman,
and went off to make war with the rest of her
offspring, who keep the commandments of God and
hold to the testimony of Jesus.* (Revelation 12:17)

Although the Russian revolution of 1917 instituted a totalitarian system that enslaved the Russian people, destroyed their freedom, and attempted to remove every evidence of Christianity, Communism failed. In 1989-90 that became clear. But for more than seventy years believers experienced bloody persecution—they were sent to Siberia, church meetings were outlawed, property was confiscated, Christians were imprisoned and killed. But was Christianity obliterated from Russia? No, there will always be a remnant of the righteous.

It is a principle of Scripture that God always has a remnant of believers (1 Kings 19:18), and it will be so even during the Tribulation. Many will be saved, and these will constitute the remnant. Revelation 7 recounts one group of the remnant that God will set apart: the 144,000 Jews that are sealed by God, twelve thousand from each of the twelve tribes of Israel; God supernaturally protects these 144,000 witnesses. Who are they, and why are they sealed? They are 144,000 "Billy Grahams" who become the evangelists during the Tribulation. Because of their witness, a host of people will be in heaven from every nation on earth "standing before the throne and before the Lamb" (Revelation 7:9).

God also sets apart two witnesses who will serve God for 1260 days—the last half of the Tribulation (Revelation 11:3). We are not told who they are. God gives them power to perform signs that people may believe their message. Since Antichrist performs signs (2 Thessalonians 2:9), God empowers the two witnesses to call down fire from heaven on God's enemies—they are modern Elijahs (Revelation 11:5). Even in the most difficult days, God does not leave Himself without a witness. Though persecuted and suffering, the Tribulation believers "keep the commandments of God and hold to the testimony of Jesus" (Revelation 12:17). What an example and incentive to faithful and holy living!

LESSON: *During the Tribulation there will be a remnant of believers: 144,000 Jewish evangelists, two witnesses, and a host of others who believe.*

December 10

GENTILE POWERS
CONTROLLING JERUSALEM

Jerusalem will be trampled underfoot by the Gentiles
until the times of the Gentiles be fulfilled. (Luke 21:24)

The Six Day War, which began on June 5, 1967, saw Israel capture and regain control of the entire city of Jerusalem. It was the first time in 2.5 millennia—since 586 B.C., when the city was destroyed—that the Jewish people gained sovereign control over Jerusalem. That "city of peace" has known only war in its history; Jerusalem has been destroyed dozens of times. And it will yet suffer a climactic battle at the end of this world's history.

Beginning in 605 B.C. and spanning history until the end of the Tribulation, four world powers have dominated Israel. This span of time when Jerusalem is controlled by Gentiles is called the "times of the Gentiles." The Babylonians were the first foreign nation to control Jerusalem when Nebuchadnezzar sacked the holy city in 605 B.C. In Daniel's explanation of the mysterious statue revealed to Nebuchadnezzar and depicting the nations controlling Israel's history, Babylon is the "head of gold" (Daniel 2:32, 37-38). It is pictured as a lion in Daniel 7:4.

But Babylon was destroyed by Medo-Persia in 539 B.C., and the union of Medes and Persians controlled Jerusalem until 331 B.C. In Daniel's statue the breast and arms of silver represent Medo-Persia (Daniel 2:32, 39). Medo-Persia is also pictured as a bear (7:5).

In 331 B.C. Alexander the Great, youthful leader of the Grecian empire, defeated the Medo-Persians and captured Jerusalem. In the statue illustrating the history of Gentile nations, Greece is the belly and thighs of bronze (2:32). The swiftness of Alexander's conquests is illustrated by a leopard (7:6). The Greek empire soon disintegrated, and Rome catapulted into prominence as the world power dominating Jerusalem. But Rome was an unusual empire; it was an uneven alliance of nations, portrayed as having legs and feet of iron but mixed with clay (2:33). This fourth empire is also pictured as a dreadful and terrifying beast that crushes its opponents (7:7).

Although Israel has gained control of Jerusalem, it is temporary. Israel will be controlled by Gentiles until the return of Christ. Then Jerusalem will be rescued.

LESSON: *Gentile powers will control Jerusalem until the return of Christ.*

December 11

THE
BEAST

And I saw a beast coming up out of the sea. . . .
And the dragon gave him his power and his throne
and great authority. (Revelation 13:1-2)

Through the centuries Christians have attempted to identify the Beast, popularly called the Antichrist. Martin Luther thought it was the pope; more recently Joseph Stalin, Benito Mussolini, and Adolf Hitler have all been nominated. Some identified a high ranking U.S. government official as the Antichrist, denominating his name as 666. But the fact is we do not know who the Antichrist will be.

The Antichrist will head a political system that will curtail Christians' worship (Daniel 7:25). Since he is lawless (2 Thessalonians 2:8), he will effect changes in the moral laws and social structures (Daniel 7:25). How will he accomplish that? By prospering through shrewdness and deceit, parading as a man of peace (8:25). Perhaps we see the foreshadowing in the breakdown of our society's moral fabric with the abandonment of the morals of the Ten Commandments (Exodus 20:3-17). Children disobey parents, murderers are rarely punished for their crime, adultery is commonplace, and dishonesty costs the country billions in lost productivity each year.

The Antichrist will control the economic system, achieving great wealth and a strong military force (Daniel 11:24, 38). During the Tribulation, all people will come under his jurisdiction, receiving a mark on their right hands or foreheads if they wish to buy or sell (Revelation 13:16). Through his conquests he will reapportion territories to his mercenaries (Daniel 11:39).

Religiously, the Antichrist will establish himself as God in the Temple in Jerusalem (2 Thessalonians 2:4). But he is Satan's counterfeit, a false messiah who blasphemes the true God (Revelation 13:5-6). How will he do that? He is energized by Satan, who gives him power to perform miracles (2 Thessalonians 2:9; Revelation 13:2).

But his success will be short-lived. When Christ returns, He will only need to speak a word, and the Antichrist will be destroyed (Revelation 19:11-16). How fortunate that we do not need to look for the Antichrist; we look for Christ, the blessed hope, and His glorious appearing (Titus 2:13).

LESSON: *The Antichrist will control the political, economic, and religious system in deceiving people during the Tribulation.*

THE KINGDOM
OF THE BEAST

*Behold, a fourth beast, dreadful and terrifying and
extremely strong; and it had large iron teeth. It
devoured and crushed, and trampled down the remainder
with its feet; and it was different from all the beasts
that were before it, and it had ten horns. (Daniel 7:7)*

Nineteen ninety-two. Europeans are talking about it, reading
about it in newspapers, and hearing about it on radio and television. What is it? It is the year the twelve-member European
Community hopes to break down trade barriers and set up a single market.
By 1992 the "United States of Europe," with a population of 350 million,
hopes to enjoy free travel between member nations, provide uniform health,
education, and professional standards, as well as a unified monetary system. The result? An economic power greater than the United States.

Why is this significant? It may well be that the European Community
foreshadows the final forming of the Roman empire. The ancient Roman
empire had its geographic roots in many of the same countries that make up
the modern European Economic Community: England, France, Portugal,
Spain, Italy, Greece, Germany, Belgium, Luxembourg, and the Netherlands.
In Daniel's vision depicting the final Gentile empire, he saw a ferocious
beast with large iron teeth that devoured its adversaries. It utterly crushed its
enemies. But it was also unusual in that it had "ten horns" (Daniel 7:7).
These ten horns are ten kings, or European nations (Revelation 17:12).

An eleventh horn, a powerful leader, emerges and subdues three of
the European nations (Daniel 7:8). This man becomes the leader of the final
form of Gentile world power. He is known as the "Beast" and is synonymous with both the man—the Antichrist—and the empire he controls, the
geography of the ancient Roman empire. Satan energizes this final Gentile
empire (Revelation 12:3), which afflicts God's ancient people Israel as well
as people who become believers during the Tribulation.

Who will stop this Beast? Christ will crush this final Gentile empire
and establish His kingdom on earth, a kingdom that will endure forever
(Daniel 2:44-45). Man's empire is temporary; Messiah's kingdom will be
eternal, and His people will reign with Him forever.

LESSON: *The final form of Gentile world power emerges from the
ashes of the ancient Roman empire.*

THE SEVEN
SEALS

And I saw when the Lamb broke one of the seven seals,
and I heard one of the four living creatures saying
as with a voice of thunder, "Come." (Revelation 6:1)

According to the annual United Nations report, the increasing demands of the world's population are damaging the basic natural resources on which all life depends. Because the world's population is increasing by 80 million each year, the earth is losing topsoil and tropical forests and creating deserts. "All countries must face the fact that the combination of population and industrial growth could destroy the land, water and air on which everything else depends," said Dr. Nafis Sadik, of the U.N. Population Fund. But this is only one possible problem during the Tribulation.

The first seal, opened at the beginning of the Tribulation, reveals Satan's counterfeit, the Antichrist, riding a white horse and conquering the nations through deception (Revelation 6:2). Symbolized by a red horse, the Antichrist removes peace from the earth while wars blanket the world (vv. 3-4). Famine follows as war devastates the crops (vv. 5-6). Food becomes scarce, a quart of wheat costing a day's wages. Food is so precious that it is weighed on a pair of scales. If a day's wages are $100, then a bushel of wheat would cost $3,200, compared to today's cost of about $4. An ashen horse, symbolizing death, emerges (v. 8). Through the ensuing wars, famine, and the diseases resulting from the famine, more than a fourth of the earth's population is killed (1.5 billion at today's population).

The scene shifts to heaven, revealing believers in heaven who have been martyred for the faith (vv. 9-11). The intensity of the Tribulation increases—God is judging from heaven (vv. 12-17). A great earthquake occurs; the sun is blackened like sackcloth; the moon becomes like blood. God lowers the lighting in the heavens to remind man He is judging the world (Joel 2:31). Stars shower to the earth like figs falling from a tree. The sky is split, enabling people to glimpse heaven, to see the enthroned Lord, judging. They panic as they suffer physically and emotionally, and they hide from God's wrath. But we do not anticipate God's wrath; we look for the rapture when we will be caught up to be with Him. He has promised, "We shall be saved from the wrath of God" (Romans 5:9).

LESSON: *The seven seals are the beginning of God's judgment upon a rebellious, unbelieving world during the Tribulation.*

December 14

THE SEVEN TRUMPETS

*And the seven angels who had the seven trumpets
prepared themselves to sound them. (Revelation 8:6)*

Waste brokers are disposing of toxic chemicals in African countries, particularly on Africa's west coast. Guinea has signed a five-year contract to buy 15 million tons of toxic waste from European pharmaceutical companies. The Congo has agreed to store a million tons of chemical waste from Europe. What is the significance? It will transform the African continent into a garbage dump for industrial waste, contaminating an entire continent.

The seven trumpets sound the destruction of the earth's environment. Although God is judging, it is entirely possible that man contributes to his own destruction by destroying the earth's environment. Hail and fire, mixed with blood, are flung to the earth, resulting in ecological devastation. A third of the earth, trees, and grass is burned up (Revelation 8:7). No doubt that results in a shortage of oxygen. The sea coagulates, turning to blood and destroying the sea life, a source of food. This judgment may well be man's own sin through oil spills and other pollution.

A star having a bitter taste is hurled into the rivers and streams, polluting the drinking water source (vv. 10-11). Is this man's own act? Perhaps. God further decreases the light by darkening the sun, moon, and stars by one-third (v. 12). Since sunshine affects man's moods, this judgment will affect people emotionally as they function in semidarkness. The earth will become an eerie place.

In the following judgment a den of demons is unleashed upon the earth, inflicting pain upon the people (9:1-11). People will desire death, but it will escape them. An army of 200 million, perhaps a horde of demons, coming from the east, kills one-third of all the remaining people on earth (9:12-21). The earth's population is now reduced by more than one-half.

What is the result of these judgments? Do people repent? No. Although a minority turn to God in faith, the majority do not repent of their idolatry, demonic worship, murder, sorceries, immorality, and thefts (9:21). Man's heart is hardened; only the grace of God can soften him and turn an unrepentant one to faith in Christ.

LESSON: *The seven trumpet judgments intensify God's retribution on a Christ-hating world during the Tribulation.*

THE SEVEN BOWLS

And I heard a loud voice from the temple, saying to the seven angels, "Go and pour out the seven bowls of the wrath of God into the earth." (Revelation 16:1)

Charles Zinser and his family lived in a suburb of Cincinnati, ten miles from a nuclear weapons plant. Charles rented a garden and often took his two sons along as he worked the vegetable garden. Two years later, both sons developed cancer, the eight year old had leukemia and the two year old had part of a leg amputated. The Zinser's garden was contaminated with enriched uranium 235. The amputated leg contained ten times more uranium than would be accumulated naturally over a lifetime. That tragic story reminds us how tragic is man's pollution of the earth.

The seven bowl judgments unleashed by God in quick succession near the end of the Tribulation may also reflect man's sin of polluting the earth. The first bowl results in malignant sores on men who have the mark of the Beast—perhaps it is a form of cancer (Revelation 16:2). These people choose the mark of the Beast, but God gives them another mark.

With the second bowl, the sea becomes congealed, apparently world-wide, resulting in the death of all sea life (v. 3). Food becomes even more scarce, and disease and stench are rampant. The rivers and springs also become completely polluted (v. 4). What was true of only part of the rivers, streams, and seas (8:8-11) is now worldwide. Fierce fire and heat from the sun scorch the people (16:8). Is this the result of the ozone layer's being depleted? Is it melanoma skin cancer? Possibly. God judges the Beast and darkens his kingdom, anticipating his final destruction (16:10). The Euphrates River dries up, luring the Eastern armies to converge on the Middle East and the War of Armageddon with the Beast. This event is initiated by Satan and his demonic hordes (vv. 13-14). The climax comes with an unprecedented earthquake, causing entire cities to fall. God rains 100-pound hailstones upon the earth (vv. 17-19).

The effects of the bowl judgments once more reveal man's hard heart—people refuse to repent. Yet Jesus said, "Unless you repent, you will all likewise perish" (Luke 13:3). Do not presume on God's patience. Come to Him in repentance and faith today.

LESSON: *The bowl judgments occur simultaneously and swiftly near the end of the Tribulation.*

December 16

THE SECOND
COMING OF CHRIST

*The Son of Man is coming at an hour when
you do not think He will. (Matthew 24:44)*

When former President Eisenhower was vacationing in Denver, the local newspaper mentioned that a six-year-old boy dying of cancer wanted to see the president. One Sunday morning President Eisenhower's big limousine pulled up outside the boy's home. The president knocked on the door. Unshaven, wearing blue jeans and an old shirt, the boy's father answered. The president talked with the overjoyed boy for a few moments and left. But the father would never forget the way he met the president of the United States. The opportunity would never come again.

That will be the experience of many people at the second coming of Christ. Although the signs will point to His soon return, the people will be going along with life as usual. It will be like the days of Noah. The people ignored Noah's preaching; they considered the mundane things of life— eating and drinking—more important than God. Then the Flood came and took them all away. That is what Christ's coming will be like (Matthew 24:39). It will be unexpected, catching people unawares.

People will be going about their business: two farmers will be working in the field and one will be taken away in judgment, whereas the other will be left on earth to enter Messiah's millennial kingdom. Two women will be grocery shopping; one will be taken away in judgment, and the other will be left on earth to enter Messiah's glorious kingdom (Matthew 24:40).

It is not wrong to be farming; it is not wrong to be grocery shopping— or marrying or eating—but indifference to Christ and His return *is* wrong. We look for the rapture, which will occur before the Tribulation; Christ's second coming is at the end of the Tribulation. His warning goes out to those living in the Tribulation. Just as the people ignored His first coming, so some will be stunned at His second coming. The principle applies: the Lord wants us to be faithful stewards of His household, prepared for His return (Matthew 24:45-46). Are you a faithful servant, awaiting your Master's return?

LESSON: *Those that are unprepared at Christ's second coming will be taken away in judgment; the prepared will enter the millennial kingdom.*

THE
RESURRECTIONS

In Christ all shall be made alive. But each in his
own order: Christ the first fruits, after that those
who are Christ's at His coming. (1 Corinthians 15:22-23)

When he was in Russia, Billy Graham heard a story concerning a small village. After the Bolshevik Revolution, the local Communist leader was sent to explain the virtues of Communism and to change the people's thinking about religion, which Karl Marx called "the opiate of the people." After the Communist had harangued the crowd for a long time, he said to the local Christian pastor rather contemptuously, "I will give you five minutes to reply." Replied the pastor, "I do not need five minutes; only five seconds." He rose to the platform and gave the Easter greeting, "The Lord is risen!" With a united voice the villagers thundered back, "He is risen indeed!"

The resurrection remains the believer's hope. Christ Himself promised that all people, both good and evil, would be resurrected. Some will be resurrected to eternal life and bliss, whereas others will be resurrected to condemnation and eternal punishment (John 5:28-29).

Christ is the first in the order of resurrections (1 Corinthians 15:23). Although there were resuscitations from death, as in the case of Lazarus, Christ was the first to be raised with an immortal body. On the first Easter Sunday, Christ was raised with an immortal, glorified body (John 20:20).

At the end of this church age and before the Tribulation, all church age believers will be raised to receive new resurrection bodies. It will occur suddenly and simultaneously with the rapture (1 Thessalonians 4:16). Since only the "dead in Christ" are raised at this time, Old Testament believers and believers who died during the Tribulation will be raised at the end of the Tribulation (Revelation 20:4-5). At the end of the Millennium, all unbelievers will be raised to face the great white throne judgment, where they will be condemned to eternal suffering in the lake of fire (Revelation 20:11-15).

What a blessed hope the resurrection is for believers! Death has lost its sting. The grave no longer has any victory over Christ's own. We look for the day when this mortal body becomes immortal, when this perishable body becomes imperishable.

LESSON: *There is a resurrection of life for Christ, the church, Old Testament and Tribulation saints, and a resurrection of condemnation for unbelievers.*

TOMORROW

*And He will judge between the nations . . . And
they will hammer their swords into plowshares,
and their spears into pruning hooks. (Isaiah 2:4)*

Marguerite Higgins, a war correspondent, received the coveted
Pulitzer prize for international reporting in her coverage of the
Korean War. She wrote an account of the 5th Company of Marines, originally 18,000, in their combat with 100,000 Chinese Communists: "It was particularly cold, 42 below. The weary soldiers, half frozen, stood by their dirty trucks eating from tin cans. A huge marine was eating cold beans with his trench knife. His clothes were stiff as a board; his face covered with a heavy beard crusted with mud. A correspondent asked, 'If I were God and could grant you anything you wished, what would you most like?' The man stood motionless, then raised his head and replied, 'Give me tomorrow.'"

Everyone longs for a better "tomorrow." A utopia, a serene, secure place of peace and comfort. God has promised us a greater tomorrow, and it is no Disney World, no fantasy land. It is real. On what basis can we have this hope? It is based on four unconditional covenants in the Old Testament. In the covenant with Abraham God promised the aged patriarch a land, a large posterity, and a spiritual blessing (Genesis 12:1-3). In this land from eastern Egypt to the Euphrates River, God promised to bless Israel and, through Israel, believing Gentiles. In the Palestinian covenant, God promised to bring the Israelites back into the land, restoring them from suffering and oppression in foreign lands (Deuteronomy 30:1-10). God promised to prosper them in the land where they would love and serve Him. In His covenant with David God promised that Messiah would rule over them, ushering in an era of peace and tranquillity (2 Samuel 7:12-16). No wars, no anarchy, no lawlessness, because Messiah will rule over the nations. And all of this is possible because God will give His people a new heart enabling them to love Him (Jeremiah 31:31-34).

This world, with its injustices, immorality, and anarchy, is not all there is. Look up. Look ahead. God has given us tomorrow.

LESSON: *There is a great tomorrow for believers.*

December 19

JUDGMENT
OF ISRAEL

*I will enter into judgment with you. . . . And I shall make
you pass under the rod . . . and I shall purge from you the
rebels and those who transgress against Me. (Ezekiel 20:36-38)*

In returning to earth to establish the millennial kingdom, Christ will judge the living Jews and Gentiles to determine who enters His kingdom. God will discipline His elect people as a father takes his wayward son into the woodshed. He will separate the rebels from the believers, and the rebels will not enter Christ's kingdom (Ezekiel 20:37-38). The believers will pass the disciplinary test and enter the kingdom.

In Christ's parable of the ten virgins (Matthew 25:1-13), the wise virgins were ready for the bridegroom; they joined the bridal procession to the bridegroom's home and entered into the wedding celebration. Christ was illustrating that some Jews will be prepared for His coming—they will be converted (Matthew 25:13) and will enter the millennial kingdom. On the other hand, the foolish virgins were unprepared for Christ's coming; they will not enter Messiah's banquet hall.

In the parable of the talents, Jesus taught the importance of faithfulness (Matthew 25:14-30). In entrusting his estate to his servants, a landowner gave one of them five talents, another two, and another one. When he returned from his journey, one servant had gained another five talents, the other had gained two, but one had buried his talent. This parable teaches the Jews' stewardship of the truth that was entrusted to them (Romans 3:1-2). Those who gained more talents are believing Jews who will spread God's truth during the Tribulation; they will enter Messiah's kingdom (Matthew 25:21, 23). The one who buried his talent is an unbelieving Jew who does nothing with God's truth; he is an unbeliever and will be cast into outer darkness (v. 30).

Preparation is extremely important. If Christ were to come today, would you be ready? Proper preparation comes by trusting in Christ. As children of God we are to be His faithful stewards. Then we will be prepared and not ashamed at His coming.

LESSON: *At the end of the Tribulation, Jews will be judged concerning their preparedness for Christ's return by whether they believed in Him.*

December 20

JUDGMENT
OF GENTILES

And all the nations [Gentiles] will be gathered before Him;
and He will separate them from one another. (Matthew 25:32)

I declare a holy war, my Moslem brothers! Murder the Jews! Murder them all!" So said Haj Amin el Husseini, mufti (spiritual leader of the Arabs) of Jerusalem in 1948. In the same year Azzam Pash, secretary general of the Arab League said, "This will be a war of extermination and a momentous massacre which will be spoken of like the Mongolian massacres and the Crusades." On March 29, 1970, Yassir Arafat, chairman of the PLO declared, "The goal of our struggle is the end of Israel and there can be no compromise" (Howard Snyder, *St. Petersburg Times,* January 18, 1988).

Those are harsh words, reflecting the animosity held against the Jewish people. And the malevolence is not by Arab people alone. Over several millennia Jews have been fiercely persecuted by many nations. But a day is coming when the Gentiles will be judged for their mistreatment of the Jewish people.

At His triumphant return, Christ will judge the living Gentiles at the end of the Tribulation (Matthew 25:31-32). Why will they be judged? For persecuting the Jews, for expelling them from their own land, for enslaving them, and for murdering them (Joel 3:2-3). During the Tribulation the Jews will be persecuted more than ever, but some Gentiles will have compassion on them and give them food and lodging, placing their own lives in jeopardy. Why would Gentiles do this? It is a reflection of their faith in Christ. To those Christ will declare, "To the extent that you did it to one of these brothers of Mine [Jews], . . . you did it to Me" (Matthew 25:40). They will inherit eternal life. Those refusing them hospitality and lodging, thereby showing their unbelief, will be cast into the lake of fire (vv. 41-46).

The Jews forever remain the chosen children of God; they are the apple of God's eye. To persecute the Jews is to provoke Jehovah. Do you have Jewish neighbors or coworkers? Go out of your way to befriend them. The best thing you can do for them is to bring them the good news that Jesus is the Messiah. We have an obligation to them because the gospel is "to the Jew first" (Romans 1:16). Have you shown your love for the Jewish people by bringing them the gospel?

LESSON: *At the end of the Tribulation, Gentiles will be judged for their treatment of the Jews, demonstrating their response to the gospel.*

SPIRITUAL LIFE
IN THE MILLENNIUM

*Behold, the tabernacle of God is among men, and He
shall dwell among them, and they shall be His peoples,
and God Himself shall be among them. (Revelation 21:3)*

Who has not read the gospels without wondering what it must have been like to walk with Christ for three years as did the apostles? What a privilege to hear His words, see His works, hear Him teach the Word of God, hear Him interact with audiences. Think of the disciples whom Jesus engaged while they were on their way to Emmaus. What an exposition of the Scriptures they must have heard (Luke 24:27)!

The apostles were limited to but three scant years in close communion with the Lord. But a future day is coming when all believers —not just the twelve—will be favored with fellowship with the Lord for eternity. As John viewed the new Jerusalem, the truly eternal city, he saw that the dwelling of God is with people: "Behold, the tabernacle of God is among men, and He shall dwell among them . . . and God Himself shall be among them" (Revelation 21:3). Three times John reinforces that God will be "among" His people. That word is important. It means "in close association with someone." It is the same word used to describe the disciples in their close association with Christ. What a privilege! Think of it—just as the disciples interacted with Christ for three years, we will be with Him for all eternity. There are no bleacher seats in heaven, no back row pews. We will all enjoy the intimate presence of the triune God as members of His family. We "shall see His face" (Revelation 22:4), meaning we will enjoy His intimacy, presence, and fellowship. And we will belong there because His name is on our foreheads, revealing His ownership of us.

But why wait for heaven to enjoy intimate fellowship with the Lord? It is our prerogative now. But sin separates us from Him. Without trusting in the meritorious death of Christ we cannot have communion with Him. Have you trusted in Jesus alone for your salvation, enabling you to enjoy fellowship with Him now and for all eternity?

LESSON: *Believers will enjoy close communion with Christ in the Millennium and for all eternity.*

December 22

SPIRITUAL CONDITIONS
IN THE MILLENNIUM

And a highway will be there, a roadway, and it
will be called "the highway of holiness."
The unclean will not travel on it. (Isaiah 35:8)

A woman was fired from her office job because she had an affair with the president of the firm. Irate readers discussed the subject in Ann Landers's column. Thousands suggested the woman should file a lawsuit for sexual harassment. Ann Landers agreed. There was no mention of moral wrong. Only her "judgment" was regarded as wrong. Surely that reflects the world's thinking, ignoring God's standard. But such will not be typical in the millennial kingdom.

There will be no adulterers in the kingdom. "It will be called 'the highway of holiness.' The unclean will not travel on it" (Isaiah 35:8). Only the righteous will be there (received through faith in Christ), those with "clean hands and a pure heart" (Psalm 24:3-4). Because the millennial citizens are righteous, they will be obedient (Jeremiah 31:33). All the inhabitants will know the Lord; no longer will they need human teachers to enlighten them. The Lord has given them a new heart, and they will have His Word written on it. No longer will there be lies; truth will pervade the Millennium, because the God of truth inhabits it (Isaiah 65:16).

The Millennium will be characterized by joy (12:3-4). The joyful singing at Israel's harvest festivals anticipated the joy of the kingdom age. All the inhabitants will have the Holy Spirit indwelling them, enabling them to walk in God's statutes and observe His ordinances (Ezekiel 36:27).

LESSON: *Believers will live righteously in the Millennium.*

PHYSICAL ENVIRONMENT
IN THE MILLENNIUM

*And the wolf will dwell with the lamb, and the leopard will lie
down with the kid, and the calf and the young lion and the
fatling together; and a little boy will lead them. (Isaiah 11:6)*

One pleasant summer day a man was swimming in a lake in
Hanna Park near the Atlantic Ocean in Florida. Noticing a turtle, he swam alongside it and pounded its shell. To his horror
he discovered it wasn't a turtle. It was an alligator! There was a race to the
shore, and although the swimmer made it, he left a crimson trail behind
him. It took more than one hundred stitches to sew him up.

Since Adam's sin, the animal kingdom has not been at peace; it is
hostile to humans. But in Messiah's kingdom even the animal world will be
subject to His authority—it will be at peace. Animals that do not naturally
live together—the wolf and the lamb, the leopard and the goat, the calf and
the lion—will then live at peace. A little boy will safely walk at the head of
those animals. In that day a cow and a bear will graze together, and small
children will play with once-but-no-longer-deadly snakes (Isaiah 11:7 8).
Why will this be so? Because Christ's Word will go forth from Jerusalem,
filling the earth and subjecting all the earth to His authority (2:3; 11:9).

Nature will also respond to Messiah's authority. Crops will be so abundant that "the plowman will overtake the reaper" (Amos 9:13). Because of
the enormity of the crop, harvesting will be so slow that the plowman preparing for the next crop will overtake the reaper. There will be a building
program for granaries to store the vast quantities of grain because "the
threshing floors will be full of grain, and the vats will overflow with the new
wine and oil" (Joel 2:24). No drought, no disease, no devastation will destroy the crops because the effect of Adam's curse is reversed. All nature
will respond to Messiah's rule.

But that day has not yet arrived; it awaits Messiah's glorious entrance
into our world for a second time. Meanwhile even creation groans as a pregnant mother, awaiting deliverance from bondage to decay (Romans 8:21).
We too wait for the glorious, complete redemption of these finite bodies
from bondage to corruption. Messiah's coming will fulfill that hope.

LESSON: *In Messiah's kingdom the animal world and nature itself
will be restored to perfect, peaceful conditions.*

December 24

HUMAN LIFE
IN THE MILLENNIUM

The eyes of the blind will be opened, and the ears of the deaf will be unstopped. Then the lame will leap like a deer, and the tongue of the dumb will shout for joy. (Isaiah 35:5-6)

After experiencing severe backaches, my brother went to the doctor, who placed him in the hospital for an examination. X rays called for an exploratory operation. When the doctors cut him open, they could do nothing more than sew him up again. Cancer had permeated his liver, stomach, and pancreas. He died eight months later. Who has not felt tears trickle down his or her cheeks in a hospital room? Who has not cried with grief at a grave site? All our physical sorrows are traced to Adam's original sin. Sickness and death have been the result—but a future day is coming when that will be reversed.

In Messiah's kingdom there will be no cancer or heart attacks—not even headaches. There will be no cataracts or blindness; no one will suffer from multiple sclerosis or rheumatism or arthritis. All will have hearing ears to enjoy Handel's *Messiah*. All will enjoy youthful limbs to walk, run, and jump. How will that be possible? Messiah will open the eyes of the blind and unstop the ears of the deaf—He will heal all diseases (Isaiah 35:5). When He was on earth Jesus offered a preview of the kingdom by performing kingdom signs—healing the sick and raising the dead.

There will also be longevity in the kingdom. In that day threescore and ten will not be an average age. In the Millennium, one who is a hundred years old will be considered a youth, and one who dies will be considered a sinner (Isaiah 65:20). It appears that believers, living on earth in their physical bodies, will not die; only those born during the Millennium who refuse to believe in Christ will be judged in death when they rebel.

In Messiah's kingdom there will be no hospitals—they would be empty! There will be no wheelchairs, medical insurance, hearing aids, or eyeglasses. Take comfort, grieving child of God. In Messiah's kingdom there will be no tears, no sorrow, no death. There will be no separation of loved ones. He will wipe away every one of our tears (Isaiah 65:19; Revelation 21:4).

LESSON: *In Messiah's kingdom there will be no sickness, suffering, or death for believers.*

GOVERNMENT OF
THE MILLENNIUM

A throne will even be established in lovingkindness, and a judge will sit on it in faithfulness in the tent of David; moreover, he will seek justice and be prompt in righteousness. (Isaiah 16:5)

E motions are fueled by political views. In Beijing, China, students indicate their political views by angrily throwing rocks at soldiers; in Romania coal miners who support the government are enticed to beat and terrify the citizenry; in Guatemala a tense exchange of government from Communism to democracy is effected; in Berlin revelers rejoice at the destruction of the Berlin wall; at home the front page tells it all as our governments and leaders are criticized. Whether Democrat or Republican, Communist or democracy, conservative or labor, citizens cry for change, looking for the humanly impossible— a utopian government.

A future day is coming when the perfect government will be inaugurated to legislate laws and rule righteously. It will not be a democracy; it will be a theocracy—a rule of God, a monarchy in the highest sense because Jesus Christ, as a descendent of King David, will rule as King. In that day the government will rest on the shoulders of the Son that was given to mankind (Isaiah 9:6), and He will rule with righteousness, fairly administrating justice to the poor and oppressed, who have not previously received justice (11:4).

Children will be born during the Millennium, and in their unregenerate state will attempt rebellion, but Messiah will crush it. Some suggest that David will rule as regent, but "David" may also be a title of Messiah (Ezekiel 34:23-24). Since Jesus will be "King of kings and Lord of lords," there will be nobles and governors reigning under Messiah (Isaiah 32:1; Revelation 19:16). The twelve apostles will rule over the twelve tribes of Israel (Matthew 19:28). Lesser authorities will also rule, administrating Messiah's kingdom (Luke 19:12-28), among them judges rendering righteous decisions (Isaiah 1:26).

Messiah's reign will blanket the earth, bringing peace and justice to the world (Zechariah 9:10) because the truth flows from Jerusalem to the nations (Isaiah 2:2-3). The cry of the hungry human heart will be satisfied, for Messiah will feed the nations with His lovingkindness and truth. True peace will prevail.

LESSON: *The government during the Millennium will be a rule of God, Messiah as King, with subordinate administrators throughout the world.*

December 26

JERUSALEM
IN THE MILLENNIUM

*In the last days, the mountain of the house of the Lord will be
established as the chief of the mountains, and will be raised
above the hills; and all the nations will stream to it. (Isaiah 2:2)*

What is the most prominent city in the world? In the past decades we might have identified London or New York. Today other cities have surpassed these historic megalopolises. In 1985 Tokyo-Yokohama was the most populous urban agglomeration with an estimated population of 29,272,000 people. The metropolitan population of Mexico City in that year was 17,321,800. But the premier city in the world is not destined to be London, New York, Tokyo, or Mexico City. It will be Jerusalem.

When Christ returns to inaugurate the millennial kingdom, He will rule on the throne of David from the city of Jerusalem, the spiritual and political center of the world (Matthew 25:31). In that day all the world will recognize Jerusalem as the capital because it "will be raised above the hills" (Isaiah 2:2). There will be topographical changes in the world to reflect Christ's administrative rule in Jerusalem. The hills surrounding Jerusalem will be leveled to a plain to draw attention to that city's prominence. From miles distant, people will see the prominent position of the eternal city of God. People from the nations of the world "will stream to it" (Micah 4:1). Why? They will acclaim Messiah's authority and come to hear God's truth that will flow from Jerusalem.

The removal of the hills will allow the living waters to flow from Jerusalem toward the Mediterranean and Dead Seas (Zechariah 14:8; Ezekiel 47:1-12), creating a beautiful, fertile plain. Whereas that is literal, the waters also symbolize the spiritual blessings that will flow from the Holy City.

Cities may be depicted as havens of sin and rebellion against God (Genesis 4:17; 19:1-11), but a day is coming when cities will no longer be dens of iniquity and cities of Sodom; they will be centers of sanctification. And Jerusalem will be the preeminent city in pointing people to the Messiah. In that day Jerusalem indeed will be "the Holy City."

LESSON: *In the Millennium, Jerusalem will be physically elevated to draw attention to its prominent position among the nations of the world.*

GREAT WHITE
THRONE JUDGMENT

And I saw a great white throne and Him who sat upon it.
...And I saw the dead, the great and the small, standing
before the throne, and books were opened... and the dead
were judged from the things which were written in the books,
according to their deeds. (Revelation 20:11-12)

I t is really going to be nice down there [in hell]. . . . The company
we will have. We will be entertained by Al Jolson, Jack Benny, the
Marx Brothers, . . . We will not have to be sorry about polio because of Jonas Salk. . . . The ball games down there will be broadcast by
Howard Cosell. . . . I think being in Hell would be a lot more fun than being
in Heaven." So wrote a reader of the *Los Angeles Times* (July 4, 1987). Tragically, hell will not be a place of enjoyment; it will be a place of suffering

At the end of the millennial reign of Christ, all unbelievers will be
raised to face Christ as their judge at the great white throne (Revelation
20:11-15). All the unsaved dead of all ages will be there. No unbeliever will
escape this judgment. Famous people and ordinary people, those who
drowned and decomposed in the depths of the sea and those who were
buried on land—all unbelievers will be there.

As they face Christ in judgment, the books are opened (v. 12). What
are those books? The books contain a record of their deeds; their sins are
recorded and reveal that they deserve eternal judgment. The record will also
determine the degree of punishment. To whom much light was given, more
will be expected (Luke 12:47-48; Matthew 11:22). All at the great white
throne will be condemned and sentenced to eternal torment in the lake of
fire (Revelation 20:15).

This is a most serious section of Scripture. It is a solemn reminder that
no one can escape the final judgment. Christ will either be our Savior and
Deliverer or our Judge. Cremation and decomposition will not prevent this
final tribunal. Christ is able to raise all the dead to life to face Him in judgment. Dear reader, if you have never resolved this issue do so now. When
you trust in the death of Christ as payment for your sins, He becomes your
Deliverer and not your Judge. Hear and heed His call to you today.

LESSON: *All the unsaved dead will be raised to life to be judged and
condemned to eternal suffering in the lake of fire.*

December 28

JUDGMENT OF FALLEN ANGELS

And the devil who deceived them was thrown into the lake of fire and brimstone, where the beast and the false prophet are also; and they will be tormented day and night forever and ever. (Revelation 20:10)

The cross of Christ marked the judgment and ultimate doom of Satan and his fallen angels. In anticipating the cross Christ declared, "Now the ruler of this world shall be cast out" (John 12:31). Through His death, Christ rendered Satan powerless (Hebrews 2:14); his destiny was determined. At the cross Christ not only canceled our spiritual debts, but He also destroyed Satan's hold on us (Colossians 2:15).

Some fallen angels are already confined to Tartarus (hell), which is the subterranean abyss in classical mythology where rebellious gods were confined (2 Peter 2:4). Apparently those angels committed some grievous sin for which they were immediately confined. Jude 6 may refer to the same confinement. They are "kept in eternal bonds under darkness for the judgment of the great day." These angels will be transferred from Tartarus to the lake of fire at the final judgment.

Some fallen angels are temporarily confined to the abyss where Christ sent some demons when He cast them out (Luke 8:31). During the Tribulation some of these demons ("locusts") come forth from the pit to torment unbelievers (Revelation 9:1-11).

God prepared the lake of fire for the devil and his angels (Matthew 25:41). At end of the Millennium Satan and the fallen angels will be cast into the lake of fire (Revelation 20:10). Since it is an eternal fire, Satan and the fallen angels will never be released from it but will be tormented in hell forever (14:11).

God's judgment of the angels is a reminder of His holiness. Sin is serious with God. Those that indulge must expect to pay the penalty.

LESSON: *At the end of the Millennium, God will cast Satan and his fallen angels into the lake of fire where they will be forever.*

December 29

THE NEW
JERUSALEM

---

*And I saw the holy city, new Jerusalem, coming
down out of heaven from God, made ready as a
bride adorned for her husband. (Revelation 21:2)*

Anyone who has ever been to Jerusalem will never forget it. Seeing the most important city in the world takes one's breath
away. A prominent professor said, "I will never forget the first
time I saw Jerusalem. We came from the south, crested a hill and there it
was. I couldn't hold back the tears, I was so overcome with emotion."

Think of seeing the new Jerusalem! John the apostle is the only one
who has ever seen the eternal city, the dwelling place of God and the saints
for all eternity. John has given us an enticing description of it in Revelation
21. This is the place Jesus promised to go and prepare for His people (John
14:2).

What is it like? It will be a place of fellowship. God will dwell there in
a face-to-face fellowship with His redeemed (Revelation 21:3). What does
that mean? "He shall wipe away every tear from their eyes" (v. 4). Since God
will dwell with men He will remove all physical and emotional suffering.
There will be no sorrow—forever!

The city itself will be brilliant because the effulgence of God's glory
will radiate forth from the city. It has "the glory of God" (v. 11). The city has
a high wall with twelve gates, guarded by twelve angels—all suggesting security (vv. 12-13). The wall has twelve foundation stones bearing the names
of Christ and the apostles (v. 14). The city is a cone or pyramid, 1500 miles
long, wide, and high (vv. 15-18). The city and the wall cast a brilliant splendor from its resplendent gold and stones (vv. 19-21). And there is no temple
because the Lord God and the Lamb are the temple (v. 22). Nor is there any
sun or moon, for Father and Son illuminate the city (v. 23). A river flows
from the top, the throne of the Father and the Son, with a tree of life on each
side of it—a reminder of eternal life in the city (22:1-2). But the focus of the
city shall be the Lamb who provided redemption (22:3-5). Glory to Him who
has removed the curse; there is no more sin, evil, or death.

Who enters the city? Only those whose names are written in the
Lamb's book of life (21:27). And the invitation goes out: "Come." And let the
one who is thirsty come; let the one come who wishes take the water of life
without cost" (22:17). Don't delay. If you don't know the Savior trust Him
today and become a citizen of the eternal city.

LESSON: *The new Jerusalem is the eternal city, the abode of God and
the redeemed for all eternity.*

HEAVEN

And I saw a new heaven and a new earth; for the first
heaven and the first earth passed away. (Revelation 21:1)

In the early morning of his last day on earth, Dwight L. Moody, awoke suddenly and began speaking: "Earth recedes; heaven opens before me." His son Will thought his father was dreaming. "No, this is no dream, Will," Mr. Moody replied. "It is beautiful. It is like a trance. If this is death, it is sweet. There is no valley here. God is calling me, and I must go." Having seen the portals of heaven, Mr. Moody entered his heavenly home.

Heaven! Believer and unbeliever alike recognize it as a place of celestial bliss and peace. The word *heaven* can actually be used in three different ways. The atmospheric heaven is the troposphere that surrounds the earth to a height of about six miles. From this heaven God sends rain, wind, and snow—gifts of God (Isaiah 55:10; Matthew 5:45). The celestial heaven describes the celestial realm of the sun, moon, and stars that God created (Genesis 1:1, 14).

Heaven is also known as the dwelling place of God, the third heaven (2 Corinthians 12:1). Paul was caught up to the third heaven (also called Paradise) where he heard "inexpressible words." In the Spirit John was caught up to heaven and saw the Lord, brilliant in majesty, sitting on His throne while twenty-four elders worshiped Him (Revelation 4). From His throne in heaven God carries out His sovereign plan for the earth, His footstool (Psalm 2:4-12; Isaiah 66:1). From heaven God rains down judgment, as on Sodom and Gomorrah (Genesis 19:24), but blessings also come from heaven, as the manna in the wilderness (Exodus 16:4).

Heaven is also the dwelling place of angels. From that place the angels carry out God's will (Genesis 21:17; 22:11). How many angels are in heaven? "A host"—an innumerable number, which is necessary to properly adorn the throne of God and praise its occupant (Luke 2:13). Old and New Testament believers also indwell heaven. When Christ was transfigured, Moses and Elijah appeared from the presence of God, or heaven (Matthew 17:3). The repentant thief was also promised, "Today you shall be with Me in Paradise" (Luke 23:43). Heaven is a prepared place for prepared people. Because God so loved the world, He sent His Son that we might share the glories of His heaven forever!

LESSON: *Heaven is the home of God, inhabited by angels and believers.*

LIFE
IN ETERNITY

Behold, a great multitude, which no one could count,
from every nation and all tribes and peoples and tongues,
standing before the throne and before the Lamb ... and
they cry out with a loud voice, saying, "Salvation to our
God who sits on the throne, and to the Lamb." (Revelation 7:10)

God created us as social creatures; we need the fellowship of
one another. In eternity fellowship will find complete fulfillment
as we meet with the Lord. God will live with us and fellowship
with us (Revelation 21:3). The fellowship the twelve knew with Jesus is the
fellowship we will enjoy with Him. As Moses mirrored the reflection of God,
so we will mirror the likeness of Christ because "we shall see Him just as
He is" (1 John 3:2).

His presence will bring eternal comfort. Think of the tears shed in this
world! Death, war, broken homes, wayward children, poverty, persecution,
sickness, loneliness—the list is endless. But no more. God will take His
divine handkerchief and wipe every tear from our eyes (Revelation 21:4).
The troubles we have here will vanish—no more death, no more pain, no
more grief.

In eternity we will enjoy rest. In this life "we have this treasure in
earthen vessels," and they feel very earthen at times! Eternity will provide
physical and emotional rest (14:13). God's people will have relief from their
toilsome labors. Are you tired, weary? Look ahead, God has provided an
eternal rest for us!

We will be satisfied and fulfilled (Hebrews 11:9-10). Our longings, our
aspirations, our journey will be over. Although we may lack satisfaction
here, in eternity we will be fulfilled in His presence and in His fellowship.

In eternity we will worship God by serving Him (Revelation 22:3). We
will lead productive, fulfilling lives in worshiping our Lord. Worship will be
at the heart of our eternal existence because God has created us for Himself, not for our independence. We will join the innumerable multitude of
people from every nation on the globe, worshiping and praising our God
and blessing His holy name forever (Revelation 7:9-12).

Have you prepared for eternity? The only way you will inherit these
blessings is by trusting in Jesus Christ as your substitute for sin.

LESSON: *For believers eternity will be a time of rest, comfort, peace,
and fulfillment in worshiping our God forever.*